SOME MIGHT SAY

THE DEFINITIVE STORY OF OASIS

oasis

CREATION

Richard Bowes

The Official Book of The Oasis Podcast

A catalogue record for this book is available from the British Library.

ISBN: 978-1-9162582-5-9

Second Edition

Front and back cover design by Liz Sánchez. Book design by Gary Bishop

Printed in the UK by Sound Performance

This Day In Music Books Bishopswood Road, Prestatyn, LL19 9PL

www.thisdayinmusicbooks.com

Email: editor@thisdayinmusic.com

Exclusive Distributors: Music Sales Limited 14/15 Berners St London W1T 3JL

CONTENTS

SYNOPSIS

Across the country and all around the world, millions of people felt a connection to these five working-class lads from Manchester. With anthemic songs crafted by possibly the greatest songwriter of their generation, delivered with intensity and swagger by definitely the greatest frontman of their generation (his brother), they set out with an insane level of arrogance, outrageously proclaiming themselves to be the best band in the world. And for a shining moment in the mid-1990s they were.

'Live Forever.' *Definitely Maybe. (What's The Story) Morning Glory?* 'Wonderwall.' Knebworth. A level of success not seen by a British band since a certain Liverpool quartet in the 1960s. Beyond that, the ushering in of a new cultural zeitgeist. Britpop. Cool Britannia. New Labour. And at the centre of it all, the soap-opera antics of the warring Gallagher brothers and their band of merry men.

But the story didn't end there. Throughout the late 1990s and 2000s they continued to inspire generations of fans with subsequent albums and tours, while controversy was never far away. Band members were left behind, as were a handful of Liam's teeth in a Munich hotel. New members joined, bringing a different dimension to the sound and ethos ... and then one eventful day in Paris in 2009 the whole thing came to a screeching halt.

With exclusive in-depth interviews extracted from the annals of The Oasis Podcast, including contributions from those involved (Alan McGee, Tony McCarroll), journalists with first-hand coverage (Paolo Hewitt, Colin Paterson) and celebrity fans (Ricky Hatton) amongst many others, this is the ultimate story of Oasis.

The rise of Oasis in the mid-1990s was nothing short of stratospheric. Yet what made Oasis truly special was that they were the people's band. This is their story, told by the people that lived through it and detailing how our lives were changed forever.

CAST OF CHARACTERS

Alan McGee - Head of Creation Records. Offered Oasis a record contract after seeing them perform at King Tut's Wah Wah Hut in Glasgow in 1993.

Alan White - Drummer for Oasis from 1995 to 2004. Brother of Steve White (see below). Replaced original drummer Tony McCarroll.

Andy Bell - Guitarist and co-vocalist of Ride. Joined Oasis in 1999 and served for the following decade. Also featured on guitar for Liam Gallagher's post-Oasis project, Beady Eye.

Anjali Dutt - Sound engineer for *Definitely Maybe*. Also worked with fellow Creation acts The Boo Radleys, My Bloody Valentine and Swervedriver.

Brian Cannon - Graphic designer. Designed artwork for all Oasis sleeves and images from 1994-1998. Other notable clients included Ash, Inspiral Carpets, Suede, and The Verve.

Chris Griffiths - Guitarist, vocalist and songwriter for Liverpool band The Real People, a big influence on Oasis.

Chris Hutton - Original singer for The Rain, the band that were reborn as Oasis.

Chris Sharrock - Once with The Icicle Works, The La's, World Party, Lightning Seeds and Robbie Williams. Oasis' final drummer. Later with Beady Eye and Noel Gallagher's High Flying Birds.

Clint Boon - Keyboard player and occasional vocalist for Inspiral Carpets. Later a DJ and radio presenter.

Colin 'Gem' Archer - Guitarist/former songwriter of Heavy Stereo. Joined Oasis in 1999, served for the following decade. Later with Beady Eye and Noel Gallagher's High Flying Birds.

Colin Paterson - BBC journalist and broadcaster.

Damon Albarn - Frontman, songwriter and singer for Oasis' Britpop rivals Blur. Also fronted Gorillaz and The Good, the Bad and the Queen.

Dave Sardy - New York musician and producer. Worked with Oasis on *Don't Believe the Truth* and *Dig Out Your Soul*, and with Noel Gallagher's High Flying Birds.

David Batchelor - Produced 'Slide Away' on *Definitely Maybe*. Other notable production clients include The Sensational Alex Harvey Band, Dr Feelgood, and Skids.

Iain Robertson - Oasis tour manager from 1994-95. Former Para. Also worked with George Harrison, Gary Moore and John Lydon.

Jason Rhodes - Oasis roadie and guitar technician.

Jay Darlington - touring keyboard player for Oasis from 2002 for the band's remaining seven years. Also featured on mellotron and electronics on the single, 'Falling Down.'

Jeff Slate - US musician and rock journalist.

Jill Furmanovsky - Notable UK rock photographer.

John Squire - Musician and guitarist for The Stone Roses. Went on to form The Seahorses, becoming a full-time artist before returning to his first band.

Johnny Marr - Lead guitarist/co-songwriter for The Smiths, turned solo artist. Worked with Electronic, The The, Kirsty MacColl, and many more, including collaborations with Noel Gallagher.

Johnny Sharp (aka Johnny Cigarettes) - *NME* journalist from 1992-2000. Later a freelance writer and author.

Liam Dennehy - Manager of the Grove, a club and rehearsal space in Longsight, Manchester, where the early Oasis made their first demos.

Marcus Russell - Managed Oasis from 1993. Founder/co-partner of London-based Ignition Management. Clients also included Latin Quarter, The Bible, Johnny Marr and Crowded House.

Margaret 'Peggy' Gallagher - Irish-born mother of Paul, Noel and Liam Gallagher.

Mark Coyle - Friend of Noel Gallagher. Co-produced *Definitely Maybe.*

Mark Feltham - Harmonica player, primarily known as a session musician and for his work with UK rhythm and blues outfit Nine Below Zero.

Mark 'Spike' Stent - co-produced *Standing on the Shoulder of Giants.* Clients also include Madonna, U2, Beyonce, Bjork, Depeche Mode, Ed Sheeran, Spice Girls, Lady Gaga, Coldplay, and Moby.

Mary McGuigan - Sister of co-founding Oasis guitarist Paul (aka Guigsy).

Mat Whitecross - Film director. Directed 2016 feature-length Oasis documentary, *Supersonic.*

Matt Deighton - Guitarist. Featured with Oasis in 2000. Started out with The Wolfhounds and also worked with Paul Weller and Mother Earth.

Meg Mathews - Activist and entrepreneur. Girlfriend then wife of Noel Gallagher. The couple were married from 1997 until 2001.

Mike Flowers - Real name Mike Roberts. Singer of easy listening band The Mike Flowers Pops, best known for their hit cover of 'Wonderwall.'

Mike Rowe - Touring keyboard player with Oasis from 1996 to 1998, then again in 2001.

Nick Amies - British writer and journalist.

Nick Ingman - British arranger, composer and conductor, and Oasis string arranger.

Nick Mercer - Singer and guitarist for Scottish indie-rock fourpiece Sergeant (2004-10). Later a solo artist.

Nicole Appleton - British-Canadian pop star actress and TV presenter best known for All Saints. Girlfriend then wife of Liam Gallagher (2000-2014).

Noel Gallagher - Middle child of the Gallagher family. Inspiral Carpets roadie turned chief songwriter of Oasis, on board from 1991 through to their 2009 demise. More recently fronted High Flying Birds.

Owen Morris - Engineer/producer. Co-produced the first three Oasis studio albums.

Paolo Hewitt - Music writer/author, whose first published book was an authorised biography of The Jam.

Patsy Kensit - Actress and Eighth Wonder singer, married to Liam Gallagher from 1997-2000.

'Paul 'Bonehead' Arthurs - Guitarist and founding member of The Rain and Oasis, staying on until 1999. Has also featured with Parlour Flames, Beady Eye and has played live with Liam Gallagher.

Paul Ashbee (aka The Big 'Un) - Friend of Liam Gallagher and Paul Arthurs, credited with introducing key members of Oasis.

Paul Gallagher - Eldest child of the Gallagher family. Big brother of Noel and Liam.

Paul 'Guigsy' McGuigan - Bass player and founding member of The Rain and Oasis, staying with the band until 1999.

Paul Slattery - Music photographer. Active in the photographer's pit since 1975 and with *Sounds* from 1977. Notable subjects include The Clash, Joy Division, Ramones, The Smiths, The Stone Roses and U2.

Paul Weller - British songwriter and Mod icon. Co-founder of The Jam and The Style Council. Established solo artist since 1991.

Pete 'Digsy' Deary - Songwriter and musician from Liverpool. Lead singer of '80s bands Cook Da Books, Smaller and most recently The Sums.

Pete Mitchell - Manchester-born broadcaster, radio presenter and documentary maker.

Peter Hook – Co-founding bass player for Joy Division and New Order.

Phil Smith – Long-time friend of members of Oasis. Tour DJ who also roadied for The Stone Roses.

Rick Witter – Lead singer of York '90s Britpop successes Shed Seven.

Ricky Hatton – Former World and British light-welterweight and welterweight boxing champion. Later a boxing promoter and trainer.

Scott McLeod – Bass player for Liverpool band The Ya-Ya's. Guested with Oasis in 1995 when Guigsy quit.

Simon Mason – Close associate of Oasis, aka 'The Cat In The Hat'. Described by Alan McGee as 'The Rock'n'Roll Doctor'.

Steve Cradock – Guitarist and multi-instrumentalist for Ocean Colour Scene and Paul Weller. Has also featured with The Specials in later years.

Steve Lamacq – Former *NME* journalist and broadcaster on BBC Radio 1. Later joined BBC Radio 6 Music. Also a published author.

Steve White – Drummer, formerly of The Style Council and with Paul Weller. Brother of Alan. Sat in for his brother for Oasis on tour in 2001.

Terry Kirkbride – Drummer, played with Proud Mary and occasionally with Oasis. Also featured with Noel Gallagher's High Flying Birds.

Tom Hingley – Lead singer of Inspiral Carpets from 1989-1995. Originally with Too Much Texas.

Tommy Gallagher – Irish-born husband to Peggy, father of the three Gallagher boys.

Tony McCarroll – Founding member and drummer for The Rain, who became Oasis. Left in 1995.

William Gallagher (Liam) – Youngest of the Gallagher brothers. Lead singer of Oasis right through from 1991 to 2009. Also featured on tambourine and occasional guitar. Later fronted Beady Eye.

Zak Starkey – Played with The Who since 1996, and the third drummer to appear in Oasis. Son of The Beatles' drummer Ringo Starr. Also worked with Johnny Marr and Paul Weller.

Zeben 'Zeb' Jameson – Keyboard player. Featured with Oasis on tour from 1999 to 2001.

FEED YOUR HEAD WITH ALL THE THINGS YOU NEED WHEN YOU'RE HUNGRY

I love Oasis. As a teenager when I really got into music, both listening to it and making it with my band Vision, they meant everything to me ... and for a while it felt like they meant everything to everyone. In those halcyon days of the mid-'90s we knew *our* band would go down in history as one of the greatest of all time and that their exploits would be remembered, collated and debated forever. They reached incredible peaks of popularity throughout that 1994/97 period, culminating at Knebworth Park in August 1996, then sonically through the incredible bombast of *Be Here Now*, arguably the most anticipated album of all time.

Then the backlash. The line-up changes. The mediocre response to new material. Time passed, tastes changed and while the band still retained a huge fanbase and had continued levels of success throughout the 2000s they never hit the peaks, both commercially and artistically, of those early years. In 2009, amid acrimony and broken splinters of guitar the band split, some might say (including some band members) around 13 years later than they should have. Is it better to burn out than Fade Away?

I also love podcasts. As a medium for receiving information they are second to none. Forget old-fashioned radio shows, tired old TV programmes ... only podcasts give the flexibility for creators to put together the content they want to in the way that suits them ... and the accessibility for the listener to consume it how and when they choose - even if they're driving, washing the dishes or running marathons. Plus, there is an intimacy with podcasts where the listener can become part of a community. You can contact the show, have your thoughts read out, have your audio message played, even become part of the show. I loved that community aspect.

I also love The Beatles, and therefore it stands to reason I love podcasts about The Beatles. It was such a joy to discover shows such as *Something About The Beatles* - hearing people talk about how this band inspired them, analysing the music and legacy of this remarkable group. I couldn't get enough of it.

So where was the equivalent for Oasis? OK, so they don't deserve the scholarly analysis The Beatles or Dylan do - but the music they made and the impact they had throughout their existence is worthy of collating and debating. Every now and then, while searching for podcasts, I would search for Oasis. Occasionally episodes would come up with Oasis-related guests (such as from the fantastic *StageLeft Podcast*), but I wanted a regular fix! Absolute Radio has a *Noel Gallagher and Oasis Podcast*, but this was basically a collection of interviews ... not a podcast in the true sense - independent, in depth and in rapture with its subject.

Then I watched Mat Whitecross' wonderful documentary *Supersonic*. While I knew much of the story, the film featured never before seen footage that was so exciting, stories I'd never heard, and a level of analysis that was exactly what I was looking for. But it was only two hours long, and it stopped at Knebworth. There was still so much more of the story to tell.

If no-one else was going to tell the story, I decided I would give it a go myself. Which is what I did.

Initially I wasn't sure what to expect. I have friends that are musicians or involved in creative pursuits, and I was expecting it to primarily be us talking about what Oasis meant to them and going through the discography, analysing each song. Stuck in traffic one day I pressed record on my iPad and started talking to myself about my musical background and what I hoped the podcast would be. I got home, downloaded free editing software recommended by my friend Casey from the *Movie Multiverse Podcast*, threw in some clips of the band plus other random stuff I thought fitted well, and with minimal editing or fanfare threw it up online. What happened next surprised me. People were actually listening ... in decent numbers and geographically spread all around the world.

I carried on going, and listener numbers kept increasing. Turns out there was hundreds of people like me, desperate for that regular hit of Oasis goodness. Within a few weeks, hundreds became thousands.

I was confident enough with the initial episodes to drop some tweets and emails out to a few people that worked with Oasis, and very quickly got responses, including those from harmonica player Mark Feltham, so important on records like 'The Masterplan,' live on *MTV Unplugged* and at Knebworth. Then there was Brian Cannon, who designed Oasis' record sleeves throughout the 90s, names like these elevating the podcast from some random bloke in Oxfordshire talking to himself to a significant part of the online Oasis/Britpop community. So many more great names I could mention, but major highlights would be interviewing an actual Oasis member, Tony McCarroll, and the man who discovered them, music industry legend, Alan McGee, both of whom I'm now very proud to call friends. I still can't quite believe it when I look in my phone contacts. And while I haven't interviewed Liam, I've had audio messages from him, which adorn the start of every episode. As you were.

But it wasn't just about people involved with the band. I wanted to give equal billing to the fans, as Oasis are a band of the people first and foremost. Therefore the podcast has heard tales of how Oasis changed people's lives, including dealing with mental health problems and helping beat cancer, plus we've heard from other musicians and people successful in other fields, such as sport and journalism, on what the band meant to them.

In 2019 we started to take the show on the road. Live events in London,

Berkshire and Glasgow were absolutely amazing and the response was truly inspiring. I even reformed my Oasis-inspired band, performing on stage for the first time in almost 20 years ... at The Water Rats, no less - a dream come true for me (not so much for people in the audience).

Pretty much from the beginning of the podcast, Richard Bowes was there. He was in contact from the early days, offering to help and writing articles for our Patreon page. I spotted straight away he was a great writer with a level of knowledge of Oasis and the Gallaghers far greater than mine. I'd always loved the idea of having a book on the history of Oasis and over the years the idea came together. I would keep going with the interviews and Richard would write the whole damn book by himself! Seemed like a great deal to me. I'm so happy with how the book has turned out and so proud for it to be 'The Official Book of The Oasis Podcast'. I hope you enjoy it.

However, just because the book is out, there's no plan for the podcast to stop. We keep on keepin' on. The Masterplan is ... there was no masterplan, but with loads of effort and the help of an amazing and ever-growing community of wonderful people, we continue to build. I'll try to get bigger and better guests with direct Oasis connections, and I live in hope of getting more members of the band itself. I'll continue to speak to Oasis fans like you that have their own story to tell, that is just as worthy of inclusion, and we'll keep going with the live events. I hope to see you at one soon.

But right here, right now - thank you for listening to the show and reading this book.

Stay in touch, stay engaged and Stay Young.

JC @OasisPodcast

oasispodcast.co.uk

THERE WE WERE. NOW HERE WE ARE.

Saturday, August 22, 2009. Liam Gallagher, clad in black Pretty Green parka, stands impassively at the centre of the stage, as ever not moving a muscle and staring out the crowd. His brother and lead guitarist, Noel, resplendent in uniform leather jacket and jeans, is playing sky-kissing guitar for set closer 'I Am the Walrus', just as he's done probably hundreds of times before. The rest of the band are following suit; Gem Archer on guitar is the solid foundation allowing Noel to venture into the unknown, while the rhythm section is the vital cog that keeps the gig flowing. Both Andy Bell and Chris Sharrock, on bass and drums respectively, display the experience that only their combined years in the rock industry can give. Keyboard player Jay Darlington adds progressive, psychedelic keys to the glorious noise that fills the night sky. The extended outro has been going on for five minutes and could go on forever. The headline act of the V Festival 2009. The mighty Oasis.

It was a good day. Ocean Colour Scene blew the cobwebs away early in the afternoon, then James and Elbow provided good singalongs for the crowds. But there was only one show in town. Objectively, it wasn't the best performance but then the V Festival, with its perennially odd mix of disposable pop and rock royalty, of a crowd made up of chavs and Mods, has never provided life-changing performances. Not only that but Oasis were in the upper stratosphere of rock bands. There's a reason U2 and the Rolling Stones very rarely do festivals, as it means relinquishing control of the set-up and the sound. Oasis were much the same. Their own gigs were rites of passage, communal experiences for the masses. The opportunity to embrace your fellow man and bawl out those anthems at the top of your voice. Saying it loud and singing it proud. It was always about the fans, and a partisan crowd never generates the same intensity.

A few weeks previously I'd seen them on the last of their three-night stint at Wembley Stadium. It was one of those nights where band and crowd come together in simpatico, channelling one another's energy to create enough power to almost be spiritual for a few wonderful fleeting moments. The V Festival gig wasn't like that. It was competent but unspectacular, but then it had been a long and troublesome tour. Cancellations, power failures and stage invaders over the course of a year had perhaps taken their toll. One of the consequences was that Liam's voice seemed strained and sometimes off-key, yet he made up for it with punk passion, spitting the words into the microphone. He never stops meaning it and to sing in the manner he does, never at less than 100%, must take its toll on the larynx.

Even so, what a set. 'The Masterplan', 'Slide Away', 'Roll With It' and 'Cigarettes &

Alcohol' all dispensed with in the first half. A closing quintet of 'Supersonic', 'Live Forever', 'Don't Look Back in Anger', 'Champagne Supernova' and their cover of 'I Am the Walrus' to close proceedings. Some of the greatest songs of the last 30 years performed by their makers is all one can really ask for. On the points Liam's voice did fall short, there was a ready and able crowd willing to pick up any vocal slack. This was what made Oasis exciting. Going to the gigs was always a gamble. They could be transcendent or turgid, rarely occupying the space in between. That night wasn't the best of their gigs I'd been to (Wembley Stadium a few weeks previously) nor the worst (Wembley Stadium, 2000). It was somewhere in the middle. With the benefit of 15 years' fan experience I chalked this down to being fatigue on the band's part. I had no doubt the next time I saw them they'd be back to their vital best.

'This is the last one. You've been biblical. I Am the Fucking Walrus.'

The V Festival was a split-site event, taking place in Staffordshire and Chelmsford, the line-ups swapping locations over a weekend. Living in the south of England we generally chose to attend the Essex show, but for reasons that are lost in the mists of time, my friends and I went to the Weston Park leg in 2009. It must have been fate, as not only did Oasis have to cancel their appearance in Chelmsford the following night but one week later, Noel Gallagher had left the band and Oasis were no more.

Looking back, the signs were there. Liam had recently told the *NME*, 'It takes more than blood to be my brother.' In his hilarious blog posts (*Tales From the Middle Of Nowhere*), Noel had stopped referring to Liam by name. Liam would respond via Twitter. There's a case to be made for social media destroying Oasis, one of the earliest of the now long list of crimes it's responsible for.

Rumours were flying around that the brothers were not even talking, travelling on separate tour buses. But this was par for the course with Oasis and had been from the moment they barged into our lives. Yet the whole tour had the feel of a victory lap, the venues primarily being stadia all around the United Kingdom. Noel even let slip onstage that night the end may be nigh, introducing Chris Sharrock as 'our fifth and final drummer'. Alternatively, that may also have been revealing the intention that Sharrock was too good to ever be allowed to leave. We'll probably never know.

It's somehow fitting that the last song Oasis ever performed was their bombastic cover of 'I Am the Walrus'. Not because it's a Beatles song (Oasis were fans, as you may have heard), but because it had been the closing number in their set even before they were signed back in 1993. Not only that but the original recording was released in 1967. The year one Noel Gallagher, the man with the masterplan, was born.

PHOTO CREDIT: WILL CAMDEN

oasis

Creation

EARLY YEARS

'KICKING UP A STORM FROM THE DAY THAT I WAS BORN'

Pete Mitchell (broadcaster): 'It was extraordinary how far that band of working-class kids from a council estate on the edge of Manchester could get. That's pretty inspiring if you think about it.'

Brian Cannon: (Oasis sleeve designer): 'The whole point of Oasis was; we grew up on a council estate. We are never going to shy away from the trappings of fame. This is what we set out to achieve in the first place. The bigger and madder it gets, the better. Bands who come from wealthier backgrounds, they tend to dress down once they've made it. Yet working-class outfits who make it good go in the opposite direction. It's inevitable. Oasis were the first band in goodness knows how long to say, 'Yes, we've made it and we've become pop stars. This is what we set out to do. We're going to have it until it stops.' In the case of Oasis, I don't think it ever will stop. It'll never die. I would never compare them to The Beatles musically, but in terms of the phenomenon ... it'll be a long time before that happens again.'

Simon Mason (part of the Oasis entourage, known as The Cat in the Hat): 'I think they encouraged a lot of people who perhaps might not have picked up guitars to pick up guitars. If you're a fan of Kasabian or The Libertines, you have Oasis to thank for that, for sure. I don't think we'll see that happen again. I don't think it's conceivable for something like that to happen again. I'd like to be proved wrong.'

Tony McCarroll (first Oasis drummer): 'It's a tough place to grow up, depending where you came from. It was a tough little place, and nobody took any bullshit. You had to stand up for yourself or you'd get ripped to pieces. It was in us all, the attitude.'

Irish migration to Britain has been a mainstay since the beginning of recorded history. The volume of people crossing the Irish Sea depended on the various circumstances of the time, be they to the individual or either of the respective countries. The post-war boom of Great Britain's economy made it an attractive proposition for natives of its closest neighbour, particularly the expanding cities and towns.

In 1962, shortly after her last Christmas in the west of Ireland, Margaret Sweeney, of Charlestown, County Mayo, moved to one of the more prominent cities in England, Manchester. That following January at nightclub The Carousel in the centre of town, she met fellow Irish immigrant Tommy Gallagher, originally from County Meath. They courted for two years and were married in 1965. Their first child, Paul, was born in 1966 and 10 months later (two days after The Beatles' seminal *Sgt. Pepper's Lonely Hearts Club Band* was released) on 29th May 1967, they had a second son, christened Noel Thomas David.

Paul and Noel were typical brothers, with the younger of the pair taking more attention by virtue of *requiring* more attention, as often happens in families around the world. Just under five years later, Margaret (or Peggy) fell pregnant again and on September 21, 1972, a third son, William John Paul, came into the world, Slade's stomp classic 'Mama Weer All Crazee Now' topping the UK singles chart at the time.

Immediately young William took over from his older brother as centre of attention amongst family and friends. Liam, as he became known, thoroughly revelled in this role and was always quick to entertain. An example of his gregarious attitude took place early in his life; during a nativity play, a traditional mainstay of primary schools the length and breadth of the UK Compensating for forgetting his lines, he broke into an impromptu Elvis Presley impression which had the audience in raptures. It's easy to surmise that the appreciation from the crowd made a lasting impression on the boy.

Pulling rank, eldest brother Paul had a bedroom to himself, forcing Noel and Liam to share the other bedroom in the Gallagher's family home. As is often the case for middle children, whereby the eldest rules the roost and the youngest demands the attention, Noel was the more introverted of the brothers, being very quiet and a dreamer. He and Paul were also the victims of Tommy's ire, their father often beating the pair upon his return from work or the pub. For whatever reason Liam was left alone, untainted (at least physically) by his father's violent tendencies. Eventually, Peggy was brave enough to leave her husband, taking the three boys with her and moving to Burnage, a suburb four miles to the south of central Manchester, and was fortunate enough to never see Tommy again.

Music was a big part of the Gallagher family; Tommy was a local DJ and used to take the boys to his local men's club, which would be playing Irish music of all varieties. Paul Gallagher was into the punk and new wave music sweeping throughout the nation during the late 1970s, adoring bands such as The Jam and The Damned. Noel swiftly followed suit and, when he was old enough and being of the right mentality, seemingly like every young rock music fan from 1976 onwards, became a big fan of the Sex Pistols. In stark contrast, Liam didn't really have much patience with music, although through osmosis he would become familiar with the classic artists his brothers were listening to. Liam was more into football (like his brothers he was a mad Manchester City fan), causing typical mischief along with his fellow teenage friends. During those teenage years he was accosted by a gang of kids near his school, and hit in the head with a hammer, which he later speculated, 'knocked the music into him.'

Pete Mitchell: 'He (Noel) really aligns himself with The Smiths, because I would imagine by the time The Smiths started to come through, he was just getting into his mid to late teenage years. They were from Irish families, they were a phenomenon, although not as big as Oasis turned out to be. Noel very much aligned himself, especially with Johnny (Marr). He was part of that community of Irish clubs around Manchester.'

THE SMITHS 1984

Liam attributes the catalyst for his feud with Noel to another escapade of the time. According to what has become part of the legend, Liam claims to have come home from a night out, apparently his first, and unable to find the light in their shared bedroom, instead opted to urinate over big brother's stereo. Understandably, Noel was less than impressed.

After leaving school (either by choice or not) and with the possibility of further education not an option, Noel went into the world of work, taking on a number of different jobs. One of which was working for British Gas and during his employment Noel received an injury, a large piece of metal landing on and breaking his foot, leaving him unable to engage in physical work and, primarily housebound or based at the site office, handing out screws or other equipment when required to other members of the workforce.

With very little in the way of entertainment during the day (a wealth of televisual choice not being an option in the 1980s in the UK), Noel took to playing his dad's acoustic guitar, and in time taught himself to play it competently to stave off boredom and escape both the mundanity of everyday life and the toxic atmosphere at home caused by his father.

One unremarkable evening, listening to 'Shine A Light' by the Rolling Stones, he noticed a melody from the song worked well with one of his own chord progressions. He revised the lyrics on the line in question to, 'Maybe I don't really wanna know.'

He also started socialising in Manchester, clawing his way into becoming part of the local music scene, regularly attending both the legendary Hacienda nightclub and gigs by upcoming local bands.

Pete Mitchell: 'Noel talks about it when I've spoken to him. He's mentioned that The Hacienda is important because it was the one and only nightclub. Noel says it was The Hacienda and Factory Records that began to create in Noel's mind and life that he wanted to do music.'

The Hacienda was a mecca for both aspiring and successful musicians. Members of Mancunian acts such as New Order and Happy Mondays would mingle with attendees of the club, no care given to status. As such, it was easy to strike up a conversation with your local hero of choice at the epicentre of *Madchester*. One of the many bands on the scene was Inspiral Carpets, who in 1989 had recently parted ways with lead singer Stephen Holt. Hearing of this, Noel, by now actively seeking to make inroads into the music business, approached the band and then auditioned for that role, having seen countless gigs and becoming recognisable to them as a fan.

Despite being impressed with his strength of character, and even offered some of his own compositions, the consensus amongst the group was that Noel's style wasn't a good fit for the music. But, undeterred, he managed to coerce himself into a position as a roadie instead, in itself a valuable opportunity to learn the machinations of the music industry. His duties included lugging instruments, selling merchandise and even answering fan mail when the band couldn't be bothered. He has since been described as 'loyal but lazy' by members of the group.

It was during this scholarship that he crossed paths with another face on the Manchester scene, a tall lad named Mark Coyle. Being of similar mindset to each other and the Inspirals themselves, the pair were given full-time roles as roadies and surely couldn't believe their luck when they accompanied the band as they toured the world, being paid a wage to travel to such glamorous locations as Japan, Argentina and the United States. Often the pair would jam with the Inspirals' instruments post-soundcheck. Meanwhile, the role of lead singer eventually went to the frontman of indie outfit Too Much Texas, Tom Hingley.

Tom Hingley (frontman, Inspiral Carpets, 1989/95): 'They auditioned Noel as one of three people. I don't think any of them would have been right for the band. Noel didn't like Clint's lyrics to a song called 'Whiskey.' He didn't like his lyrics for the band and Clint's lyrics are very good. There's a line that says, 'She gets prettier by the pint,' and I don't think Noel liked that.

'I didn't know Noel had auditioned for the band. Then he didn't get in. Three months later I auditioned and got in, but they never told me. It was a secret that wasn't exposed to me until three and a half years later when we sacked him. I don't think I would have been very happy having him as a roadie if I'd known that.

'Noel was never a scally. He was always very smart. Very intelligent. Very funny. Very motivated in a great way. He went off and became a million times more successful than us and that's fantastic. They could have had him as a singer but that would have been a more 'scally' band. Which I don't think would have been good for the band. It's a good thing for Noel he didn't do that either.

'I'm not sure Noel would have been famous if he hadn't worked for us. He used to work for British Gas. Then a pipe got dropped on his leg so he couldn't work, so he started working for us because he couldn't do his other job. It provided an income for three years. He probably learnt a lot about the business because we used to let him attend meetings. And he learned a lot about the music on stage and watching us perform and what we played, and then deciding to make sure HE sure as hell never did any of that and did his own music!

'They didn't choose him to be the singer in the band. The band didn't tell me because I wouldn't have been entirely happy at having Noel work with us for all those years. I wonder whether at some point they were planning to get rid of me and have him sing instead.

'He was canny. He was a great person to have around. A bit of a guru. He always had good suggestions. I think we just took him seriously and I'm not sure anyone at that point had taken Noel seriously in his life. I don't mean that in an insulting way.

'I think we were quite sussed about business, so I think Noel learnt a lot. He did the opposite of what we did; we shared everything equally, but he kept most of the money for himself.'

Pete Mitchell: 'He became a runner with the Inspiral Carpets. When I first knew him, I was on the radio and he would bring the white labels around from New Mount Street, where their offices were. Noel would be the guitar tech for Graham Lambert (Inspiral Carpets), I think. They (Inspiral Carpets) weren't touring or leaving Manchester a great amount at that time. They kind of got left behind when everyone really took off, but Noel was their runner into Piccadilly Radio.'

While Noel was studiously observing the travails of an indie band, picking up numerous tips which would stand him in great stead later in life, back in Manchester his little brother Liam, who previously showed little interest in music, attended a Stone Roses gig at the Boardwalk. Amid the throng, watching the local heroes in close proximity, Liam had a revelation; from there on he too wanted to be in a band, preferably and probably only as a singer. Ian Brown and co. were an inspiration to the youth of Manchester, being aspirational but also fiercely Mancunian. Pop stars of the 1980s were often found in leather trousers or all black gothic attire whereas the Roses took to wearing more regular, unremarkable clothing - jeans, shirts, T-shirts, etc. To their burgeoning fan-base this made them even more accessible. As such the streets of Cottonopolis were strewn with inspired young men.

From there on at every opportunity Liam would let it be known to anyone who would listen that he wanted to join a band. But in the meantime, he had a day-job. Whilst working with his friend Paul Ashbee for the latter's car valeting business, they would often discuss the future and how determined Liam was to break into the music world. Ashbee had managed to acquire a valeting contract working with Manchester United. He and Liam would spend their working days at United's training ground, cleaning the players' cars whilst apparently they were put through their paces. Unbeknown to anyone at the time, two of the biggest British icons of the 1990s may have been close every day, before the eyes of the world fell upon them.

Paul Ashbee (friend): 'Liam was always dead curious about David Beckham. I remember one day Beckham was playing his music and it was R'n'B and all that. I remember Liam having a conversation with him, saying, 'Here y'are mate, what is this fucking shit you're listening to?' Beckham tried to explain what it's all about and Liam's having none of it. I was like, 'You cheeky little cunt!', but that's what he was like.'

THE STONE ROSES

SILVERTONE RECORDS

WATERFALL

7" (ORE35)   12" (ORE ZT 35)   CD (ORECD35)

1991

'I WAS LOOKING FOR SOME ACTION'

Word reached a typical music quartet, themselves inspired by attending the legendary Stone Roses gig at Spike Island gig, that a young recognisable face around town had expressed public aspirations of fronting a group. This particular group of lads had taken to calling themselves The Rain, after the revered Beatles B-side to 'Paperback Writer'. Ashbee was a friend of Paul Arthurs, better known as Bonehead, and, during one of their many conversations about the future, claims he proposed to put the boisterous young man in touch with the aspiring four-piece.

Paul Ashbee: 'Back then, in the '80s, Thatcher's Britain and all that, we were all out of work. Me and Bonehead weren't working, so we were sat in the park and someone had a big ghetto-blaster. We were listening to Big Audio Dynamite. I think the first conversation between me and him was, 'I want to start a band.' I knew Bonehead was always musical. He could play anything - spoons, anything. He was amazing at what he did. I went up to his house one night, and we were sat in his bedroom and he pulled a bass out. He was trying to teach me to play it. I remember him teaching me 'Love Will Tear Us Apart'. He was desperate for me to be in a band, and then six months later The Rain started. I just couldn't do it. That's where it all started.'

Mary McGuigan (Paul McGuigan's sister): 'The first one of the band I really knew was Bone. The person I'm closest to is Bone because I've known him longest and he's always treated me like a sister. He's a good man. He was a fucking awesome musician, he can play the piano accordion! Honestly, the man is a genius.

'Paul (McGuigan) knew him, as far as I'm aware, from the Milestone Pub. The Milestone is a pub in Burnage that Paul, Bone, Chris Hutton and Tony all used to drink in. I don't know who else was there. I guess that's how Paul and Bone became really good mates, and he used to come 'round our house and we knew him. To us he was Bonehead. He was a plasterer, that's what he did. He was just a fixture, part of our lives. He would come around in his van.

'Bone and Guigs were going to the Milestone pub pretty much every night or every other night, because there was nowt else to do. Our kid says, 'I'm sick of this to be honest, what else can we do?' Paul worked for BT, in HR. He was doing pretty well but didn't really like it. It wasn't really him, but he didn't know what *was* him. So, they had a chat and Bone says, 'Why don't we start a band?' Paul says,

'Because I can't play an instrument,' and Bone says, 'You can play bass.' The two of them were holed up in Bone's mum and dad's garage, just the two of them, playing bass and guitar for a while. We went to the legendary Johnny Roadhouse music shop and bought a bass. It went on for a while then it got to the stage where Paul said, 'We can do something with this.' Tony Mac could play the drums and Chris Hutton used to drink in the Milestone too, and he could sing. So that was that, that was The Rain.'

Tony McCarroll: 'I think I was the only fucking drummer in a two-mile radius. That was probably the only reason I was asked to do it! I had my own kit and all that shit. The original line-up for The Rain was Guigs, Bonehead, Chris Hutton singing and then a drum machine. They needed someone who could play drums and could play live. I went down to watch them. I can't say I was massively impressed, but it was next steps. I was going to be in a band. (I was) very impressed by Bonehead at the time; that man could get a tune out of a radiator.

'I will say that wall of sound carried into Oasis, without a doubt. That was all Bonehead. His rhythm turned up to 10. I found myself competing with that, hence I probably started hitting really hard. Quite simple but quite hard.

'It was very straight-forward music. No Grade A musicians in there, but it was that simple that there was space for us all to be heard.'

Consisting of Chris Hutton on vocals, Paul Arthurs on guitar, Paul McGuigan on bass and Tony McCarroll on drums, The Rain were functional if unspectacular, with most of the songs apparently written by Arthurs (although Chris Hutton laid claim to devising most of the material in his book, *Don't Look Back in Anger*). According to other accounts, songwriting was claimed to be something of a group effort, with McGuigan (Guigsy) also said to offer his fair share.

Tony McCarroll: 'Bonehead and Guigs and a lad called Chris Hutton approached me. The only one I didn't know was Bonehead. I'd known the others since I was nine or 10. I was invited to join their band.

'I felt something immediately, even with The Rain. That wall of sound. It was Bonehead's energy and me and Guigs behind it all. I felt it initially. We needed a good frontman, direction and some good songs.'

Mary McGuigan: 'The Rain played their first gig at the Milestone, which doesn't exist anymore, sadly. There's a video somewhere of that gig. I've seen it, so I know it exists. I don't know who owns it, but it's definitely out there in the world.

'I don't know what they did after that, but I know they played what was at the time Times Square in Didsbury. It was an over-21s bar, so it ended up being about five of us in the audience. They only had three songs, one of which was 'House of the Rising Sun.' They played the same three songs three times!

'Not long after that was the Strangeways riots, and I know there are various versions of the story of the song, 'We're Having A Rave on The Roof' I know because Paul and I wrote it together in my mum's living room'.

Finding their feet, The Rain eventually came to the realisation, amongst the instrumentalists in the band, that Chris Hutton wasn't going to fit the style of the band, and was coerced out. It became known within their social circles that they were in the market for a new singer.

Tony McCarroll: 'I've got great respect for Chris (Hutton), but for many months we recognised, being on stage with him ... he started doing stuff on stage. He'd get the microphone and do tricks with it. He can't be our man. We heard through the grapevine that Liam was mad for joining a band, so we gently pushed Chris away. We all knew Liam from early teens, and instantly it was like, 'He'll work. He's definitely got the look, the walk, the talk, the girls. Everyone's after him.' All we needed to know was could he sing?'

Paul Ashbee: 'Liam pops up and I've seen something in that kid and thought, 'You know what? Let's see if we can do this.' Liam then was quite shy and unassuming, but he was a listener. He was a fucking top lad. He just needed someone to put a bit of belief into him at that point, and that's where I came into it. I gave him that passion to go on and audition for Bonehead's band.

'The funny thing is, back then, when we used to be in the valeting van, we used to chat. We were talking about being in band and all that, and I said, 'I'll get you an audition.' When I did, I remember him coming out the next morning to start valeting and I said, 'Look, I've got you an in here.' And he said, 'Nah, fuck that.' I said, 'Are you for fucking real? What do you mean, 'Fuck that'? You've been on my case for the last two months, we've talked about everything. I've got you in and now you don't want to do it?' It became a battle. Me being me, I thought, 'I'm not having this.' Bonehead had sacked Chris Hutton and everything.

'I was like, 'Liam, you've got to fucking do it. You can't make me look a cunt here. Come on.' 'Oh mate, I don't know, I'm not ready for that shit.' I said, 'You've been fucking telling me you want it! What do you mean?' Anyway, the battle went on for probably two weeks. If he put his hand on his heart, he'd said that. I said to Coatsey, his mate, 'You're going to have to speak with him.' So, me and him went 'round and both got him in Coatsey's car and drove round to Bonehead's. He walked in and, as the story goes, Bonehead cracked open the case of a tarantula, (his pet), threw it at him and he went, 'What the fuck?' It broke the ice, so he said to Liam, 'Right, do you want to be in a band? Can you sing?' And I remember him saying, 'Yeah, I fucking sing in the shower.' I thought, 'For fuck's sake.' We never even thought about that!

'I'd always seen it in Liam. Liam demanded attention. We created a band once called The Moochers. It was pretty mad. We'd go 'round telling people we were in this band. We copped off once with two birds one night, telling them we were in a band. About six months later at the Astoria in London, I was stood outside having a fag and a bird came bowling up to me. 'Do you remember me?' I said no. She said, 'You do! We copped off in that bar, you were with that Liam guy.' It was mental. It just went from that, and that's where it all came from.'

By the time Liam Gallagher entered their orbit he had fine-tuned his style of casual clothes and regulation moptop. But more than that, and intrinsic to his appeal, he had attitude and belief, key components of any frontman. It surely didn't take much persuasion amongst the group to replace Hutton with Liam, who took his first bite of the cherry readily but with one caveat; changing the name of the band. Seeing the word Oasis on one of his brother's Inspiral Carpets tour posters in their room, Liam suggested it as a replacement band name. And so, a nondescript leisure centre in Swindon ended up cementing its place in the annals of rock history.

Mary McGuigan: 'We were all Levenshulme-based. The first of them I met was Liam, I remember meeting him when I was really quite young. I remember this boy coming into our house in a pair of sunglasses and being smuggled upstairs like he was a rock star.

'They got Liam involved, and Liam is God-like in so many ways. He's had that swagger since he was nine years old. That is not a man who is trying to be cool. He just *is* cool. And who knew he could sing? If I'm going to be controversial, they could have potentially made it without Noel, because that boy was good enough. Bone is just a genius of a musician. Yes, Noel came in with amazing songs, and thank God he did. But without him they were still tight. Bonehead is the tightest rhythm guitarist I have ever heard. Liam was born to be a superstar.

'They weren't thinking about Noel. These are not criminal masterminds! They were just a bunch of lads who were trying to do something else other than get pissed in the pub.

'Liam, Paul and Bone were really close. The three of them were like the Three Musketeers.'

The group may not have been the most talented, but they were committed to honing their craft and used their spare money to book practise time at the Grove, a club and rehearsal space in nearby Longsight, managed by local lad Liam Dennehy.

Liam Dennehy (manager of the Grove): 'He (Paul Gallagher) used to come in and say, 'Our kid's in a band.' He had a bigger mouth than Noel and Liam put together. He asked to use the space at the back because no-one's using it. They used to come in on a Tuesday night and gave us £20. Because we were a big cabaret club, with all the stage set-up and all the gear. They just used to plug in and play.

'I used to sit at the back turning the sound on for them. To be honest, they were pure shite. Noel weren't there, it was Liam. Noel came in a couple of times to call in for something. He was with Inspiral Carpets.'

Tom Hingley: 'The only songs they could play, as far as I can remember it very early on, was 'One' by U2, 'Saturn 5' by Inspiral Carpets (which hadn't been released at that time), and a house record. I still can't work out what it was. ('Better Let You Know' by Two 4 U). Those were the only songs they could play when Noel joined them.'

Paul Ashbee: 'When Liam joined, we started rehearsing at the Grove. Paul Gallagher got us in, and I always remember we had a lighting system. I was stood messing about with the lights and they were all strumming. Liam was sat playing his tambourine with his head in the clouds, not really knowing what was going on. We didn't really have any songs, we were just trying to find our sound. I always remember something happened that night, and then the sound became Oasis. That distinctive sound just came from that.'

While overseas with Inspiral Carpets, Noel Gallagher made one of his regular calls home to speak to his beloved mum, primarily to keep her reassured that he was surviving the strains and excesses of the rock'n'roll lifestyle. Enquiring about his younger brother, he was surprised to learn that, having previously shown no interest in music to the best of his knowledge, Liam had joined a band. Shortly after being fired by the Inspirals (part of a record label initiative to clean up the band's image and to save money), Noel went to see his brother's band's first gig, at the Boardwalk in Manchester on August 18, 1991, supporting local act Sweet Jesus. Noel was impressed, though no doubt played the situation as if he was doing the band a favour by attending. After their set, the motley crew asked this apparent veteran of the rigours of rock 'n' roll if he would be interested in becoming their manager.

Mary McGuigan: 'Nobody spoke to him (Noel) because he was the kid who had met The Smiths and we couldn't comprehend that.'

Pete Mitchell: 'Around about that time, Noel came into Piccadilly (Radio) one day and said, 'I've joined Liam's band.' I went, 'Oh right, OK. Will you play me something?' And he went, 'No.' I've never forgotten that! There was kind of an attitude then. Probably looking back, I know why he said no. The demos weren't very ... they were a starting point. They were highly influenced by the likes of U2 at the time.'

Tony McCarroll: 'We needed Noel. That's it. Any band who goes into the stratosphere will say there's always some kind of madness and lunacy there. An extra element if you like. We definitely needed him, he was essential. It finished off the equation.'

Oasis reasoned that he would have contacts within the music industry and would be able to assist them with landing a record deal. Noel declined but, seeing an opportunity present itself, instead offered to join the band as songwriter and ostensible leader. He had amassed a collection of songs over the years and, seeing as the band only had a small number of tracks written between them (the most notable 'Take Me', a Stone Roses imitation written by Liam and Arthurs), the collective were more than happy to bring him on board to steer the ship.

Tony McCarroll: 'When we initially got to the Boardwalk, I don't know how much of *Definitely Maybe* we had. 'See the Sun', 'Take Me', 'Better Let You Know'...'

Paul Ashbee: 'They went to the Boardwalk, and I turned up with Noel and Louise, his first girlfriend. I was stood at the back with Noel, and I was watching him watching them. I could see his eyes light up and I knew he'd seen something. But afterwards he went backstage, and he was fucking slagging it off. This, for me, is where the power thing came in. They wanted that respect from Noel. They wanted Noel to be impressed with that. He pretended he wasn't, but I knew he was. Liam was like, 'Fuck off, what do you mean it's shit?' Noel was like, 'You need my songs in there.' Straight away they said yes.

'I remember saying to Bonehead that night, 'Don't let this guy come in and take control, because he will. He'll kill it.' Literally, he came in and created that monster that we have of Oasis. But he created a horrible vibe. I used to sit in this old chair and look at him and you had Liam to the left, Noel, McGuigan and McCarroll on drums. I used to sit there watching this day in, day out. (In a sense, I was listening to) *Definitely Maybe* for six months before anyone had ever heard it.'

Tony McCarroll: 'We only had one or two tunes when Noel came on board. Bonehead did write 'Take Me' but Noel added to it. When Noel joined, he started moulding the sound and different songs. None of them (early songs) crossed over to *Definitely Maybe*. We just matured as a band. Songwriting, structures of songs, advice from The Real People, it kind of moulded us ready for the road and for a recording contract.

'We used to rehearse Sundays, so you'd come up straight from a rave, somewhat 'up there.' We were just energy. We jammed a song for 15 to 20 minutes. We knew where everyone was going to steer it to. It was a great natural band, we all knew what to do.

'We knew them for many years, before Oasis was formed, within a two-mile radius, my mum knew Peggy. It was a very cliquey, Irish community. We knew years before, again meeting Noel, that everyone was envious of him being a roadie. He was a cool guy, he slipped in and got a job. Toured the world and got the experience that was essential for the next step.

'We only had three or four songs. We recognised that was our weakness; the line-up was good, we needed a songwriter. We needed the songs. Initially Noel was going to come in as the bass player. But that didn't quite happen, and he ended up coming down one Sunday afternoon session.

'That pump the air Celtic rock we grew up with. I'm very sure it had an effect on every member of Oasis, without a doubt.'

Simon Mason: 'Noel was already 27 when it started to happen. I wonder sometimes if Noel thought it was this, or that was it. I think Noel kind of knew the superficialness and the vagaries of the music industry. Nothing was going to stop him, he got what he needed around him and he was on his mission. Liam was at the centre of that. The other guys were like, 'Let's just stay with us because we ain't going to get a better offer.' And of course, they were all friends, hence the gang mentality. That's what they were, they spoke in their own language. It was remarkable to behold.'

Oasis first phot session in Castlefield, Manchester
©peterjwalsh.com

1992

'I KNEW EXACTLY WHAT I WANTED TO BE. NOW I'M SURE'

Pete Mitchell: 'If you're looking for an answer as to why it happened, there was a very strong infrastructure (in Manchester) where people could go to somebody and people would record them. Somebody would take a punt, somebody would promote the record for them, and somebody would play it. That's what happened.'

Having seen at first hand the mechanics and requirements of the music industry, Noel was adamant that the band wouldn't get anywhere without good old-fashioned hard work and insisted on daily rehearsals to formulate their sound and setlists. Virtually all the band were holding down full-time jobs but dedicated all their spare time to rehearsals. Only Tony McCarroll had any familial responsibilities to speak of, being married and having a young daughter. The rest had no such commitments and were more than happy to comply with their new leader's instructions. After a few rehearsals, the expanded band played more intermittent shows, again at the Manchester Boardwalk, in October and then two nights in January 1992. The setlist for the latter gig was:

'Columbia'
'Take Me'
'Must Be the Music'
'Life in Vain'
'I Will Show You'
'Better Let You Know'

Tellingly it seems that Noel hadn't taken complete control of the music by this point, as 'Take Me' was still in the set. However, that and 'Better Let You Know' were the only songs not written by him, so one imagines Liam and Bonehead had probably downed tools on that front. The band then had their first gig outside Manchester on April 19, 1992 at, of all places, Dartford Polytechnic (such was their dedication that a 450-mile round trip to leafy Kent for a gig was readily taken up), and then the following night at Oldham's Hippodrome.

According to records, these gigs were the only ones played outside Manchester for the rest of that year, the band only playing the Boardwalk on a bi-monthly basis. At this point they were without a manager, relying purely on their own initiative including blagging a support slot with New Order bassist Peter Hook's side-project Revenge. Tony Wilson, a local legend and the owner of Factory

Records, home to New Order and Happy Mondays, turned the band down, citing them as 'too baggy.'

Tony McCarroll: 'It was a progression. The room was only five metres by five metres, and we practiced three nights a week. Obviously, you're going to improve and get better.

'For us they were 10-minute jams. We'd start something and all join in. It was all for progression, but we were dedicated. Something needed to happen in our lives. There was nothing else in Manchester, that's a fact. We needed to get out. If it only lasted for one album, we'd had a go.'

Paul Ashbee: 'He (Noel) had a vision and believed it. We all did. In our heads, when Oasis were in the Boardwalk, they were superstars. That's the belief that they had. It was there long before anyone knew it.'

Mary McGuigan: 'Even when the boys (Noel and Liam) were involved, they used to get into a Transit van, drive to London and then drive straight back. They'd go to work and then drive to Newcastle, do a gig then drive straight back. They worked bloody hard. It's a story that couldn't exist anymore but it's not how the music industry works anymore. They just grafted and did it because they enjoyed it and wanted to do it. I was so proud of them because they were cracking on, trying to get their voice heard and tell a story. When maybe no-one wanted to listen. But they kept going and kept going. I think that relentlessness is phenomenal. There was no overnight thing there!

'There was a point at which they were rehearsing three times (a week) in the evening and both days on the weekend. Noel said, 'We're not working hard enough, we need to give it more.' Paul phoned me one day and said, 'Noel's saying we need to up the game. What do you think?' Then he said he'd just been offered voluntary redundancy. I said, 'Follow your dreams, Paul.' It was difficult for everyone because Bone was self-employed, Tony was labouring, but they did it. But it was tough.

'I don't know if at any point they thought it could be big. They just thought, 'Let's do it. We'll just live from moment to moment.' They didn't have a measure of what success looked like. They were a band of brothers.'

Tony McCarroll: 'We were a natural band, if you like. We'd grown together, matured together somewhat musically.'

Noel had always been a big fan of Factory Records and on his frequent visits to The Hacienda would spark up regular conversations with someone who would regularly badger Noel to give him a demo tape so he could present it to his brother. Separately, in attendance at some of those early Oasis gigs was Johnny Marr, formerly of indie icons The Smiths and a true figurehead of Manchester's music scene. Persuaded to go along by a friend, Marr was impressed with what he saw. And it transpired that the guy from The Hacienda badgering Noel for a demo tape was his brother, Ian Marr.

Tony McCarroll: 'He was very helpful in the early days in many ways, giving Noel a leg-up here and there with equipment and so on. Advice. And obviously the best management in the world when they came on board.'

After introducing himself to Noel, Marr advised him that he was taking too long between songs tuning up, Noel replying that because he only had one guitar, he had very little choice. Seeing the band's potential, Marr gave Noel the Les Paul guitar on which he had written classic 1986 single, 'Panic'. Perhaps inspired, Noel started writing songs on the guitar itself, and one evening came up with one he knew to be a cut above most of those he had written up to that point. He called the song 'Slide Away' and it represented a significant step up in the quality of his songwriting.

Not that everything written prior to that had been sub-standard. The song inspired by the Rolling Stones' 'Shine A Light' was now complete and ready to be presented to the band. It was now a life-affirming ode dubbed 'Live Forever'.

Tony McCarroll: 'He walked into the Boardwalk. Straight away you knew it was different class. We were all throwing our little bits in. I think he was still finishing the lyrics at that point.'

Tom Hingley: 'I know Noel gave a demo to Johnny Marr and he passed it on to his manager. They were talking about Johnny Marr producing or writing some stuff with them, and that was before the Alan McGee thing. You can't mythologise a rubbish band.'

Paul Ashbee: 'He'd learnt a lot with Inspirals, he knew the scene, from the House scene and band scene, everything. Noel used to come to my gaff, he'd get his weed and come over. I remember one night he turned up with this tape, he had some fucking dodgy sideburns, and he said, 'Do you want to go and see a guy called Johnny something? He loved this acoustic kid. So, me and him went to Manchester University. That was the first time we spoke about getting a band together and he was trying then to do it. It wasn't happening but he never gave up.

'Noel started to gather things like videos, and different things. He was either

oasis
A
B
Noise Reduction
EQ High(CrO2) : 70μs
A
B
THE FIRST DEMO TAPE
A
90
Noise Reduction
IN OUT
TDK
SA90
EARLY RECORDING SESSIONS 1992

getting rid of them or keeping hold. I remember one time we went 'round his flat in town to watch United against Villa. I was stood at his windowsill and I saw the videotape of a gig and said, 'That's not yours, I'm having that!' He fucking kicked off about it. 'That ain't leaving here.' Even then he was on it. He didn't want shit like that getting out there. He got hold of anything and got rid of it or dismantled it. He knew what was happening even then.'

Pete Mitchell: 'They wanted to sign to Factory Records. If you think about the inspiration for driving Noel forward - and Noel was obviously the driving force - it is Factory Records. It's The Hacienda. It's the infrastructure. It's Tony Wilson.

'I think there was that musical education and being in the right place at the right time. Noel says, 'If we came from Ipswich, we wouldn't have been famous.'

THE COPYRIGHT IN THIS SOUND RECORDING IS OWNED BY BIG BROTHER RECORDINGS LTD. ALL RIGHTS OF THE MANUFACTURER AND OF THE OWNER OF THE WORK PRODUCED RESERVED. UNAUTHORISED COPYING, HIRING, LENDING, PUBLIC PERFORMANCE AND BROADCASTING OF THE RECORDED WORK PROHIBITED.
oasis
COLUMBIA
WRITTEN BY NOEL GALLAGHER
(OASIS MUSIC/CREATION SONGS LTD/SONY/ATV MUSIC PUBLISHING)
PRODUCED BY OASIS AND MARK COYLE
ADDITIONAL PRODUCTION & MIXING BY OWEN MORRIS
℗ & © 2004 BIG BROTHER RECORDINGS LTD.
45RPM RKID006TP
FOR PROMOTIONAL USE ONLY.
WWW.OASISINET.COM

1993

'ALL MY LIFE I TRY TO FIND ANOTHER WAY'

As planned, Noel's experience in the music industry was put to good use; during his time with the Inspiral Carpets he'd met and become friends with The Real People, a Liverpool indie act influenced by The Stone Roses and Inspiral Carpets as well as channelling their home city's '60s roots. They had released an album and a handful of singles and compilations which hadn't broken them into the mainstream but had given them a cult following. They also possessed a key requirement when recording music: a studio. Noel asked one of masterminds behind the band, Chris Griffiths, if Oasis could use their recording studio, christened Dock Road, to record a professional-sounding demo with the intention of sending it on to record companies in the hope of the band getting signed.

Tony McCarroll: 'Noel was on tour with them, and that's where it started. He seemed to get on well with them. They invited us to do a demo in Liverpool. They'd been thrown off their label as far as I know. So they had lots of time on their hands and lots of experience. We needed that. Our songs could be 10 minutes long and they structured everything and took minutes off. We didn't have a clue.'

Chris Griffiths (guitar/vocals, The Real People): 'I have heard (the early demos) them before, yeah, and had to turn them off halfway through. I said, 'Come on lads, fucking hell.' We went to see them at a gig at the Boardwalk. I went to see them in the praccy room underneath, and we talked about them coming up. I said, 'Listen, just come up and record live. Everything sounds great.' It took a little bit of, 'Listen, you're doing that too many times' and 'Let's repeat that good bit, 'That riff's good,' a little bit of guidance and stuff like that. That's all it took.'

In the spring of 1993, when playing a few more gigs in Manchester and Liverpool, (with songs such as 'Up in The Sky,' 'Bring It On Down' and 'Rock 'n' Roll Star' added to the set) Oasis went to Dock Road studio and laid down about a dozen tracks, of which four made the cut for a tape that would be called *Live Demonstration*. The other two tracks featured were recorded at the home of Mark Coyle, by this point acting as co-producer along with Noel. There were 10 cassette copies said to be made of the tape, which were adorned with a swirling Union Jack and the band's logo, distributed to record companies to no avail.

Paul Ashbee: 'Liam personally gave (Manchester United footballer) Brian McClair one of them. Liam was always on at him, 'What do you think?' McClair said, 'Yeah, it's good, man.' Brian McClair's still got that tape! He tells everyone today.'

The eventual final track list was:

'Cloudburst'
'Columbia'
'D'yer Wanna Be A Spaceman?'
'Strange Thing'
'Bring It on Down'
'Married with Children'
'Fade Away'
'Rock'n'Roll Star'

Chris Griffiths: 'We'd just finished recording *Marshmellow Lane* when we started working with them. We finished it in '92 and were working with them in '93. When we were touring with the Inspirals we played a lot of the songs we'd been recording for *Marshmellow Lane*. They were listening to it at the time, 'cos it never got released, you see? It only got released when we got the rights back a few years ago. So obviously they've known that album for years and years.

'Even when we were doing the demos, one of the very, very first demos, you've got to remember this is the first time they've ever been into a studio. It's called *Live Demonstration* because it was all recorded live. There may be a few things over the top, but it was only done on a little Tascam 8-track. I've still got a reel-to-reel of 'Rock 'n' Roll Star' and 'Columbia' as well, which had me singing the verses with the words I wrote at the time. You can hear on the drum takes, you can hear the spill of all the guitars. You've got to have those guitar takes in, otherwise it would spill from a different track.

'('Columbia') was completely instrumental, it was recorded as instrumental. This track was too good to not have lyrics and be an instrumental that you walk on to. So, I grabbed the mic and, in one take, sang 'There we were, now here we are. All this confusion, nothing's the same to me'. All of the first verse. Liam comes down, likes it and wrote the chorus. And then Noel wrote the second verse, and I wrote all the 'yeah, yeah, yeah', and all them little ad-libs. The thing was, when we were more or less trying to get our name on the record, and we were badly advised by solicitors and everything, we signed off on them. I took an out of court settlement for that, and for 'Don't Go Away', which was a lift from a song of ours called 'Feel the Pain'.'

The demo version of 'Columbia' isn't markedly different from the finished version but includes much more effects and psychedelic splashes that wouldn't make the final cut.

Chris Griffiths: 'It was all from me, I used to collect when I was on tour different CDs of, you know, Tibetan monks or weird little chanting things. I always used samples and demos. So, the thing with ... was it Tony Benn?... doing some sort of talk - that was live. I used to just turn the radio on and tape them through the radio, and that came on and just fitted right in. The little chants were some sort of Tibetan or weird tribe, and you just put them on underneath the track, and when you're looking for some atmosphere you turn it up now and then. I used to do it all the time, put a mic on the telly then turn it up now and then for production's sake.'

Tony McCarroll: 'There's a version where Liam sings one verse then he (Noel) sings the chorus, and it just goes 'round and 'round.'

Chris Griffiths: 'What a lot of people don't realise about that session ... they were only just coming down, like at weekends and stuff like that, and it wasn't just the four songs that made the album that we recorded. We done 'Rock 'n' Roll Star', 'Bring It on Down', 'Columbia' and 'Up in The Sky' that made *Definitely Maybe*. We also demoed a version of 'Whatever', which wasn't on an album, and we also demoed B-sides, and a track called 'Alive', 'Cloudburst', 'Fade Away', 'Strange Thing', and we done a track called 'Coming On Strong' which got put into The Chemical Brothers' tune 'Setting Sun.' We done another song called 'Lock All the Doors', which was another lift from bloody *Marshmellow Lane*, where we've got a track called 'Space', (actually 'My Own Dream') which says, 'Lock all the doors.' They also covered a Real People song, one of our very first demos, called 'Heaven Knows.' So, all in all there was eleven tracks that have been used from that session, which is unbelievable from a few weekends. If you put all the weekends together it was probably only a week or two. It was over a few months, they were coming down and either staying in one of our flats or staying in the studio or driving back to Manchester.

'We were the ones with the record deal when we met them. They were coming to our tours when we first met them.'

When drawing comparisons, it seems difficult to deny that The Real People contributed a healthy amount to the gestation period of what would become recorded Oasis music. As their star ascended, no real credit was given by any member of the Oasis camp.

Mat Whitecross (director, *Supersonic*): 'You only have to look at the books to see how crucial they (The Real People) were. They gave the band confidence. There was a crucial thing of them turning up at just the right time and showing Oasis how good they were and the potential they had.'

Tony McCarroll: 'They were thrown off the bus at some point. These lads did us massive favours. They came to the end of their recording contract, and I guess they had that bug of, 'Can't let it go.' I can't credit them lads enough, and I do wish other members of Oasis would give them a shout sometimes.

'You'd come out in a bloody state from that studio and four in the morning. I'd have to go to work two hours later, down the M62 to go to work. Driving on the cat's eyes.'

Pete Deary (aka Digsy, friend): 'The song ('Digsy's Dinner') was already written, and Noel never had the title for it. We were down at The Real People's studio one night and we were all just jamming, and I farted. So, I started singing, 'Guess what I had for my tea? It was lasagne, lasagne!' The next day he 'phoned and said, 'What was that you were singing? I said, 'I dunno, I was just making it up on the spot.' 'Well, I've got a song, and I wanna call it 'Digsy's Dinner'.'

Paul Ashbee: 'The fucking atmosphere with Noel ... Liam wanted Noel's attention and respect ... he'd never give it to him. Just because he's bringing in 'Live Forever' and 'Rock 'n' Roll Star'... me and Bonehead used to wonder where he was getting these fucking songs from. But it was easy because he was a poet. He was writing these songs long before. He never gave them that respect. Any of them. He used to sit there and slag Tony off. Paul McGuigan used to shake in his shoes, he was scared to death of him. I remember one night, we walked back, and Noel said to me, 'I can't have him in my band. That fucking McGuigan.' I said, 'Why, he's fucking sound!' And he said, 'Not for me, mate.' That's what he was like.

'He started with Tony, but Tony fought back. That was the problem. He used to put him down constantly. I was like, 'No need, Noel.' But going back to when Noel was a kid, we used to call him Nobody Knows Me-Noel. He was a loner. But I always had respect for him, he was a fucking good kid.'

Rick Witter (singer, Shed Seven): 'When we started getting in the top-10 *NME* 'Best Unsigned Acts' list and all this business, we started seeing the name Oasis quite a lot. It got to the point very early on where we were releasing stuff, they were releasing stuff. There was an awful lot of gatherings.'

Despite getting tentative interest around the city, Oasis couldn't seem to make an impact on their own doorstep.

Tony McCarroll: 'We had Factory Records coming down to the rehearsal room to see us. They'd just walk away; 'Too Madchester'. If you look at Liam back then, his haircut, everything, was Ian Brown. The attitude, the walk, the talk. They just couldn't recognise it, they couldn't see it. It took someone like McGee to recognise it. And obviously he knew what he was doing, he was going to make that band massive. It was needed.'

Having been working on the Manchester music scene for 18 months or so, Oasis had become friendly with other bands on the circuit, one of whom was Sister Lovers, a similarly guitar-driven act they shared rehearsal space with. Frontwoman Debbie Turner invited Oasis to play a support slot for them at a gig in Glasgow on May 31, 1993. Happy to accept, the band found some money to hire a van and made the five-hour drive up to Scotland with the intention of playing their 13th gig, on a fateful night when Alan McGee, head of Creation Records, was in attendance.

Tony McCarroll: 'We shared the room with Sister Lovers. They said, 'We've got a gig in Glasgow, can you make it?' As usual with us lot, we started the day in the van leathered. We got all the way up to Glasgow and the bouncers on the door said, 'No way, you're not playing. We've got three bands on, and it's a tight gig.' We did kick off, but whether or not it made a difference, I haven't a clue. Eventually we agreed they'd let us on for a 15-minute slot beforehand. Now that was lucky. It's got to be fate. Alan McGee then walks in the door and by the third song he'd decided he was going to sign us.

'It was more of an experiment, I'd say, because we were getting no response in Manchester. I think that was down to the Madchester scene having totally burnt itself out, and no-one was interested in signing us. We used to get, at all the little gigs we did in Manchester, 'You sound like The Stone Roses, you're this, that and the other'. It was a bit of an experiment, we thought we'd get out of town and see what happened. Lo and behold, it was the best gig we ever turned up at.

'We were struggling. We were begging to get any kind of record deal, just to get a single out even. At the time that would have done us, or would have improved our lives somewhat, even with just a short run at it.'

The legend goes that Oasis arrived mob-handed with a gang in tow and, after being initially turned away by security at King Tut's Wah Wah Hut, informed them that, as they were considerably outnumbered, they would 'smash the gaff up' if they weren't allowed to play. Whilst this is a great story, it has been revealed to be slightly incongruous, an alternative version of the truth being that the doorman and management of the venue were persuaded to let Oasis play as there was enough time for them to play before Sister Lovers, 18 Wheeler and headline act Boyfriend.

A further alternative version is that 18 Wheeler and Sister Lovers agreed to perform shorter sets to accommodate Oasis. The gig was on a Sunday and, owing to Glasgow's licensing laws, the first band was due to play at 10.30pm.

Creation Records was an independent record label with a handful of successful releases to their name, including the seminal *Screamadelica* by Primal Scream, from two years before. Other acts signed to the label were The Jesus And Mary Chain, My Bloody Valentine, Ride, Slowdive and Teenage Fanclub. A native Glaswegian though based in East London, McGee prided himself and the label on having artistic integrity and giving the acts they represented total creative freedom. McGee went along to see Sister Lovers, being a friend of Debbie Turner, with time to kill as he had missed his train back to London. In the venue McGee claims to have noticed 'a young Paul Weller in an Adidas tracksuit' seated at the bar. He thought the lad, who he later discovered was the singer in a band, looked cool, though McGee wasn't thinking of him as a musician, rather he was under the impression he was a drug dealer.

Oasis took the stage and opened with 'Rock 'n' Roll Star'. McGee's immediate reaction was that he wanted to sign them to Creation. On hearing second song 'Bring It on Down', he was convinced, and this was cemented by the time the third track, 'Up in The Sky' had finished. Concluding the set with a Beatles cover ('I Am the Walrus') was the cherry on the cake, as the song has some occult allusions, an interest of McGee's at the time. After Oasis finished their set, McGee approached Mark Coyle, who was still in his role of sound technician and recently fired from Teenage Fanclub, and asked if they had a record deal, to which Coyle replied in the negative. On finding out that Noel was ostensibly in charge of the band, McGee strode up to him and offered them a six-album deal on the spot. When Noel discovered who McGee was, he too was decisive and accepted there and then. Noel offered McGee a copy of *Live Demonstration*, but the Glaswegian's mind had already been made up. The pair chewed the fat for a while and history had been made. So excited by the possibility that he had discovered the future of rock'n'roll, McGee called Creation's PR man, Johnny Hopkins at his home in London at regular intervals from midnight, unable to contain his excitement.

Alan McGee (founder, Creation): 'The demo that he gave me on May 31, 1993 was The Real People (demo). After the gig, Noel gave me that and I said, 'I don't need it, I'm gonna sign you. I saw that gig, I know what's good.' Which was kind of brave, but Oasis were so good that night ... for a little band, that's a phenomenal gig. And they only played three songs, and I said I'd sign them. I got this demo, and the thing that really hooked me in off the demo ... I was still drinking and taking drugs at that time, so I was pretty hammered when I saw Oasis. So, I was thinking 'maybe I got that wrong.'

Tom Hingley: 'I don't really believe the story about McGee signing them in King Tut's. There was a band on Creation that used to rehearse in the Boardwalk called Metal Arc 11. I think Alan McGee would have been going to the Boardwalk for up to 18 months before he signed Oasis. The very idea of him getting within 100 yards of the Boardwalk and not being able to hear them playing at 1000 watts was extremely unlikely. The only thing that was louder than the band would have been Noel and Liam's personalities. So, there's absolutely no way that Alan McGee wasn't aware of them.'

Johnny Sharp (*NME* journalist, aka Johnny Cigarettes): 'I remember a couple of people at *NME* saying, 'Bollocks, did he discover them.' They said they'd already signed a publishing deal with Sony. I'm not sure whether that's true, I think that was a little bit of a confusion. What I did find out was that they already had Marcus Russell interested. They'd already met Johnny Marr. I slightly doubt that Alan McGee hadn't heard of them from Adam. I think he got a tip-off and decided to get there early.

'I defy anybody to see much in them (based on recorded footage from a handheld video from King Tut's taken that night). If McGee did, I take my hat off to him. But still, you've got to put your money where your mouth is and actually sign them. Nobody else was at that point, so fair enough.'

Tony McCarroll: 'McGee said he only signed us up for one album, thinking that he'd get himself out of debt.

'Obviously we made a massive impression on Alan McGee. I don't know if he was pissed or whatever, but by the second song he was like; 'I'm signing you.'

Pete Deary: '(Oasis covering 'I Am the Walrus') worked in their favour because a lot of Scousers warmed to it. It was a tribute, if you like.'

Simon Mason: 'People didn't know what to do with them. Only people like McGee got it and went, 'This is a bit special. I don't want to change them, I don't want to smooth out the rough edges, I don't care what they look like.'

Alan McGee: 'I put on the tape and the thing that grabbed me and what really made me love them was 'Columbia.' I love Happy Mondays, to this day I think they're the most important band to come out of Manchester, and it reminded me of them. At that point I didn't have the Mondays! I thought, 'Great, you've got a really good-looking singer, sounds a bit like the Mondays. I have to have that.'

Hearing of Creation's interest, other labels started courting the band, most notably Mother, home to U2, and Go! Discs, who had Paul Weller on their books, the former Jam frontman having made something of a comeback in the early 1990s with a strong debut solo album. However, Noel was good to his word and the next week he, Liam, and Bonehead went down to London to visit Creation's HQ in Hackney, at the time a low-rent, high-risk part of town, a far cry from the affluent, hipster utopia it is today. Essentially the meeting was so the band could suss out Oasis and their aspirations, and presumably vice versa but without the power of the purse-strings. McGee had big plans for the band and had already begun lining up managers and publicists. Johnny Hopkins was brought in as the latter, and other names were bandied around for the former, but Noel had his own suggestion; Marcus Russell of Ignition Management, who represented Noel's by-now friend Johnny Marr, as well as New Order's Bernard Sumner, and therefore came highly recommended. McGee knew Russell by reputation and agreed it was to be a good fit. All the parts for a sustained push were falling into place, though Russell was very keen not to push the band too soon, before they were ready.

Tony McCarroll: 'McGee started the ball rolling, and then it was a bit of a fucking panic after; 'We need management, we need this, that and the other.' Ignition Management came on board. (There was) a fateful meeting with Noel and Ian Marr at The Hacienda and they started chatting. (Ian) let him know that Johnny was on Ignition, that's how the connection was made, and the rest is history.'

Although they were signing to Creation Records, the label's cash-flow was in such dire straits that McGee had to borrow money from a major, Sony Records, then in turn licenced Oasis to them. Come the day the band actually signed the record contract, which took place at Sony Records' HQ in London, the fivesome had various stipulations, including that a photograph of Liverpool indie act The Farm, which adorned the walls, be reversed. Noel apparently didn't deem the Scousers as being worthy of witnessing such an event. Afterwards, all present went for some celebratory drinks in North London and tumbled into a pub hosting a gig by run-of-the-mill indie act Whiteout. Liam insisted on performing with them, which didn't go down well with his brother. They ended up having a big argument. Even at this early stage, success wasn't going to change them.

Tony McCarroll: 'Liam was the only one that would ever give him (Noel) some of his own medicine.

'I was working right up to the record deal as far as I'm aware. Guigs was, I think. Bottom line is, if someone put enough money in our pockets, we could do what we liked. It was about money, a few quid in your pocket and surviving. Truth is, in the early days of Oasis, that's all we did; survive. We got about £15 a day to eat and stuff like that.'

Yet dividing lines were starting to be drawn within the band. With his nous, and wielding the power he had in the band, Noel was fully immersed in financial affairs and overseeing the advances Oasis would start to get from Creation.

Tony McCarroll: 'Before we got signed, that was when it started with Noel. There was £1,000 sent up by McGee to do a mini-tour. He said, 'Put all your gear back in order.' I didn't get any of that money, but I got a £600 tax rebate. I went out and got a kit at Johnny Roadhouse Music. Me, Liam and Noel couldn't afford a taxi to take it back to the Boardwalk, so we carried it on our shoulders.

'So, I'd spent my own money and this £1,000 comes in. Noel's like, 'What do you need?' I just said, 'Get me skins, I don't need drums.' Sorted. Come Thursday night, there's a brand spanking £800 Les Paul in the corner. I said, 'Where's my fucking drum skins?' 'I got you a gold-plated drum kit, you prick!'

'I went away and chewed on that. Next day I phoned him and gave him the verbal. I just leathered him verbally. Apparently, he didn't sleep for two days. It was all fucking building up, his sarcasm and everything. 'Fuck you, this is our band. Oasis is our band.' Basically, I give it him. Come Monday I get a phone call off Liam, who was quite sheepish, saying, 'Me and our kid don't want you in the band no more.' I went, 'For fuck's sake. If that's the case, then you hear me out.' Everything I pointed out to him, he said, 'You're right, you're right, you're right.' Next thing, I was reinstated.'

Pete Deary: 'He (Noel) gave me a guitar when he first got signed, an Epiphone Les Paul. Alan McGee gave them a grand to tide them over and he bought himself a guitar for £500. I think he Liam a mic stand, Tony McCarroll drumsticks, Guigs bass strings. I've still got the guitar, Christie's offered me about six grand for it years ago.'

The touring continued across the north, Oasis regularly hitting Leeds and Liverpool as well as continuing to play Manchester, new songs sporadically dropping into the set. 'Digsy's Dinner,' 'Slide Away' and 'Shakermaker' were included as Oasis began to play higher up the bills and, logically had to play longer sets. Noel's songwriting was also beginning to gather pace. As well as the aforementioned, he had composed a song built around a familiar riff; 'Cigarettes & Alcohol' opened in a strikingly-similar fashion to 'Get It On' by 70s glam-rockers T-Rex. When playing it for the first time for the rest of the band, Bonehead admonished Noel for shamelessly ripping off such a classic song. Noel's response was one of indifference, reasoning that no-one would ever hear their version anyway, which clashes with his notorious self-belief of the time.

Brian Cannon: 'The first time I ever saw them play was at the Hop & Grape in Manchester. I think they were supporting Liz Phair. I hadn't done any work with them at this point, '93, they hadn't had a record obviously. Noel had been mithering me for ages to go and watch his band. I liked Noel and got on with him. I didn't want to go because 99% of bands are rubbish and I thought they were bound to be shit. What was I gonna say to him afterwards? So, I kept putting it off, but in the end capitulated and went along to this gig. As I remember the only people who were there were me, Marcus Russell, Johnny Marr and a couple of students knocking about. That was basically it. I missed the first couple of songs, but then got in for the middle couple, and just thought, 'Fucking hell.' There was nobody there, it was in a tiny room. They obviously didn't have this amazing backline that they would have later on. But it was just like a juggernaut coming through the wall. It blew my cap off completely, it was incredible. Right from the very beginning they were that good.'

Oasis started to pick up support in the local press and in August recorded a programme for Radio 5 at the BBC's studios in Manchester, part of a series of shows called *Hit the North* which were focussing on the music scenes in various parts of the north of England. The programmes were presented by child of the North and Radio 1 DJ Marc Riley. The band played five songs; 'Bring It on Down', 'I Will Believe', 'Digsy's Dinner', 'Cigarettes & Alcohol', and 'Rock 'n' Roll Star'. It was their first-ever broadcast, and the first two performances would later become B-sides. There was also an interview, and if the band felt any shyness or nerves at being on national radio for the first time, they certainly didn't show it; Noel mocking New Order's Peter Hook (present in the studio), while Liam's message about the band's burgeoning reputation was simply, 'Don't believe the hype'. The music, however, spoke for itself.

Brian Cannon: 'There was no doubt in my mind that they were going to be massive. Having said that, it's the most-fickle industry in the world and quality is no guarantee of success. But I just couldn't see it not happening.'

Tom Hingley: 'Both Noel and Liam were a bit rude about us in the early days, because they wanted to completely separate themselves from us. Which was completely understandable.'

Plans to lay down some material for the band's first general releases started to formulate and, once the band had been officially signed to Creation, they entered Pink Museum studios in Liverpool to record their first single, at this point set to be 'Bring It on Down.' The B-sides were pencilled in as 'I Will Believe' and an acoustic number called 'Take Me Away,' performed solely by Noel. Unfortunately, this plan was soon nixed as Noel was unsatisfied with the drumming by Tony McCarroll for the lead track, so they only recorded 'Take Me Away' as intended.

Determined not to waste their time (or money) in the studio, the band tried a completely different song, then started playing a jam they had tried out in a soundcheck. As the jam progressed, Noel shouted the chords across the room to Bonehead, who in turn relayed it to Guigsy on bass, Tony providing a steady beat the entire time. Noel took to another room to compose some lyrics, while the rest of the band tucked into a Chinese takeaway. The elder Gallagher had decided to have a drink whilst composing and had opted for a gin and tonic. All the while, the dog belonging to engineer Dave Scott, Elsa was breaking wind at regular intervals. All these references were incorporated into the lyrics Noel was writing. After listening to Noel's guide vocal melody, Liam recorded his part in one take. With a few tweaks and adjustments, the whole process comprising 11 hours from start to finish, 'Supersonic' was complete. Pleased with what he heard, and apparently pouring a bottle of Jack Daniel's whiskey over his head in celebration, Alan McGee booked them in for further recording sessions.

Tony McCarroll: 'I was soundchecking at The Real People's studio. I was just playing with the simple beat, then Noel cracked open the door and says, 'Keep that going,' and 'Supersonic' came together within minutes. Whether it was one he had up his sleeve, or it came together that night ... I haven't got a clue. We all had our own input.

"Supersonic' was accidental. We went to The Real People's studio in Liverpool to record the first single, which was to be 'Bring It on Down.' That wasn't coming together so we were soundchecking different kits that night. Tony (The Real People's drummer) said, 'Do a soundcheck,' so I did and kept it simple. The next thing, the doors kick open and it's Noel saying, 'Keep that going.' Then 'Supersonic' just folded together.'

Rick Witter: 'Certainly with *Definitely Maybe*, they had the opportunity to go back and fix things which weren't quite right, which probably cost Creation a lot of money.'

Alan McGee: 'These were great times. It was a lot of work. Everybody thinks that album ... everybody thinks the rise of Oasis was really fast, but it wasn't. It took a long time coming. We had to dig a lot. Initially I was the digger and eventually we got there. Initially I was the one saying it wasn't good enough.'

The sessions were to be at Monnow Valley Studios near Monmouth and were to be produced by Dave Batchelor, whom Noel knew from his days with the Inspiral Carpets in his role as sound engineer.

Alan McGee: 'Noel had been on tour with Dave Batchelor, the producer. Dave wasn't getting any work around 1992/93. Noel met him as Inspiral Carpets' roadie, doing sound (I think). Noel promised that if he ever got signed Dave Batchelor could produce the album. When I met Noel, and Noel was amazing right off the bat, they were really big friends, he said, 'McGee, on the first album I have to let Dave Batchelor do it.' I wasn't wanting to get him to do it but I went along with it.

'I can't remember where we went, I think it was Monnow Valley. We spent £50,000 and it was fucking rubbish.'

Tony McCarroll: 'Dave Batchelor was chosen on his merits. He done his best job, but it was too clean. The studio was daunting. This was the first professional studio we'd been in. I was in what I can only describe as a steeple, where the sound went. I had 5,000 mics around me. The doors were closed, and I could barely get the eye contact we were always used to. The songs were dead slow. I would say the nerves got to all of us, and we were under pressure. We got to the end and it just didn't sound like us.'

Those sessions never quite hit the mark; everyone involved with Oasis was determined that the recordings should capture the ferocity of their live shows, and for whatever reason Batchelor was unable to do so, Bonehead later stating, 'It wasn't happening. He was the wrong person for the job. We'd play in this big room, buzzing to be in the studio, playing like we always played. He'd say, 'Come in and have a listen.' And we'd be like, 'That doesn't like it sounded in that room. What's that?' It was too thin. Weak. Too clean.'

Brian Cannon: 'It was Dave Batchelor, who'd done the Kinks, producing it and his recording style, which was a traditional recording style whereby everybody would be separated and record all the parts at different times and then mixing it all together. They'd only ever played live together, or even demoed together, so that was all binned.'

Tensions between the producer and everyone else in the studio can't have helped; Noel was made to record a number of different guitar solos for 'Live Forever', and Batchelor was adamant that one of the key tracks, 'Slide Away', had the wrong tempo and was determined to slow it down, despite protests from all concerned. With some suggestions from recording engineer Dave Scott, a new tempo was hit upon which went completely against Batchelor's ideas, so Scott was fired. The sessions were costing Creation £800 a day and, on Noel's recommendation to Marcus Russell, Dave Batchelor was relieved of his duties.

Alan McGee: 'I think one thing got kept off the Dave Batchelor sessions, and that was 'Slide Away'. Owen (Morris) mixed it, but they got 'Slide Away' right. So it wasn't a complete waste. It was nearly a waste of time, the whole session, but we got 'Slide Away' from it.'

Panicking, Noel - who had recently moved to Chiswick, west London, to have more ready access to the mechanics of the music industry - and Mark Coyle took the recorded demos to a few studios in the capital to mix them. On playing them to Creation, everyone was in agreement that the tapes simply weren't a reflection of Oasis as a live band. Indeed, the overall consensus was that the recordings weren't as powerful as *Live Demonstration*. Alan McGee made the executive decision that everything was to be scrapped and they would start again in the New Year.

Alan McGee: 'Me and Noel had got the tapes and we had come on in on the Dave Batchelor thing. Ride were recording with John Leckie. John's recorded with John Lennon. He's done XTC, Magazine, Public Image. He's done loads of great records. He was amazing with The Stone Roses. It showed you where my brain was, thinking logically. I came into the studio, I can't remember what studio Ride were recording at, doing their third album. I came in and said, 'John, we've got to get you. We should be recording with you.' And John turned us down. John turned down Oasis! He does now regret it.'

But away from the studio, momentum was building. During a short pre-Christmas tour the band got their first mention in the *NME*, a review of a gig at Birmingham Institute. The review itself was quite small, which was just as well as writer Johnny Cigarettes was hardly complimentary, but exposure was exposure:

'If Oasis didn't exist, no one would want to invent them. For a start, they look and sound like they're long overdue product from a bankrupt Polymer Records' Manc scally also-rans' factory. Vaguely trippy guitar almost-tunes with vaguely late-'60s rock tendencies, vaguely Ian Brown as Tim Burgess frontman, singing in a vaguely tuneless half-whine, vaguely shaking a tambourine, vaguely … er, yes, well, you get the picture.'

Johnny Sharp: 'I was wide of the mark on a few levels. But one thing I would say … you know when they say, 'The first time I saw them, blah blah blah' … that may well have been the case if you'd seen them maybe later on, when there was a real buzz around them, and they were starting to walk the walk and talk the talk. But I did that review when they were supporting St Etienne on tour in 1993 at Birmingham Institute. At that point they came on stage … to me they just looked like … the baggy thing was quite important. I'd only be writing for the *NME* for a year and a half, but I would get sent tapes and stuff like that from a lot of bands. You hear a lot of new acts that were very post-baggy. You thought, 'That ship has sailed.' Then you saw Liam do that Manc swagger, and let's face it, he did inherit a fair few mannerisms from Ian Brown and Tim Burgess. He did, in the end, completely make his own style in a brilliant way, and I totally didn't recognise that. But at that time, it was a little bit embryonic. The whole thing that annoyed me about them was that they reminded me of too many bands around that time who looked vaguely embarrassed to be on stage. They all stood stock still stage on stage, including Liam. My bank manager could stand on stage in a £600 anorak or whatever it was, and he could be a member of Oasis.

'Just hearing them once, I didn't think the songs were that good. The only thing I'd heard was a demo they sent into the office. People were supposedly raving about them. Geoff Barrett for example, who had discovered loads of bands and is unquestionably an important figure in music, was apparently raving about them.

'The one thing we'd heard was 'Columbia.' It sounded like that cliched indie lyric. When I went to see them, I had that slightly in mind.

'Oasis took umbrage at that review, and the subsequent reaction forms part of the 'Wibbling Rivalry' interview.'

The tour took in dates across northern Britain, stopping at Sheffield, Wolverhampton, Glasgow, Warwick, Birmingham, Preston, Newcastle and Bradford. For part of the tour they supported Wigan space rockers Verve, and the experiences they shared would become the foundation of a long-lasting friendship.

Brian Cannon: 'When Oasis supported The Verve, that was '93. It was an incredible tour. Support bands and the main acts invariably have separate dressing rooms, they are separate entities. The support act is almost looked down upon. On this tour there wasn't the segregated dressing room situation, we all just mucked in together. Whoever had the bigger dressing room, we'd all just congregate in there. They played a gig in Preston at the Mill, and I got a phone call. I think it was from a service station near Oldham. It was Noel on the phone, saying, 'We can't make the gig, the van's broke down.' I said, 'Leave it with me.' I told Richard Ashcroft, who said, 'We can't have this.' He mustered the troops and had the Verve's roadie and driver get their van, drive all the way to Oldham to pick up the Oasis guys and their equipment, and drive them to Preston for the gig. It was that kind of camaraderie.

'The night in Newcastle, the power went so the crowd were getting a bit restless. Bonehead came on stage, sat on a bar stool and started playing the spoons with somebody holding a torch above his head. He played the spoons with Richard Ashcroft singing, 'I'll Be Coming 'Round the Mountain' with him. It was a laugh. It was an adventure. It was just good fun.'

Three days before Christmas, Oasis were invited to record some tracks for the *Evening Session* on BBC Radio One, at Maida Vale studios, London. They did a six-song set where they introduced 'Cigarettes & Alcohol' and 'Supersonic' to the wider world, with the show pencilled in to be broadcast in January. Despite their troubles so far, McGee had complete faith in his new prodigies, all the pieces starting to fall into place for a full-throttled attack on the charts in the New Year.

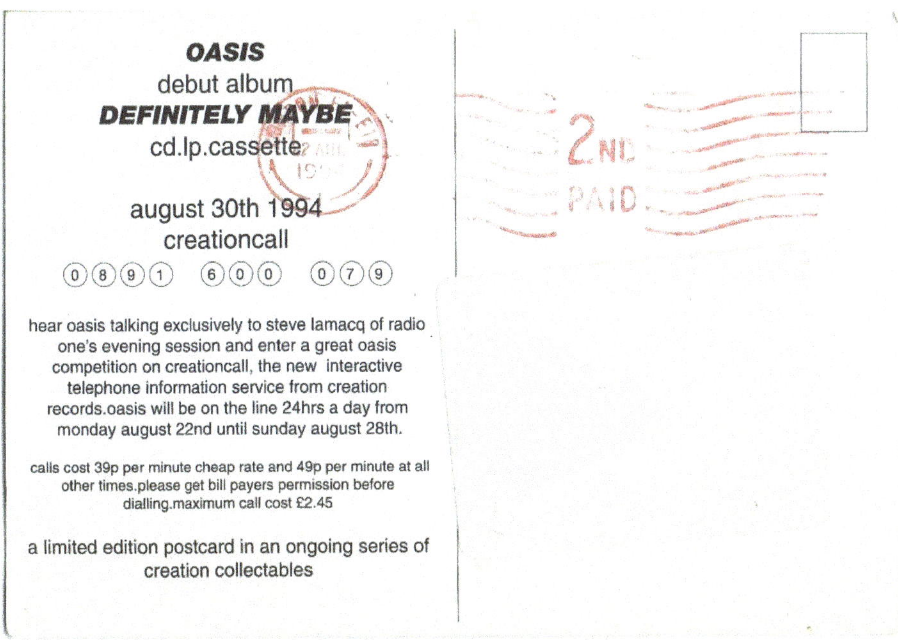

Photo credit: peterjwalsh.com

1994

'WAKE UP, THERE'S A NEW DAY DAWNING'

Pete Mitchell: 'It was definitely at the point where their reputation grew outside of Manchester with 'Columbia.' Radio One were playing it. It got picked up pretty well. Everyone began to play it. If it wasn't suitable and they weren't good enough, people wouldn't have picked up on it.'

In early 1994 Creation launched their first Oasis salvo on the general public - the demo version of 'Columbia.' Lifted directly from *Live Demonstration*, it was given a limited edition, white label release and ended up being picked up and played on BBC Radio One around 20 times over a two-week period. This kind of exposure for an unknown band was unheard of, and everyone within the Oasis camp, specifically those at Creation Records, were jubilant. Alan McGee claims that to be the moment he knew they were going to be massive.

Alan McGee: 'It must have been because I loved it. I fucking loved that track. But you are talking to the man that went with 'Morning Glory' as the first single in America, and it fucking bombed. We stuck out 'Wonderwall' and it sold two million off the back of me putting it out. I've made some legendary mad moves, and ultimately it must have been that I really loved it. I shoved it, and they let me have it. It was really successful. It nearly got 50 spot plays on Radio One, which is phenomenal. When 'Supersonic' came out in April '94, we charted probably off the back of getting the white label out.'

Simon Mason: 'That white label of 'Columbia' is, to this day and always will be, one of the most remarkable pieces of music ever.'

No recognition on the music scene would come without performing in London, and so Oasis were booked to play their first gig in the capital at The Water Rats, near King's Cross station, on January 27. Only 200 people attended (although it has to be said that was the capacity) and because of the buzz surrounding the band it was the 'must have' ticket in town that night. Once again it was a six-song set, but had been refined to contain four future singles:

'Shakermaker'
'Bring It on Down'
'Digsy's Dinner'
'Live Forever'
'Cigarettes & Alcohol'
'Supersonic'

Simon Mason: 'When I saw Oasis in the Water Rats, I had a sit-up moment. I was standing there with a couple of hundred people in this room going, 'Fucking hell.' It felt like what they'd done was taken the essence of every band I'd loved that were no longer in existence. I just stood in the Water Rats and went, 'This is my band.' I had goosebumps all over.

'It absolutely had the same impact as that first Jam gig, seeing The Smiths on TV, seeing the Roses in '89. It was like, 'This makes sense to me.'

'The room was full of A&R men that had missed the boat. They were all standing there chatting shit to each other, with their ponytails and really ill-fitting suits, going, 'How did we miss this?'

Pete Mitchell: 'I do remember the band breaking out of Manchester at the time, and the fallout of Liam and his antics and everything ... every kid walking down the high street aping Liam. Liam had aped Ian Brown, and Tim Burgess prior to that. So, we had this kind of caricature thing for a while which still maintains itself. That kind of caricaturing, if you want to call it that, didn't actually exist until the point that Liam Gallagher began to become well-known.'

With London under their belt, the next significant stride Oasis were due to take was an international gig, pencilled in for Amsterdam in late January. A roadie was required, the appropriately-named Jason Rhodes assigned to the task. In the morning, he picked the group up in a Transit van. After establishing there was cash in the float that Rhodes had been entrusted with, the gang scoured Manchester for cheap drugs, then set off for the ferry terminal. Not only did they have the float, but Guigsy had received redundancy money (in cash) from British Gas. Somehow, even though they were as drunk as skunks and high as kites, the van was allowed on the ferry that Thursday night, with all the fixtures and fittings required for late-night jaunts, including a casino.

Alas, also on board was a group of football fans who, after a few hours drinking champagne and Jack Daniel's slammers, the band and some of their entourage managed to butt heads with. First to jump into an affray was one Liam Gallagher. After swinging a few punches, Liam managed to attract the attention of the on-board constabulary. Bonehead also claimed that his clothes had been stolen by the hooligans. Eventually, Liam and several other members of the party, including Bonehead and long-term friend Phil Smith, were arrested and spent the rest of the night in the hold.

Absent from the shenanigans was Noel, who awoke the next morning to be told his band had been deported and sent back to the UK. Marcus Russell was furious when Rhodes called him to break the news, Alan McGee less so. A canny operator, McGee advised the allocated PR representative, Johnny Hopkins, to ensure the story became widespread. Fortunately, the *NME* had assigned a photographer and reporter to cover the gig, so there was the opportunity of ready-made coverage. McGee knew this would only enhance Oasis' burgeoning reputation and was pleased. The story made headlines across the music press, grabbing the prime news article in the *NME* (with accompanying photograph of Noel without band in Amsterdam), and national radio. The moniker of 'bad boys of rock' was more than readily attached to them from this point on.

Tony McCarroll: 'If there was a journey, then it started about 8.30am in Manchester. You'd whizz around Manchester to get a few extra bits and bobs for the journey. We got absolutely leathered. We got on the boat and it was like a day trip to us. Our first international gig and it was for Sony. With Amsterdam being a ship-holding hub, they decided that all the delegates from around the world would land there for a convention for European labels. We were so leathered that it wasn't long before the security was watching us. Apparently, there were £50 notes going through the till, bottles of champagne missing. I do remember drinking champagne and JD slammers, and I didn't buy them. Chances are someone in our lot was pilfering away. But security watching us enticed Liam. He was getting all excited, running away, and they were running after him. It was just mayhem. It resulted in 80% of the band except Noel being arrested. Only Oasis could fuck up the most important gig in their career. The only thing I remember from the next morning was being handcuffed in a room and Noel walking past us, (thinking he's) not going to be happy!'

After Amsterdam, Oasis played some gigs in Scotland, including one at Gleneagles. Before the gig, they played 'I Am the Walrus' in their soundcheck, this version later the official release (rather than a version at Glasgow Cathouse, as later claimed). To sustain the momentum triggered by the 'Columbia' white label, Creation worked in conjunction with the *NME* to release a cassette tape free with their February 12 edition. On it were four tracks, all from the label. A forthcoming B-side from The Boo Radleys, a reworked album track from Teenage Fanclub, a live version of John Lennon track, 'I Don't Want to Be A Soldier' performed by Ride, and a demo of one of the Oasis tracks in consideration for the album, 'Cigarettes & Alcohol.' The tape was dubbed *Mutha Of Creation*.

Alan McGee: 'That was nothing to do with me. It was all my bands, the Primals, Valentines and Fanclub. And Oasis were the little band on it. I can't remember what version went on, probably The Real People version.'

Yet all the touring, promotion and extra-curricular activities couldn't distract from the fact that there was still an album to be recorded, so more session time was booked, this time at Sawmill Studios in Cornwall.

It was decided that the recordings would be produced by Noel and Coyle and a new engineer was drafted in, Anjali Dutt, regarded as a safe pair of hands by Creation, having worked with My Bloody Valentine.

Tony McCarroll: 'Coyley could appreciate the energy that was in a gig. He recognised that, tried to bring it to the desk and record it that way.

'In Sawmills he locked us in. There was no getting to the local pub, it was a three-mile walk down a dark railway track. The only alternative was when the tide was in, and we had to get a boat to the pub. None of us ever bothered. I think they did it on purpose.

'We were fishing outside in the pond. It was like a holiday for us!'

Alan McGee: 'Oasis live were fucking phenomenal. So, I thought, 'OK, get Coyley to mix it like a gig. Record it, then mix it like a gig. That's got to work. And it did, 50 per cent of the way. Coyley recorded it like a gig, amazing live performances. But he couldn't fucking mix it. So, then the next person we got in was Anjali (Dutt), and she mixed it. She never got it, and she was a big mixer at that point. She'd just done The Boo Radleys, a big record for me. She was brilliant at mixing. She'd done Valentines ... all the shoegaze bands. She was really good with sonics.'

Dutt made the decision to scrap everything and start again, and felt the best approach to replicating their live sound on record would be to simply record together, without sound proofing between instruments, Noel adding overdubs of guitars to the material after recording had finished.

Anjali Dutt (studio engineer): 'I think they came from Manchester and they hadn't particularly been out and about very much and so, when we went to Sawmills in Cornwall, because it wasn't a complete luxurious studio, it did have this feel of a school trip field centre. They hadn't been away from home in particular, so they were liable to do crazy stuff like wake up late, go to bed late but still want their food put on the table.

'The album feels like a bunch of school friends playing a record. Noel was very clearly focussed on the music and the thing is with Noel, he can play everything. In the countless hours we were waiting for people to wake up, and managed to get into the same room, at the same time together. I cannot emphasise enough how difficult that one thing was to do. You could hear Noel playing drums or playing a bit of bass. You realise he was actually quite a good multi-instrumentalist. Noel definitely stuck out, because he was the most mature and serious out of all them.

'There was a bit of bluster coming out of Liam, but then Liam only talks in blusters. None of the others were.....you have to remember they were a bit tired, because it was the third time they'd recorded this album and they were slightly under pressure to get it done. They were also not entirely sure why it was that the album wasn't sounding good. Was it them? Was it the recording? Nobody actually knew. And there was a tour imminent, so it had to be done within a certain time. And they were in the middle of absolutely nowhere.

'Liam just sang. You couldn't get many takes out of Liam and they weren't desperately necessary either. He always sang in tune. He didn't have any direction with his voice, I just remember he just sang it, usually in one take. Sometimes you'd ask for a second or third take. He wasn't keen on singing for very long. He was an unusually good tambourine player. I know they did some of the vocals again with Owen (Morris) though.

'Bonehead and Guigs were very consistent, they were very good. There wasn't much scope for messing up, because I think they just recorded every single thing they played because we couldn't keep them together in one place for long enough. There was definitely a couple of places on the bass where it did have to get replaced. Noel did love putting layer after layer of guitar on, and Bonehead's guitar got lost sometimes with it. They played best when they were live. To get them to play it separately with an overdub wasn't quite as effective as it was with other bands. I think on 'Up in The Sky' Noel replaced the bass, and you can hear it sound quite different. 'Slide Away' might have been replaced on the bass. But generally, at the time the takes were OK.

'There was actually lots of trouble with 'Slide Away'. It had a very slight, sort of, Neil Young feel about it, and it was never quite coming together. It was done over and over and over. In the end, we went back to the Monnow Valley version. It dragged on a bit. It always gave trouble.'

Alan McGee: 'For a band that inexperienced to get it ('Slide Away') so right is brilliant.'

Brian Cannon: 'They went off to Cornwall to Sawmills Studio and recorded as live, pretty much really. I think Liam was in a booth on his own, but apart from that they recorded live.'

Tony McCarroll: 'It was a mish-mosh of an album. I can't say there's two tunes that are somewhat the same on there. It was built up over a couple of years. The energy, the rawness ... the budget we'll say. I think after my time there was a lot more money involved, but then it was, 'Get in there and do that in two takes and shut up.'

'It was quite nerve-racking, the whole experience was something new to me. Back in the studio, surrounded by five million mics, it's like, 'Don't fart, don't do anything wrong.

'Owen (Morris) used to say, 'I'll do no more than five takes, because you may be losing your energy then.' The majority of the time we nailed it.'

One of the most problematic tracks to commit to tape was 'Bring It on Down,' with Tony not quite able to capture the energy of the live performance. With the clock ticking, it was decided that a session drummer would be drafted in.

Tony McCarroll: 'It was the second time round recording, and a lot of the record companies back then used to play games like that. 'That ain't good enough, you're going to have to do it again.' But you're living in their pockets for years. Noel pretty much said, 'I've got to get this done.' Fair play to him for once, he did phone me and say this is happening. It was more of an order. I said, 'Whatever, it's got to be done.' And then I got it right in the end. Maybe I was tired, you don't know.

'It was the only track we had to get down. The drummer gets blamed for fucking everything by the way! Tony (from The Real People) is stood in front of me with the meanest stare, to get the muscles going. 'You're going to record this, don't give him your fucking money, blah blah blah.' Then I recorded it in one.'

But, again, the results weren't up to expectations. Alan McGee was prepared to allow the band another go, and he was determined to get it right, but rather than throw good money after bad straight away, a last-ditch attempt was made to salvage what they had. Marcus Russell made contact with engineer-turned-producer Owen Morris, who previously mixed the album's songs for the first recording attempt. Morris was unimpressed with what he heard but was given free rein to do whatever it took to improve the recordings, his first choice being to remove all the guitar overdubs. He then went to work on mixing the album and used a method he takes credit for pioneering, which he christened 'brick-walling.' This was a relatively simple act of turning up all the levels of the instrumentation, which are normally varied to allow nuance and for the music to breathe, to maximum, creating a cacophonous wall of sound. It worked a treat. The music sounded equally as bombastic coming out of car stereos as it did from six-foot high speakers found in the recording studio.

Brian Cannon: 'Owen only mixed it. Owen had no part whatsoever in the recording of that album. He just mixed it. He was given the recorded parts that were done in Cornwall because they just couldn't mix it, they didn't know what they were doing, as Mark Coyle freely admits. As a last-ditch attempt to salvage the record Owen Morris was brought in and he just worked his magic and saved the entire project, if you ask me.'

Tony McCarroll: 'I don't know what he did. He had a special machine that he put the sound through or something. Owen brought energy to us. The session with Dave was flat. We'd done demoes with Owen before, so he was more than aware of us. He did a brilliant job on *Definitely Maybe*. The final product was amazing.'

Owen Morris (record producer): 'Marcus Russell was managing Johnny Marr and also looked after me for a while. But I was getting a bit frustrated working for Johnny and got a different manager just before Marcus got involved with Oasis. The theory was that I should have been involved with Oasis from the start, but they went with Dave Batchelor first.

'The multi-tracks I got were well recorded multi-tracks, with good guitar sounds and separation. I think maybe with Dave Batchelor they might have over-tidied everything up in a '70s style with absolutely no spill and stuff like that. Whereas when they redid the backing tracks with Mark Coyle they probably just set up in a live room and bashed the backing tracks out quickly, live together. I think that's what they meant when they were talking about a live style.

'I think it got to the stage where Creation didn't want to spend any more money on it. So Noel paid, from his publishing advance, my mixing fees and the studio time. He probably paid 30, 40 grand out of his own pocket. That's my understanding, I don't know if it's entirely true. I assume he got recouped and paid back very quickly. That was a loan to the band from himself. I think he had a pretty good publishing deal. It was easier for them just to take control.

'There wasn't really any A&R input from Creation with Oasis. I think Alan McGee listened to the initial songs, but I think he went into rehab or something during the making of *Definitely Maybe*. I never really saw Alan McGee in the studio apart from maybe one time when he came in to listen to *Morning Glory* near the end. So, it was basically Noel choosing the songs and running the band, with Marcus Russell managing the whole thing.

'Noel really had it sussed with arrangements and song choices. He just wasn't experienced in the studio so I kind of filled in the gaps, as far as putting takes together, overdubbing methods and getting vocals done, which was quite important as Noel wasn't that into spending time.....once he'd shown Liam the song, he just buggered off and let Liam sing. Which was fine actually, because it was a cool way of doing it. I'd be producing the notes and compiling and just general production techniques. Basic production techniques which were just filling the gaps.

'I wasn't a very good engineer, but I was engineering. I wasn't technically adept! But I didn't really like working with anyone else, it was always quicker to do it myself.'

Alan McGee: 'I was tearing my hair out. I was also trying to come off drugs, so I was in this self-imposed rehab in my house. Marcus and Noel would come 'round to my house, and Marcus says, 'I'll get Owen Morris to do a mix on spec.' I was like, 'Really, would that work?' I mean, what's he done? I really didn't see how it was going to work. But it was costing us no money, so of course I let it happen. I got 'Rock 'n' Roll Star' back and they'd fucking nailed it.

'With *Definitely Maybe*, if I hadn't have said it's not good enough, fuck knows what would have happened. Although to be fair, Marcus totally thought the same and he was probably thanking God that I was conscientious and saying it's not good enough, it's got to be better. Noel would have put it out because he didn't understand the business at that point, he thought there'd be a second chance. There ain't a second chance baby, this is it. This is the chance. It's not even about me not picking up the option, it's nothing like that. The music business pays attention for five seconds. You've got to be good. I pulled the record and made them record it again. By the time Noel was nailing it, by the time success was happening, Noel was pretty much it was a joint thing between Creation and Oasis at that point.'

With *Definitely Maybe* finally in the can, it was time for Oasis to start seriously flogging their wares around the country. A co-headline tour with Scottish rockers Whiteout was booked, spanning the end of March to the end of April, from Glasgow to Southampton, most nights consisting of a nine-song set. Amidst the tour, they made their first appearance on national television on March 18 for late-night magazine show *The Word* on Channel 4. It was a blistering performance with the hallmarks that would define Oasis; confrontational but nonchalant, loud and full of attitude. Though his voice was now fully rounded, Liam had yet to define his stage presence; he holds the microphone on its stand but is moving (albeit on one spot) throughout, and films the crowd through hand-held camera, presumably for personal use.

Their second London date at the 100 Club on Oxford Street was declared as a triumph by the *NME*: 'At times tonight Oasis assume the mantle of Best Live Band in the Country with joyous, arrogant Mancunian confidence. They may never be this good again and they may never have been this good before but, four rows from the front, they sound like the most astute, important signing Alan McGee has made since Ride.'

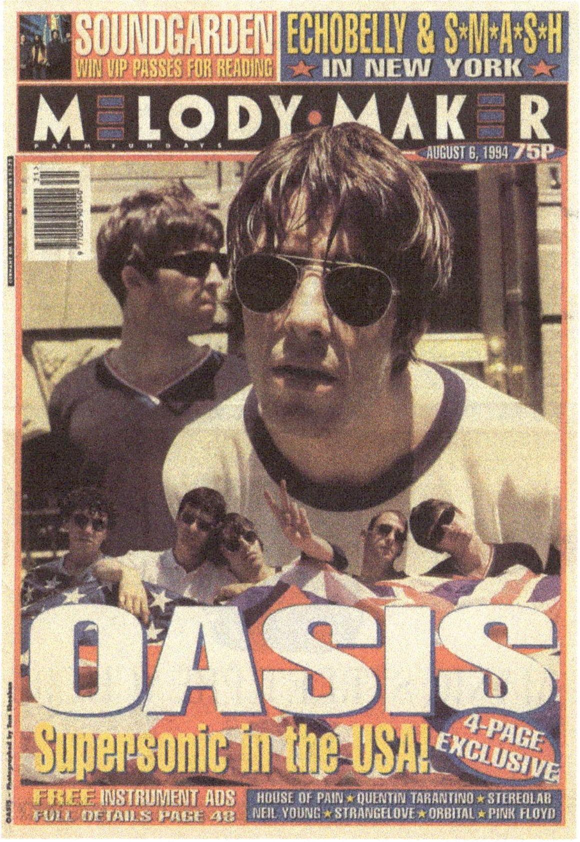

Alan McGee: 'The joke was, there wasn't a lot of money behind it. These things work the way they're going to work.

'The biggest problem that anybody has got looking at it after the fact is that you think that everybody knew what they were doing. That's not really the case. We were guessing a lot of the time. We didn't know that 'Supersonic' was going to go in the top-40. We wanted it to, but we never knew it was going to. When

Marcus booked that (early) tour, he played it safe as he should do. To put them into thousand capacities as a new band, you'd have got everybody going, 'Who the fuck do you think you are?' So, what was good was that they were ramming it out that whole tour. They were selling everything out. They weren't even the only band on the tour. There was a little Scottish band called Whiteout and they flipped the bill. By the end of the tour Oasis were going on at the end every night because it was too ridiculous.'

Paolo Hewitt (music writer): 'It was one of those things that was word of mouth. No, I tell you what it was ... I used to hang out with Jeff Barrett at Heavenly Records, I was round to his house and he was listening to 'Live Forever'. I was like, 'This is one of the most amazing records I've ever heard.' Then I saw them on *The Word* and thought, 'Yeah, this is good'. There was a real buzz around London about them, that word of mouth, so we got tickets to The Forum, and it was just great. The thing that struck me was that they were making this huge sound that nobody was making on stage. They just stood there, staring at the audience, and had this huge sound coming from them. It was quite unique. And of course, Liam with his hands behind his back, his vocal style. It was, 'Wow!' You knew it was something.

'It was Noel that I first got to know and was probably closest to, then going on the road, I met the rest of them. Liam was very stand-offish with me. He was very suspicious of everybody in those days, which is fair enough, I understand that totally. Guigsy was lovely. Bonehead and (Tony McCarroll's imminent replacement on drums) Alan White were just lovely guys. Funny. We had a lot of fun then. Everything was new. 'We're going on tour in Japan!' But four years later, 'Japan, ugh ... we're staying in that shit hotel again, are we?' But at that time everything was brand new, and it was all groovy. Everything was adventure after adventure. Noel would come down and say, 'I got stopped at the border, and we had to hide everything.' I mean, it was just funny.

'His writing was just one of those streaks. His writing had value to it. I would say some songs weren't as effective as others, or as big, or as epic, but the little ones had something about them. He was just on this incredible roll really. I think he had been waiting and waiting so long that when he saw his chance, he just took it with both hands. But they had no idea how big they were going to get.'

The tour was ostensibly to promote debut single 'Supersonic', which was released on April 11, 1994, and eventually reached No.31 in the UK singles chart. The lead track was backed by 'Take Me Away', 'I Will Believe (Live)' and the white label demo of 'Columbia', while the video was typically low-budget for a debut effort, the band playing on the roof of a hotel next to King's Cross Station in London. The radio stations would brief (or were harassed by) the staff at Creation on when the single was to be played, and the band made it a ritual to listen out for it where possible. They also got together on the Sunday it charted to listen to the top-40 on Radio One, and on hearing of its placing, no doubt celebrated into the night.

Even though it was presumably unintentional, the opening lyrics (*'I need to be myself, can't be no-one else')* were a mission statement that are often commented upon as being perfectly representative of the band's outlook. It was sleeved in the first of many designs by Microdot's Brian Cannon, the band dotted around a studio with a blue hue.

Brian Cannon: 'Traditionally, and I'd had this before from major labels throughout my career, they would insist that not only is the name of the record on the front of the cover, but it's in the top third, and it has to be a certain per cent ... honestly, it's like a mathematical science. When I was first asked by Noel to do the artwork, I actually got a phone call from the in-house designer for Creation Records at the time, and he said, 'I believe you're doing the image for the 'Supersonic' sleeve. Send it through to me and I'll put the rest of the package together.' I said, 'No, I'm doing the lot.' This went back and forth, and I said, 'I'll just give Noel a quick ring.' So, I called him and told him the story. He said, 'Give me five minutes.' He rings up Creation, gets the guy on the phone, not being bolshy about it, and basically says to him, 'If Brian Cannon doesn't do the artwork it's going out in a brown paper bag and that's the end of it.' So, he gave me a ring back and said, 'Get on with it, Brian.' So, I never really had anyone interfere, and that was down to McGee really. It was literally between me and Noel, all of it.

'The whole Oasis gig was a branding exercise. The whole point being that a blind man on a galloping horse could see that it was an Oasis record. It (the logo) didn't need to be any bigger, it just works.'

April was a big month for Oasis; not only was their debut single released but they also had the first of many, many controversial interviews. For their first interview with the *NME* the band, but primarily Liam and Noel, were interviewed after a gig at the Tramway in Glasgow by John Harris. The interview was intended to cover the debut single, the band's influences, and the usual vignettes, but quickly transcended into a dialogue about their fledgling reputation, the focal point being the incident on the ferry to Amsterdam.

As would soon become commonplace, it descended into an argument between Liam and Noel which Harris was lucky enough to be recording. It was a standard interview until the pair get side-tracked into a vociferous disagreement. Both make valid points; Liam believing that getting into trouble and scrapes is part and parcel of being a rock'n'roll band, with Noel's stance being that such behaviour is beneath artists and ultimately their reputation should be built on music above all

4 June 1994 75p $(US)3.75
READING FESTIVAL line up – Page 3
NME
NEW MUSICAL EXPRESS
The Great GLASTONBURY Ticket Giveaway Part Three
Ready steady Gobi
THE OASIS BAR
LUSH ★ THE ORB
NINE INCH NAILS
VAPOURSPACE
FUTURE SOUND OF LONDON
NICK KENT
MEGADOG
DOWNSET
SABRES OF PARADISE
CREATION UNDRUGGED
ARRESTED DEVELOPMENT
TOTALLY COOL
OASIS:What the world is waiting for
Liam out of Oasis photographed by Kevin Cummins

else. Both would be proved right in their own ways. Looking back on the interview now, with the knowledge of where both Gallaghers are in their respective solo careers, it's the expression, 'The more things change, the more they stay the same' writ large. The interview would later be released as a CD single called *Wibbling Rivalry*.

Also in April, another tour began, this time with Oasis headlining in their own right. The first date at Hull's Adelphi saw more people turned away than were able to fit in the venue. The same thing happened the following night in Coventry, and those that were allowed in took to stage-diving. Noel had to climb onto the PA to escape. Step by step, Oasis were becoming undeniable.

Paul Slattery (photographer): 'It was mad. Completely mad. Bonehead was driving the van, Salford Van Hire as I remember. I remember driving down from West London to a gig in Southampton. I'd known the band for about a month or two by then. I got into Southampton and saw this Salford Van Hire van just going 'round and round the ring road in Southampton. Then suddenly there's a face at the window going, 'Eh, Slattery, where's the fucking gig?' It was Bonehead driving the van. That's how it first started.

'I remember the Old Trout pub in Windsor, where there was a huge crowd of kids who wanted to get in. We all had to give our passes to Noel, who went outside and gave them to all the kids. It was a small cognoscenti of fans who were turning up to all the gigs. It was great. I loved it because they were playing small venues, which I always loved. I saw this band playing and after half a dozen gigs, I thought, 'I think they're going to be quite big'. At that time, it was only Noel who has the vision of how great they were going to be. Quietly!'

Alan McGee: 'They played New Cross (May 13, '94) and Noel and Liam came 'round to see me because I was really ill. Well, I was fucked, I was a fucking mess! They were lovely and cool, and I was a bit mental. Fuck knows what they really thought! They said, 'We're giving the guy from The La's a gig - John Power. Will we get you a tape?' Which they never bothered doing.'

Rick Witter: 'I do remember we (Shed Seven) had a joint headline gig with Oasis at The Venue in New Cross in '94. We turned up at soundcheck time, they're already there. So, we walk in and we were almost a bit excited because we'd heard this name quite a lot. They were all just stood in a group next to the stage and immediately Liam comes up, saying, 'You're not using your backdrop, and we're going on last.' 'Alright, nice to meet you, Liam.' Obviously, they went and skyrocketed, great stuff. Maybe in the early days there might have been a threat from us, which is why they were a bit like that.'

Simon Mason: 'I saw them at the 100 Club, I saw them at the old Marquee, which is where I met them for the first time. Someone said, 'Can you pop backstage, someone wants something?' I walked into an argument between Noel and Liam about why Liam didn't have any money, and Noel just went, 'I write all the fucking songs.' He went 'Yeah, but I'm the star.' 'Yeah, but I write all the songs.' 'Yeah, but you're a knobhead.' 'Yeah, but I write the songs.' 'You'll get yours when the album comes out.' 'When's the album coming out?' 'Dunno.' And I'm standing there going ... 'You rang?'

'In the audience that night was Richey (Edwards) from the Manic Street Preachers. I was standing next to him and I remember as Oasis were finishing with 'I Am the Walrus', people with mouths open, and Liam walks off. This is just a theory, but I looked at Richey and he was looking at them. He disappeared a few days later, never to be seen again. He was clearly impressed. It wasn't that long after the Water Rats, a couple of months maybe, and they'd got even better. There was more confidence, and more swagger, and the volume had got louder. This is an unstoppable force.

'He was Liam. Absolutely confident. Just that belief. A belief that they were going to be bigger than The Beatles. Completely unshakable, funny, charming, didn't suffer fools, entertaining, cheeky. He had this sense of, 'Nice to meet you, get out of my way.' I think he may not have realised it, or admit it, but there was a genuine excitement. Noel had been in the music business for years by this point, he'd seen it, done it, and knew what was going on. Whereas I think Liam, at the centre of the storm, had a genuine excitement about everything.'

May and June saw the band continuing to tour in small venues throughout the country, with Noel playing a short acoustic set as part of a special event at the Royal Albert Hall for their new label (*Undrugged - Creation Records' 10th Anniversary Special)*. In the latter month the second single was released; 'Shakermaker'. A 12 bar-blues number, the song was a woozier, more psychedelic offering than 'Supersonic', with almost dream-like lyrics. The lyrics and melody were 'borrowed' from 'I'd Like to Teach The World To Sing (In Perfect Harmony)' by '70s pop pickers The New Seekers. So much so that, for the first time and certainly not the last, Oasis were sued, and forced to change their composition, including the lyrics. Legal troubles would become an ongoing concern. However, with word-of-mouth and significant airplay, the single charted at No.11 in the top-40.

Top of the Pops, which at that point was airing on Thursday nights on BBC One, was not only a national institution but a rite of passage for British music acts. The programme had a policy that new entry singles entering in the top-25 would have, if possible, a live (or more likely, a mimed) performance on that week's show. The performance by the rest of the band was indeed mimed, but Liam sang live. The way the band were set out on stage was interesting though; Tony McCarroll and his drums were positioned at the front, with Liam behind and the three guitarists positioned at the sides. Noel was apparently furious at this decision. But Oasis had been beamed into the nation's living rooms and had made a significant step into the mainstream. Which was all part of the masterplan. It also helped sales, 'Shakermaker' doubling 'Supersonic''s figure to 45,000 copies, which enabled them to play again on the following week's show.

As if their first *Top of the Pops* appearance wasn't enough, June also brought Oasis their first *NME* cover and lead interview. The cover was of Liam on his own, in a bar in a hotel in Newport which was, no doubt entirely coincidentally, called The Oasis Bar. Following them for three days, the article was the first detailed insight into the rigours, or more pertinently the antics, of a band in their first flush of success. Liam and Noel fought, a hotel was trashed, drugs were consumed, and the gigs were glorious.

At the end of the month Oasis were booked to play the Glastonbury Festival in Somerset. The biggest festival in Britain, Glastonbury had several stages and prided itself on giving good exposure to up and coming bands. However, the 1994 festival was in doubt as, less than two weeks before, the famous Pyramid Stage had burnt down. Fortunately, a temporary replacement was found, and the festival went on as planned. It was also the first year Glastonbury was shown on television, on Channel 4, so it was a good opportunity for record labels to maximise exposure to their current crop. Creation were never ones to turn down such an opportunity and had a number of acts performing on various stages, one of which was Oasis. In the early afternoon of the last day of the festival, the band were second on the bill, sandwiched between Echobelly and Credit to the Nation. The set was well received and was another step on the ladder.

Tony McCarroll: 'Madness. We were backstage so we didn't see that crowd before we came out. If you notice I've got no fucking neck, because I was so nervous. It was the same on *The Word*. The early performances, where you have to get it right and the cameras are there, are so nervous.

'Glastonbury was up there with our best gigs. An iconic festival.'

Pete Deary: 'They were like a breath of fresh air, I suppose. Liam being Liam, you couldn't take your eyes off him. All he done was stand with his hands behind his back just singing, but he had that little aura about him.

'Oasis brought Manchester and Liverpool together. They got on with Scousers and I think a lot of Oasis fans became warm to it.'

A huge step (or hurdle, depending on the label's attitude) to success for UK bands is 'cracking' America. It's commonly understood that to do so, there has to be a lot of effort put in. With their ambition this was a challenge Oasis were never going to shy away from, and their first American appearance was to be at the Wetlands Festival in New York, a music industry seminar for Sony executives (Sony also representing the band in America). And the jaunt was put to good use, as they filmed a video there for their next single.

Paul Slattery: 'As the months wore on into the summer, I went over to New York to see them play at the Wetlands. That was their first gig in the States and was a wild night. As far as I don't remember! It was a great gig and a great party afterwards, put on by the New York Rock Chicks. A never to be forgotten party. I've never been to a rock party like that, before or since. It was just a party beyond anybody's wildest dreams. Oasis lapped up every second of it until about 5am, when the sun came up. Guigsy said to me, 'Are we really in New York, Slats?'

'It was a lot of fun. But also, Noel was the music master. Every soundcheck he'd be looking at the band. He was the man who was keeping it together musically. It was his vision. Liam turned up at soundchecks and the great thing about him is that he has perfect pitch. He would turn up, sing and just know the correct tone. It was amazing. I've never, ever known anyone to do that. Before Noel had even struck a guitar chord. He had an incredible voice. He hit the correct note all the time. He could get right up to those high notes without any problems at all.'

But as their trajectory continued, practicalities had to start being considered, and if crowd safety was a concern, things needed to change. Marcus Russell was simply unable to look after all the affairs of the band, and as the venues were becoming bigger so was the itinerary. It was decided that a tour manager would be required, someone who would be accountable for ensuring the band would fulfil their appearance commitments, both onstage and off. Stepping into the breach was an ex-military, brick outhouse of a man called Iain Robertson.

Iain Robertson (tour manager): 'I was in New York for a series of music shows. The New Music seminar I think it was called, at a place called the Wetlands on the Lower West Side if memory serves. I knew Marcus, he and I were friends already, so it was nice to see him. I picked up on the buzz there was. I hung around to watch the Oasis set and they were blistering. In that small club they were absolutely astonishing. It was punk. Liam's voice then was still crystal. At the end of the night I ended up in a hotel with Marcus and Bonehead in New York. I just said, 'I really wanna work with this band, and I don't care in what capacity.

'The whole Oasis thing was a real challenge. There was an intensity there in those early days that you genuinely cannot begin to imagine. The point at which I started working with the band, I already had a pretty decent track record. I had

Johnny Rotten under my belt, I had George Harrison under my belt. I'd worked with some pretty serious bands. But to be with a band in those very early days when frankly every day was a surprise. What's really interesting for me is if you look at the kind of rhetoric Noel was using; 'It's written in the stars, it's inevitable', the kind of arrogance that the mainstream media picked up on. I can tell you categorically that every single day was as much as a surprise to him, to Liam, to the rest of the band as it was to the rest of the world.

'Unlike anybody else from the early years within the management structure, he (Tim Abbott, Creation MD) was there. Marcus had his hands full. Marcus got out as often as he could, but he had a whole lot to deal with, and so he was at Ignition Headquarters or at Creation. Or he was out at the big shows, London, Los Angeles. But when we were out fully on the road, we were just like this little gang. Tim, out of that kind of management hierarchy, was really the only person that we saw with any regularity and shared a tour bus and kind of stayed up late with us.

'There were some people who did incredible things for the band; the Brian Cannons of the world. But we didn't see a great deal of them, and we certainly didn't see them when we were in Salt Lake City. We might see them in London, or in Manchester or Glasgow, but we didn't see them in Frankfurt or some crappy little club in France. On those instances it was half a dozen, maybe seven or eight people max.

'They absolutely were (a gang) with shared experiences. All coming from the same side of the tracks, that was a very real thing. The incredible thing about Liam; I had nothing but admiration for anybody who has the courage to go into the world and not filter anything. It would be a really messy place if we all did that, but Liam's never gonna do that. He's going to tell you exactly what he thinks, or what he doesn't think. Sometimes the brain doesn't get involved in the process. But you're gonna get a completely emotional and honest response to whatever the hell it was you asked or whatever the hell it is that's happening around him.

'He was never that difficult or challenging apart from a number of occasions, most of which are fairly well documented. The real drama and the greatest difficulty on the road was the sibling thing. That was genuinely damaging to be around for anybody who was very close to it. And notably for other members of the band, because it was real. There was no pretend about it. They didn't wait for the cameras to fall out, they'd fall out whenever the hell they fell out. Sometimes it was genuinely a violent thing to be around. There were occasions when my role was to protect one or other against one or other, and not the great British unwashed.

'Any tour, no matter how small or how big, your role as one of rock's worker bees is to make sure whatever time the show is scheduled, it happens, and the band are ready to do what they're supposed to do. The other thing I don't think people realise is how incredibly hard they work when they're hot, because everybody wants a piece of them. At that point in the early stages, you need the *NME* and whatever press is out there. You can't be cavalier with them in a way you can be when you've sold 100 million records. If you have to do a tiny radio station in France, you have to. Those things are challenging, and that's a work ethic that, with the best will in the world, groups of people didn't have.

'Bonehead, Guigsy ... they were where they needed to be when they needed to be. To be fair to Tony, in those early days he was as well. They were where they were supposed to be, eyes rolling at why Liam wasn't. But they would be where they were. It was really just about making sure that Liam was where he needed to be, from a logistics point of view. Which wasn't without challenge, but I'm not going to pretend it was a quest for world peace. I think if you're going to work that closely with the band then it becomes critical that you are emotionally connected with what it is you're doing that day, and that you admire them as artists. That makes it that much more easy. I could forgive Liam anything when I saw him do what he was there to do.'

Another festival appearance, this time back in the UK, took place at the inaugural T in the Park festival in Hamilton, Scotland at the end of July. The team of Oasis 'people', i.e. an entourage, was expanding, and the latest recruit would be someone able to facilitate their requirements for their extracurricular activities. Eventually falling into the frame was Simon Mason, present at some of their early gigs, known as The Cat in the Hat.

Simon Mason: 'We were going to the first T in the Park festival, in Strathclyde County Park in Glasgow. We'd been out the night before - me and Liam went to a rave in Hulme. It was one of the most bizarre nights of my bizarre life. It felt like we were on the set of Mad Max or something. It was a partly-demolished shopping centre with a couple of thousand people absolutely off their tits. Point is we stayed awake. We headed up towards Scotland. Get to Carlisle to refuel the van, and the driver of the van either puts diesel in a petrol engine or petrol into a diesel engine. We got 500 yards back on the motorway and the van just says, 'Nah, not having that.' And we break down. I have my equipment for the weekend, shall we say, in a bag. I suppose that's probably about 20 years' worth of jail. We just need to keep our heads down here, stay in the van, wait for the AA to turn up, and everything will be alright.

'Liam wasn't there, it was Noel and the rest of the band. Paul Gallagher was there, Phil Smith was there, Owen Morris and his girlfriend. They decide that rather than keep a low profile, Noel and Phil decide it would be a perfect time for a game of frisbee. They proceed to have a game of frisbee across the motorway, with six lanes of fucking traffic. I'm sitting in the van going, 'I'm going to jail.' It went for a while, but thankfully the AA turned up. The guy from the AA turns up and says he can sort it, but he only has four spaces in the van. So, Noel obviously gets in. Being the gentleman he is, he insists Owen's pregnant girlfriend gets in, and Owen gets in so Noel can't run off with his girlfriend when she's pregnant. That wouldn't be a good look. So, there's one seat left. There's the rest of the band minus Liam, a couple of roadies and me, sitting in the van paranoid thinking the police were going to turn up and I was going to spend the rest of my life in jail. And then Noel just looks at me and says, 'Get in the van.' I remember feeling a little bit guilty that the rest of the band weren't in the van. They did get there and went on to play one of the best gigs they ever did.

'I don't think I needed any encouragement, but Marcus Russell said to me before, 'Why don't you go out and gee the crowd up a little bit?' So, not to shy away from opportunities like that, and the fact that I was absolutely off my tits, I went out in front of. It was a marquee remember, it wasn't a main stage gig. They'd been booked way back, earlier in the year. Tiny Monroe were on after them. That

was contractually where they were due to play. So, a Saturday afternoon in a reasonably-sized marquee, a couple of thousand people sized. It was five times that amount, there were people hanging off the roof, footballs flying ... you could feel it, it was going to off. We were all there having the best times of our lives. This is the absolute truth, I said, 'Please make some noise for the greatest rock'n'roll band in the world.' Because they were. They absolutely were. They came on and started playing 'Shakermaker' and I'm still stood in front of Liam's microphone.

It's not until Liam taps me on the shoulder and says fuck off for those five seconds I was the singer in the greatest rock'n'roll band in the world. It was a phenomenal gig. It was everything you'd want in a band; pure celebratory, dirty scuzzy singalong. Nothing else. We could have walked outside of that tent after that gig and there could have been a nuclear war, and no-one would have given a fuck. That's how good it was.'

The next single chosen was 'Live Forever' (although in truth the song chose itself), written as a riposte to Nirvana's 'I Hate Myself and I Want to Die.' Although a fan of lead singer Kurt Cobain, Noel wasn't impressed with the message of the song and, in particular, it transferring to British teenagers: 'It seems to me that here was a guy who had everything and was miserable about it. And we had fuck all, and I still thought that getting up in the morning was the greatest fucking thing ever. Kids don't need to hear that.'

Noel cites the moment he wrote the song as the point where everything changed, saying, 'I knew enough about music to know that was a great song, and the songs just flowed from there.' The single was released on August 8, 1994, the last before the debut album was due at the end of August. The accompanying sleeve carried a black and white image of John Lennon's childhood home, the band firmly nailing their flags to the mast as obsessive Beatles fans.

Brian Cannon: 'That's the only Oasis sleeve we did where the image wasn't specifically shot. It was an image that we already had. I was just racking my brains, we couldn't think of it. Then we noticed that we had that shot. The photographer I was working with had taken it, so we had the copyright. It just worked, didn't it? It's the only Oasis sleeve I did that didn't have a back sleeve to it, it's just a black back cover. If you didn't know (it was John Lennon's house) you'd just think it was somebody's house. Oasis were the kind of band that people got so into and researched things like that.'

The following day, Oasis were booked to play the Riverside in Newcastle. The band were by now familiar faces and the gig was broadcast live on Radio 1, so exposure for the show was at a maximum (for 1994). It was another rowdy occasion but there was something unsavoury about the whole atmosphere. The 'bad boys of rock' reputation was starting to have unwanted consequences. Objects were thrown early on, then a fan leapt on stage and went for Noel. The guitarist retaliated by going for the young man with his guitar, which unfortunately was the one given to him by Johnny Marr (who in turn had bought it from Pete Townshend).

It was claimed that Noel was struck very near his eye, and Liam jumped into the crowd to find and presumably attack the perp. Alternative recollections claim Noel actually struck himself in the eye with the guitar, which seems entirely possible, as the entire incident would have been over in a matter of seconds. The gig was abandoned but news of the fracas travelled fast. As the gig had been broadcast live, the tabloid press immediately jumped on the story and the complicated relationship Oasis had with the mainstream press was born, red-top journalists more than happy to push the aggressive reputation of the band for good copy. On the other hand, it was priceless promotion for 'Live Forever', that week beautifully exemplifying the dichotomy at the heart of the band.

The single charted the following Sunday and hit No.10 in the UK chart, an impressive placing for a band's third effort, breaking another glass ceiling. All these years on, it regularly tops 'best song ever' charts and defines Oasis. Once again, *Top of the Pops* beckoned and there was an appearance on MTV show *Most Wanted.* In an incredible show of confidence, despite the fact that the performance was to promote 'Live Forever' and *Definitely Maybe*, Noel, Liam and Bonehead debuted a new, non-album song, 'Whatever'. And after the performance, the band headlined their biggest gig to date, at the Astoria in central London, following shows at Rock City in Nottingham and the Forum also in the capital.

Paolo Hewitt: 'I met the band in '94. They had just started their ascent into super-stardom, and it was just brilliant to be there and watch it all unfold. It was a unique experience and I'm very, very grateful for it.'

Rick Witter: 'They were a breath of fresh air at the time. But the key word here is controversy. If they were going to have scraps, if they were going to get into trouble, it's rock'n'roll. It's going to get written about, they're going to get more front covers. It's just part of the game, and they were brave enough to crack on and do it.'

Paul Ashbee: 'They lost all sense of direction with it. A lot of innocent people got hurt. Good people who wanted nothing from them but a guestlist, and they didn't get it. Oasis trampled over everyone from their past. It's fucking sad.'

Not only did Oasis now have the fans and press onside, but they were starting to get noticed by musicians too. Noel was invited to join Crazy Horse, Neil Young's backing band, for an onstage jam on their next visit to London. Noel hadn't been shy in interviews about his admiration for Young and readily accepted, but Liam was unimpressed: 'So my twat brother thinks he's Eric fucking Clapton now, does he? He's in Oasis now and that should be enough.' Noel's musical promiscuity would become an ongoing point of tension between the brothers that would never be resolved.

That quote from Liam came from an interview with *The Face* magazine, one of many Oasis made in the lead-up to the release of their album as, engineered by Creation, they hit the press campaign very hard. Images of the band graced numerous magazines in August 1994, from *NME* to *Select*, as well as many broadsheet newspaper articles. They did live performances on 2FM in Dublin, BBC Radio One and, on the day of the album's release, an in-store gig at Virgin's flagship megastore in Marble Arch, London, joined on tambourine, bizarrely, by Evan Dando of The Lemonheads, who had declared himself a super-fan. Noel and Evan had struck up a friendship, fuelled no doubt by alcohol and drugs, leading to the once-witnessed, never-forgotten sight of Dando dancing and swinging his head as if at Woodstock whilst the band adopted their by-now signature lack of animation.

Creation were operating on a strict budget for the marketing of the album, with the label more than £2m in debt and having £60,000 - comparative peanuts - to spend on the promotion. Creation's promoter, Tim Abbot, either by accident or design, stumbled upon a unique idea and, rather than using the music press, which had by now taken care of itself, they placed adverts in other publications. Football programmes, various other magazines and more traditionally dance-music based monthlies all contained adverts for *Definitely Maybe*. *Mixmag*, the dance music bible, in turn gave the LP a five-star review. Shrewdly, Abbot had realised Oasis had a broader appeal than just indie fans, and it worked a treat.

Other reviews were equally hyperbolic; *Melody Maker* gave it album of the week status, *Mojo* called it 'addictive', *Q* claimed it was 'an outrageously exciting rock/pop album.' Most memorably, the *NME* likened it to, 'Opening your bedroom curtains one morning and discovering that some fucker's built the Taj Mahal in your back garden and then filled it with your favourite flavour of Angel Delight. Yeah, that good.'

Johnny Sharp: 'I wish they'd put that ('Rock 'n' Roll Star') as a single. It's such a statement of intent. Such a fantastic introduction. It's one of the great rock'n'roll records, a great blast of joy.'

Ricky Hatton (boxing champion): 'I just heard it on the radio, like you do. Then as time goes on you get your CDs and get more into it. As you get more into it and you love the music, you get more into Noel and Liam's characters and what they were all about. The reason it was good for me is that they were council estate lads just like myself. They were really good at what they were good at. No airs and graces. Say it how it is. They made successes of themselves. There's a lot I can relate to in Noel and Liam and I think that's why we get on so well.'

Notoriety, critical acclaim, sold-out gigs, superb live performances, word of mouth and, most importantly, great songs; there was only ever going to be one outcome. *Definitely Maybe* hit the top spot on September 4, 1994, selling 86,000 copies in its first week, the fastest-selling debut album of all time at that point. It outsold its nearest rival that week, *The Three Tenors in Concert*, by 50%. It was safe to call it a smash hit, and accolades such as 'the biggest/best band since The Beatles' were regularly being thrown Oasis' way. On the day it was confirmed they had a No.1 album, Oasis played their first gig in Northern Ireland. Unfortunately, the man who 'discovered' Oasis, Alan McGee, was unable to participate in any celebrations, having not long before suffered a nervous breakdown, mainly put down to excessive drug use, and was keeping a low profile. A shame for him, but he no doubt felt a significant sense of pride and justification.

Iain Robertson: 'I believe that to be with that band at that time, when the blue touchpaper had been lit, was a real privilege. It's playing those small shows and watching the crowds grow, and the swell. And riding that swell, and the chaos of it, and the maelstrom. The not knowing; it was impossible to plan things because things were moving so very quickly.'

Mat Whitecross: 'When *Definitely Maybe* came out, we played that, and played it and played it. That was the soundtrack to a whole year.'

There was further proof of what was now becoming a phenomenon when, in early September, Oasis embarked on their first tour of Japan. Japanese fans are known for being passionate about most British or American acts, such is their adoration of certain elements of Western culture. So, when the latest hot property landed, they were not left alone, from airport to hotel to gig. For left alone, read not given any breathing space whatsoever in transit from airport to van, van to hotel, etc. It's an oft-used phrase but the only comparable reference point was Beatlemania. They played six headline shows and, as well as playing the debut album, 'Fade Away' and 'I Am the Walrus,' the time required was bolstered by short acoustic sets from Noel. 'Sad Song,' a track only released on the vinyl edition of *Definitely Maybe*, and early B-side 'D'Yer Wanna Be A Spaceman?' helped fill the set out. And so, a precedent was set, Noel gaining more and more confidence every time he played live.

Tony McCarroll: 'The maddest, most beautiful place I've ever been to in my life. We got off at the airport and there was hundreds of fans there. We had gifts of Walkmen, Game Boys, all these modern things, and we didn't have a clue what they were. What a beautiful nation.

'Then we got to the hotel, there were hundreds there. You try to go for something to eat and they are coming out of doorways. Absolute madness. Even in the big hotels you'd open the window and hear (screaming). Beatlemania is the only way I can describe it.'

MELODY MAKER, July 23 1994 5

NEWS

HEADING FOR THE OASIS

OASIS have lined up another tour to coincide with the release of their debut album at the end of next month. And they have also issued details of their third single.

The new tour dates open at Buckley Tivoli on August 31, continuing at Dublin Tivoli (September 3), Belfast Limelight (4) and Manchester Hacienda (5).

These dates follow hard on the heels of the previously announced UK tour which opens on July 31 in Glasgow and finishes at the London Astoria on August 18.

Details of the album are still unconfirmed.

The single, "Live Forever", is released by Creation on August 8 – 25 years to the day after The Beatles' famous Abbey Road photo shoot. The limited edition seven-inch is backed with an acoustic version of "Up In The Sky", and the 12-inch adds a new song, "Cloudburst". The CD also carries a live version of "Supersonic".

Creation president Alan McGee has said "Live Forever" is "Single Of The Year and a 'Wild Horses' for the Nineties".

Finally, Oasis have announced that the tickets for their September tour of Japan sold out in two days – despite the fact that they have never released a record there.

Paul Slattery: 'Japan was very mad. I told the band it was going to be mega, and it was. It was unbelievable. There was a lot of love for the band. It was really overwhelming. The gigs got better and better. The first gigs at Club Cheetah were incredible and the band just fed off the audience. By the time of the last time in Nagoya, all the arms were stretching out for the band at the end of the gig and the band were almost in tears. I remember seeing Guigsy wiping his tears with his arm. They absolutely loved Japan, the whole emotion of it. Of course, this was one of the problems; they went straight from Japan to the USA, where it just wasn't happening for them. And of course, there was a rift in the band then, because the Americans didn't treat the band with the respect they deserved. It didn't work for them at first. But Japan was amazing. I'll never forget it. I can still feel the emotion from it. The gig in Nagoya was probably one of the best I've seen in my life and that was because of the feedback between the crowd and the band. It was something so special and unique. It could only happen in Japan.'

While the Japanese fans were ecstatic, American fans were somewhat harder to please. The first American tour was pencilled in for early September. The first set of gigs on the tour went well, although Oasis were unwilling to play to the crowd by attempting to earn their love. Rather, their attitude was the same as it was in the UK; play the songs with minimal fanfare but maximum noise. Static bands are something of harder sell in the States; the audience want to be entertained. There was also the multitude of press engagements that had to be fulfilled, including a joint interview on a San Francisco radio station with another one of British music's hot properties, Blur.

The four-piece from Colchester, after several years operating as a mid-level indie band, were suddenly hot property thanks to the success of their third album, *Parklife*, released earlier in the year, which managed to capture the zeitgeist of Britain with its intoxicating blend of observational lyrics and dexterous musicianship. Not to mention that they had a good-looking, pop-friendly frontman in the form of Damon Albarn. The interview itself was one of mutual respect between Blur and the brothers Gallagher (the remaining members of Oasis not being present), all obviously quite amused at the cultural differences between presenters and interviewees. Liam even went as far as to suggest playing a Blur song, and so it seemed like what would be a useful friendship for all parties was blossoming.

Tony McCarroll: 'I think I walked up with Liam the night before, there were a couple of crew dragging behind. By the time they caught us they told us (that) someone had been shot.

'I think a lot of ex-pats turned out. The actual Americans didn't quite get it until 'Wonderwall.'

For the first four dates (Seattle, Portland, San Francisco, and Sacramento) the tour was going as well as could have been expected, but once again overseas, drama was around the corner. The next gig, on September 29, 1994, was at the Whisky a Go Go on Sunset Strip, Los Angeles, the go-to destination for up and coming acts in the world's most glamorous city. As a band on the up, drugs would have been rife and by this point it's reasonable to assume cocaine was constantly on the menu. As per normal, the band indulged on the night before their gig. Unfortunately, what they were ingesting up their noses wasn't cocaine but the much stronger stimulant methamphetamine, more commonly known as crystal meth, so they'd been awake for a considerable amount of time and were a bit worse for wear when they took to the stage. Not only was the band in such a state, but roadie Phil Smith and engineer Mark Coyle had also been partaking.

They opened with 'Rock 'n' Roll Star', but the song only lasted for a minute before there was a problem with the bass amp. For some reason there was a mess up with the setlists, meaning Noel had a different setlist to the rest of the band. There is a question to be asked to why the leader of the band didn't know the set by heart by this point, but then several days without sleep (according to legend) will probably have a negative effect. And so, there was the incongruous sight of the band playing different songs. They had to stop and start on several occasions, with Liam snorting more lines of crystal meth as the gig went on. Tempers were starting to fray, and Noel took Liam to task about something, to which Liam responded by tossing his tambourine in his brother's direction. Watching it back, it looks like a relatively meaningless gesture, but in the heat of the moment (loaded with mood-enhancing drugs and having gone hours without sleep), Noel was deeply outraged. 'Shakermaker' was dropped at the last minute because Liam and Noel refused to sing the song together, but they did manage to complete the set.

Ever the perfectionist and disgusted with his bandmates, Noel sought out the tour manager, insisted on taking what was left in the tour float, and disappeared to Las Vegas. He made contact with Melissa Lim, a girl he had met a few days earlier whilst in San Francisco, who took him in for a few days. Extremely upset, Noel was adamant that he was going to call it a day and split the band up, with the appealing side effect of the band entering into legend. By taking him for walks to Huntingdon Park, going record shopping and to all intents and purposes looking after him for a few days, Liam convinced Noel not to do anything rash, especially as they were on the cusp of greatness. 'San Francisco has a reputation of being a place where bands come to die, like The Band and the Sex Pistols. I wasn't going to let it happen on my watch. I told him, 'You can't leave the band, you're on the verge of something big!"

Noel claims the deciding factor in his decision to return was being alerted to a tour poster for the next trip around the UK, whereby all the dates were sold out. Meanwhile, back in LA, the rest of the band and the crew were in limbo as to whether or not the tour, or indeed the band itself, was to continue. Eventually, Noel contacted Marcus Russell and reconvened with the rest of the band for their next gig in Minneapolis, and the US tour proceeded until the end of October. The incident had long-lasting effects and is a defining moment of the Oasis story; not only were three songs written during his sabbatical (two of which, 'Talk Tonight' and 'Half the World Away' are ranked amongst his most popular) but Noel claims that from that point on he always felt separate to the rest of the band; 'Before that it was always us, after that it was me and them.' Mark Coyle agreed, saying, 'We all had to be with him. The new era started when he walked back into that hotel.'

The tour resumed, taking in the key cities in America before culminating in another show in New York's Wetlands Preserve.

Jeff Slate (US journalist): 'I was a big reader of *Q* and *NME*, so I saw rumblings of this band and I remember hearing 'Columbia.' I was in New York and saw they were playing at the Wetlands, a club I used to frequent. It was just a local place a lot of musicians used to hang out at. I thought, 'I'll go check these guys out' and it totally blew my mind.

'It was really loud and my memory of it was that they weren't great, but the songs blew me away. Liam was completely riveting. He didn't do anything, he just stood there. The Wetlands was a really small club, a place that was lengthwise, it wasn't a very deep club. No matter where you were, you were only about 20 or 30 feet from them. I was a fan instantly. How could you not be?'

The tour also factored in an appearance on *The Jon Stewart Show*, their first American TV appearance, where they performed 'Supersonic' and 'Rock 'n' Roll Star.'

Colin Paterson (BBC broadcaster/journalist): 'They came to Philadelphia, they played a venue called JC Dobbs' pub on South Street. Suede were also touring and played the bigger venue down the road as they were a bigger deal at the time. It was a Sunday night and it was absolutely packed. When I saw the gig, I spent the next four days afterwards thinking, 'I can't hear what anyone's saying.' On the Thursday my ear went pop, and suddenly I realised I'd been deaf because of that gig. It was incredibly loud.

'I managed to blag this interview with Oasis through the student plugger, who would come to you and offer you acts. I asked, 'What British ones have you got?' 'There's some band called Oas …' 'Yes, I will have them!'

'The debut album came out in August and I remember buying it the day before I moved to the States. It was one thing I had to do. I remember listening to it on the plane.

'In traditional way, they foisted the bass player on me. I got Guigsy. He was very good. He said, 'We're not necessarily the best at playing our instruments. I mean, I can hardly play my guitar, Tony can't drum, Liam complains about his own singing. Noel admits he is not the best guitarist in the world, and Bonehead says he just smashes on his guitar for fun. You don't have to be the best musicians to be great. I mean, Hendrix wasn't in The Beatles, but they were still the best band. It's when we come together, we're something different.

'At this time, they were spinning it in the States as 'are they the new Beatles (or) are they the new Sex Pistols?' Guigsy said, 'I don't see how you can judge us next to The Beatles. With them you've got a whole career to look at. Their progression to *Sgt. Pepper* and beyond. It's our first album, so to compare us to The Beatles, look at their debut! Our first album is better than The Beatles' first album.

'He talked about their celebrity fans, saying, 'Evan Dando is a top bloke. Liam thinks he's John Waters on acid. He's excellent on his own, just with an electric. I hate The Lemonheads though. We've told him to leave them, but he won't listen. He described Suede's Brett Anderson as a 'middle-class kid who pretends he's working class to sell records.' Then, The Stone Roses, who were, 'old men whose new record sounds like Rare Groove.'

'I was also allowed to watch the soundcheck. Liam left the stage, sat down and watched the soundcheck, so I went up to him. I remember thinking that they loved Man City, so I would print out the football results from Saturday's games and give them to them, but only if Man City won. So, I went up to him and said, 'I've brought you the football results.' He said, 'Yeah, know them. We beat Spurs 5-2.'

'Liam gave me one quote which I started my article with, 'A year ago I was on the dole in Manchester spending my giro the day I got it and being nagged by my mum. Now, 12 months later I'm a star' is the arrogant claim of Liam Gallagher of the explosive British pop group Oasis. The turn in their lives really has been that quick.

'They were so excited to be in the States at this time. They'd had all the No.1 success. A few days before they'd play *The Jon Stewart Show*.'

It was while they had a couple of free days whilst in Austin, Texas, that they took the opportunity to record some B-sides, which would mainly consist of songs

Noel had written on his sabbatical. By this point, Noel's frustrations with Tony McCarroll's drumming were becoming more and more vocal, going so far as to physically threaten him. Believing McCarroll would be incapable of using brushes for 'Half the World Away,' Noel sent the drummer out for a break then did the part himself. Tony himself was struggling with being away from his young family.

Tony McCarroll: 'A phone call is indirect contact. I'd phone her (his daughter) and say, 'I'm on *Top of the Pops* tonight, I'll wave to you.' She actually glued herself to the TV. I always sent her letters and drew her pictures of me on drums.

'I think my goal at the time was to buy a house, and that was it. If I can make a house out of it, then I'm laughing. So that was it. No-one ever thought it would last that long.'

Back in Britain the success of *Definitely Maybe* prompted a fourth single to be lifted from the album. Noel was hesitant to sanction this, believing four singles from an album to be overkill, and they already had 'Whatever' in the bag. His arm was eventually twisted and 'Cigarettes & Alcohol' was unleashed, backed with three staples of the live set; 'I Am the Walrus,' 'Listen Up' and 'Fade Away.' The version of 'I Am the Walrus' was listed as being recorded at Glasgow Cathouse, but later revealed to have been recorded at a conference at the Gleneagles Hotel Sony Seminar, a showcase event for executives to hear Creation Records' new signings. Noel confirmed that the band loved the particular recording but were mortified it was made during rehearsals at a corporate event. They chose a recording sounding as similar as possible, in this case the Glasgow gig, lifted some crowd noises from a Faces bootleg album, and hoped no-one would notice the deception.

Anjali Dutt: 'Yes, there definitely was (a studio version of 'I Am the Walrus'). It was great, because they always do that one really, really well.'

Fortunately, no-one noticed. Having three fan favourites included on the single and undertaking a cunning marketing ploy (packaging the cassette version in the style of a cigarette packet) all helped the single reach No.7 in the UK charts. Even though it had been helped by their strongest set of B-sides released by this point, all of which were legendary amongst fandom, for a song people had already owned for a number of weeks to chart higher than anything else they recorded was astonishing. As Noel himself said, 'Now we're talking. This is going to get stupid now.'

Alan McGee: 'Every jump was ridiculous. They were ridiculous, Creation was ridiculous, we were all ridiculous at one point. Everybody believed it, and it was great, but it was delusional. They were as deluded as me, they all thought it was going to go on forever.'

Tony McCarroll: 'The drugs and alcohol weren't exaggerated in the slightest. We concentrated on the drugs and beers more than the music!'

There was a fly in the ointment; for the second time Oasis were accused of plagiarism, with the main riff identical to 'Get It On' by T.Rex, as well as being very similar to 'Little Queenie' by Chuck Berry and Humble Pie's cover of 'C'mon Everybody'. Noel's rationale was that when he wrote the song it didn't matter who they were ripping off, as no-one was going to hear it anyway. 'Cigarettes & Alcohol' was also a good contrast to the mild psychedelia of 'Supersonic' and 'Shakermaker', and the melodic aspiration of 'Live Forever'. It was and remains an undeniable party anthem, and the line, 'Is it worth the aggravation to find yourself a job when there's nothing worth working for?' struck a particular chord for disenfranchised youth. Sadly, because they were overseas, with BBC bosses probably relieved on account of the lyrical content, there was no *Top of the Pops* performance to mark the achievement.

Brian Cannon: 'That was mental, because that (single cover) was shot in the Halcyon Hotel in Holland Park, west London, quite a swish part of town. Quite an expensive hotel was that. I managed to convince Alan McGee we needed to book the room for two nights, so we could have a practice warm-up the night before! Minus the band I may add. The band were in Sweden the night before. Liam jumped off the top of the tour bus, I believe, and broke his ankle. That's why, if you look at the shots, he's sat on the floor and doesn't move. Noel's on the bed jumping about, Bonehead's up and down, but Liam is just sat on the floor, because he's got a pottled leg and can't move.'

Simon Mason: 'I almost made the cover of 'Cigarettes & Alcohol'. I was going to sit on the floor, but then Noel said, 'You might get arrested, we'll put Tim Abbot there instead.'

Touring continued into November back into Europe, with the band playing gigs in France, Sweden, Germany, the Netherlands and Belgium before heading back to the UK to play progressively larger shows, the first of which was the Guildhall in Southampton, a 1,850-capacity venue. Other gigs on the pre-Christmas UK tour included the Barrowland in Glasgow (three times in the month), the Civic Hall in Wolverhampton and Hammersmith Palais. At one of the Barrowland gigs, Liam lost his voice mid-set and stormed off stage. After some debate, to placate a baying Glaswegian crowd, it was agreed Noel would complete the gig with just his acoustic guitar for company.

Paul Ashbee: 'The fact is that Noel only started singing Oasis songs when Liam got that bad throat. He would never have been a frontman. He always tried it. When he used to come into rehearsals back then, he'd come in and give Liam a sheet of handwritten lyrics. Because Noel was dyslexic, Liam used to copy them out. Liam would get them instantly, with no second chance. He'd hit it. It was unbelievable. I used to say to Bonehead that those two were rehearsing it, they'd done it before they'd even come in. Liam was bang on it.

Noel Gallegher and Jarvis Cocker ©peterjwalsh.com

'Then Noel would try it. It wasn't the same. He'd try singing it, and I thought, 'No, you're not a singer.' But he always wanted to be. I remember Tony saying to me one day, 'Listen, I've got an idea. Why don't I do the backing vocals?' And Noel went, 'Are you for fucking real? With that haircut?' Tony said, 'Fuck off, you cheeky bastard!' He nearly fell off his stool. I've never seen Tony McCarroll so insulted in his life!'

Tony McCarroll: 'There was friction all the way. One day it was me, the next day it's Liam. You're in a little bus, someone's going to step on each other. I fell out with Guigs for a short period, but he's a lovely man and I fell out with everyone.'

Larger venues mean longer sets, so not only was *Definitely Maybe* now being played in its entirety, as well as 'Fade Away' and 'I Am the Walrus,' but Noel's now regular acoustic set also comprised 'Sad Song,' and 'D'Yer Wanna Be A Spaceman?.' The final addition to the set was the next single 'Whatever,' which often included the chorus from 'All the Young Dudes' by Mott the Hoople as part of its outro.

'Whatever' was one of Noel's oldest songs, written long before the band had a record deal, and had been rehearsed along with other unreleased tracks such as 'All Around the World' at their practice rooms at the Boardwalk. It presumably wasn't selected for inclusion on the debut album because there wasn't the budget to record it. As the track was an out-and-out pop song, Noel was adamant he wanted to go the whole hog with the song, including a string section (he himself cites this point as 'when the obsession with the strings started'). Paul Weller, by now a friend of the band, described the strings as 'shit,' Noel having arranged them himself. To keep momentum going, it was selected to be released as a single in December 1994.

Owen Morris: 'We recorded 'Whatever,' and that was the first time we'd recorded all the band. That was a good session. We did B-sides like 'Listen Up' and 'Fade Away' and we demoed 'Some Might Say' and we recorded 'Whatever,' all in about five days. It was a very creative session, with the intention of me making the next record.'

Tony McCarroll: 'We had it for years, so we were gelled with that one. The band was that tight at the time that with any jam we seemed to know what the next person was going to do. We just felt it.'

Nick Ingman (string arranger): 'I'm sure Noel won't mind me saying this; he absolutely loved The Beatles, to a point of obsession. The hard rock bands didn't want anything other than the three guitars and the drums. Noel wanted to reproduce The Beatles' sound. I don't mean copy but reproduce the vibe that was there. When I first met him, essentially what he wanted me to do was to be George Martin, in an arrangement sense. I remember when I first met him, he did say to me at one stage, 'Can I get the original musicians who played on...' such and such record, which was tricky because most of them were dead. That was his level of involvement, that he really wanted to do that. And it was him, I don't sense that Liam was that involved at that point, and certainly not the other members of the band. It was definitely Noel driving.

'Our booker got a call from Creation Records saying what they wanted, and they didn't really know what they were saying, but their client (Noel) wanted this thing called 'strings.'

'I met Noel, I think at his house, and he was very clear about what he wanted. He sang me the part that he wanted. Admittedly it was just the melody, but he wanted a string quartet, because that was the sound of, for instance, 'Yesterday', and that was what he wanted. I say he was very clear, but only on a melodic basis. He didn't know - and why should he? - the mechanics involved.

'Owen Morris was the producer. They played the tape of a basic backing track and we played the arrangement. This is standard stuff. We ran it through, and one of the musicians was talking through it. I think a music stand fell over at one stage. It was mild chaos and I said to Noel, 'Right, well, let's do it properly.' 'No, see you in the pub.' He said, 'No, it's fine.' 'No, it's not, we haven't done it.' His view, and it has a lot to be said for it, was that too careful is too un-rock'n'roll. Don't be careful, don't be too precise. It's too soft, it's too polite. And of course, he's absolutely right. (On the record) is the first take. No wrong notes, fortunately. And then it sold a million records, so he knew what he was doing.

'He knew that he didn't know enough to tell me what to do. The melody was there, and he was clear about that. The rest he said, 'You do your thing.'

Promotional appearances included a pre-release performance on *Top of the Pops*, that week's edition presented by Damon Albarn who, continuing his enthusiasm for the Mancunian comrades, described the song and band as 'wonderful.' The band also made their debut on *Later with Jools Holland*, the more mature BBC2 companion to *Top of the Pops*. A showcase for 'real' artists, i.e. those that are able to perform live, the show was in its infancy in 1994 and had a regular influx of guests that were part of a movement dubbed 'Britpop.' For their turn, Oasis performed 'Whatever', 'Sad Song' and 'I Am the Walrus', neatly encompassing several sides of the band but also already consigning *Definitely Maybe* to the past. The boys also dressed up for the occasion, perhaps to appeal to the more mature viewership, in smart matching black blazers, one of the only times they undertook anything resembling uniformity. They also performed on Radio One's Evening Session, giving '(It's Good) To Be Free' and 'Talk Tonight' their live debuts.

Unfathomably, 'Whatever' was also a contender for the coveted Christmas No.1 spot, in competition with professional warbler Mariah Carey's 'All I Want For Christmas' and hard-hitting gritty boy band East 17 and their ballad 'Stay Another Day.' How Oasis were even being mentioned in the same breath as the pop stars of the day still takes some believing, but there they were. In truth, despite the success the band had enjoyed to this point, as would become apparent later in their careers, if they were to compete against a pop phenomenon they would lose, as was the case this first time. However, 'Whatever' charted at a very respectable No.3, easily their highest-charting single by that point. It would become one of the most successful Oasis singles, spending over 100 weeks on the UK singles chart (although no doubt due to it not appearing on any album until 2010).

Sadly, as was now becoming par for the course, a songwriter took umbrage. Neil Innes of The Rutles, Bonzo Dog Doo-Dah Band and Monty Python fame, was quick to point out similarities between 'Whatever' and his track, 'How Sweet To Be An Idiot.' The similarity was too uncanny to be coincidence, despite Noel's insistence that it was, and Innes was given a co-writing credit. But that couldn't take the gloss off what had been a phenomenal year, one rounded off with a gig at Brighton Centre with Creation label-mates Ride as main support, and The La's also on the bill. It would turn out to be the last Ride gig for more than 20 years.

As Noel put it, '1994 is our year. No one can touch us.' Indeed, only one other band in the Britpop movement could even make a similar claim; art school poppers Blur, who had, after a couple of false starts, found significant mainstream success.

Noel and Liam with fans

1995

'IS MY HAPPENING TOO DEAFENING FOR YOU?'

Oasis activity for 1995 commenced with a second tour of the US, this one much lengthier than the first, spanning nearly two months and 32 shows, including a night at the legendary Fillmore in San Francisco. By this point Noel was becoming as much the face of the band as Liam, doing most of the interviews Stateside. This would have most likely been down to Noel's more considered approach to answering questions, as opposed to Liam's more impromptu attitude. There was only one incident of note, in New Jersey, where the band were heckled for being English. It was by all accounts a bad-tempered gig, Liam confronting the crowd with the offer of a fight and Noel leaving the stage with a barbed, 'You don't deserve us. Thank you. Fuck you.' The setlists were generally made up of 13 songs from the 25 that had been released and recorded. During the tour Tony would confide to room-mate Bonehead that becoming the butt of people's jokes was starting to take its toll.

The first UK appointment in Oasis' calendar for 1995 was to attend the *NME* Awards, where they picked up three awards; Best Album, Best New Band and Best Single for 'Live Forever.' They certainly made a splash at the inaugural awards; in what would become his default setting for award ceremonies, Liam was heckling everyone and anyone, and was told to 'shut the fuck up' by James Dean Bradfield of Manic Street Preachers as the Welsh outfit picked up an award.

Liam and Noel had somewhat different approaches to their acceptance speeches; Noel was gracious and doffed his cap to Paul Weller, label-mates Primal Scream and promising newcomers Menswear. Liam on the other hand expressed his pleasure that Shed Seven and Elastica didn't win the awards Oasis picked up. The front cover of the following week's *NME* depicted Noel and Damon Albarn celebrating their respective awards.

A few weeks later the more mainstream Brit Awards took place, where Oasis picked up Best Newcomer, presented to them by one of their heroes, Ray Davies of The Kinks. Traditionally, the Brits were a night for the record labels to pat themselves and the acts they've marketed most effectively on the back, but by 1995 Britpop had crossed over to the mainstream and guitar music was back in the public eye. The big winners on the night were Blur, and in the press conference after Damon Albarn declared, 'I think this award (Best Group) should have been shared with Oasis.' It appeared that mutual respect was now evolving into what would be described as a one-sided 'bromance.'

Four further dates were pencilled in to round off the *Definitely Maybe* tour; two in Paris at the Bataclan, with a date in Southend sandwiched in between, and their first arena gig, at the Sheffield Arena. As the band were a bigger deal in Europe, they were back to performing larger sets, and some new songs were debuted. The gig in Southend was recorded for posterity and later released as a live video, *Live by The Sea*. Amusingly, during his now-regular acoustic set, Noel messed up his performance of 'D'yer Wanna Be A Spaceman?'. To his credit, the full incident was included in the video.

Sheffield was a big deal for a number of reasons. Firstly, very few other traditionally indie acts were able to perform in arenas at this point, with Blur, Suede and The Stone Roses the exceptions. Officially, the *Definitely Maybe* tour commenced at The Angel in Bedford, Hertfordshire, a 100-person capacity venue, whereas Sheffield Arena could hold 13,500 attendees. Those that dubbed the rise of Oasis meteoric weren't wrong and were able to add this number to their argument. Secondly, it was the last gig for original drummer Tony McCarroll. Lastly, it was the debut performance of a song Noel had written earlier the same day, called 'Don't Look Back in Anger.' Noel performed the song during his three-song acoustic set, to a no doubt muted response. It's almost impossible to quantify those facts together; a song which had been written less than 12 hours previously and is now heralded as something of a national anthem was performed for the first time in an arena. Such was the confidence of Noel Gallagher and the madness of their lives.

Iain Robertson: 'When Rob Ballantyne and Simon Moran at SJM first booked Sheffield Arena, and we went to see it for the first time, Liam turned on him and said, 'You fucking idiot, we will never ever sell this venue.' Because it was so much of a leap from what we were used to playing. We'd just come back from Europe, where we were playing to 200 people max. And not always to full houses. Rob Ballantyne just turned and said, 'Well, actually, you've already sold it. The tickets went in hours.' That whole kind of thing where they always knew; they really didn't. It was as much of a surprise to them that it was happening as it was to everybody else. That was an amazing thing to be around.'

Tony McCarroll: 'Sheffield Arena, when our parents came - our Mams were there thinking, 'How the fuck did they get here?'

Noel Gallagher ©peterjwalsh.com

The setlist for the first Oasis arena gig was:

'Rock 'n' Roll Star'
'Columbia'
'Digsy's Dinner'
'Some Might Say'
'Shakermaker'
'Live Forever'
'Up in The Sky'
'Acquiesce'
'Headshrinker'
'(It's Good) To Be Free'
'Cigarettes & Alcohol'
'Married with Children'
'Take Me Away'
'Don't Look Back in Anger'
'Talk Tonight'
'Whatever'
'Slide Away'
'Supersonic'
'I Am the Walrus'

Despite the rapid succession of singles and B-sides, the well of songs Noel was able to produce was still overflowing, and another single was quickly selected for UK release. 'Some Might Say' had been demoed during sessions for 'Whatever'. Work was done on the demo with a view to releasing it as the next single, but both Noel and Owen Morris were unsatisfied with the speed of the recording (it being too fast) and re-recorded the whole thing, with Liam nailing his vocals in two takes.

Owen Morris: 'We recorded 'Some Might Say' just after I finished the Verve record. That was the last session with Tony McCarroll. I think we did 'Some Might Say' and 'Acquiesce' that week.'

The single was backed with strong B-sides that are rightly now seen as quintessential Oasis; the aforementioned 'Talk Tonight', a moody, introspective lovelorn ballad; 'Acquiesce' the first of only two duets between Liam and Noel, taking verse and chorus respectively and a heady slice of melancholic, fist-clenching rock; and 'Headshrinker', which was very much in line with their punkier material. It's probably also the fastest-paced song Oasis ever recorded and would be the last time they were quite so raw. 'Acquiesce' and 'Headshrinker' were both debuted during the European gigs.

Alan McGee: 'There was a funny moment between me and him once when he'd done 'Some Might Say'. I'd just come back out of rehab and I hadn't got with the programme that Noel was now in control. I went, which is still to this day the truth, "Acquiesce' is better than 'Some Might Say'." I wish we went with that. He was really affronted. No, affronted is slightly the wrong word for it, but he was like, 'McGee, get back in your cage.' Then I went, 'You know what? There's a lot of money to be made here, I'll get on side'. It depends what day you really wake up. I love 'Some Might Say', so it doesn't really matter.'

Brian Cannon: 'From top to bottom ('Some Might Say') was the best one I ever did. That's my favourite Oasis sleeve, that and *Definitely Maybe*. I was in a tour bus with them in Southampton and Noel gave me a handwritten sheet of all the lyrics, and said he wanted all the lyrics of the song illustrated in one image. I thought, 'No pressure there then'. The starting point was that we needed a location, a setting, for 'standing at the station in need of education'. I thought, 'Well if you're standing at a disused railway station you need educating for the fact there's no train coming.' So, we got hold of a map of the South Derbyshire area, an old map, pre-'60s before they shut all the railways down. I traced off where all the stations were and transposed that to a modern-day map, and where the x's fell, where there was no railway station, where there was once upon a time a station. As it happened, the one we used was semi-in-use, because the opposing platform was still used. Every 20 minutes a train would pull in and everybody on the train was like, 'What the hell's going on here?'

'There's little things that people don't notice. If you look closely at it, the windows of the disused station house itself, there's photocopied enlargements of bits of Noel's guitars in each window. All the lyrics on are on there, obviously. It was my Dad with the wheelbarrow with all the fish. That station is literally as far from the sea as you can get in Great Britain. We had to find, on the morning of the shoot, a load of fish that still had their heads and tails on. This isn't like being in Grimsby or Hull, where fishmongers are 10 a penny. It never crossed my mind. We had to drive all the way to Bakewell to find a fishmonger so we could do the shoot. The wheelbarrow was a sink which my Dad made himself. The umbrella with the pots and pans on the end of it was made special. This was for a single, not even an album, before they'd even had a No.1.'

Tony McCarroll: 'That was demoed just after the 'Whatever' session. It was just floating an idea about. As far as I remember, Owen got his claws into that and said we had to do it.'

Cromford railway station, the location of the cover shot for Some Might Say

In the weeks leading up to the single's release, promotion was required. Best of all was a performance on short-lived music show *The White Room*. Oasis were performing on the same show as Paul Weller, and after tearing through 'Acquiesce' and '(It's Good) To Be Free', Weller joined Noel on keyboard and backing vocals for a moving performance of 'Talk Tonight'. Noel and Weller had struck up a firm friendship; Weller was undergoing something of a renaissance after a fallow 1980s and had been dubbed 'The Godfather of Britpop'. His third solo album was imminent, and Noel had been invited to play acoustic guitar on a cover of Dr John's 'I Walk on Gilded Splinters'.

Mark Feltham (Nine Below Zero harmonica player/session player): 'I think I did *The White Room* with them. The phone went one day, and they said, 'They're (Oasis) doing some live stuff'. Whatever I did they asked me to do it live as well. It wasn't only me, there was about six of us with brass as well. The lead trumpet player actually played on *Sgt. Pepper* (Derek Watkins). He was part of the brass ensemble we had with Oasis.'

Oasis were on an unstoppable trajectory and there was quiet optimism that a No.1 single may be within their grasp. Released on a Monday, the track was performed on *Top of the Pops* as an exclusive three days afterwards, which would only have helped their chart performance. In the singles-led 20th century, most impartial fans would buy the singles on the Saturday after release, thus television exposure would have been invaluable.

On April 30, 1995, boy band of the moment and perennial chart-toppers Take That were at No.1 in the charts, and had been for four weeks, with 'Back for Good', an admittedly mature and sophisticated effort for a pop act. But on Sunday May 1, they were displaced at the top of the charts by Oasis, a seismic achievement considering Oasis were an 'indie' band and their debut single was only released a year before. It was also the real signalling of a change in the guard in the pop charts. Previously, indie acts would regard a top-20 entry as a hit. Now anything less than top-10 was regarded as a failure. Britpop was now an all-encompassing title to be given to any band that wrote and produced their own music, and the 'Brit' part could easily be removed.

By this point it was very apparent that Noel was at the end of his tether with the drumming skills of Tony McCarroll, vocalising his dissatisfaction to anyone and everyone, not just amongst those within the band's inner circle. Any mention of drumming within Oasis was met with disparaging comments or, at best, indifference. There was always a sense that Tony was an outsider within the band, not least because he had a child and as such couldn't fully indulge in the party lifestyle, as he had, quite understandably, other priorities. Noel had also long held the belief that Tony's drumming had limitations that wouldn't be acceptable for his latest batch of songs, to be recorded for their second album in spring 1995.

And so, with unfathomable cruelty, on the day before 'Some Might Say' topped the charts, Tony received a call from Marcus Russell, who broke the news to him that his services were no longer required. A story was concocted, presumably to present the remaining members in a good light, that Tony and Liam had a fight, but this was swiftly dropped for the more honest version. 'I like Tony as a geezer, but he wouldn't have been able to drum the new songs' was Noel's party line, which seems half-true. Tony claims that he finally snapped and in a recent argument had told Noel exactly what he thought, his fate finally and firmly sealed as a consequence.

Tony McCarroll: 'We knew it ('Some Might Say') was going to go to No.1. It was that weekend that I got the call from Marcus saying, 'Are you sat down? I've got some bad news.' I thought he was going to say we didn't get to No.1. He said, 'The lads want to move on,' and I'm thinking 'Noel wants to move on.' I had a major argument with him weeks before that. For full effect, when we've gone to No.1. He knows how to create the headlines.

'I was given an itinerary for the recording sessions, the tours we were going to do. I was getting a full diary for the year. But I did have a fateful argument with Noel in Paris. At the time I was seeing a girl from America. We had a drunken argument, but I didn't realise I was next to Noel. The next day, rather than a quiet word, he's doing his acoustic soundcheck. I'd just finished soundchecking and he said, 'Next time you fucking keep me awake, I'll fucking sack you,' or whatever. I just kicked the kit out of the way, fronted him and said, 'Don't ever fucking speak to me like that again.' Lo and behold, that was probably the last time I spoke to Noel Gallagher.'

Mat Whitecross: 'Noel acknowledged that he was ruthless in his pursuit of being the best band in the world. He considered that he didn't want Tony to be in it anymore. His first thing with Tony would be that he'd be very flippant and very dismissive. Then he'd go, 'Well, he's a lovely guy, but that's not what rock'n'roll is about.' Then he'd reconsider and go, 'Maybe I just didn't like him.'

'Similarly, with Tony, he was quite hurt by that time and would have loved to have relived it again and to have stayed on. He did wind people up, you can see it in his book that there was a lot of friction. It's the classic thing in every single band, from Pete Best to Will Champion in Coldplay to Tony, that every single drummer, because it's the most fundamental thing that keeps the whole band together, that's the engine room of any band, and it's the first thing you notice when it doesn't work. Most drummers are going in with a level of proficiency that's about the same as the singer and the guitarist, but they are the ones who get it in the neck because you notice when it's wrong immediately. That's happened with most bands. I feel bad for him in that sense. His thing was, 'If they'd just given me one more chance.' But then depending on who you speak to, he had a million and one chances.

'Mark Coyle said, 'I think a lot of us regret the way Tony was treated.' It wasn't just to do with musical skill, there was a friction of personalities.'

Tony's card was marked from the early days and his dismissal came as no surprise. Whilst the question marks over his ability and limitations may have been valid, the way he was treated seemed, from the outside looking in, callous at best, especially the timing. However, as would soon become apparent, the decision to remove him from duty was vindicated, and he certainly wouldn't be the last to fall in the line of duty. Meanwhile, Oasis had to find a new drummer, and sharpish.

Simon Mason: 'I think Tony was almost over-awed by the whole thing, perhaps. I'm happy for him to correct me, but I don't think he had any idea what was happening until it started to happen. I may be wrong about that, and if I am, I apologise to Tony. Guigs was too stoned to really give a fuck. Bonehead was happiest on stage and after the show with a nice glass of red wine and a cig. He used to hang around with Owen Morris more than anything. He was incredibly funny. I remember one night we were in the Columbia Hotel and Bonehead decides he's going to give us his Elton John impersonation on the piano. I should point out that Elton John is a better piano player than Paul Arthurs. It may have been the fact that he'd had about five bottles of wine. He took on the role of the entertainer. The whole lounge was just in hysterics. I would imagine he enjoyed it for most of the time because he wasn't centre of attention, for obvious reasons. But give him an opportunity and he seized it.'

Regardless of their vacancies, the band celebrated their No.1 success with a party in central London at the Mars Bar in Covent Garden. Blur were on the guest-list and, perhaps wary of having a growing association with the Colchester outfit, Noel was uncomfortable with the idea. Liam had no such reservations and, upon their arrival, bowled straight up to Damon and goaded him with taunts about their No.1 single. Ambitious people are by their very nature competitive, and this act rankled with Damon and would have huge repercussions.

Back to the problem in hand; the lack of a drummer. Alan White, younger brother of Paul Weller's long-term collaborator Steve, had previously auditioned to be in a band called Whirlpool, fronted by Gem Archer. He had also done the circuit, playing on the solo album of Ride frontman's Andy Bell's wife Idha, and with acts including Starclub and The Blow Monkeys' Dr Robert. On recommendation from Weller, Noel called White's mother to offer him the gig. After one rehearsal he was advised that he was in, if he wanted it. White accepted, and his first performance with the band was on *Top of the Pops*, performing their No.1 single 'Some Might Say', their second drummer in two weeks playing the song.

Steve White (Paul Weller/The Style Council drummer/brother of Alan White): 'Because he's that much younger, by the time he started to show interest in the drums, I'd moved out. I'd got my own place and I was gigging and touring. So, all my old bits and bobs that were still left at my mum's house, he kind of acquired. The very first Pearl kit he was using when he first started working with Oasis, that was one of my old drum sets. He also had the Rogers kit that ended on the front cover of 'Don't Look Back in Anger.' That was something he bought when he was working at Foote's in London. And I would put a bit of work his way. Like he got to play with Dr. Robert, did some recording with Robert before he joined Oasis. Alan did that and was kinda coming through behind me. He had just finished in Japan with Dr. Robert and came back, and that's when the notorious meeting or call happened, and he joined Oasis.

'And Oasis were on, and that was the original line-up of Tony and Guigsy and Bonehead. And I got on really well with everybody. I'm still really good friends with Bonehead to the day. We see each other quite regularly because of my connections in Manchester. So, I met them then and kind of got sort of a strange wind that something was afoot. I didn't pry too much because it wasn't my business in band politics, but essentially it wasn't too long after we did *The White Room* that it became apparent that Tony was going to be replaced. And the way I hear the story, I think Paul Weller did mention to Noel that my brother was a good drummer, and I don't know if Noel took it on board but I'm sure there are people out there that know much more about it than me, but I'm pretty sure Noel heard Alan playing with another artist that was signed to Creation and Alan was doing some session work with her in a studio in Fulham.

'I think Noel heard the drumming and asked Alan McGee, 'Who's that playing drums?' And Alan said, 'Oh, is that Alan, Steve's brother?' 'Yes, I think it is.' So that's where the connection was actually made. I think Noel managed to get hold of my mum's number and left a message for Alan to call. He phoned and spoke with my mum, that's how it happened. I remember my mum saying, 'This bloke Noel Gallagher's just phoned up for you, Alan.' That was it really. He went down to a rehearsal and they liked what they heard and the next thing they did the Plymouth Pavilions, and then they were doing Glastonbury. That was very, very soon into his tenure with the band. He just grabbed the bull by the horns and went for it. I told him when he said he was going to do an audition, to 'Get everything you can of the band's, learn them all, find out if there's B-sides and learn them.' But he went to the audition and I don't know if they actually played anything by Oasis. I think it was all Beatles tunes, and that was it. I'm sure that's been elaborated on over the years. But that's the skeleton of the way I remembering it all happening and then that was it, he was gone.'

Alan McGee: 'By the time we got to (*What's the Story*).., and we'd probably done seven million *Definitely Maybe*s at this point, Oasis were in definite control and I was putting the records out. Which was fine as we still made the same amount of money!'

With a new drummer on board, and buoyed by every new success, it was time to capitalise with a second album. This time Rockfield Studios in Wales was the chosen venue, with Owen Morris and Noel again producing. Compared to the frustrating and often tortuous *Definitely Maybe* sessions, the sessions for the second album were a breeze, taking place over around two weeks, with a completion rate of one song per day. There were obviously disagreements between Noel and Liam, but such incidents were par for the course. A smaller matter at the time, but one which would have a longer lasting effect, was over lead vocal duties.

SINGLE OF THE WEEK

OASIS
Some Might Say
(Creation)

OK, SO it's no 'Whatever', but what is? Anybody would have difficulty following a record like that, but don't let the recent brilliance of Oasis blind you to the charms of their new stuff. 'Some Might Say' is still one the finest examples of pop music you'll hear this year, up there with The Boo Radleys and Take That singles.

What's strangest about this song is that on the first couple of hearings you convince yourself there's no hook, nothing going on at all. Then, a few hours later, you find yourself humming a tune which you genuinely can't remember hearing before. It's certainly a deceptive little f—er. Noel Gallagher is back on the barmy lyrics bus again, however ("*She can do the dishes/She's got little fishes on the brain*"), and it's nice to hear Big Bro joining little Liam on the neat call-and-response coda.

Noel makes his presence felt strongly on the rest of the EP (four new quality tracks, basically one-third of an album), and gets to do his John Sebastian solo acoustic thing on 'Talk Tonight', as previewed at live shows late last year, while 'Acquiesce' – for which he takes the chorus on his own – is a song which could be read as a peace plan for the Brothers Gallagher: "*We need each other/We believe in one other*". Meanwhile, Liam sounds more like Lennon than ever before.

We close with 'Headshrinker', a slight steal from The Faces' 'Stay With Me' on the intro and quite possibly the fastest song you'll ever hear by Oasis.

Ah, I remember punk rock, like it was only yesterday.

OK, so they're no Beatles. But who is? Er, are? Whatever...

Owen Morris: 'I remember him (Noel) telling me on the 'Some Might Say' session - which was March time and we started *Morning Glory* at the start of May, so there was only two months in between - he had songs like 'Hello' and 'She's Electric' for years and years.

'We went to rehearse the week before *Morning Glory*, and I think they only really practiced 'Roll with It' and 'Hello'. I think that was basically wanting to spend a tiny bit of time with Alan White, because he'd joined the week before they started recording.

'I did a lot of learning with Johnny Marr, so I put these tricks together. Noel was fantastically musical, he had it all anyway. All he needed was a bit of trimming round the edges and guidance on how to structure the dynamics of a recording. Noel's songs were obviously quite classic arrangements, so the dynamics were fairly obvious really.

'I think the first week is almost well documented. We went in on a Monday and on the first day we recorded 'Roll with It', apart from a few overdubs. On the second day we did 'Hello', pretty much all recorded and done. On the third day Noel said to Liam, 'Which one do you want to sing, 'Wonderwall' or 'Don't Look Back in Anger'?' I think because Noel had already sung 'Don't Look Back in Anger', Liam said he'd sing 'Wonderwall'. So, Noel said he would sing 'Don't Look Back in Anger', having made the decision he was going to sing one of them. So, we recorded 'Wonderwall' that day. We pretty much finished it apart from one little piano overdub at the end. That was recorded in eight hours, maybe less.

'The only track that was recorded live, as the band playing together, was 'Roll with It'. It was actually the first take they did. They did another half-dozen takes but I ended up liking the first take.'

As on *Definitely Maybe,* Noel took on some additional musical responsibilities.

Owen Morris: 'Usually Noel would put the bass down. I think Guigs played bass on maybe a few tracks. Guigs, God bless him, wasn't the best musician in the world. He was great live, but it was just quicker for Noel to do a bass take, which he'd do in one or two takes with maybe a couple of drop-ins. So, things would happen very quickly. By mid-day you'd have drums and bass down. If Bonehead was playing electric guitar, he'd get his takes down very quickly. I'd normally get two tracks of Bonehead down so that would be another half an hour to an hour, maximum. Then Noel would overdub maybe three, four, five guitar parts, if they were electric tracks.'

With enough studio nous, Morris and Noel had perfected a technique to get the best out Liam's vocals; not to over-stretch them. The younger Gallagher had an unerring gift of listening to Noel's demo once, going through it to make sure it scanned properly, then making it his own within three takes.

Owen Morris: 'When I was recording with Liam he was singing very well, and his voice was very open. So, he was doing takes very confidently and very quickly, he was so easy to record.'

Noel had two songs which required more nuance in the vocals; the aforementioned 'Don't Look Back in Anger' and a new ballad, apparently written about his new girlfriend Meg Mathews, called 'Wonderwall.' Liam couldn't understand why he wasn't allowed to sing both, but Noel gave him an ultimatum. Liam eventually opted for 'Wonderwall' so big brother took the other song. Liam did have some involvement in 'Don't Look Back in Anger' though, suggesting the opening line to the chorus, 'So Sally can wait.'

Owen Morris: "Wonderwall' got finished very quickly. I think it was after we had the vocal, then the mellotron was there. Bonehead wasn't going to play his usual strum along bar chords on this track. So, I went and picked out the root notes and showed him where those were. Then I just got him to play those on the cello, which we all liked. We picked out a harmony for the bridge and chorus, to build it and things like that. I think I did the delays and we were finished by dinner time. The one little piano line which comes in at the end I think Noel did a few weeks later. We just said it needed something to keep it going.

'The next day we did 'Don't Look Back in Anger.' We finished on pretty much the same basis as 'Wonderwall.' It probably went longer into the night because there are more electric guitars on there, and I put quite a few more string parts on it. That would have been a genuine 14-hour session.

'Noel got Bonehead to play it like 'Imagine,' and that made us all laugh. No-one really cared, it was funny. The whole derivative Noel Gallagher/Beatles thing, he was quite happy to be compared to The Beatles.

'I think maybe we would have done a couple of extra takes with Noel. I was never that convinced he should be singing, I didn't think he sounded as good as Liam. Certainly not back then. Liam was such a great singer at the time. I was never that convinced it was that brilliant really, but it works obviously, people like it. I just always thought Liam should have sung it.

'Liam was quite happy to have a break. He knew that Noel wanted to sing one of them. He sang three lead vocals in three days, so was quite happy to have a day off.'

Most ambitious of all was a new, seven-minute track called 'Champagne Supernova.' The song started simply with verse then chorus, before expanding into a sprawling epic.

Owen Morris: 'Oasis used to work from Monday to Friday, and then everyone would bugger off down the pub on Friday night. So, I think we started the backing track for 'Champagne Supernova' on the Friday and we probably got to the stage of basic acoustic guitars, drums, bass, Bonehead's electric guitar and a couple of Noel's guitars. I think we probably left it there that day. 'Champagne Supernova' took maybe three or four sessions, because that Friday night is when Liam brought lots of people back from the pub and he and Noel had a bust-up or whatever.'

The other notable disagreement was said to be the biggest physical altercation the brothers ever had. As songwriter, guitarist, backing vocalist and producer, Noel was required in the studio at all times. Likewise, Bonehead, Guigsy and Alan White had to be readily available. Such was the uncanny ability that Liam had to nail his vocals in a couple of takes, he would often spend time being surplus to requirements. As was his wont, he would often fill that time by going to the nearest pub. On one occasion, undoubtedly a few sheets to the wind, Liam invited half of the local pub back to Rockfield. Noel was seething at this, and even more so when one of his guitars was broken by one of the crew. So a fight broke out between Noel and Liam, which involved the elder brother hitting his sibling around the head with a cricket bat and then jumping out of a window. Alan White drove Noel away as Liam followed them on the drive, throwing a bin at the car. No long-lasting damage was done, although Noel didn't re-enter the studio for another three weeks, the incident being just another day in the life of the band.

Owen Morris: 'Liam had no problem with Noel singing 'Don't Look Back in Anger.'

'I think it was my birthday on the Friday. Liam went down the pub. Me and Noel were still doing guitar overdubs on 'Champagne Supernova' at maybe nine in the evening, something like that. Me, Brian Cannon and Noel decided to have a few drinks for the first time in a week and listen back to what we'd done. I think Noel came into the studio and Liam apparently turned up at the accommodation part of Rockfield, which was about 500 yards away from the studio, with maybe 20 people. I think he was getting off with some girl. I think me, Noel and Brian knocked it on the head about one in the morning in the studio, fairly drunk. We'd had a listen to the music and locked the studio up. I went to my bed, I was exhausted after a week's work. I went straight to sleep and missed all the aggro.

'Apparently, Noel kicked off at Liam when he saw all these people having a party at his accommodation, which upset Liam. There are various stories of what happened after that, I don't Liam trashed any of Noel's equipment as he couldn't get into the studio to do anything like that. I think it was more about Noel trying to get rid of Liam's supposed new friends and stuff and Liam being angry at being told off by his older brother in front of people. Liam tried battering Noel's door down to fight him in front of these other people, and that's when I think Noel got a cricket bat and hit Liam. Liam always came out worse in their fights because Noel always battered him.

'Noel buggered off and got Alan White to drive him to London because Liam had kicked his door in. I just remember waking up the next day and Liam looked very sheepish. He'd broken his foot kicking the door in. Noel had disappeared so everyone buggered off. It was a good week's work.

'So, Noel had a week off and Liam had a week off. It was about 10 days later that everyone reconvened. Liam and Noel had a big hug and we just got on with it. They'd been breaking up regularly by then, I think it was just another brother argument. There wasn't an atmosphere at all.'

So much larger in scale was 'Champagne Supernova' that it required an equally sky-scraping vocal performance from Liam.

Owen Morris: 'Then Liam had a go at singing it. The high note on 'Champagne Supernova' was burning his voice out, so he was getting croakier on each take. By the time he got to the end of the song he sounded very Rod Stewart-y. Noel liked it, bizarrely, and Liam liked it. But I didn't. At the very end of the session in Rockfield, with just me and Liam in the studio, I got him to re-sing it. We did it piece by piece, half a dozen times. We did all the softer bits first to build it up in sections. Once he'd got his softer bits done, we did the first chorus a bunch of times. So, the high bits we did last, so we could burn his voice out then. That was the last session in Rockfield.

'There was another session somewhere in the middle where Liam got really drunk and did all the 'aahs.' He got drunk and had the inspiration to do it. Having the luxury of all the tracks meant you could put lots of stuff down.'

Mod legend Paul Weller, by now firm friends with Noel, joined to play on two tracks, an instrumental later to become known as 'The Swamp Song' and the aforementioned 'Champagne Supernova.' Some 15 songs were completed in the sessions, which would make up the album and B-sides. The sessions were finally concluded in the middle of June. Just as well, because at the end of June there was the trifling matter of a headline slot at Glastonbury Festival.

Owen Morris: 'Noel put a bit of lead guitar on but wanted Paul Weller to do lead on it. I think he said from the start he wanted Weller on one of the tracks. They were big mates straight away. Noel was a big fan and they'd met quite a few times at Glastonbury and stuff like that. I think they just got on very well. He was quite definite that he was going to play on it. After the Rockfield sessions, which was mid-June, they went off and did Glastonbury. After that we went to Orinoco (Studio) near Elephant & Castle to mix it. I think Paul Weller came down on one day, which was all he needed. Weller probably did four solos and then let me pick the one I preferred. Noel let me pick as well. I think he also did stuff on 'The Swamp Song.' I think Weller played harmonica and some lead guitar.

'We had a lot of freedom. Total freedom. There were no record companies demanding remixes or interfering or wanting things changed at all.'

Back in those days Glastonbury wasn't such a pivotal part of the summer calendar as it is now, and it wasn't unusual for a band to headline on their first album. That said, it was still something of a big deal for Oasis to be playing last. Having not played a gig for two months, a warm-up gig was arranged at Bath Pavilion, Alan White's first official gig with the band. The setlist was freshened up to factor in the new songs and prevent the existing ones from becoming stale. Debuts were given to 'The Swamp Song', 'Hello', 'Roll with It' and 'Morning Glory'.

Publicising their headline slot, Noel did a lengthy interview with the *NME*, where he slated sub-headliners, Black Crowes, who they would later embark on an American tour with, and David Bowie, describing him as an 'old git'. He also ventured, 'I see Oasis as three albums and that's it. There's only so many anthems you can write.'

The headline slot itself was something of a mixed bag. The band played pretty well, with Alan White's ferocious drumming adding serious weight to the older numbers, including a storming version of 'Live Forever' which would later become a B-side. However, the gig itself was met with satisfactory reviews, but as it contained a wealth of unfamiliar material, including five songs yet to be released and two B-sides, that was understandable. Watching the footage now, seeing 'Don't Look Back in Anger' met with virtually no acknowledgement is a surreal sight. An even more surreal sight was Robbie Williams from Take That sauntering onstage to 'dance' with the band during 'Shakermaker.' He and Liam were drinking buddies for the festival and Williams was desperate to be released from the shackles and pressures of being a pop star, so the incident was allowed, although one would have paid more than a penny for Noel's thoughts on it.

The setlist was:

'The Swamp Song'
'Acquiesce'
'Supersonic'
'Hello'
'Some Might Say'
'Shakermaker'
'Roll with It'
'Slide Away'
'(It's Good) To Be Free'
'Morning Glory'

'Cigarettes & Alcohol'
'I Am the Walrus'
'Don't Look Back in Anger'
'Live Forever'
'Rock 'n' Roll Star'

The following night, having stuck around and appearing on the BBC's coverage of the festival, Noel gave a first performance of 'Wonderwall.'

For the rest of June and July the band embarked upon a string of summer dates across Europe, including support slots with R.E.M., and also played festivals in Italy, France, Switzerland, Germany, Belgium and Spain, after Noel had completed the mixing and mastering for the second album, at this stage simply called *Morning Glory*. Oasis once again supported R.E.M. at Slane Castle in Ireland, movie star Johnny Depp watching from the side of the stage before partying with the band after.

With the album in the can and a release date of early October pencilled in, further singles were slotted into the calendar. The first was 'Roll with It,' released in mid-August. As ever, Brian Cannon was in charge of sleeve design.

Brian Cannon: 'I had the idea that they should be uniform in the shot. All great bands are gangs. That uniformity was something I was interested in. One of them had a Burberry duffle coat, which I thought was particularly smooth, so I contacted Burberry and asked if they'd lend us five duffle coats. I got quite a curt reply saying, 'No, but you can buy them at £900 apiece.' I thought we'd give that a miss, so we bought some. I can't remember where we got them from in the end. They obviously liked them, because the night after that gig they played Glastonbury and, if not all of them, certainly Noel wore his onstage.

'Another mad thing, bearing in mind that Oasis were signed to Creation, which was owned by Sony - I asked Sony if we could borrow five televisions for the shoot. They turned us down. Talk about missing a branding opportunity! So, I had to hire five televisions from a shop in Wigan, and purposely didn't pick Sony. They were all Panasonic tellies.'

Tom Hingley: 'Oasis was pop music at its best. My favourite period of Oasis was when they were releasing three-minute pop singles. Rebellious singles, punky singles, but it's pop.'

Rick Witter: 'In the '90s there was as little bit of competition (between bands). I don't know if Oasis had a bit of blame for that by just creating animosity. I think that's just the type of people they are.'

Meanwhile, galvanised by the astonishing success of *Parklife*, Blur were gearing up for an album and single release of their own. The first single for their fourth album, 'Country House', was also scheduled for an August release. The lines of communication between Creation and Food, Blur's label, had been good, with an understanding that the release dates wouldn't clash and both singles could have a clear run at No.1.

Johnny Sharp: 'I realised that clearly they had really good songs. The whole Blur-Oasis rivalry was bullshit. I didn't buy the whole idea that Blur were public-school southern poshos, because they weren't. They weren't privately educated, and even if they were, they wouldn't have been the first rock stars to do that. Also, this idea of Oasis being salt of the earth, working-class boys. They kind of were, but you meet five Liam Gallagher-esque blokes in every playground in the North. I got the feeling that a lot of more London-based journalists were enamoured, just like they were with Shaun and Bez, with these Northern scally creatures.'

Accounts of this story vary depending on who is interviewed; the Blur camp are adamant that 'Roll with It' was brought forward by as much as six weeks, to be perilously close to the Blur single, possibly the week before. Andy Ross of Food, was working on the premise that if 'Roll with It' was released the week before 'Country House', not only would Blur be up against Oasis, they would also be up against a No.1 single, which could have added 50% more sales because of all the resultant exposure. Devising a plan at the pub, where all best-laid plans are made, it was apparently Damon Albarn's decision to go head-to-head with Oasis. Liam in particular had a problem with Damon, and in subsequent years there were fleeting comments from those involved about deeper undertones to the rivalry, which were never disclosed.

From the perspective of the Oasis camp, it was great publicity. Alan McGee felt that, as successful as Oasis had been thus far, Blur were in the next level of popularity, and this move would put his proteges on an even keel. Ignition management were also very keen on the idea and aimed to milk the publicity as much as they could. They were adamant that they weren't going to move.

The *NME* leapt on the story and put together a front cover of their August 12 edition with Liam Gallagher and Damon Albarn in a 'big match' boxing mock-up, christened 'The Battle of Britpop'. The following Monday, Oasis released 'Roll with It' on 7" vinyl, cassette and CD, with the accompanying B-sides 'It's Better People', 'Rockin' Chair' (one of the few Gallagher compositions with two writers credited - Noel Gallagher and Chris Griffiths) and 'Live Forever' (live at Glastonbury, 1995).

Chris Griffiths: 'Rockin' Chair' was another...it wasn't a sit-down co-write. It was a complete lift off a song I had, that we were recording at the same time we were doing 'Live Demonstration,' a song called 'Growing Old.' My brother went along to this session in London, and Noel said to our kid, 'I've got some new B-sides here, I'll play you them.' My brother said, 'That's our kid's song, what are you doing?' He just went, 'Oh yeah, I thought I'd heard it somewhere before.' He said, 'You fucking know it is, you only listened to it a few months ago.' It was just a complete lift. It wasn't asked for or anything. It was only when we actually went to court ... this is

the sort of thing - 'We'll give you a little bit of money, forget about the other two songs, because your legal fees are really high at the moment.' Noel just sent my solicitor a letter, my solicitor sent one back. We couldn't get legal aid at the time 'cos we'd just wrote a song for Cher and had a little bit of money in the bank. They were more or less trying to make us go bankrupt, sending letters to solicitors.

'In the end our legal fees were astronomical, (and it was like) 'I don't think these two little scallywags from Bootle are going to be able to pay this bill. Let's just accept a deal, so they get paid and we get a bit of money.' All I was fighting for was my name on three of the tracks. So the payback, the percentage we agreed, whether it be 10%, 5%, I wasn't really bothered, I just wanted my name on the track and a payment of that percentage. It never really happened, I got badly advised, and I took my name getting put on to 'Rockin' Chair' and a small pay-off for the other two tracks, a really silly thing to do at the time. In the end, everyone knows the truth anyway.'

The same day, Blur released 'Country House,' their first single for nine months, also on 7" vinyl, cassette and CD. There was also an extra version of the CD, featuring live recordings from their show at Mile End earlier that summer. A small detail but one which would be important. Then all hell broke loose.

The timing was perfect; Britpop, such as it was, was in full swing and the associated acts were enjoying chart success. Sheffield's Pulp, toiling in the background for a decade and a half, had finally found success with their single 'Common People,' and stepped into headline Glastonbury when The Stone Roses had to withdraw. At the other end of the scale, newbies Supergrass had written the anthem of the summer with the upbeat 'Alright.' Meanwhile, Elastica's self-titled debut album had broken *Definitely Maybe*'s record of fastest-selling debut album earlier that year, and their front-woman Justine Frischmann was dating Damon Albarn, so they were the 'power couple' of the movement.

It was the midsummer, known in the UK press as 'silly season.' With Parliament in recess there's often a news void for the mainstream media to fill, and the Battle of Britpop filled it perfectly. There were larger connotations as well, with Blur deemed middle-class, art school attending Southerners, compared to the working class, council estate aesthetics of Oasis. The story could easily be spun as a North/South class divide debate. The chart battle made the BBC News as a headline story, compared to the Beatles vs the Stones (even though no such chart battle ever occurred between those legendary acts). In midweek, BBC2 showcased a number of bands in a special show called *Britpop Now*. As well as performing 'Country House,' the show was hosted by Damon Albarn. Notable by their absence were Oasis, who refused to, wary of becoming too associated with the movement, seeing themselves as classic rock'n'roll.

Tellingly, Oasis kept a low profile all week. As had often been demonstrated, Liam and Noel weren't backward in coming forward when offering opinions. On the other side of the ring, Damon Albarn was everywhere; not only on the aforementioned *Britpop Now*, but happy to do interviews on news programmes. He also appeared on BBC Radio 1's Breakfast Show, presented by Chris Evans, who played 'Roll with It' which Albarn, on air, compared to Status Quo's 'Rockin' All Over the World.'

Symptomatic of the whole affair was a press article about a couple who had taken sides then fallen out, the female (Oasis fan) smashing her partner's merchandise and records. All very silly, not to say questionable, but it sold. All week the singles were neck and neck, the *NME* producing covers for each outcome, and the bookmakers never revealing a clear favourite, although 'Roll with It' just about shaded it in any predictions.

The top-40 countdown took place on Sunday, August 20. It was already the biggest week for UK singles sales in a decade. Over the course of the show stories began to leak to the press and the labels that 'Roll with It' sales had been hit by faulty barcodes, so not all sales were recorded. To firmly milk the anticipation, in a break from tradition, rather than counting down from 40 to 2, Radio One halted at No.3, ratcheting up the tension.

Then came the news the world had been waiting for, the No.2 single that week was 'Roll with It', with sales of 217,000, 'Country House' straight in at No.1 with sales of 270,000. Blur had won the 'Battle of Britpop'.

The barcodes story was never clarified but the general consensus was that Blur owed their success to releasing four different formats of the single to Oasis' three. Die-hard fans, of which there would have been many, would have bought all formats, so by basic mathematics Blur were always going to win. In most other weeks 'Roll with It' would have made No.1 without question, indeed it sold more than many No.1 singles that year. Aside from the obvious indignity of 'losing' out to their 'rivals', there weren't really any losers from the whole affair ... in the short term.

The irony of the situation was that neither offering represented any kind of creative zenith for either band. 'Roll with It' could stake a claim for being the weakest Oasis single up to this point, being a throwaway pop song (albeit with a very Beatles-like structure). Much better songs were to come on the second album. 'Country House' was, by some distance, the worst Blur single in this period. Even worse was the video, which portrayed Keith Allen, Matt Lucas, a wealth of Page 3 models and the band in a sordid, Benny Hill environment. Directed by artist Damien Hirst, it was no doubt intended to be ironic but straddled the line between irony and vulgarity too closely. That said, it was memorable, certainly in comparison to the 'Roll with It' video, effectively a live performance by the band.

Amid the fallout, Blur were understandably jubilant, apart from guitarist Graham Coxon who, at the party to celebrate in London and in the throes of alcoholism, attempted to throw himself out of a window and had to be talked down. Shortly after, Liam saw bassist Alex James, and said, 'I met Alex in the pub, so bombed over and said, 'Congratulations on No.1 – it's about fucking time, mate', and he goes 'Oh yeah. But both our songs were shit anyway'. And I went 'No, this is where you're wrong. And this is why I fuckin' hate your band, and you. I thought our song was top.'

Top of the Pops later that week was compulsory viewing for those with even a passing interest in the story, and, whilst it would have been entertaining

enough as it was presented by Pulp's Jarvis Cocker, it didn't disappoint. Both bands treated the incident with good humour; Liam and Noel swapped around their positions in the band for their performance, poking fun at the idea that people were struggling to tell the brothers apart. As you'd expect, having written the song, Noel's performance as frontman was impeccable. Liam taking lead guitar, specifically the solo, less so.

For their part Blur gave the audience a nod and a wink, with Alex James wearing an Oasis T-shirt. Following *Top of the Pops*, Oasis jetted over to the Far East to play a short tour of seven gigs. After being painted as 'losers' in the press, returning to over-excessive adulation would have been a good tonic.

Mat Whitecross: 'Alan McGee said, 'Basically, it's boxing. You're the heavyweight champion of the world, or champion of the UK in the case of Blur. You don't go into the ring with the young upstart, because even if you beat him, then he's now at your level. What have you got from it? But if he beats you, you're really screwed.' What happens in the next fight, then what it comes down to is the next album; Oasis had the classic album and Blur didn't. It's a great album but it wasn't their best.'

Before that, on the same Radio One show as the culmination of 'The Battle', an announcement was made for a special project to aid the charity *War Child*, specifically their efforts in war-stricken areas such as Bosnia and Herzegovina. The concept was that an album would be recorded in one day, mixed the next and be in the shops within four. The great and the good of the indie scene were all involved; Radiohead, Suede, The Stone Roses, Manic Street Preachers and Blur were amongst a stellar cast. Oasis were also involved, recording an acoustic version of 'Fade Away'. Under the banner Oasis and Friends, movie star Johnny Depp played guitar, with then-girlfriend, Kate Moss adding backing vocals.

More excitingly for fans, and no doubt Noel Gallagher himself, was the formation of a special, one-off 'supergroup', the Smokin' Mojo Filters, to record a cover of 'Come Together' by The Beatles, consisting of Noel, Paul Weller, Steve Cradock of mod revivalists Ocean Colour Scene, Steve White, soul singer Carleen Anderson and one Paul McCartney. The hook was 'three generations of British music'. The cover itself was unremarkable, but it would be churlish to dismiss the cause, and the glee on Noel's face in the photographs as he posed with two of his heroes was obvious.

Another bump lay in the road ahead; with another huge tour on the horizon Guigsy was forced to withdraw from the band for health reasons, citing 'nervous exhaustion'. Iain Robertson, Oasis' tour manager at the time, later put this down in part to Liam's vitriolic attacks; 'more than anybody, Liam's venomous poison surrounds him.' Unlike with Tony, there was no categorical statement that Guigsy had left the band, and the door was left open for him to return. But the tour had to go ahead, and a replacement had to be found. Scott McLeod of Liverpudlian band The Ya Yas was drafted in on bass. A short tour of the Far East took place at the end of August.

Iain Robertson: 'I remember saying to Liam in Tokyo when we had a really important set of press commitments to meet on the Wednesday morning. Liam wanted to go berserk on the Tuesday night. I remember saying to him, 'It's Tuesday. It doesn't matter where you are in the world, it's Tuesday. Nothing good is going to happen'. It had no effect whatsoever, he stayed up until stupid o'clock and nothing happened. It was just a procession of trawling from empty club to empty club.'

In the early autumn the promotion for the second album, now with a longer title of *(What's the Story) Morning Glory?* commenced. There was much to discuss; the opening track, 'Hello' 'borrowed' the chorus from glam rocker Gary Glitter's hit 'It's Good To Be Back'; 'Cast No Shadow' was dedicated to frontman of close friends The Verve, Richard Ashcroft; 'Don't Look Back in Anger' had a distinctly-similar piano intro to 'Imagine' by John Lennon. One track, 'Step Out' had to be dropped at a very late stage because of its similarity to Stevie Wonder's 'Uptight.' By this point, accusations of plagiarism were water off a duck's back. Despite all the comparisons, it was undeniable that the band had stepped up a level in terms of songwriting and musicianship. Proof of Oasis starting to properly infiltrate the mainstream was an appearance on the cover of *Smash Hits*.

Said promotion included a lengthy interview with Noel in *The Guardian* on September 17, covering a wealth of subjects, including songwriting, wealth, musical heroes, his brother ... and Blur. Finally offering an opinion after a month of silence, Noel gave it, and then some: 'The guitarist I've got a lot of time for. The drummer I've never met, I hear he's a nice guy. The bass player and the singer... I hope the pair of them catch AIDS and die because I fucking hate them two.'

There was no further mention of the comment in the article. There were however lots of comments in the days that followed, and something of an uproar in the mainstream media about the crassness and insensitivity of the comments. If the piece had been in the *NME* a year earlier no eyelids would have been batted, but their meteoric rise and the headline-making battle had changed everything, the Gallagher brothers fair game to the British media. Noel eventually recanted and said AIDS was no laughing matter and had to write a letter of apology. He later confessed, 'My whole world came crashing down in on me then. If it wasn't for our kid, I don't know what I would have done'. 'It's alright, you said something daft.' This is my little brother, who I keep looking after, putting his arm round me and saying, 'It'll be alright, man."

The comments gave an insight into his feelings about the whole 'Battle of Britpop' circus and his frustrations at losing. If it hadn't already, Britpop was turning nasty.

The early reviews of *(What's the Story) Morning Glory?* were lukewarm at best. *Q* said of the lyrics, 'They scan, they fill a hole, end of story'. *Melody Maker* claimed 'The whole album sounds laboured and lazy. On this evidence, Oasis are a limited band.' The general consensus seemed to be that the Oasis bubble had burst, the rip-offs were now demonstrating a lack of guile rather than being charming, and that, having shaved some of the more punk elements and moved into anthemic string territory, Oasis would lose their fanbase. Undeterred, two large shows at London's cavernous Earl's Court were booked in for early November. The shows were the largest indoor gigs in Europe, with each night allowing a capacity of 20,000. Both gigs sold out within minutes.

As with *Definitely Maybe*, Oasis performed in-store at Virgin Megastore's flagship outlet in London the day before the album's release, although only one song from the new album was performed ('Cast No Shadow'). The second album finally landed on Monday, October 2, 1995. Despite the bad press, the album flew off the shelves. The HMV store in central London was said to be selling two copies per minute at one stage. Unsurprisingly the album hit No.1 in the UK album charts, a first week haul of 347,000 copies making it the second fastest-selling album in British history, behind *Bad* by Michael Jackson.

Tony McCarroll: 'To be honest, when that album first came out, I was like, 'What have they done? What's going on?' I find that Oasis tracks are growers. You could tell there was money spent on there.'

In the week of release the band sandwiched four UK shows in between numerous media appearances to promote the album, at the legendary Empress Ballroom, Blackpool, Trentham Gardens in Stoke, the Bournemouth International Centre and the Leisure Centre in Gloucester, with Scott McLeod in tow, before they went to the US for a quick promotional jaunt including an appearance on the legendary *Letterman Show*, as well as other gigs. 'Cast No Shadow', 'Champagne Supernova' and 'Rockin' Chair' found places in the set, as well as another new song, 'Round Are Way.' On the outro to the song Liam would often sing the verses of 'Up in The Sky', such was their similarity. In the US, 'Wonderwall' became part of Noel's acoustic section.

'Wonderwall' was selected as the third single to be lifted from *(What's the Story) Morning Glory?* Unlike anything else the band had ever released, complete with expensive looking video, the package was tailor-made for the US market. The single was ostensibly about Noel's girlfriend Meg Mathews, although Noel later said, 'The meaning of that song was taken away from me by the media who jumped on it, and how do you tell your Mrs it's not about her once she's read it is? It's a song about an imaginary friend who's gonna come and save you from yourself.'

As ever, the single was backed by three new songs; the aforementioned 'Round Are Way', a full version of 'The Swamp Song' (snippets of less than a minute made up two tracks on *(What's the Story) Morning Glory?)* and a composition written by Noel called 'The Masterplan'. Noel had been asked to record new B-sides for the next singles by Creation. On hearing the latter track, Alan McGee was of the opinion it was too strong to not be included on an album. Noel's response was typically bullish, saying, 'He called me up and said, 'That's not a B-side. It's too good.' I said to him, 'I don't write shit songs, it's a B-side.'

Nick Ingman: 'What Noel's got, like the really top songwriters, is earworm melody. That's his talent. McCartney's got it, Stevie Wonder's got it, Burt Bacharach has got it ... very few people have it, but Noel certainly does. 'The Masterplan' is a great example of that. Everything in it is immediately memorable. If you played it to a bunch of guys in a pub on a Saturday night, everyone would be singing along, and I think that's the litmus test. It's immediately recognisable, not because it's a copy, but it does have what the Americans call 'high memorability factor.' It's a horrible phrase.'

Alan McGee: 'Noel was just a machine at that point, coming out with B-sides. The B-sides are probably my fault. I actually thought, 'This guy's never going to run out, let's just put them all out!' If we'd kept back 'The Masterplan' and things like that...'Round Are Way,' what a song. If we'd been clever about the B-sides, we'd have had three great albums before *Be Here Now*. But still, the first two are shockingly good.'

By this point, with the hubris that comes with hundreds of thousands of sales, Noel Gallagher's word was final, and McGee reluctantly agreed to put it on the single of 'Wonderwall.' Interestingly, Blur's next single 'The Universal,' was released the week after, but with little acknowledgment of the rivalry by any party.

Meanwhile, all the hysteria and rigours of the celebrity lifestyle were becoming too much for stand-in bassist Scott McLeod. After a show in Pittsburgh, the night before the *Letterman* show, he told tour manager Maggie Mousaitikis that he was quitting, with his primary reason being that he missed his girlfriend too much. With little choice, the band played *Letterman* with Bonehead on bass but had to cancel the remaining US gigs. Some weeks later, McLeod made contact with Noel, admitting he thought he had made a mistake. Noel's typically brutal response was, 'I think you have too. Good luck signing on.' Fortunately, they were able to coerce Guigsy back into the fold, just in time for the shows at Earl's Court in early November.

Buoyed by the astonishing and continuing success of *(What's the Story) Morning Glory?* there was a celebratory mood in the air in west London. Making a mockery of all Beatles comparisons in the press, Oasis had tribute act The Bootleg Beatles as their main support and the foursome later joined in for set-closer 'I Am the Walrus,' all playing their respective instruments apart from 'Ringo,' who had to make do with a tambourine.

London was abuzz all weekend. Not only that, no doubt sensing that Oasis were now where it was at, all forms of celebrities started began attending their gigs, or more specifically appearing backstage. The Edge from U2, George Michael and Kate Moss were all seen floating around a free bar.

Effectively a stadium gig, changes to the set were necessary. The band performed 11 songs, all sung by Liam, then Noel had his three-song acoustic set ('Wonderwall', 'Cast No Shadow' and 'Morning Glory') before the rest of the band returned for 'Don't Look Back in Anger.' Liam would have been offstage for the best part of half an hour and when he returned to the stage and started introducing the next song ('Whatever'), Noel also began talking. Liam quickly admonished his big brother, saying, 'Piss off, this is my job.' Perhaps conversations were starting to be had about Liam's frustrations.

On the other hand, during 'Whatever', he quite sweetly looked to his brother for permission to sing the chorus of 'Octopus's Garden' for the outro. A brass and string section assisted with 'Don't Look Back in Anger', as well as 'Whatever' and 'I Am the Walrus'. To be able to command such luxuries when performing requires a lot of kudos, and Oasis were starting to flex their muscles.

Alan McGee: 'When I got played 'All Around the World', it was the two nights we did at Earl's Court (October 1995), a big fuck-off party. Liam found me, and I was just sitting down. I was sober and quite a shy person at this point. All the drugged, bullshit bravado had disappeared by this point, which was good. I was sitting at the edge of the dancefloor, minding my own business, when Liam came up to me and goes, 'Do you want to hear 'All Around the World?' I'm thinking 'how am I gonna hear it?' and he just fucking sang it to me! That was the first time I'd ever heard it and he was just singing in my ear. It was fucking great. 'It sounds amazing, Liam.' Great times.'

On the same weekend as Earl's Court, 'Wonderwall', accompanied by a surreal black and white video with clowns and musicians playing saws and featuring the already-departed Scott McLeod, charted at No.2. This time, rather than being held off by a direct competitor, it was thwarted by a cover of 'I Believe' by TV actors, Robson & Jerome. Still not a bad performance for a song that had already been released. Ordinarily the dedicated following of Oasis fans would buy a single in the first week, eager to hear new songs, the first-week position would be the peak position, and it would then fall away back down the charts. But 'Wonderwall' didn't go away and stayed in the top-10 for the rest of 1995. No.1 singles came and went, but it held firm in the top-five for most of that period.

The cover shoot for the single didn't quite go to plan, however. After formulating the idea of Liam Gallagher adorning the cover on Primrose Hill, North London, within a photo frame, influential rock photographer Michael Spencer Jones

SINGLES

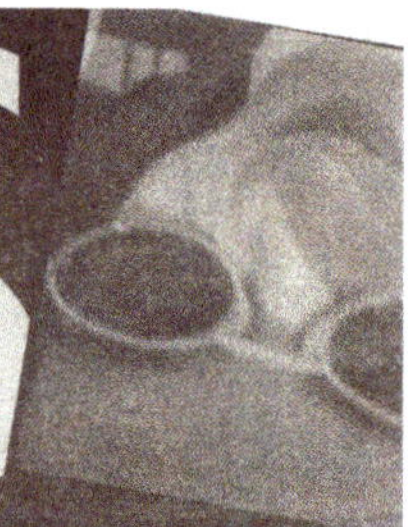

REVIEWED BY MICHAEL BONNER

SINGLE OF THE WEEK 1

OASIS
WONDERWALL (Creation)

A MESMERIC declaration of love – haunting, beautiful and effortlessly simple – and, unless you've been locked in a coal cellar for the last two months, you should know it forwards, backwards and sideways by now.

Anyway, anyway, anyway . . .

Single Of The Week.

You want a reason? Slip inside my private life for a minute. There's a girl I've been in love with for eight years. She means more to me than anyone has, *ever*, and, for a while now, she's been staying at my house. After the last time we went clubbing, we crashed out listening to Portishead, the "Blade Runner" soundtrack, Jam & Spoon's "Tripomaptic Fairytales 2002" and the three mellow tracks off "(What's The Story) Morning Glory". We were lost, floating in our own bubbles of blissed-out numbness, the only sensation to permeate mine being a soul-swallowing yearning when Liam sang, plaintively: *"I don't believe that anybody/Feels the way I do about you now."*

(You're so beautiful, you're just so beautiful . . .)

"Wonderwall", to paraphrase the French philosopher, Chateaubriand, is the sublime pressed to its furthest limits. And "Round Are Way", its all-singing, all-dancing, all-new B-side, isn't far behind.

and Liam went to the location. A few photographs had been taken, but by sheer coincidence Noel happened to be passing in a taxi. Seeing his younger brother being photographed, he jumped out of the taxi and demanded the shoot be abandoned. His argument was that 'Wonderwall' was a love song and it would be inappropriate at best for his brother to be on the cover, and it required a female. Creation employee Anita Heryet was drafted in as replacement.

Mark Feltham: 'I didn't know anything about them, I have to be honest. I'm on the B-side of 'Wonderwall'. Apparently, they recorded 'Wonderwall' a couple of hours before I went in ... 'Round Are Way'. I'm on that.

'When I went in to do my parts (in the studio), on everything I ever recorded, it was rarely ever with the band. It was always as an overdub at mix stage. Traditionally a harmonica player would always go on last. So, the band had been and gone, I didn't meet the band. The only times I ever met the band was when we did the live shows, and even then, it was only very sporadically. I only spoke to Liam once in the whole time I worked with Oasis. That was in a bank in Manchester. I walked in and he walked in behind me, came up to me and went, 'Hey Mark, you alright?' He gave me his funny old straddle and his walk, then went, 'Alright, see you later', gave me the thumbs-up and that was it, he was gone. I never spoke to him again. It was always very much that the band was kept very special. They were very segregated from the rest of us. I think the Mums, girlfriends and the others were always there in the VIP enclosure. We never travelled with them, we never saw them.'

It was a true crossover hit; not only did the die-hards love it, but pop fans loved it too. Parents loved it. Such was the success of the single that the release of the follow-up, 'Don't Look Back in Anger', had to be continually delayed. Being accompanied by such a strong song as 'The Masterplan', which Noel acknowledges as, 'One of the few times where everything went right; the songwriting, the production, the playing, everything' wouldn't have harmed sales, with word of mouth giving that song a legendary reputation. 'Wonderwall' also reached No.8 on the Billboard Chart in the US, yet another impressive achievement. It finished the year at No.10 in the yearly chart. It was everywhere for the next six months.

So successful was the song that, in the Christmas chart, two versions of it were in the Top-10, including a version by an act called Mike Flowers Pops, the song reworked as an easy-listening, Burt Bacharach-esque rip-off.

Mike Flowers (real name Mike Roberts, frontman, Mike Flowers Pops): 'At the time, without any consideration as to what's legal or not, we just did it. I'd heard of Oasis a bit. They were big, but not as big as they'd become a year later.

'I wasn't aware of its ('Wonderwall') resonance really. It went well with our concept: I was a slightly clueless old band leader trying to stay with it. I think our ironic comment was on pop music generally, not just Oasis. It was almost just to say, 'This is a soppy love song. They're pretending it's a rock song but it's not. It worked out very well, I was very pleased about it. We made good decisions about how to present it.

'I did bump into Noel on Hanley Street in London, by Tottenham Court Road. I introduced myself and he shook my hand and said, 'Thanks very much, I think you bought me a swimming pool. At the time I was very relieved we weren't (the Christmas No.1), because it was pretty full-on for a couple of weeks. In retrospect it would have been funnier.'

The Mike Flowers Pops' version of 'Wonderwall' was briefly in the mix for that Christmas No.1, before being overcome by Michael Jackson and 'Earth Song.'

After the Earl's Court mega-gigs there followed a quick jaunt around Europe, stopping in Germany, Sweden and a handful of dates in France. Over the course of this short tour the band parted ways with tour manager Iain Robertson.

Iain Robertson: 'Everybody had an awful lot to drink throughout the course of the day, which never helps. We were being interviewed for a little radio station in Paris with Eddie Izzard. He was coming to Paris later to do a show. It was fine until Eddie started asking questions in fluent French, which completely charmed the radio host. Suddenly the conversation became much more about Eddie and much less about Liam and Oasis. In the room was Bonehead, Guigs, Alan and myself, but Liam was the only one doing the interview. The rest of us were hanging out, having a drink and chatting to some French birds. You could see the situation going south. In the end Liam literally stood up, threw his chair across the room and kicked off severely, I think live on French radio.

'After that had happened, I thought, 'Let's get out of here, this doesn't end well.' Liam wanted to leave, I said, 'I'll come with you.' He and I had a couple of cars ferrying us around town, so we took one and went to a bar that we as a band used to like. He and I sat there, and he calmed down and we were getting to a place where I thought, 'This will end as well as this could ever end.'

'Then unfortunately the record company representative turned up, and Liam and she ended up in an incredible row in the back of the car. Liam, in fairness, was pretty much out of order so I was trying to reconcile the pair of them. Liam took that as a personal slight and literally threw himself out of the car when the car was doing 20 miles an hour. I followed him as my job is to look after him. So now we're both rolling down the street and then from nowhere he just punched me. I didn't see it coming, and he punched me again. So, I lifted him up, carried him across the road and bounced him off a bus stop. We stood and looked at each other and that was pretty much it. I knew that was it.

'Unfortunately, those kind of run-ins were happening between he and I with greater frequency. That was in part my fault. Without creating any excuses, I believe my job was not to just nod and say, 'Yes, how high?' I believe my job was to get stuff done, and the things we were doing were important and we couldn't just sack them off if we didn't feel well or had a hangover.

'Most of the time the reason we were late for something was because of something Liam hadn't done. Why not, he's a rock star, that's his job. But my job is to get us to here or there, so increasingly we were having run-ins with each other, and I wasn't as diplomatic as I could and should have been. There were times when I was unreasonable, unfair, and probably harsh and schoolmasterly, with Liam particularly.

'I called Marcus and I called Noel. I got a voicemail from Marcus and I was able to speak to Noel. This was immediately after the event, about 45 minutes after it had happened. I wanted to jump before I was pushed, but there was never any doubt in my mind that the push would come. In a conversation Noel and I had subsequently, he said, 'Well, we're blood and because of where we are with the band, he and I are joined at the hip. There is only one way this can end.' Liam was pretty adamant that he didn't want to work with me anymore.'

Accompanying the band on the tour was esteemed rock photographer Jill Furmanovsky.

Jill Furmanovsky (photographer): 'It was an awful time when there was a lot of tension between Noel and Liam. Things had gone wrong as far as the (photo) shoot was concerned, getting them all in one place at one time. Liam was at the bar a bit too long and Noel was not in a good mood. The weather was a bit bleak. There was paparazzi everywhere. It was all going wrong. Yet it produced the most fantastic set of pictures for me. I never thought for a minute these kind of pictures, which were so full of tension, would ever be considered to be suitable press shots. But absolutely they were! I remember on the bridge Liam was running after French people on bicycles, pinching bottoms and flinging a glass of alcohol. Noel virtually had steam coming out of his head as the whole shoot had already been ruined before and they were supposed to do other stuff. He was so pissed off. I said to Noel, 'Don't worry about it, you stand there and when he comes into frame, I'll shoot it.' By this point Liam was trying to make it up to Noel, who wasn't having any of it, but the whole thing was just a press shot.'

OASIS: NO LOOKING BACK

OASIS have made it official. Their next single, released on January 15, will be "Don't Look Back In Anger", as revealed by The Maker six weeks ago. And, as we also predicted, it will be accompanied by a cover of Slade's "Cum On Feel The Noize", a new song called "Underneath The Sky" and "Step Out", which had to be dropped from "(What's The Story) Morning Glory?" at the last minute because of its similarity to Stevie Wonder's "Uptight".

Liam: man without dartboard

The seven-inch and cassette versions of the single feature only "Step Out". The 12-inch adds "Underneath The Sky" and the CD has all four tracks. "Step Out" is now credited to Noel Gallagher, Stevie Wonder, Hank Cosby and Sylvia Moy (the latter pair co-writers of "Uptight" with Wonder).

While advance copies of the LP featuring "Step Out" were recalled and destroyed, some slipped the net and are now changing hands for around £200.

In other Oasis news this week, the band are carrying on breaking records. They announced, locally, gigs at Dublin The Point on March 22 and 23, and these became the fastest-selling shows ever in Ireland. Tickets went in half an hour, with a space in the middle while repairs were made to the Dublin telephone exchange, which collapsed under the weight of calls from fans.

Two more shows, in Cardiff on March 18 and 19, were advertised locally, and also immediately sold out.

In the last 18 months, Oasis have played 200 gigs to a million people worldwide. "(What's The Story) Morning Glory?" has sold 1.5 million copies (five times platinum) and "Wonderwall" has shifted nearly half a million singles.

Oasis, meanwhile, have become involved in an anti-drug video campaign by the parents of Leah Betts, the teenager and Oasis fan who recently died after taking Ecstasy.

Her family were given permission to use "Wonderwall" in a video reconstruction of her last hours. It was played at her funeral.

Meanwhile, "Wonderwall" features elsewhere in the news with the revelation that The Mike Flowers Pops' easy-listening version of the song is the bookies' new second-favourite for the Christmas Number One.

An Oasis spokesman commented: "I know the band like the interpretation of it. It's a compliment. It shows what a strong song it is."

Oasis themselves are in America, where MTV have picked up on "Wonderwall" and placed it on "stress rotation", described as "the best you can get" for a band of Oasis' up-and-coming status in the US.

The band will be returning to the UK for Christmas, when their record company will present them with an extraordinary accolade – a copy of the December 14 Daily Star which featured an Oasis festive board game on the centre spread!

The same issue of the Star reported that Liam is hoping for a dartboard for Christmas.

He shouldn't hold his breath: it's not on Creation's shopping list.

After picking up Best Live Act at the *Q* Awards, and following more dates in France, Germany and Sweden, Oasis spent the rest of November playing UK arena dates - in Newcastle, a homecoming gig at Manchester's NYNEX Arena and at London's Brixton Academy, before jetting over to the States to capitalise on the success of both *(What's the Story) Morning Glory?* and 'Wonderwall.' There were only one or two gigs, with the rest of the time taken up by various US rock stations, such as appearances on *KROQ* and *MTV*.

In the UK their latest performance on music show *Later...With Jools Holland* was broadcast sans Liam, who was said to have a sore throat. As well as paying 'Wonderwall' and 'Round Are Way,' with Noel singing, they also debuted their cover of iconic '70s rockers Slade's 'Cum on Feel the Noize,' with Noel on lead vocals rather than the recorded version featuring Liam.

At the Creation Christmas party, with spirits no doubt stratospheric, thank you presents were given to the members of Oasis by the label for not only their success but for lining several people's pockets. With the numbers Oasis were pulling in it was entirely justified. Bonehead, Alan, Liam and Guigsy were each given a Rolex watch and Noel was presented with a chocolate brown Rolls Royce. Noel's girlfriend Meg Mathews reminded McGee that he had promised the car to Noel 'if they made it really big,' which McGee couldn't recall but did so anyway. Noel revelled in the decadence but later commented, 'Liam got a watch and I got a Rolls-Royce. Which is ironic because I can't drive, and Liam can't tell the time.'

SJM CONCERTS & MCP PRESENTS
BY ARRANGEMENT WITH PRIMARY TALENT INTERNATIONAL
oasis
plus special guests
Saturday 10th August 1996
KNEBWORTH PARK
STEVENAGE, HERTFORDSHIRE
Tickets £22.50 (inc vat) Subject to licence - Strictly no camping
Maximum 4 Tickets Per Applicant - Gates Open 12.00 noon - Show Starts 2,15pm
OASIS FREEFONE TICKETLINE 0800 614595
EXCLUSIVE 24 HOUR LINE - BOOKING FEE £1.50 PER TICKET - ACCESS/VISA/SWITCH ACCEPTED
MAILOUT CHARGE 50p PER TRANSACTION - REGISTERED POST OPTIONAL AT ADDITIONAL EXPENSE
COACH TRAVEL INFOLINE 0345 581869 (LOCAL RATE)
EXCLUSIVE 24 HOUR NATIONAL CONCERT & COACH TICKET LINE
OASIS HOTLINE (TICKETMASTER) 0171 344 4040
EXCLUSIVE 24 HOUR LINE - BOOKING FEE £1.50 PER TICKET - ALL MAJOR CREDIT CARDS ACCEPTED
MAILOUT CHARGE £1.00 PER TRANSACTION - REGISTERED POST OPTIONAL AT ADDITIONAL EXPENSE
TICKETS AVAILABLE TO PERSONAL CALLERS IN THE FOLLOWING OUTLETS:-
LONDON: Astoria Theatre • MANCHESTER: Labatts Apollo • LEEDS: Town & Country • CAMBRIDGE: Corn Exchange
WOLVERHAMPTON: Civic Hall • BIRMINGHAM: NIA • BRIGHTON: Centre • CARDIFF: International Arena
SHEFFIELD: Arena • PORTSMOUTH: Guildhall • NORWICH: UEA • DERBY: Way Ahead Shop • OXFORD: Apollo • EXETER: University
LEICESTER: De Montfort Hall • BRISTOL: Colston Hall
BOOKING FEE TO PERSONAL CALLERS MAXIMUM £1.00 PER TICKET CASH/CHEQUES ONLY
NO CREDIT CARD BOOKINGS - MAXIMUM 4 TICKETS PER APPLICANT
ALL TICKETS ON SALE & LINES OPEN SATURDAY 11TH MAY 9.00AM
BBC RADIO ONE
97-99 FM
fine art america

1996

'ALL MY PEOPLE RIGHT HERE, RIGHT NOW. THEY KNOW WHAT I MEAN'

Pete Mitchell: 'There was something they managed to capture at that time that reflected what was going on in Britain. That attitude, that kind of post-rave/ techno. When that gap arrived, Oasis were there to fill it. I remember at that point everyone was buying little home studios to make dance records. What Oasis did ... my son and all his mates wanted to pick up a guitar and play a real instrument. The kids wanted to play guitars and I solely put that down to Noel and Liam.'

Although recorded well before Christmas, on New Year's Eve a special edition of Channel 4's *The White Room* was broadcast, and Oasis had the honour of 'performing' as the clock struck midnight. Crossing over from 1995 into 1996 with Oasis blaring from the screens is as fitting an analogy as you can get for their ubiquity in this period, all thanks to the formidable triumvirate of *(What's the Story) Morning Glory?* 'Wonderwall' and the brothers Gallagher, now quote, headline and money-making machines. In early January, Noel also appeared on a short-lived show called *Hotel Babylon*, where he divulged that 'Live Forever' was in fact about his Mum, Peggie.

No rest for the wicked, Oasis were touring in the second week of January, playing two dates in Germany and one in the Netherlands. Following this, there were more arena shows, in Newcastle and Edinburgh. Perhaps due to their status as Now A Big Deal, or having learnt the lessons of the previous tour, the dates were fewer and more spread out. Two dates here, three dates there in Europe. Because of the travel required there would be more gigs in the US but even then, they were broken up to one every other day as opposed to on consecutive days previously. It was also being reported that Tony McCarroll was suing Oasis for half a million pounds in royalties, because of his presence on 'Some Might Say,' while *(What's the Story) Morning Glory?* went back to No.1 in the album charts and remained in the top-three for the next seven months.

The astonishing and unprecedented success of 'Wonderwall' was finally starting to wane, and the fourth and final single from the album could finally be unleashed in mid-February. It was backed with 'Step Out' (which was earmarked for the parent album, but had to be registered be a co-write between N. Gallagher and Wonder/Cosby/Moy; submitting royalties to the Stevie Wonder camp cost significantly less as a B-side than on an album), new track 'Underneath The Sky' and the cover of 'Cum On Feel The Noize.' The party atmosphere was translating to the music; the Slade cover ended with a huge backing chorus, among those voices a certain Robbie Williams, who had now left Take That and somehow managed to blag his way into the recording studio. Noel presented a radio show in the same week, making a tongue-in-cheek claim that Oasis had been responsible for Take That's demise, and he was going to write Williams' debut solo single.

'Don't Look Back in Anger' had already received some exposure in the public eye, aside from its place on the album. A popular BBC show at the time, *Our Friends In The North,* featured the song play over the last scene in the final episode, a pre-James Bond Daniel Craig walking over a bridge to his future, the show itself a zeitgeist moment. The producers claimed they weren't aware the song was to be released as a single. Despite similarities to other songs (Lennon's 'Imagine' the best example), the song struck a resonant chord which continues to this day. The lyrics to the bridge included a line taken from Peggy Gallagher, '*Stand up beside the fireplace, take that look from off your face,*' illustrating Noel's flexibility when it came to his influences.

The video was recorded in L.A. at a mansion with similarities to the infamous *Playboy* Mansion. Included were countless young women, ostensibly *Playboy* Bunnies, and Patrick Macnee of cult TV show *The Avengers.* It looked luxuriant and was a far cry from the black and white performance video for 'Whatever' 14 months earlier. Perhaps down to the song's exposure, the video is now one of the most recognisable images of Oasis, with Liam looking somewhat ill at ease with being surplus to requirements. One of the 'bunnies' would later become Alan White's long-term partner.

'Don't Look Back in Anger' was another smash hit and went straight in at No.1 later reaching No.10 in the US. Another astonishing return, especially for a fourth single from an album that had been out for four months. As Noel put it, 'By that point we were selling more singles than some people were selling albums.' And with two incredibly successful singles behind them, the sales for *(What's the Story) Morning Glory?* kept on coming; the album had spent the early part of the year still in the top-three of the charts. As a testament to their success, Oasis were given the honour of performing two songs on *Top of the Pops* the following week, the first band to do so since The Jam in 1982. Noel played a guitar adorned with the Union flag, and they also performed 'Cum on Feel the Noize.' For someone to quickly distance themselves from Britpop, they had no qualms using the branding itself, but it's now easy to forget how positive the arts and certain demographics of the British public were feeling at the time. The single eventually surpassed one million sales in the UK.

There was also the small matter of the Brit Awards in February. Essentially, the Brit Awards simply honour success and sales, so Oasis were in line for a good night, and a good night was most certainly had. Fuelled by cocaine, champagne and success Oasis dominated the ceremony, picking up three gongs and making the headlines. They were a little ungracious but excellent comedy value. The first award (Best Video for 'Wonderwall') was presented by INXS frontman Michael Hutchence, who had made some disparaging remarks about Oasis in the press. A bearded Liam enquired as to where 'the slap' he'd been promised from Hutchence was, who responded with a kiss. Noel was less forgiving; 'Has-beens shouldn't present awards to gonna-bes'. Clearly furious, Hutchence marched off the stage.

Their second award, Best Album, was presented by Lenny Kravitz. On taking to the mic, Liam started thanking 'all the people', before he and Noel went into an impromptu singalong of Blur's 'Parklife', changing 'park' to 'shite'. Then the band won Best Group (presented by Pete Townshend) and Noel took the opportunity to make a charged statement, 'There's seven people in this room that are making a difference to young people in this country. That's me, our kid, Bonehead, Guigs, Alan White, Alan McGee and Tony Blair. If you've got anything about you, you'll go up and shake Tony Blair's hand, he's the man. Power to the people!'

All the while Liam was bending over to the crowd and sticking the latest award up his backside. After the ceremony, Noel stated that the only award that mattered was Best Video, having been voted for by fans, with the others decided by 'corporate pigs' and therefore meaning nothing.

Tony Blair, who became leader of the Labour Party the year before, was a breath of fresh air for the party and a vital face in British politics. Years of Conservative rule and a new, younger leader made the party a more appealing prospect to voters, part of a group rebranding the party as New Labour. Ostensibly, this was a modern, forward-thinking Labour and a real alternative to the dusty, stagnant Conservatives, odds-on to win the next General Election. Part of the re-branding exercise, in a bid to engage younger voters, Blair was marketed as the 'rock'n'roll politician.' This essentially boiled down to making capital of a man of the people him who was in a band in his youth and could be seen playing football at Newcastle United's training ground, and other such PR opportunities. The largest cultural movement in Britain of the time was Britpop, by now an all-encompassing term for British music, and overtures were made to Blur's Damon Albarn and Radiohead's Thom Yorke about backing the party. Both were reticent, but Noel Gallagher and Alan McGee were staunch Labour voters, both more likely to be amenable to being associated with them.

Brian Cannon: 'In the mid-90s, knocking about with Oasis was a cross between a Laurel and Hardy film and *A Hard Day's Night*. It was bonkers. Every Friday night when they weren't away, Liam would turn up at my flat in Camden Town, because he knew whatever happened wouldn't reach the press. We were all a tight group and there was nobody selling stories. On the Saturday morning we'd get up, then go to a little Greek cafe on Parkway called George & Nicki's for lunch, literally 100 yards from the flat. In that 100 yards in walking from my flat to the cafe I saw a car run into the back of a bus. The guy driving the car was, 'Fucking hell, it's Liam Gallagher.' Another guy on a push bike went all wobbly and fell over, nearly killed himself and woman, who must have been in her late 40s/early 50s, dropped all her shopping and started screaming. This was just every day. Wherever Liam Gallagher went, absolute chaos would break out. It was mental. He loved it, he absolutely loved it.'

A week later it was the *NME* Awards, and again Oasis cleaned up. Best Album, Best Band, Best Live Act and Best Single all went to the band. Disappointingly, despite the awards having a less polished reputation than the Brits, there was very little in the way of controversy. At the end of the trophy-laden month of February, it was decided that Oasis would play two homecoming gigs at Maine Road, home to the Gallagher brothers and Guigsy's beloved Manchester City, with 40,000 tickets released for one night and selling out within three hours. A second date was then announced and sold out within 70 minutes.

A short tour of the US spanned late February and early March before another set of arena gigs, two each in Cardiff and Dublin. After a successful show at Dublin's Point Arena there was the usual drink-up after, with members of the Gallagher family, their friends and members of U2 in attendance. As has been illustrated, Oasis were meat and drink for the tabloids and the *Daily Mirror* had spotted an opportunity for the Dublin gigs. Interviews with Noel, Liam, and to a lesser extent Peggy Gallagher had revealed some details about the boys' father, Tommy. Then as now, the murky rules of tabloid newspapers suggested family controversy sold. The *Daily Mirror* managed to track down Tommy and took him to the pub where Oasis were drinking in Dublin. Word made its way to Liam and Noel that their father was present. Ever angry and keen to seize an opportunity to exorcise demons, Liam was enraged and keen to meet him.

Five years older and more at peace with the relationship, Noel stepped in to calm his brother down and advise him of the consequences. Somehow however, a telephone call was arranged between Liam and Tommy, the latter offering an olive branch, Liam giving him short shrift and threatening to break his legs. The *Daily Mirror* set up a phone-line so readers prepared to pay not insignificant charges, could listen to the conversation. It wouldn't be the most distasteful story that involved Oasis, but it was certainly the most underhanded. Liam and Noel were certainly making the most of their fame and celebrity status but, as many others had found, it came at a price. For their part, the statement from Oasis was that the incident had been 'exaggerated'.

Paolo Hewitt: 'He's got a good heart on him, Liam. And one of the things I was trying to do in both *Getting High* and *Forever the People* (his books about the band) is say this guy is not a dickhead. The perception of him is as a drunken dickhead. He's really funny. We were at Noel's and it was getting near Halloween, with Bonfire Night around the corner. We were at Noel's, me and Liam talking, and on the TV screen was this documentary about the Ku Klux Klan, and there were all these images with guys in hoods and burning crosses, and Liam says, 'They're all taking Halloween a bit seriously, aren't they?"

Somewhere amidst all this madness, long-time associate Mark Coyle decided to step away from his responsibilities as main sound engineer for live shows. This was something of a blow to the band, another person there since the early days departing, following in the footsteps of Tony McCarroll (by now deep into legal action against the band) and Alan McGee, who missed their rise during a nervous breakdown. Coyle felt that the band had become a brand and too corporate. And while that was part of Noel's plan, it had consequences.

Oasis jetted between North America and Europe playing shows, abandoning one gig in Vancouver after fans threw coins and shoes, and upon his return to the UK, Noel was interviewed on popular Channel 4 magazine show *T.F.I. Friday*, where he disclosed to host Chris Evans that because of his new-found wealth inspiration was becoming hard to find, although he had written two new songs ('My Big Mouth' and 'I Hope, I Think, I Know').

Then came the big homecoming gigs at the end of April. Support came from Ocean Colour Scene and Manic Street Preachers, the latter regrouped after the disappearance of guitarist Richey Edwards and enjoying commercial success with their album *Everything Must Go*. Oasis took Manchester over for the whole weekend, the local boys coming home in the midst of conquering the world and fast becoming a cultural phenomenon. But they also had something to prove, the two nights at Maine Road their first official stadium gigs, another milestone to add to an ever-growing collection. There were rumours flying around over the weekend that Liam had been kidnapped by some gangs, and that the venue was to be used as a battleground, Bonehead outlining the very real concerns: 'There were real threats. I can definitely remember we had extra security in. You always have security knocking about, but we had security with Dobermann and Rottweiler dogs. We were like, 'What the fuck?' and someone said, 'Yeah, there was a serious threat that they were gonna kidnap Liam, so - extra security.'

Liam was now dating singer Patsy Kensit, the actress and singer in the public eye for more than a decade, so considered fair game as far as the tabloids were concerned, with the brothers Gallagher now among the most recognisable faces in Britain. The tickets themselves featured images of Liam, Noel and Guigsy sat in the stand at Maine Road, Bonehead and Whitey not being Manchester City fans and therefore not involved. Loyalty to be admired. As Maine Road remained a functioning Premier League football stadium, with a home match against Liverpool the following weekend, a giant shipyard crane was used to safely carry the equipment over the pitch, delivered there by 51 trucks.

Saturday April 27
'The Swamp Song'
'Acquiesce'
'Supersonic'
'Hello'
'Some Might Say'
'Roll with It'
'Morning Glory'
'Round Are Way'
'Cigarettes & Alcohol'
'Whatever'
'Cast No Shadow'
'Wonderwall'
'The Masterplan'
'Don't Look Back in Anger'

Sunday April 28
'The Swamp Song'
'Acquiesce'
'Supersonic'
'Hello'
'Some Might Say'
'Roll with It'
'Morning Glory'
'Round Are Way'
'Cigarettes & Alcohol'
'Whatever'
'Cast No Shadow'
'Wonderwall'
'The Masterplan'
'Don't Look Back in Anger'

'Live Forever'
'D'Yer Wanna Be A Spaceman?'
'I Am the Walrus'
'Cum on Feel the Noize'

'Live Forever'
'I Am the Walrus'
'Cum on Feel the Noize'

The two sets were slightly different; 'D'Yer Wanna Be A Spaceman?' was included on the first night but had to be swiftly abandoned as Liam didn't know the words and was dropped for the second set. Similarly, on the following night,

OASIS MAINE ATTRACTION

OASIS sold out all 40,000 tickets for Manchester Maine Road in less than three hours on Friday morning (February 9). This makes it officially one of the fastest-selling stadium concerts ever.

The show, at the home of the band's revered Manchester City FC, takes place on Sunday, April 28, with doors open at 3.30pm. Special guests have yet to be announced.

Tickets, at £17.50, went on sale at 9am on Friday morning via a credit card hotline and at various ticket outlets in Manchester: Labatts Apollo, Ticket Master, Piccadilly Box Office at the Virgin Megastore and Maine Road itself.

People queued throughout Thursday night in freezing weather conditions outside the Megastore and the Apollo to secure their tickets, which were limited to four per applicant. Police were called to control the crowds outside the Apollo. At Maine Road, the queues began at 5am, and over 1,000 people were turned away when the tickets had sold out. British Telecom reported "significant problems" with an estimated million calls made in the first hour of ticket sales.

There is still no information on the rumoured July 13 concert at Wembley Stadium, or on any other live dates. A spokeswoman said: "Nothing at all has been confirmed on any of them. There will be less than a handful in the UK this year. There won't be any more around the time of the Maine Road one, because the band have got other commitments. If there are any other gigs, they won't be for a long while yet."

The latest gossip says that Oasis are now considering a show at Knebworth as an alternative to Wembley, and that they are waiting to find out if they can book the site in the first two weeks of August.

Noel Gallagher, meanwhile, has announced plans to become a radio presenter on GLR (94.9FM).

Noel *(left)* hosts his own two-hour show – titled "Gallagher's London Radio" (GLR) – on February 22 from 10pm, and promises special guests, sessions and "scandalous rumours about the people whose records he plays".

Two of the guests are Paul Weller and Digsy from Smaller (and of "Digsy's Diner" fame). Both will chat with Noel and play acoustic numbers.

Robbie Williams, ex-Take That, has pre-recorded an interview with Gallagher. And according to BBC GLR, one jokey exchange claims that Robbie's first solo single will be a Noel composition.

"Is it any good?" asks Noel.

"Yeah, it's top, you've come out with another banging tune," says Robbie.

Robbie also good-humouredly blames Oasis for getting him sacked from Take That by being unsuitable company, to which Noel retorts: "We planned it . . . we split them up."

Noel's playlist reportedly includes The Beatles, Ocean Colour Scene, Dr Robert, The Verve, Cast, Heavy Stereo and Northern Uproar.

The show's producer, Jim Lahat, told The Maker: "We're giving Noel a free hand, within the limits. I think he'll be a natural."

Noel has asked about the possibility of the show being also broadcast on GMR in Manchester, but this has yet to be sorted out.

Liam came in too early during 'Whatever' and it too was interrupted mid-song. The younger Gallagher challenged Noel to perform lead vocals, which he did without hesitation as Liam looked on.

Minor hiccups aside, both nights were universally accepted as glorious. Brian Cannon provided the backdrop for the sets, and during 'Live Forever' included stills images of heroes of rock heroes of the past, including Jimi Hendrix, The Rolling Stones' Brian Jones and John Lennon. None of the band knew this was to happen, with Liam visibly chuffed on seeing the late Beatle.

Noel primarily played the guitar emblazoned with the Union flag that earlier featured on *Top of the Pops*, becoming one of the iconic images of the 1990s. On the second night, which was recorded for posterity along with the Earl's Court gigs for a live video called *There And Then*, Liam wore a blue Umbro jumper, and having become a fashion icon by this point, even something as non-descript as a sports jumper had become a must-have item of clothing. The live video's cover featured a now iconic photograph: the adoring audience facing the stage, with Noel holding his arms aloft to them, as shot by Jill Furmanovsky.

Jill Furmanovsky: 'I think it was the second one. I think I'd seen the first show and thought, 'I'll go up there for the second one.' If you've got two shows you can work out what you didn't get on the first night. The reason that worked so well was because there was a quite a tall platform which was for the string and brass section that we had access to from behind. I crept up there before they came on stage. I remember shaking! My main concern is that I'm going to fuck it up. Strangely enough, that was also Noel's worry. He said afterwards he thought he was going to trip over something when he came out because there was wires everywhere. Of course, when they did walk out, I was in the right position. I didn't fuck it up, sometimes I don't.'

Brian Cannon: 'Second night at Maine Road. Of all the big gigs it was my favourite. Maine Road was absolutely out of this world.'

The gigs were as triumphant a homecoming as anyone could have expected. The atmosphere was electric, the band embracing the moment and playing out of their lives. As Bonehead said, 'We probably would have played all night if we could ... we wanted to make it the best. We really did...Maine Road meant something.'

There was only one problem; not enough people could go. Each night the stadium held 40,000. By April, *(What's the Story) Morning Glory?* had sold two million copies in the UK alone. Demand for Oasis tickets was at fever pitch. So, there was an obvious requirement to find the biggest possible venue in the UK to meet the demand. A series of outdoor summer shows in stadia and fields would have been easy to sell, but the temptation to make a statement was too appealing to the ego to refuse. Eventually Ignition and Creation settled on Knebworth Park in Hertfordshire, an hour's ride north of London, which had hosted huge bands in the past, including Led Zeppelin, the Rolling Stones and Queen, and was fit for purpose. The venue could hold up to 125,000 people, and in early May a show for Oasis was announced for August, following a large outdoor gig at Balloch Castle Country Park, on the shores of Loch Lomond, 20 miles north west of Glasgow.

Mat Whitecross: 'There was something so exciting about that moment in time, not just for the band. It felt like it was full of possibilities. We seem to be living in a mirror image of that now, where everything is fucked and falling apart.'

Tickets were released on May 11 and all 125,000 tickets sold out in four hours. A second gig was announced for the day after. The phone lines were chaos and all tickets sold out instantly. The other shows at Loch Lomond the weekend before also sold in record time. Later that week it was announced that these four gigs were the fastest-selling concerts in the UK ever. At one point during the day of release, 500,000 people called the ticket line in five minutes, with tickets selling at a rate of 10 per second, an astonishing five per cent of the population trying for tickets. Even then, demand to see Oasis could not be met.

With no more singles released (surprisingly, given *(What's the Story) Morning Glory?*'s impact) and the band taking a break from touring until those mega-gigs, one presumed Oasis would disappear from the public eye, but it was not to be. Not only was there an insatiable desire from the public on all matters Oasis, but the tabloids hadn't quite finished extracting their pounds of flesh. The stories mainly concerned Liam and Patsy Kensit, but not exclusively, such as accounts of their dates, or what food was being delivered to Kensit's flat. Literally anything and everything involving the band was made news. Even Marcus Russell was considered of interest, and he divulged some nuggets on the strategy behind breaking Oasis in America, saying, 'We've been working in the US since July 1994, and a lot of the strategy was not to release a single. We didn't release a single until year ('Wonderwall'), so we just kept making the radio play the record or people had to go and see the shows.'

A novel approach, and even today the jury is still out as to whether or not it was successful. Meanwhile, Noel divulged two track names for the third album; 'New Suede Shoes' and 'My Big Mouth.' He also took the opportunity to take a holiday, on the invitation of Mick Jagger, to Mustique in the Caribbean, accompanied by Johnny Depp, Kate Moss and Owen Morris, along with girlfriend Meg Mathews. After apparently suffering from writer's block for some time, the songs started flowing for Noel while he was away. Having written 15 songs, Noel and Morris recorded demos with a drum machine and a keyboard. The Mustique Demos would become legendary, unheard for years.

Noel also kept himself busy by remixing the 'Devil's Haircut' single by American alt-rocker Beck, and recording 'Setting Sun,' a collaboration with electronic duo The Chemical Brothers. Noel had long stated his intention to familiarise himself with more contemporary and experimental music to overhaul the Oasis sound, and it appeared they weren't just soundbites but actual intentions.

Alan McGee: 'The one thing that me, Liam and Noel have all got in common is that we thought it was never going to end. It only really lasted for three or four years, the amazing part. The rest of it was just 'rock band doing good.' The really amazing part - we never thought it was going to end. We thought it was The Beatles. In my head I thought it was the Stones *and* the Beatles. Take your pick. It was never going to end.'

Even though, to Joe Public, there was no new music to digest (although going back through the B-sides was becoming a more common pastime among teenagers), *(What's the Story) Morning Glory?* was continuing to sell incredibly well, hitting three million UK sales in early August, and could be heard in pubs, clubs and from bedroom windows across the land. There was general euphoria in Britain at the time; as well as the highly likely possibility of a new Government and the initial positivity that brings, there was also the Euro 96 international football tournament being held in England over the summer. As hosts, England were present, but Scotland also competed, so the goodwill wasn't just south of the border. While Scotland fell at the first hurdle, the England team, after a false start, did well, reaching the semi-finals. Football and music began to overlap, and the mainstream accessibility of Oasis played a significant part in that marriage.

Johnny Sharp: 'Those first two albums are absolutely incredible songwriting. They really made a glorious glam racket.

'There was a point in the summer of '96 where you would hear *Morning Glory* blasting out of every shop window. It was the absolute sound of Young Britain. You could not get away from it. All the songs were earworms, you just couldn't get them out of your head. They were massively dominant at that point.'

Sadly, the build-up to the Loch Lomond gigs was overshadowed by a tragic accident. Lorry driver James Hunter died when he was trapped between a lorry and a forklift truck. Hunter's family would later sue several individuals and companies associated with the concert for negligence. But the show pressed on, despite dreadful weather on the day. 'Columbia' was re-introduced to the set, replacing 'The Swamp Song' as the opening number. Two new songs were also debuted; 'My Big Mouth', written ostensibly about Noel's run-ins with the press, and another rocky number, 'It's Getting Better (Man!!)'.

Colin Paterson: 'I was living in Scotland at the time, so instead of Knebworth I did Loch Lomond. My abiding memory of that gig was the death, which was big, big news in Scotland. On a happier note I remember when I walked into that gig, the first thing I saw at Loch Lomond was a man with a bucket of paint and a brush, and the sign said, 'Noel and Liam monobrows, £1.' Very enterprising.'

Jill Furmanovsky: 'Liam didn't always sing at the soundchecks, but he did show up. He just didn't take part in them, just as a fan. He sat and listened. I found that quite endearing. Before Manchester and Knebworth I don't think he did any singing at the soundchecks, but he was there. Sitting at the front like he was the sole member of the audience. Except a bevy of young girls that showed up and he allowed them to sit with him.'

People that were there would argue otherwise, and the good people of Scotland certainly would, but in the eyes of the press the Loch Lomond gigs were but a precursor to Knebworth, with a date in Sweden sandwiched between the two weekends. To call the gigs historic was something of an understatement; it's not an exaggeration to say the world was watching. The gigs were the zenith of the '90s British music explosion, and to call it 'our generation's Woodstock' wasn't too big a stretch. The weekend was like a festival, albeit one with one headliner, the support bills being, in ascending order:

Saturday, August 10
The Bootleg Beatles
The Chemical Brothers
Ocean Colour Scene
Manic Street Preachers
The Prodigy

Sunday, August 11
Kula Shaker
Dreadzone
Cast
The Charlatans
Manic Street Preachers

Most of the bands were happy to be involved. The Charlatans, who three weeks earlier suffered a tragedy in the death of their keyboard player Rob Collins, found the gig to be cathartic. Liam later dedicated 'Live Forever' to him. And James Dean Bradfield of Manic Street Preachers was reflective, calling it, 'A humbling experience, we felt like a really small band compared to the biggest band in the world. It makes you realise where you fit into the big scheme of pop things.'

There was significantly more for the crowd members to complain about rather than their egos; the queues for the bars would take up to two hours. Security was everywhere, restricting enjoyment. The prices for drinks and food were sky high, and people were banned from bringing in any food or drink. Backstage was no better; a multitude of celebrities vying for attention and said to be frustrated at where they could and couldn't go. Even Alan McGee wasn't allowed in certain areas backstage and was curious as to why, when he had paid £250,000 for the tent, he wasn't allowed a Diet Coke. He was from a certain point of view paying for everything. The Monster had well and truly outgrown Frankenstein.

Alan McGee: 'We'd had bands that sell a million records, but we'd never had a band that sells 23 million. They're a really different beast. We'd had a few big bands actually. Primals (Primal Scream) had been really big for us. Valentines (My Bloody Valentine) were big for us. (Teenage) Fanclub was big for us. We'd had different people that were big for us, House of Love, (The Jesus &) Mary Chain ... that was just a few. The Oasis thing threw us into being a big label and with a big band.'

Noel insisted that Phil Smith, still part of the entourage, and Mark Coyle journeyed with them by helicopter to Knebworth Park. The build-up couldn't avoid emphasising the significance of the gigs, and as they had been part of the story since day one, Noel felt it was only right they be there for the crowning glory. Apparently, unaware that the band were playing two nights, Liam got very drunk after the first night on Saturday and claims not to remember anything of the weekend after that point.

The only concession to anything in the way of theatrics was kicking some oversized footballs in the crowd when entering the stage, and a huge firework display at the end. As before, strings and trumpets were added, as was harmonica to a number of songs, most notably 'Whatever' and 'The Masterplan.'

Mark Feltham: 'I was totally out of my depth on that gig and yet everyone speaks about it. I can assure you that nothing was rehearsed. I've not spoken to Noel since that day, that very last show that we did together. We were hired and fired as quickly as a manager in the football. We were there and then we were gone. The brass all went off to do something with Robbie Williams, the next time I saw them I'd been called in to do a bit of stuff with him, because Robbie Williams would often hang out backstage at the Oasis shows. I remember seeing him at one of the shows in London.'

The setlist was the same both nights, to ensure everyone was able to enjoy the same experience, although John Squire, who had recently left the hugely-influential (not least on Noel Gallagher) Stone Roses, played on 'Champagne Supernova' on the second night:

'Columbia'
'Acquiesce'
'Supersonic'
'Hello'
'Some Might Say'
'Roll with It'
'Slide Away'
'Morning Glory'
'Round Are Way'
'Cigarettes & Alcohol'
'Whatever'
'Cast No Shadow'
'Wonderwall'
'The Masterplan'
'Don't Look Back in Anger'
'My Big Mouth'
'It's Getting Better (Man!!)'
'Live Forever'
'Champagne Supernova'
'I Am the Walrus'

Chris Griffiths: 'I did an interview with someone recently and they said, 'What was your worst Oasis moment?', and for me it was when they opened up Knebworth with 'Columbia'. I just knew I wasn't going to get any sort of credit for it, I couldn't even get on the guestlist for it. We just got told when they got signed ... we were the white elephant in the room, that never got spoke about. Any guestlists and stuff like that we just got fucked off in the end. And that was one of the most heart-breaking things, just watching ... my brother was actually there, he phoned me up and he went, 'Chris, there's fucking half a million people here or something, and he opens up with your tune.' I was like, 'Whoa!' and then I saw it on videos, and thought, 'That's just amazing, they're just fucking huge now.'

Tony McCarroll: 'The band were at their peak then, they really were.'

Brian Cannon: 'Knebworth was almost too big as a gig, as a spectacle it was something else.

'I asked JVC if we could borrow one mini hand-held camera so Liam could film the crowd from the stage at the Knebworth gigs. They turned us down. Every magazine in the world had a picture of Liam Gallagher on that stage. And he'd have had a JVC camera in his hand. I subsequently got a letter from JVC, who could not believe we had been turned down, and he gave the person who knocked us back a serious drubbing for it.'

Simon Mason: 'Knebworth was really for me the end. It was the end for me on all sorts of levels.

'I remember leaving Knebworth, but I didn't see them. I got there, and I realised I'd left my supply of heroin in London. I walked around the backstage area of Knebworth, and it was a who's who of Z-list celebrities, which make you think, 'What are you doing here?'. On the way out I remember walking past the main stage and seeing ... you had to have 25 different coloured laminates and wristbands to access even the roadies by that point. I just had this feeling that I didn't want that really.

'As I was walking out, there was a teenage lad walking in. I took all my laminates off and stuck them around his neck and said, 'Go on, get yourself backstage. They're all cunts anyway.' I walked out mid-afternoon, and the majority of people were on their way in. It felt like I was going against this sea of humanity that were all there to go and have one of the best nights of their life.

'I've spoken to a lot of people over the years in various bands who were at Knebworth and they've said they're not really sure what it was about. Knebworth metaphorically left a brown stain on the Britpop bath. What happened next to a lot of people is that ... thankfully the majority of people decided to slow down. But there was an inordinate amount of people, musicians and fans that for whatever reason couldn't do that.'

In truth, it wasn't the best Oasis performance, possibly down to being slightly rusty. Maine Road is now regarded as the band playing at their peak, but that was three months earlier, and after more than three years on the road then three months off, to expect to recapture such fluidity was a tall order. But Knebworth wasn't about the quality of performance, or the stellar line-up. It was in fact the zenith of Oasis, Creation Records and Britpop. Britain was continuing to ride the crest of the wave, with a new Government seemingly an inevitability, along with the music and football, the two post-war religions.

Paolo Hewitt: 'The journey upwards (to Knebworth) is the most exciting bit. Once you get to the top, once you've achieved, I said, 'The trouble with Oasis was they had all these dreams about being huge rock'n'roll stars and they wrote records called 'Rock 'n' Roll Star' about those desires and they wanted to live in big houses and sleep with amazing-looking women and take the best drugs and drink the finest champagne. They wanted this classic rock star thing and they got it. And once they got it, they didn't know what to do, because they had achieved their dreams.'

With the benefit of hindsight, several key players now wish Knebworth had been the final act. Alan McGee queried at the time, 'Where do we go from here?' Bonehead says he wishes they had signed off there and then, Noel also wishing they had, 'Disappeared in a puff of smoke.' Which would have made a great story and made Oasis the stuff of legend. But they didn't - not when there was money to be made. Three days later the band played two more huge open-air gigs at Pairc Ui Chaoimh in Cork, Ireland, and an already sold-out American tour had been scheduled from the end of August.

Alan McGee: 'When it (*Morning Glory*) sold that first 20 million it was like *An Audience with Noel Gallagher*. He was completely master of his own ship at that point. As he should be. If I'd sold 20 million records and it was me that had done it, with my songs, I don't know if I'd listen to anybody.'

Mary McGuigan: 'I learnt how much the media was savagely trying to provoke him (Liam) into being a horrible person. He's not a horrible person. He's a beautiful person and they kept poking him. It's like poking a puppy, and eventually the puppy will bite. There would be times when he would be walking down a normal street, and someone would jump out a bush and punch him in the face. And there would be a photographer waiting to see his reaction. That used to break my heart. There were other things the press did to make him out as some sort of rabid thug.'

Ricky Hatton: 'I used to walk around with my sunhat on, like everybody else!'

Simon Mason: 'What happened is, they no longer had a transit van. The vans get bigger, the entourage gets bigger. There were more people trying to fit themselves in somewhere into that.'

Before the American tour, a performance at London's Royal Festival for *MTV Unplugged* was in the diary. *MTV Unplugged* is, as the name suggests, was a generally acoustic show which many legendary acts had participated in and often released albums on the back of, including Nirvana. This was an accolade and part of another attempt to crack the American market. It was required to be a more subtle showcase for the band's catalogue, and rehearsals had been going for a few weeks, with Liam apparently only attending once. In the dress rehearsal before the main show, Liam turned up drunk and was incoherent. As the band were limbering up to take to the stage, giving no regard for history or status, Liam declared he had a sore throat and walked off, leaving Noel to take the reins for the entire performance. It has to be said that he did a sterling job, not least because the first two numbers were 'Hello' and 'Some Might Say', which he had never performed live and had only realised he was going to have to some minutes earlier.

But Liam did make an appearance that night. In attendance was Mark Coyle and other close members of the band's entourage, in a box above the stage, and Liam managed to join them. Brilliantly, mid-way through the performance, drinking beer while he did so, Liam started to heckle his own band, specifically his brother. Undeterred, the band were able to complete the set, with positive reviews and Noel earning kudos from the music and wider press. A line had long been drawn in the press between the brothers and this continued to cement it; Noel was the more considered, talented and media-friendly of the two. Liam was the more unpredictable, aggressive and belligerent, but being the face of the band and dating a famous actress meant he was far more attractive a story. For his part, Noel ticked off another ambition by singing with a personal hero, Burt Bacharach at the Royal Festival Hall, Noel taking up the mike, for probably the only time without the protection of a guitar, to sing 'This Guy's in Love with You.'

Mark Feltham: 'When I did the *Unplugged* thing at Royal Festival Hall, I didn't get any guidance from Noel on that. I know he was pretty fed up because they'd had a row. I went in, and remember Noel just giving me a nod, and I just started to play. But none of it was rehearsed. I can't remember anything ... was there any sheet music? No, there wasn't! We did 'The Masterplan.' Noel just kind of went, 'Mark, do what you want on it,' He was so fed up with what had gone down. I just opened it up and closed it. That was totally, totally unrehearsed. Much like the whole of that show was, I think! I think it (Liam walking off) threw Noel, but he handled it brilliantly.'

Chris Griffiths: 'The thing was, it was around the second or third album that they released, and suddenly, boom. One, they were on *Spitting Image* and stuff like that at the time. It was like Beatlemania to me, because everywhere you looked there was people walking like Liam, with haircuts and everything. There was even Scousers talking like them, do you know what I mean?'

Mat Whitecross: 'It's inevitable that if you grew up in that time, that was just part of your life. The way you were, the way you dressed, the people you hung out with. You'd go to those kinds of gigs.'

Whilst the phenomenon that was *(What's the Story) Morning Glory?* had, alongside the Knebworth gigs, put Oasis on a nearly unsurpassable level in the UK, there was continuing success in the States. 'Wonderwall' was at No.5 in the Billboard charts, and another tour had long been in the diary. In late August, as the band were boarding the plane to North America, Liam declared that he had other priorities, namely finding a house with Patsy Kensit. The couple had been living in hotels for months, and the younger Gallagher decided at that moment to put Oasis' reputation at risk.

One can only imagine how incandescent the rest of the band, specifically and obviously Noel, were at this revelation. But given Noel's confidence in taking centre-stage, no doubt enhanced by the Royal Festival Hall incident, it's unlikely there was any danger of the tour being pulled. They would plough on with Noel on vocals, which they did on the first gig in Rosemont, Noel saying, 'We won't pull the gig, because that would be giving in. That would be letting him think he's bigger than the band, which he's not.'

Unsurprisingly, the incident made headlines in the UK, the world's press camped outside Liam's door in London (or more likely partner Patsy's), with BBC

Last Friday, OASIS appeared at London's Royal Festival Hall for a soon-to-be-legendary 'MTV Unplugged'. Liam, however, wasn't there...

WHERE'S Liam?

Liam's not here. For this, the climax of their historic summer shows, Oasis are playing at half-strength, minus their Iggy Jagger, their Shaun Rotten, their dramatic, anarchic centre. It took three months of organising by the American branch of MTV to get "Oasis Unplugged" secret gig to happen at London's prestigious Royal Festival Hall, and precisely three seconds for Oasis' songwriter to explain that it won't be quite what MTV, and the 400 kids who entered competitions to be here (the ratio of fans to liggers is unprecedentedly high for an "Unplugged", according to MM's Paul Mathur), had been led to expect.

"He's got a sore throat, so you're going to have to make do with the four ugly ones," says Noel Gallagher, almost dismissively, as cries of "Where's Liam?" pour from the audience.

The cheers for the Liam-less Oasis are considerable, but the sense of anti-climax is palpable. There are balloons wrapped in cellophane behind the stage, yet already the celebration is tinged with disappointment.

At 8.30pm, Noel takes his seat behind the stagefront mic, with Bonehead sitting to his right, Guigsy on the lip of the stage, and Alan White behind. Meanwhile, two pianists, three saxophonists, three trumpeters and three violinists assume their positions. And then we current affairs show *Newsnight* among those running a piece on it. When he did emerge, confronted by the press, Liam barged them aside and sneered in response to questions, 'You know what's going on, it's in the fucking papers.'

Liam was unrepentant; he had to find somewhere to live, and he came first, before the band and the fans. As it transpired, Liam only missed the first gig in Rosemont, Illinois, catching up with the rest of the band by the time of the second gig in Auburn Hills, Michigan. Upon landing in America, Liam was happy to report to the press, 'I'm upset the way the tour gets wrote and you got to go here, you got to go there. I need to find a house, simple as that. I come first, before any fucker. And that's my attitude, alright?'

It was the first of three nails in the coffin of this tour. Following the Auburn Hills show, gigs in Barrie, across the Canadian border in Ontario, and Philadelphia went by without incident, at least in the public sphere. Being one of the world's biggest acts, Oasis had a slot at the *MTV Video Music Awards* show at New York's Radio City Music Hall, with a worldwide audience of 300 million viewers. The selected song was 'Champagne Supernova', which had been released as a US single in May. During the performance, a particularly sullen Liam seemed to be on a mission to offend most of America. Firstly, by deliberately singing off-key, then by frequently spitting on stage and then making sexual gestures. Seemingly enjoying himself, he then spoke to the crowd, saying, 'I hope you're having a good time, but you're probably having a shit time.'

As the song closed, he punched the microphone to the floor and, with a final flourish, threw the beer can he was regularly swigging from across the stage. Liam didn't divulge why he was so belligerent but theorising from what we know, it could simply be that Liam never took to America. Two years previously, he said in an interview, 'Americans want grungy people, stabbing themselves in the head on stage. They get a bright bunch like us, with deodorant on, they don't get it.'

In addition, Liam was never one for the more corporate side of the music industry, always looking to cause mischief where possible, the Brit Awards earlier in the year being a good example. Once again, there was outrage across America, some people going so far as to insist the band were deported.

Four more dates followed in Worcester, Massachusetts; Wantagh, New York (two shows); and Bristow, Virginia; before the final nail was struck; Noel quit the tour and the band. His version of the story now is that Liam and Bonehead were having an argument, apparently about a leather jacket (which makes for an amusing tale) and he decided to leave. Other reasons cited including Liam's 'unprofessionalism' and the next gig in Charlottesville apparently being downgraded; 'Everyone was full of their own self-importance, just because we'd sold a few records. It made no difference to me. So I stayed that night in the hotel, packed me bags and said,

'Look, I'm going back to England.' If the truth be known, I didn't want to be there anyway. I wasn't prepared to be in the band if people were being like that to each other.'

'It seemed to be a never-ending circle of work. And, of course, everyone wanted to squeeze as much money as possible out of *Morning Glory* before the band imploded.'

On landing at Heathrow, shielded by security, Noel stared impassively ahead and ignored all the press surrounding him, avoiding any comment. While carrying on a US tour without Liam was possible, carrying on without Noel wasn't at this point, so all remaining dates were cancelled. The *(What's the Story) Morning Glory?* tour was finally over, but so, apparently, were Oasis.

Paolo Hewitt: 'I remember Noel said to me when *Morning Glory* was still selling after a year, 'I thought we were going to replace The Stone Roses.' That's what the idea was; they were going to replace The Stone Roses and become The Stone Roses and have their audience. It was a big audience, but it wasn't the worldwide phenomenon that they became.'

There followed a frenzied few weeks of speculation; the entire Oasis camp were silent, so the press had nothing to go on. Which of course didn't stop them reporting on it. The fans were less frenzied, having seen similar incidents before, but there were probably a lot of people at Creation and Sony that were worried. The cocktail of the pressures of fame and adulation, drug abuse and testosterone had always been a volatile one.

The media did have a few Oasis nuggets to work with; the band officially announced that they were backing Tony Blair's Labour Party, with Alan McGee appearing at a Labour Youth Experience rally to present a platinum Oasis disc and £10,000 of sponsorship for the party. In November their singles were re-issued in box set housed in silver and gold flip-top boxes, like Benson & Hedges cigarette packets. Earlier, in October, Noel Gallagher was No.1 for the second time that year, this time in collaboration with electro-pioneers The Chemical Brothers, having provided a melody and lyrics for 'Setting Sun,' originally an Oasis demo called 'Coming On Strong,' offered to the pair for their second album. The song shifted 200,000 copies in its first week as a public thirst for Gallagher music, having been starved for six months, was partially quenched. Not only that but for the second year in succession, Noel Gallagher was the recipient of the prestigious Ivor Novello award, given to the outstanding songwriters of the time, based on both songwriting and composition.

Jeff Slate: 'There's something visceral about the way he works that is unique to him. That's what's true of the great songwriters. I'm not sure what school he is in or what he does. With relative ease he writes anthems. What he has always focused on is partly the chorus; he does see things in linear form. He's a traditionalist in that. Sure, maybe his songs are simpler than The Beatles,' because he's not George Harrison, who loved to throw in the weird chords. But he is a traditionalist in the sense that there is a straight-forward structure to them that leads the listener easily to the next step - verse, pre-chorus, chorus. And that chorus is a big pay-off. He has a lot of ideas for verses and chord progressions, and a lot of them overlap. He's the first to admit that, but he's always looking for that big pay-off.

'There are very few people throughout their careers who are able to draw on a well that engages the listener, not just melodically - it's not the music, not the words, but it's the record. How does it make you feel? Noel is very focused on the end-result. He knows in his head what it's going to sound like when he starts. He had his eye on the prize from the very beginning; what is this going to sound like in a stadium full of 100,000 people in Buenos Aires. Very few people have that sensibility. He wasn't joking when he said he wanted to be bigger than The Beatles. He, whether consciously or unconsciously, had that as a goal. If you have that as a goal you can't be writing songs like The Mock Turtles. You're going, not for the cheap seats, but for mass appeal with quality. You're trying to touch people

in a unique way. Somehow this guy from Burnage hit on a formula that he's been able to draw from frequently.'

After a few weeks, as the ice was showing signs of thawing amongst its members, a band meeting was called, and it was decided that they would continue. It was eventually agreed that Oasis should return to the studio to record another album, although Noel cast doubts on whether he would tour said record. Asked what the chances were, he said, 'Very, very little I'd say. But you never know, you might see me touring.'

Studio time was booked for Abbey Road, used for the majority of The Beatles' recordings and arguably the most famous recording studios in the world. The third album was intended to primarily be made up of songs Noel demoed in Mustique, but the sessions did not start well; Owen Morris, once again donning the producer's hat with Noel, described the first week as 'fucking awful' and suggested to Noel they abandon the session; 'He just shrugged and said it would be all right. So, on we went.'

Although the atmosphere was good, bridges having been built, Oasis and their entourage brought the party with them, and so other clientele recording in the studios, for presumably not an insignificant amount, were not so happy. Complaints were made that Oasis were playing too loudly, affecting other recordings. Being so intensely under the microscope wouldn't have helped; Abbey Road Studios being so close to Central London, so anyone entering the studio, Oasis-affiliated or not, would have been subject to the press pack. Liam being arrested in early November for possession of cocaine, after celebrating Oasis winning Best Act in the World Today at the 1996 *Q* Awards, didn't help. Having to put the dream of recording in their idols' creative space on hold, Oasis opted to leave the famous studio with only a few backing tracks in the can after four weeks' work.

A more rural location away from prying eyes and controversy was required, that being Ridge Farm Studios, near Dorking in Surrey. The band reconvened with more energy, but the cocaine abuse, by now part and parcel of Oasis life, was severely compromising the quality and more exactly, the quality control.

Tony McCarroll: 'The more money you've got to spend in the studio, the less things you've got to write about.'

Owen Morris: '*Morning Glory* was very easy. Everyone wanted to be there, which was nice. Everybody's energy was good about it. We did another good session just before the album came out, where we did 'The Masterplan'. That was our last great session really. *Be Here Now* was a horrible session because Noel didn't want to be there, Liam didn't want to be there. None of the band wanted to be there, I don't think, but there was so much money flying around that they couldn't refuse. I think they should have taken some time off. That was quite an ordeal. Compared to six months of joy in Rockfield, there was 10 months of pulling teeth. Which was a shame, but it was down to people's attitudes and desires. Things had changed by then. There was so much money around, the paparazzi were around, there was always pictures of them. Noel's songs were maybe not as good as before. It all went a bit wrong. So *Morning Glory* was a definite high for me with Oasis.'

Owen Morris had originally wanted a more stripped-back approach for the album, more in line with the Mustique demos, but as time passed more and more was added to the songs, including numerous layers of guitar. He went so far as to say to Noel that he thought the new material was quite weak, but was cut down; 'I just carried on shovelling drugs up my nose.' He later expressed regret at not being able to transfer the Mustique demos and overdub the drums. Noel on the other hand wanted to make the album as dense as possible; he would dub 10 channels with identical guitar parts to create volume on several tracks. Alan McGee, at this point drug-free, commented later, 'I used to go down to the studio, and there was so much cocaine getting done at that point. Owen was out of control, and he was the one in charge. The music was just fucking loud.'

The album didn't entirely consist of new songs. 'All Around the World', which had long been mythologised and was among the first batch of songs Noel had composed, finally had the offerings of a budget that could match its ambition. 'Hey Jude' on steroids, the nine-minute opus demanded the kitchen-sink approach.

Nick Ingman: 'We had a huge orchestra. I don't think that would have been signed off if they hadn't had budgetary success. I think there was more acceptance by the record company of a budget. It was a much freer budgetary situation. There was also another, chemical element in the room, which was very much part of the environment at that point. It certainly made certain decisions that perhaps wouldn't have been made, I don't know.

'The number of guitar overdubs that were done on that after we did our stuff, I believe (a) weren't necessary and (b) possibly made it a lesser record.

'I think we had, I'm guessing, 40 or 50 (musicians). They may have double-tracked it to make it sound like it was 128.

'We had brass on it certainly, and latterly Noel said it would be great to have a piccolo trumpet. The trumpet player didn't have a piccolo, so there was a whole palaver. He had to phone his wife to have his piccolo put in a taxi. He lived miles away, it took hours for the taxi to come. Finally, the taxi came, and we put on a piccolo trumpet part. Liam, who hadn't contributed very much, leapt up and was alerted by the sound of the piccolo trumpet. He came into the studio and said, 'That's a great looking instrument. Can I play it?' Very, very reluctantly, the trumpeter said, 'Alright.' I do have this vision of Liam half-trotting around AIR Lyndhurst trying to play the piccolo trumpet.

'The song was very simple, harmonically. It was the same two or three chords going over and over again.

'Later, Noel did ask the string players to play hard and tough. For a few years after I used to say to the string players, 'Oasis', and they knew what I meant. Play hard, no gentleness.'

A name and an associate from before the time of chaos was keeping a keen eye and ear on the output of his former proteges. Chris Griffiths from The Real People had been so incensed by his treatment that he was driven by suspicion that there may be more songwriting infringements hidden amid the bluster. Eventually he was proven to be correct: one of *Be Here Now*'s plaintive ballads, 'Don't Go Away', had more than an air of familiarity about it.

Chris Griffiths: "Feel the Pain' was on *Marshmellow Lane*, so they'd obviously been listening to that. It was one of them, there was so many little coincidental things, or songs that sounded similar, little riffs or little words or sayings, that I was getting pissed off with it by then. We approached chambers regarding 'Columbia', because it was always a case of, 'No, don't worry about it, your name will be on it. We've only just done this first pressing of 100,000. Next time it comes out I'll let the publishers know. Your name will be on it, don't worry about it.' And the same with 'Rockin' Chair'. Obviously, my name wasn't on it when it came out as a B-side of 'Roll with It' and my name never got on to 'Columbia'. So, I was looking out for things, sometimes I was hearing things that weren't there. 'Is this one of my riffs?' And then I actually listened to the album on the day it came out in my ex-manager's recording studio, and just heard the, 'Don't go away, say what you say' bit, and I went, 'Is that my fucking song?' And this is no exaggeration, I punched a hole in the ceiling. But we did take an out-of-court settlement for that. I should have carried on, to get my name on the record, which was all I wanted. It didn't matter if I got 5% of it, I just wanted my name on the record.'

Meanwhile, demonstrating true mass appeal, adorning the autumn edition of the New Labour magazine was Noel Gallagher, officially backing Labour with the claim that Tony Blair's most recent speech 'had brought tears to my eyes'.

Noel Gallagher with a fan outside his home in 1997

1997

'THESE ARE CRAZY DAYS, BUT THEY MAKE ME SHINE'

In February 1997, Noel Gallagher joined Ocean Colour Scene onstage at the Royal Albert Hall, along with Paul Weller and Chris and Tony Griffiths from old friends The Real People. Yet Noel already had one controversial moment under his belt. At the end of January, he attended the *NME* Awards, at which Oasis were once again successful; the Best Band and Musical Event of the Year (for Knebworth) going their way. Tellingly, they picked up three negative awards too - Worst Dressed Person and Arse of the Year (both Liam), plus Worst Band. A key part of the cycle for any band is the backlash, which Oasis had at the time of *(What's the Story) Morning Glory?*'s release, but they largely weathered the storm. However, the *NME* had always been staunch supporters (although the vote was conducted by fans), so it was evident that more and more people were starting to turn against the band, the more successful they became.

There was a media storm at that time as Brian Harvey, lead singer of pop band East 17, had been fired for drug use. Prime Minister John Major condemned the singer in the House of Commons and radio stations banned the group. Needless to say, the media wanted Noel's thoughts on the matter, which he gladly offered: 'If Brian Harvey did do 12 Es in one night – if he did do, and he's saying he did – if he's being honest, then fair enough. If you can't be honest in this country then we might as well go and live in China, know what I mean? There's people in the Houses of Parliament, man, who are bigger heroin addicts and cocaine addicts than anyone in this room right now. And it's all about honesty at the end of the day. As soon as people realise that the majority of people in this country take drugs, then the better off we'll all be. It's not like a scandalous sensation, or anything like that. Not when you've got our Government selling arms to people who go out and kill probably relatives of somebody in this room. Drugs is like getting up and having a cup of tea in the morning, and until people realise that, it's their tough shit, innit?'

Unsurprisingly, outrage followed. It made the news on BBC1, ITV, Channel 4 and Sky, Tory Home Office minister Tom Sackville denounced Noel as 'incredibly irresponsible' and the more sanguine Gallagher was everywhere across the media for a couple of days. Conservative MP Peter Bottomley accused Noel of making the comments to 'drum up publicity' for the band, despite the fact that publicity wasn't something they were in short supply of. There were calls for Noel to be sacked from Oasis, as Harvey had been, as laughable a thought now as it was then. For his part, Noel was defiant; 'If by saying a few seemingly outrageous things has helped instigate an open and honest debate about drug abuse in this country, then I'm pleased.'

Brian Cannon: 'The thing with Oasis was there were no big secrets. It was all totally transparent.'

While sessions for the third album at Ridge Farm had been productive, managing to get down the guitars, bass and some dubbing, the band opted to leave leafy Surrey, perhaps due to press harassment once again. It had been suggested by Owen Morris and others that the sessions be completely dropped, but Noel was insistent that the wheels kept rolling. So they decamped to AIR Studios, logically back in London. Morris declared these to be the best of the three sessions. Ridge Farm and AIR Studios had one thing in common; both contained fully operational bars. By now fully in throes of success and their egos, Oasis wouldn't have needed much persuading to have a drink or 50, and with no-one around to stop them, they surely did. Yet again, the environment and temptations available got the better of them.

For the sessions, Liam was adamant that he would record his vocals (last, as always) on his own. With at least 70 minutes of music to add vocals to, it was no small task. Taking the opportunity, Noel opted to go on holiday while Liam made his contribution to the record. On his return, hearing the vocals, big brother was appalled at the quality and insisted he and Liam return to the studio to re-do them, which, with The Chief back in attendance, took two days. The album was then mixed at AIR, again by Owen Morris and Noel; 'All the things you shouldn't do when you're mixing an album, we did it 10-fold.'

The band were also losing members of the inner sanctum. Mark Coyle wasn't working with them anymore. Alan McGee had taken a back seat, and Brian Cannon saw the band less and less.

Brian Cannon: 'It just kind of fizzled out. They did *Be Here Now*, then after that I did *The Masterplan*, but it all started going funny around that phase. Up until then we had been one big gang. When they were recording *Morning Glory* I was in the studio the whole time. I didn't really go to the studio when they were doing *Be Here Now*. Nobody fell out with each other, it just wasn't the same. Liam and Noel didn't want to be in the studio at the same time, there was a bit of a bad vibe going on, so I kept away.'

Meanwhile, the tabloids were fixated on Liam's impending wedding to Patsy Kensit, the media camped outside Liam's house in St John's Wood for days. To avoid the tabloids, the couple were forced to have their nuptials at 7am on April 7.

Two hours later, Liam told his big brother by phone about the happy occasion.

In early May, Noel was contacted by Bobby Gillespie of label-mates Primal Scream, to play with them at a benefit gig for the dockers of Merseyside, unceremoniously sacked by the local council. Several notable people came out to support them in public, including footballers from both Everton and Liverpool. Also playing at the gig were Dodgy and Billy Bragg. Noel's set was a short acoustic one, with no new material. Noel also supported Paul Weller for one night at the Brixton Academy. In June he again played a benefit gig, this time in New York, for the annual Tibetan Freedom Concert. It was an impressively stellar line-up; included on the bill were U2, Radiohead, Foo Fighters and Patti Smith. More than 10 years later, that gig would come back to haunt Oasis.

Also in early May, the political class were starting to reap the rewards of Cool Britannia; after closely aligning themselves with figures in the arts and those of left-wing persuasion, the Labour Party won the UK General Election with a landslide victory, with no little thanks placed at Alan McGee's (a very public sponsor) and, by association, Oasis' door. Shortly after, following suit with his brother, Noel and Meg Mathews married in Las Vegas, an Elvis Presley impersonator conducting the service.

With the third album finally in the can, plans for the launch campaign started to form. Rather than adhering to common practice of the label (either Sony or Creation) being in charge of promotion, Ignition Management took control, an unusual amount of power for a management company to have. But seeing as their clients were the Gallaghers, they could wield such authority. Ignition were adamant that the whole album was embargoed and insisted anyone and everyone who heard the album should be made to sign non-disclosure agreements. This raised a lot of journalistic hackles from those who believed themselves to have played a huge part in the rise of the band. Indeed, there were several reported disagreements between Creation and Ignition. After declaring that the album (by this point christened *Be Here Now*) would sell 20 million copies, in usual hyperbolic fashion, Alan McGee was excluded from involvement in the campaign.

The rationale within Ignition was this; they didn't spend a huge amount on marketing and were keen to downplay any hype, presenting *Be Here Now* as an everyday collection of tunes, while with glorious irony insisting that NDAs were signed - adding to the hype and mystique. To avoid too much exposure, the first single ('D'You Know What I Mean?') was given a short-lead time between its debut on the radio and the physical release. Unfortunately, shortly before the embargo was to be lifted, three radio stations broke it by a few hours, which was considered a disaster. Joe Public wouldn't have noticed.

Images of the cover for *Be Here Now* started to be released to the press. Shot in a hotel in Hertfordshire, the band, Brian Cannon and others utilised a number of meaningless items from the BBC props department, such as a globe, large keys, a scooter, and other paraphernalia, with the band surrounding a Rolls Royce partially submerged in the hotel swimming pool. The Rolls Royce did not have a number-plate, so someone came up with the idea of copying the plate of a police van from the cover of The Beatles' *Abbey Road*. It was then decided that every item on the cover had a significant meaning, *The Sun* and *Daily Mirror* double-page spreads itemising everything.

Brian Cannon: 'The idea behind the Rolls Royce in the pool, that's obviously a rock'n'roll cliche from old. For all the rest of it, we literally went down to the BBC props department in White City with Liam and Noel. I just said, 'Pick whatever you want, this will get everybody at it.' I saw *The Sun* newspaper did a breakdown of it and analysed every piece and gave an explanation. Got ya! It doesn't mean anything, it was just absolute nonsense.'

To warm themselves up for the third album world tour, Oasis played some dates in the US, two of which were supporting U2. Presumably the only band Noel would agree to support, U2 had become friends with the Gallagher brothers over the preceding years. The sets consisted of the greatest hits, with 'Wonderwall' and 'Cast No Shadow' played on electric guitars rather than acoustic. More importantly, after what seemed like an eternity, two new songs were debuted; the forthcoming single 'D'You Know What I Mean?', the first time anyone had heard

OASIS fans went mad for the band's new album yesterday — snapping up one every TWO SECONDS.

Hundreds of shops opened at 8am to cope with the rush for Be Here Now.

Some sold well over 500 copies in the first 20 minutes. Many fans bought the album on CD, vinyl **AND** cassette.

At the HMV store in Oxford Street, **London**, Swedish tourist Gabriel Bjerner got his £13.99 CD at just 23 seconds past 8am.

The 18-year-old student, who had queued since 4am, said: "I feel great. I love Oasis and can't

By JANE ATKINSON, Showbiz Reporter

believe I'm the first to buy it."

In **Manchester, Liverpool** and **Leeds** there were queues of 300.

At HMV in **Manchester** – the band's home city – Martin Harrison, 17, waited nearly 11 hours.

Record

Martin, of Rochdale, said: "I've been a fan since the first album Definitely Maybe. The new one is just as good."

The album – Oasis's first in two years – is set to break records by reaching No 1 in three days.

That would beat Michael Jackson's Thriller, which took four.

Be Here Now is expected to trounce Oasis's last album (What's The Story) Morning Glory?, which sold 3.5million.

Tony French, of HMV in London, said yesterday: "I've never seen crowds like this." Nicki Strange, 16, queued from 6.30am, leaving her GCSE results unopened in **Ilford,** Essex. "I know they're bad anyway," she said.

HMV is confident of selling 100,000 copies of Be Here Now by the end of this week – making it the fastest selling album of all time in the UK."

● **DAD** Bob Drake – working in Bangkok for a Bradford firm – paid £40 to have the album flown out for daughter Sarah, 16.

The Sun Says— Page Eight

THUNDERWALL FINED

A GUITAR-playing Oasis fan was fined £100 for driving his neighbour up the Wonderwall.

Mark Hoey, 26, entertained pals by singing hits like Don't Look Back In Anger in the early hours.

But sleepless Melanie Gutman complained to council officials who told him to quieten down. When he struck up again he was fined and ordered to pay £250 costs by JPs in Abingdon, Oxfordshire.

Mark said: "My family is crazy about Oasis so we had a singalong." Miss Gutman, in her forties, refused to comment.

● **NOISY fans should "spare a thought for neighbours" before playing Be Here Now, said the Chartered Institute of Environmental Health.**

OASIS SPOT

SUN reporter Chris Pharo, 28, has named his son Connor Liam after girlfriend Kirsty, 27, gave birth in Bristol as Oasis played on TV in the background.

the song, and the title track of the album, 'Be Here Now', with hand-held camera recordings of the new songs played on the news.

In celebration of their ascension to Government, New Labour held a thank you party at Downing Street to their fiscal and verbal benefactors, with Alan McGee, Noel Gallagher and a wealth of other celebrities who had backed the party invited. The photograph the press really wanted was of Noel and new Prime Minister, Tony Blair, and they duly obliged. One of the most famous images of the 1990s, it's now regarded as the death of Britpop, the movement becoming a key ingredient of the Establishment rather than the outsider scene it started as. Noel now justifies the evening, 'I was 30, off me head, and everyone was telling me we were the greatest band since who knows. Then the Prime Minister invites you round for a glass of wine. It all becomes part of the high.'

'I asked him how he managed to stay up all night (on election night). He leaned into me and said, 'Probably not by the same means as you did.' I thought he was a geezer after that.'

Pete Mitchell: 'My one defining moment of Cool Britannia would be Noel, Meg and Alan walking down Downing Street to this champagne drinks (thing) at No.10. At this time, I thought, 'This has gone too far.' It's extraordinary that you can work at the gas board and in the space of six/seven years, maybe not even that, you're going into No.10.'

Back to the day-job, the single, 'D'You Know What I Mean?', described by Noel as a 'call to arms to the fans', was a sprawling monster of a song. Seven minutes long, with the first minute and a half consisting pretty much purely of feedback, it was anthemic rock of the mightiest kind. The production values had obviously increased, with a lot of money thrown at effects and the video. There was a lot of hype in the lead-up to its airplay and inevitably it was immediately A-listed on all mainstream stations. Some stations chose to play the lead B-side, 'Stay Young' rather than the single, given it was a lot more listener-friendly and shorter. Such was their arrogance, Oasis refused to provide an edit for the lead track to make it more palatable. As well as 'Stay Young', the other B-sides were 'Angel Child', a demo from the Mustique sessions a year previously, and a cover of David Bowie's 'Heroes', with Noel on lead vocals. Yet Liam wasn't happy with the inclusion of the latter, saying, 'I haven't got an ounce of Bowie in me, and neither have you.'

The single was released on July 7, 1997 and went on to sell 370,000 copies in its first week, and topped the charts for one week, knocking Puff Daddy's tribute to his long-time friend Notorious B.I.G., 'I'll Be Missing You', from the top slot, although the rapper returned the favour the following week. But that was now three No.1 singles, and three weeks at No.1.

The *Top of the Pops* performance was quite under-stated given the monumental scale of everything else surrounding the band, although they allowed the audience to take to the stage at the end. Noel was already starting to sound disparaging about the forthcoming album though, saying, 'I just wish the rest of the album sounded like that ('D'You Know What I Mean?'). It's good, but the next one will be better.'

Promotion for both the single and the album had begun in earnest, the first port of call a large interview and cover feature in the *NME*. It didn't take long for the interview to be picked apart by the press, specifically Noel's section, and for a headline to be found: 'Some of the pop stars I like are more important to me than God, so yeah. I would hope we mean more to people than putting money in a church basket and saying 10 Hail Marys on a Sunday. Has God played Knebworth recently?'

It was the usual story - headlines, controversy, outrage. All par for the course. What wasn't widely reported was that the answer given was to the question, 'Do you think Oasis are more important to the youth of today than God?' One suspects it was something of a trap, but Noel was as honest as ever. He also gave his thoughts on previous controversies: 'It's like when we were leading up to Earl's Court and there was all the stuff I'd said about Damon and AIDS. The Terence Higgins Trust wanted all the profits from those gigs. What profits?'

'And I suppose, it's about like when I said that thing at the Brats (*NME* Awards) about drugs being like a cup of tea. Right, well, I had Leah Betts' parents (a teenager who died after taking ecstasy) on the phone giving me a hard time. It starts off with this compassion and guilt thing and then at the end of the line it all boils down to, 'How much money are you going to give us?"

More details began to emerge about the forthcoming album. Johnny Depp played slide guitar on a track called 'Fade In-Out,' while 'All Around The World,' which the band used to rehearse at The Boardwalk in Manchester, was to be unveiled as a nine-minute opus, featuring several orchestras, backing vocals supplied by the Gallagher brothers' partners Patsy and Meg, and Richard Ashcroft of The Verve among others (Liam returned the favour for The Verve's forthcoming album *Urban Hymns*, appearing on closing track 'Come On.'). The track also had a reprise to close the album. 'My Big Mouth' and 'It's Getting Better (Man!!),' both debuted at Knebworth, were also included, 'Magic Pie' referenced a Tony Blair speech ('there are but a thousand days preparing for a thousand years'), and it was going to be 20 minutes longer than the band's previous albums.

The promotion and secrecy around the record was ongoing, with BBC Radio One given a CD of three tracks to play on air, with the condition attached that there would be a lot of talking over the tracks to avoid bootlegging. After the first day, DJ Steve Lamacq received a call from Ignition informing him he would not be able to preview any further tracks, because he hadn't spoken enough over the first batch of songs on his radio show. Creation publicist Johnny Hopkins insisted that, upon giving members of the press cassette copies of the album, the recipients sign a contract containing a clause that they weren't to discuss the music with anyone, including partners.

The album's release date (August 21) was, unusually, a Thursday. This seemed to contradict Ignition's tactic of keeping things low profile, bringing out the album on a day when no other albums were to be released. The night before, the BBC broadcast a documentary, *Right Here, Right Now*, featuring interviews with all of the band, spanning the lead-up and recording of the album. Highlights of the 40-minute show included full band performances of 'Be Here Now' and 'It's Getting Better (Man!!)', as well as an acoustic version of 'Stand by Me'. It took the band back to Maine Road, saw them in the pub, behind the scenes of the 'D'You

Know What I Mean?' video shoot and in the rehearsal studio. Noel proclaimed in the documentary: 'This is probably going to be the most important album of our career. It's either going to be the one that sends us up to U2's level or it'll probably see us back on the dole.'

Eventually the album was unleashed upon a salivating general public. At the end of the first day, it had sold over 424,000 units. The reviews were virtually all overwhelmingly positive, the music press perhaps very cautious of being caught out as they had been with *(What's the Story) Morning Glory?* Inevitably it hit the No.1 album slot after being available for three days. Both Liam and Noel went on holiday that week, presumably to avoid the hype and let the music speak for itself.

Brian Cannon: 'Oasis lost three days of sales and were still No.1, hands down. That's ridiculous. I've never heard of anything like it. In terms of sales, that'll never be beaten. Never.'

Paolo Hewitt: 'Over half a million people went out and bought *Be Here Now* the first day of release. It was just craziness. Absolute madness. And like they say in that documentary, they were suddenly surrounded by a lot of men with man bags saying you've got to do this, and you've got to do that. I remember thinking after Knebworth you should just ... Sunday night at Knebworth, you should have said, 'That's it', and then it would have gone down in history as just amazing. Instead it just sort of slowly began to disintegrate.'

Between the release of the album and the tour, what was to be regarded as a national tragedy engulfed the UK; Princess Diana, along with her lover, Dodi Fayed, killed in a car crash in Paris. Unprecedented levels of grief followed across the country, the optimism of a new Government overshadowed.

Earlier in the summer, one of the music scene's darlings, Radiohead released their opus, *OK Computer*, which had been lauded as the future of rock music with its melancholy overtones and pre-millennial anxiety. Meanwhile, old friends of Oasis, The Verve finally struck gold with the release of their third album, *Urban Hymns*, its lead singles, 'Bittersweet Symphony' and 'The Drugs Don't Work', having impressive showings in the charts, No.'s 2 and 1 respectively. *Urban Hymns* was also a more reflective, despondent work - a far cry from the euphoria of Britpop. These two albums seemed to capture the public mood in the wake of Diana's death, and anything else was considered ill at ease. *Be Here Now*, with all its cocaine-driven bombast, couldn't have seemed any more incongruous.

Not that the band were bothered; the party was about to start once more. The first date of the tour was to be in Oslo, Norway, in September. The world's press descended, to get a view of the band, and for once they had more than just the band to lay their eyes on. For reasons that are now lost in the mists of time (drugs), Oasis indulged in some visual theatrics. The entire stage was made up to look like the album cover. All the significant props were there; Alan White played drums inside the Rolls Royce, the clock was present and correct, and the band made their entrance from a red telephone box centre-stage (a butler opening the door for them after hyping up the crowd). There was even a fully-functioning bar.

As for the songs, if they were harbouring doubts about *Be Here Now*, they didn't shy away from it; seven new songs were included, alongside the old favourites. The first set list was:

'Be Here Now'
'Stay Young'
'Stand by Me'
'Supersonic'
'Some Might Say'
'Roll with It'
'D'You Know What I Mean?'
'Magic Pie'
'Don't Look Back in Anger'
'Wonderwall'
'Live Forever'
'It's Getting Better (Man!!)'
'Champagne Supernova'
'Fade In-Out'
'All Around the World'
'Acquiesce'

Further dates in Stockholm and Copenhagen followed before the tour reached the UK. There were arena shows in Exeter, Newcastle, Aberdeen, Sheffield, Birmingham and another residency at Earl's Court, this time for three nights, with support from The Verve, continuing their close association. The *NME* tried to make this into another 'Battle of the Bands' yarn, even though the two mighty acts weren't on the same bill by accident. On an earlier tour date in Scandinavia, Liam dedicated a performance of 'Live Forever 'to the late Princess Diana. Noel, something of a Republican, thought little of this gesture, and it became an issue later in the tour. They then jetted over to the US for some promotion and two gigs at the Hammerstein Ballroom, New York City. Meanwhile, during the British leg, London's criminal arm began registering that, with the Lord of the Manor away, Noel's Primrose Hill home, dubbed Supernova Heights, was ripe for the picking. Yet another element of fame that isn't often mentioned.

The second single to be lifted from the album was 'Stand by Me,' a slower, more traditional rock ballad that Oasis had now mastered. The video debuted on popular ITV show *The Chart Show*, which was unique in its field in only playing music videos. In keeping with the theme of the album title and accompanying promotion, the video included CCTV footage following incidents in a town centre. The timing on that footage was the exact time that the video was debuted, as they had done with *Be Here Now*, showing the date of release on the cover.

The single was backed by the abrasive '(I Got) The Fever,' the more sedate, Bacharach-esque 'Going Nowhere,' and 'My Sister Lover,' paying tribute to Debbie Turner's band, Sister Lovers (who had invited Oasis to join the bill in Glasgow that fateful night in May '93 when they were spotted by Alan McGee), its melody taken from early demo track, 'Lock All The Doors.' . The single was held off the top spot by Elton John's reworking of his '70s hit 'Candle in the Wind,' the new version a tribute to Princess Diana,

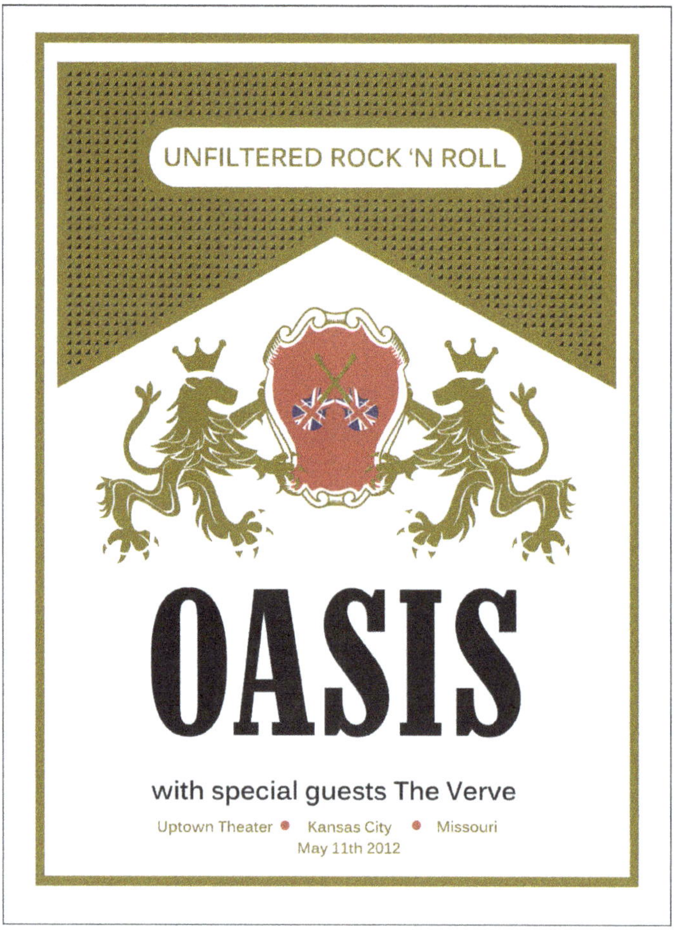

becoming the biggest-selling UK single of all time. The *Top of the Pops* performance was recorded at the same time as 'D'You Know What I Mean?' was, due to anticipated commitments.

Nick Ingman: 'He was almost equally as into Bacharach as he was into The Beatles. That ('Going Nowhere') may have been Noel saying to me, 'Be Burt Bacharach.'

'Stand by Me' wasn't the only Gallagher-penned single in the autumn of 1997. Liam had co-written a song for John Squire's new band, The Seahorses, which was selected as their third single. The track, 'Love Me and Leave Me', contained some brother references that could only and surely have come from Liam. Despite being Liam's first songwriting credit, the track only made No.16 in the charts.

Owing to Liam's onstage tribute to Lady Diana early in the tour, Oasis briefly became associated with her, and were, one guesses, one of the first names on a list to be asked to participate in a tribute concert. When asked, to have said no would have appeared churlish and bought them more bad headlines, so begrudgingly, coerced by his manager, Noel agreed to participate at the event in Paris. As it turned out, the benefit concert was scrapped after a lorry drivers' strike brought the whole of France to a standstill. For all concerned it was probably a bullet dodged.

Back in the UK, Liam and Noel conducted an interview for BBC Radio One, on Steve Lamacq's *Evening Session*. The interview was scheduled to be a one-to-one with Noel, but when his little brother showed up in the studio everyone knew fireworks were on the agenda. The interview went out live, and the Gallagher brothers rolled into the studio very, very drunk.

Liam and Noel disagreed over several things, including the merits of *Be Here Now*. Noel made the announcement that the album was to be the last Oasis album of the '90s, and once again he was planning to overhaul the sound entirely. They waxed lyrical about the success of The Verve's *Urban Hymns*, and Noel made a few comments indicating that Oasis, as a whole, had become boring and conceded that they were now part of the Establishment. Liam on the other hand had some personal grudges to settle.

The previous year, one of the band's idols, George Harrison, made disparaging comments about the frontman, saying, 'I think he's a bit out of date. It's just silly, I feel a bit sorry for him really, because I think he's totally missed the bus and I think it's proven when you see the band without him singing. You know, they're more in tune and he's just excess baggage, I think, and all he does is make people think what a bunch of prannies they are.'

For whatever reason, Liam took the opportunity the interview provided to set the record straight:

Steve Lamacq: 'Noel and Liam Gallagher are with us. Noel, you were saying this is the first time you've been interviewed together since 1994.'

Liam: '1964.'

Noel: 'Yeah. Was that before I left The Beatles or before you joined The Beatles?'

Liam: 'It was before I was born.'

Steve Lamacq: 'You've been away in America. When did you get back from there?'

Noel: 'We got back about 10 days ago and went to the studio to do some B-sides. Then we came out of the studio on Monday.'

Liam: 'And we had a lot of flashbacks.'

Steve Lamacq: 'B-sides for 'All Around the World'?'

Noel: 'Yeah. We've actually done a cover of 'Street Fighting Man,' just to piss Keith Richards off, 'cos he's been slagging us off.'

Liam: 'Just to make them more money that they've already got. Obviously, they ain't got enough.'

Steve Lamacq: 'I was going to say, do you have to clear something like that before you do it?'

Noel: 'No, as long as you don't change the arrangement, apparently you don't need permission.'

Steve Lamacq: 'They had quite a run-in with The Verve, didn't they?'

Liam: 'Yeah, and they're going to have a run-in with me when I meet them down Sainsbury's.'

Noel: 'I think it was Andrew Loog Oldham who had a run-in with The Verve about that.'

Liam: 'Can I interrupt? We're here to....'

Noel: 'You interrupt away.'

Liam: 'We're here to celebrate Bonfire Night and stuff like that, cos I'm silly, aren't I, George?'

Noel: 'Not before Halloween. You can't celebrate Bonfire Night before Halloween.'

Liam: 'All these snegs coming out the closet at the moment, right ... I'm going to shoot me mouth off to this.'

Noel: 'I bet you won't.'

Liam: 'John's been a bit rude in the past.'

Noel, pulling money out: 'All that says you won't shoot your mouth off. That's about 95 quid. And a platinum case.'

Liam: 'I've got me own, man. Listen, before we go any further, all these old farts who get out the day centre....'

Noel: 'Gimme the money back.'

Liam: '... and a microphone comes out. 'You've got a ploblem with a kid...''

Noel: 'Ploblem?'

Liam: '... a *problem* with a kid out of Oasis, obviously. I ignore all that 'cos I dig all their music, I dig them as personal human beings, right. But, at the end of the day... (Noel attempts to interrupt) you shut up a minute right, songwriter. At the end of the day, they almost want a scrap. And I will offer them all, right out here on radio. If you want a fight, right, Primrose Hill, Saturday morning, 12 o'clock. I will beat the fucking living daylight shit out of them, and I'll still give them a steak pie at the end of it...'

Noel: 'To answer your question, yes we have been to America.'

Liam, still talking: '... that goes for George, Jagger, Smichards, and the other cunt who gives me shit. You calm down over there, I've got to say my bit. Any of them old farts who've got a problem with me, leave your zimmer frames at home and I will hold them up with a good right hook. And that's the end of it.'

Steve Lamacq: 'Who's the person who's most hurt you out of those?'

Liam: 'Oh, fucking ... gotta be Jesus Christ, innit? But no-one's hurt me, 'cos I still dig their music. I love George Harrison's music, I love Keith Richards, I love Mick Jagger's music. I love whoever else wants to slag me off and all that tackle but at the end of the day it's getting childish. It's like being in the playground. I left the playground years ago. Now they want a push-about on the fucking swings and that. I'll push them and I'll put them in them little swings. I just want a fight with them, me.'

Steve Lamacq: 'Do you think they say these things because they're goaded into saying them?'

Liam: 'I think they're jealous and I think they're senile and they ain't getting enough meat pies and that.'

Steve Lamacq: 'Does it bother you? Because you're bigger than that, aren't you?'

Liam: 'I'm bigger than everything, me. Me personally, I'm bigger than that but obviously they want a scrap. And I will beat them up if they want a fight.'

Steve Lamacq: 'And the venue is ... Primrose Hill ...'

Noel, in hysterics: 'Shut up, man! Shut up.'

Liam: 'I told you I was going to say that.'

Noel: 'Next question.'

Going out live, the swearing was an immediate problem. Steve Lamacq and his producer asked Liam to tone it down, but he refused. Eventually, after being dismissed by Noel on several occasions while making points, Liam left the studio for the presenter and Noel to conduct a more traditional interview. But of course, the damage was done, and they were on the front pages once more.

The European leg of the tour took up the entirety of November, spanning France, Spain, Switzerland, Italy, Germany, the Czech Republic and the Netherlands.

Despite their fame and popularity, for those in the hospitality industry the name Oasis carried a level of notoriety, and hotel managers across Europe weren't reluctant to ban the band from hotels at the first opportunity. Most issues were resolved, but the band's entourage had a few close shaves when it came to accommodation. There was logic to their reasoning; while in Spain, Bonehead was caught on camera baring not only his backside, but something else in very close proximity to the world's media.

It was also around then that Noel started being referred to as The Chief. From the outside looking in, the nickname appeared tongue-in-cheek but, fuelled by cocaine paranoia from all parties, Noel's word became law and his mood dictated levels of conversation. He would often snap to people, 'Don't forget you work for me, mate.' It's easy to imagine that could have been taken many ways. That said,

BUY HERE NOW

Fans in stampede for Oasis album

Record seller . . . cover of Be Here Now

By JANE ATKINSON, Showbiz Reporter

OASIS fans went mad for the band's new album yesterday — snapping up one every TWO SECONDS.

Hundreds of shops opened at 8am to cope with the rush for Be Here Now.

Some sold well over 500 copies in the first 20 minutes. Many fans bought the album on CD, vinyl **AND** cassette.

At the HMV store in Oxford Street, **London**, Swedish tourist Gabriel Bjerner got his £13.99 CD at just 23 seconds past 8am.

The 18-year-old student, who had queued since 4am, said: "I feel great. I love Oasis and can't believe I'm the first to buy it."

In **Manchester**, **Liverpool** and **Leeds** there were queues of 300.

At HMV in **Manchester** – the band's home city – Martin Harrison, 17, waited nearly 11 hours.

Record

Martin, of Rochdale, said: "I've been a fan since the first album Definitely Maybe. The new one is just as good."

The album – Oasis's first in two years – is set to break records by reaching No 1 in three days.

That would beat Michael Jackson's Thriller, which took four.

Be Here Now is expected to trounce Oasis's last album (What's The Story) Morning Glory?, which sold 3.5million.

Tony French, of HMV in London, said yesterday: "I've never seen crowds like this." Nicki Strange, 16, queued from 6.30am, leaving her GCSE results unopened in **Ilford,** Essex. "I know they're bad anyway," she said.

HMV is confident of selling 100,000 copies of Be Here Now by the end of this week – making it the fastest selling album of all time in the UK."

● **DAD** Bob Drake – working in Bangkok for a Bradford firm – paid £40 to have the album flown out for daughter Sarah, 16.

The Sun Says— Page Eight

THUNDERWALL FINED

A GUITAR-playing Oasis fan was fined £100 for driving his neighbour up the Wonderwall.

Mark Hoey, 26, entertained pals by singing hits like Don't Look Back In Anger in the early hours.

But sleepless Melanie Gutman complained to council officials who told him to quieten down. When he struck up again he was fined and ordered to pay £250 costs by JPs in Abingdon, Oxfordshire.

Mark said: "My family is crazy about Oasis so we had a singalong." Miss Gutman, in her forties, refused to comment.

● **NOISY fans should "spare a thought for neighbours" before playing Be Here Now, said the Chartered Institute of Environmental Health.**

OASIS SPOT

SUN reporter Chris Pharo, 28, has named his son Connor Liam after girlfriend Kirsty, 27, gave birth in Bristol as Oasis played on TV in the background.

Noel *was* now in full control, being consulted on everything from TV appearances to logistics, wanting to stay in charge of what was now a fully-fledged business.

Backed by The Seahorses in Europe, John Squire would join Oasis onstage on a handful of occasions, the irony of one of Noel's heroes doing him a favour a perfect demonstration of the hierarchy.

Some people were allowed into the operation, and respected journalist and long-time friend of the band, Paolo Hewitt joined the tour as a DJ and later released a book outlining the experience.

Paolo Hewitt: 'It wasn't an open goal, but it was like, 'I've got to put this into the back of the net, because if I miss this it will be such a missed opportunity.' I call one of the chapters 'In The Eye of the Storm,' which is a George Harrison quote, I think. I was there in that storm so I would never, ever, ever again be in that storm. I will never be witness to this, I had to get it absolutely right, so it was pressure. And I was doing things like, you know... like the conversations that go on, it was me running back to my hotel room at four in the morning, scribbling down everything I could remember. And of course, waking up the next day looking at my notes, not being able to read one word. My handwriting was so bad, I probably had a couple of shandies. Yeah, there was a lot of that going on, and that took me a year. I think I started in '96 and wrote from January to October and was working like 10, 15-hour days.

'They're musicians. They play music to a very large amount of people, in itself a huge skill. That's what they did. What I did was DJ'd on tour with them, which was a really smart move because what it did was, if I'd gone on tour with them as the writer... if I'd walked into the dressing room, they would shut up. 'Oh right, the writer's here.' But they didn't, because I was Paolo the DJ. They kind of forgot I was writing a book, because they couldn't see me actually do it. At the end of each night, I'd go back to the hotel and write down everything I could remember, so there wasn't a sense of, 'Oh, be quiet, he's here,' but, 'There's Paolo, he's the DJ.' 'But musicians are honestly far looser. There was a lot of rows going on, a lot of fighting, there wasn't any, 'Calm down, don't do this in front of him,' Everything just evolved organically.'

Oasis closed the year with arena shows back home, three shows at The Point in Dublin, two at the SECC in Glasgow, two at Cardiff's International Arena, two at the G-Mex in Manchester, then three dates at Wembley Arena. The set was tweaked slightly from the earlier dates; 'Whatever' came and went, and 'Magic Pie' was replaced by 'Don't Go Away.' The second gig in Manchester was shown live on MTV, support for the tour provided by up and coming Scottish indie act Travis.
Zeb Jameson (touring keyboard player): 'A friend of mine, Ian McAndrew at

Wildlife Management, was managing Travis at the time and asked me to help them out on their first tour. We had some stadium shows with Oasis, so we were hanging out with them. They were great at supporting up and coming bands. That was really important to them, because they knew the journey themselves.'

Unfortunately, the first gig of this leg turned to misfortune, with Liam horrendously below scratch. It later became apparent that he was having problems with his throat, rather than extracurricular activities having an effect, and was ordered to rest to prepare for the big UK dates, and the next shows in Dublin. For the second and third shows Noel took over the responsibility of lead singer as well as guitarist, performing the majority of the standard set and reintroducing an acoustic set, comprising of 'Stand by Me' and 'Don't Go Away', with 'The Girl In The Dirty Shirt' added for night three. Later that night, Noel and mother Peggie were interviewed on Irish TV programme, *The Late, Late Show.*

More trouble occurred in Glasgow the same week; in the latter part of the set bottles were thrown on stage, and the band walked off stage, not to return. Tensions were high; combined with this, Liam reportedly didn't take his brother's success in Dublin well, and in Glasgow had a physical altercation with Mani, bassist of Primal Scream and formerly The Stone Roses. Having vented his frustration, Liam disappeared to Loch Lomond to mentally recharge. The ship had steadied by the time Oasis rolled into Manchester, the second night at the G-Mex broadcast on MTV, one of the only professionally recorded shows on the tour. They then wrapped up 1997's touring commitments at Wembley Arena, the 'doorman' hyping up the crowd dressed in a Santa Claus costume in acknowledgment of the season.

Elsewhere, on Christmas Day, BBC Radio One aired a special pre-recorded show called *Back to Mine* with DJ Sean Rowley (one of the figures on the cover of *(What's the Story) Morning Glory?*) interviewing Noel about his musical influences at Supernova Heights, his home base in Primrose Hill, north west London.

By the end of 1997, *Be Here Now* had sold eight million units, the band having achieved one No.1 and one No.2 single. The tour dates, entirely arena shows, all instantly sold out. But the tide was certainly starting to turn; after the elation of the third album simply existing, fans were coming to terms with a realisation that it simply wasn't as good as the first two. The critics took no time in validating those claims, and Oasis were now being spoken of in disparaging tones more frequently. But they just kept on rocking.

Thursday 4th December • Thursday 4th December • Thursday 4th December • Thursday 4th December
MCD PRESENT by arrangement with Primary Talent International
oasis
PLUS SPECIAL GUESTS
DUBLIN POINT THEATRE
THURSDAY 4th DECEMBER 1997 DOORS OPEN 7PM SHOW STARTS 8PM
ADMISSION £19.00 + booking fee (up to £2 maximum)
003446
STANDING AREA

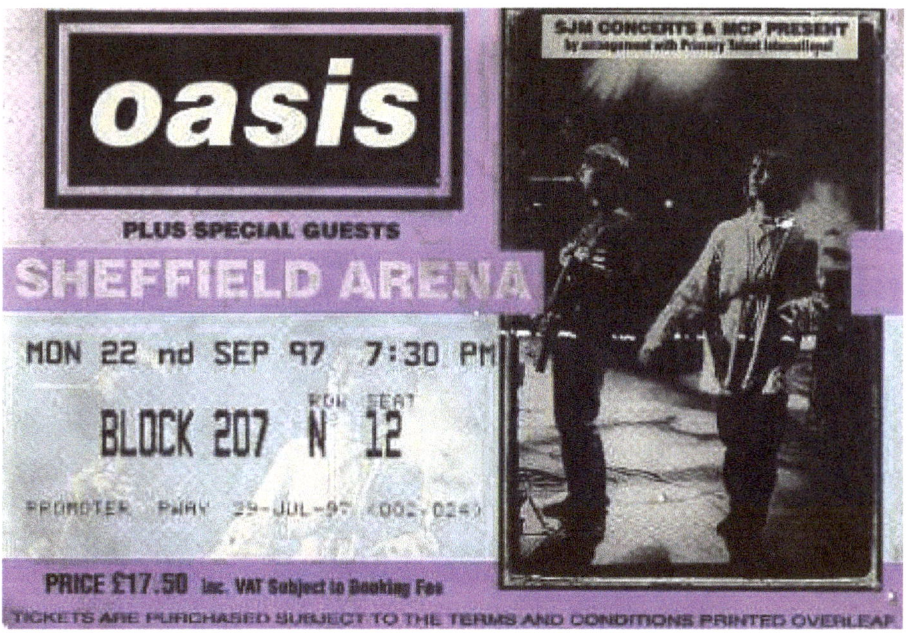
oasis
PLUS SPECIAL GUESTS
SHEFFIELD ARENA
MON 22 nd SEP 97 7:30 PM
ROW SEAT
BLOCK 207 N 12
PROMOTER PWAY 29-JUL-97 (002.024)
SJM CONCERTS & MCP PRESENT
PRICE £17.50 inc. VAT Subject to Booking Fee
TICKETS ARE PURCHASED SUBJECT TO THE TERMS AND CONDITIONS PRINTED OVERLEAF

OASIS
1998 CALENDAR

1998

'IN YOUR HEAD, DO YOU FEEL WHAT YOU'RE NOT SUPPOSED TO FEEL?'

The tour headed back over the Atlantic in early 1998, rocking through 13 North US and Canadian cities in January. The setlist was altered slightly, with Noel's cover of The Beatles' 'Help!' incorporated into his acoustic sets, as were 'Don't Go Away' and 'Talk Tonight'. At a later stage of the tour an acoustic version of 'Setting Sun' was also added. During the West Coast leg, Noel dropped into the King's Head pub in Santa Monica, California to play a short solo set on electric guitar, giving 'Slide Away' a rare airing. An acoustic version of 'Fade In-Out' was included in Atlanta, with Anthony Saffery, the sitar player of support band Cornershop joining Noel onstage. They then ventured over to Japan and Hong Kong, where the itinerary included three nights at the Budokan in Tokyo.

Jeff Slate: 'I loved that *Be Here Now* tour. It's their *Glass Spider* tour that people put down, but I thought they were on great form. That was the best moment live for that edition of Oasis. The way they tell it now is that it wasn't as much fun, but I think they were still having fun. It was pretty special. They'd cracked America a little bit at that moment. There was a core of diehard fans - especially in New York City, Philadelphia, Boston, DC, Chicago - who really loved them.'

Paolo Hewitt: 'There was a hint ... the drug thing is boring now, blah, blah, blah ... but by then it was a different kettle of fish. That *Be Here Now* tour was a slog. It wasn't fun anymore and, I think I say in (his book) *Forever The People,* all they kept talking about was 10 years previous, being stuck in a van going up to Leeds to play to one man and his dog and getting caught by the police or shenanigans like that. Because suddenly it became a job, it felt like a slog. It's funny, because I'd been on tours before, I think everything leading up to Knebworth was just magical and after Knebworth it started to become something completely different than what it had been. The fun kind of went from it really.'

Back on home turf, another unlikely collaboration was unveiled, Noel playing guitar on UK jungle icon Goldie's latest single, 'Temper Temper'. He also appeared in the video, with his now iconic Union flag guitar. Possibly a result of some of the parties at Supernova Heights, the single didn't receive much airplay despite the Oasis connections, but most likely because it wasn't radio-friendly. Largely ignored, it still managed to reach No.13 on the UK chart, Goldie's biggest hit.

Meanwhile, a third single was lifted from *Be Here Now* and, in an outrageous display of confidence, 'All Around The World' was the track selected (with 'Don't Go Away' later released as the third single in Japan). On the one hand, 'All Around The World' was the most pop-centric track on the album, so perfectly logical as a single choice, but on the other it was over nine minutes long. There were radio edits which condensed the best elements, but they failed to do justice to its grandeur. Backed with two tracks recorded prior to their fateful BBC Radio One interview ('The Fame' and 'Flashbax'), the release also contained a cover of the Rolling Stones' 'Street Fighting Man.' The accompanying video was the most daring and ludicrous by the band yet; essentially a *Yellow Submarine* pastiche, it consisted of the band performing in a spaceship, flying through a world of Terry Gilliam-style surrealism. And despite coldness towards the band from the mainstream press and the near hostility they were getting from music journalists, 'All Around The World' went straight in at No.1.

By this point *Be Here Now* was becoming regarded as a huge disappointment and apparently the most frequently found album at UK second-hand shops, while in America it struggled to stay in the top 100. Oasis were very much derided as being out of step with the times; as well as the aforementioned *OK Computer* and *Urban Hymns*, electronic pioneers The Prodigy's most recent LP, *The Fat Of The Land*, made big waves worldwide, fusing dance and rock together for a more exciting, innovative sound. Elsewhere, Blur completely turned their back on the wave of national pride Britpop had been such a focal point of, their self-titled fifth album embracing the lo-fi American sounds of Pavement and Dinosaur Jr. And Pulp were set to release what would be seen as their comedown album, *This Is Hardcore*, dealing with the trappings and negativity of fame. Meanwhile, normal service was resumed in the top 40; worldwide phenomenon the Spice Girls blazing a trail for pop acts to outsell guitar music once more.

Against this backdrop, the success of 'All Around The World,' although expected, set a standard. Oasis would have several more No.1 singles, but artistically to the media and general public they were now regarded as irrelevant, naught but a pop act who wrote their own songs. And as always, Noel sensed the mood, saying, 'Yeah, it's started. People are getting fed up with us, or we're not trendy anymore.'

Not that they cared. The *Be Here Now* tour was going well, with few signs of the trouble that plagued them on previous tours. The amount of cocaine coursing through the camp's veins ensured they were unmoved by any criticisms, Noel confirming, 'I don't resent people for not enjoying it. That doesn't matter to me. I'm going to enjoy whatever I do, because I could get run over by a bus tomorrow. This is like a party for us.'

That it was, but the back-lash did have a positive effect on Noel and Liam's relationship. In every interview they conducted around that time, the brothers were keen to mention the barbed comments Oasis had received from the rock fraternity. As well as George Harrison's words, Paul McCartney declared Oasis 'derivative,' saying, they 'mean nothing to me', while Keith Richards advised them to 'grow up.' Noel and Liam were both on the same page, albeit different editions; Liam continued his threats, while Noel took it all on the chin but defended his brother, arguing, 'You have to remember he's only 25. He's still a young kid. If you were 25 and in one of the biggest bands in the world, you'd probably be a bit of an arsehole as well.'

The siege mentality of 'us against the world' was back. The majority of those interviews took place in the US, but by the time of publication Oasis had moved on to the Far East, their three Japanese dates followed by another in Hong Kong.

Next up was a trip to Australia. Upon arrival in Perth, members of the entourage stepped off the plane and were immediately hit by the press, at a time when being mobbed at airports was still an occupational hazard. Members of the Oasis crew had apparently boarded the flight drunk, and over the course of the flight were said to have 'abused cabin crew and passengers, lit up cigarettes on a non-smoking flight, used obscenities, and behaved offensively' on the seven-and-a-half-hour flight.

Apparently, during the flight - thoroughly under the influence - Liam started throwing various items, one of which hit a fellow passenger. He then asked the stewardess for a scone, her refusal prompting Liam to hurl abuse at the woman. The pilot was brought out, and he also felt the wrath of the younger Gallagher brother.

Confronted by press the next day, Liam readily informed them that he had been told to calm down by 'some panhead who wants stabbing.' The Australian press then scrutinised every move the band made, primarily their internal flights. Liam was later banned from all Cathay Pacific airlines, yet the story didn't seem to put many people off; they played eight dates across Australia and New Zealand, in Perth, Adelaide, Melbourne, Sydney, Brisbane, Auckland and Wellington. On the interview circuit, Noel made disparaging comments about the still news-worthy Lady Diana, and Supernova Heights once again became a target, this time from Royal loyalists, according to the UK's Metropolitan Police.

Australia was surely to be the most troublesome part of the whole *Be Here Now* tour. As well as the Cathay Pacific incident, Liam was arrested for allegedly punching a child, the intended recipient a photographer who wouldn't leave the frontman alone. Allowed to walk free from court, he was released on bail for headbutting a minor. Trouble continued to mount as Huw Richards, the sound engineer who replaced Mark Coyle and had worked with Oasis for quite some time, quit. By happenstance though, Coyle had joined the band Down Under in a social capacity and was able to resume his old duties.

The various pressures were starting to get to Liam, who arrived onstage in Wellington absolutely plastered, missing vocal cues and generally shambolic. So bad was little brother that Noel threw his guitar to the floor and left the stage, the rest of the band following suit, with Liam booed as he left the stage. After a backstage confrontation, they concluded the set, with Liam continually booed as his brother was cheered. All concerned were happy to leave Australasia behind.

The last leg of the tour encompassed South America, specifically Chile, Argentina, Brazil and Mexico, taking them to the end of March. However, Liam's court appearance in Australia was still pending, and one evening he demolished a lift after a combustible cocktail of alcohol and frustration. This occurrence provided yet further insight into how much Liam was starting to mentally fray. It also saw them barred from another hotel.

More pleasingly, the brothers Gallagher were able to meet Argentinian footballing legend Diego Maradona, described by both as a life and career highlight. Elsewhere, Noel took a personal pilgrimage to Teotihuacan, a Mesoamerican pyramid site outside Mexico City, which he described as a spiritual experience. And at the last show in the Mexican capital, Noel announced to the crowd before 'Acquiesce', the closing number, 'Thanks to everyone that's come to all the gigs. We won't be coming back for a while but when we do come back, we'll be having it extremely fucking large.'

Although it had been troublesome, the tour ended on a pleasant note, Mark Coyle married his long-term girlfriend Ruth Farrell in Mexico, with Noel acting as best man and Liam as witness. The tour had taken in many corners of the world, spanning seven months and was regarded, by band members at least, as the most successful and fun time they'd had, despite the problems of its parent album. Now it was time to take stock and have that promised break. Noel could think about what direction he wanted Oasis to take, Liam could enjoy married life and maybe even write a song or two, and Bonehead, Guigsy and Alan could go back to their private lives. Ultimately, everyone went home happy, but things would never be the same again.

Paolo Hewitt: 'The *Be Here Now* tour kind of really did my head in a bit. It just wasn't fun anymore and they'd become rock stars, but I thought the idea was *not* to be rock stars. What disappointed me was they got into this Manc thing and it was all about ... I became the cockney cunt. I thought the whole thing was to escape where you were from, to be who you want to be, where you want to be. It just became cynical and, like I said, a machine.'

And then the silence. For the first time since the release of 'Supersonic', Oasis largely disappeared from the public eye. Their shadow still loomed over the music industry though, with West Yorkshire band Embrace in particular frequently compared to Oasis, by virtue of the fact they played anthemic rock and featured two brothers. Also, communal gatherings in the form of music festivals or open-air gigs soon become a regular fixture of the summer season, so the gaps were filled.

A large part of Noel's summer consisted of watching the FIFA World Cup, France '98, with one of his few public appearances as a guest on the popular David

Liam Gallagher in 1998

Baddiel and Frank Skinner-fronted TV success *Fantasy Football League*, newly switched to ITV, where Noel looked noticeably thinner than during the previous tour. He revealed how matches were often watched at Supernova Heights, ostensibly as the backdrop to massive parties with the great and the good. Noel later claimed that, at some point during the tournament, he woke up and greeted the new day by opening a can of Red Stripe and snorting a line of cocaine. And it was at that point that he decided enough was enough, announcing to his inner circle that he was giving up cocaine and drugs in general, saying, 'The giving up of gear itself was just, 'Do you want to be a junkie anymore?' 'No, I don't.' 'Let's stop taking drugs.' It was easy, but then I wasn't doing smack, and I wasn't an alcoholic.'

'I just wasn't gonna do it anymore. It wasn't doing my health any good and I couldn't focus on anything. I came off the road in March and carried on taking drugs every day, 'cos I had fuck all else to do. But by the end of April I thought, 'If this carries on, I'll be dead by Christmas.' So I packed it in, and about six weeks later I started writing songs.'

Noel later claimed that drug-taking had simply become boring, having spent around £1 million on cocaine, his decision having huge ramifications in his life. The party scene at his Primrose Hill home had to stop, and he began to move away from the circle of people that attended gatherings there.

Noel and partner Meg took action, moving out of London, ironically to buy himself a house, a very big house in the country ... on the edge of the Chiltern Hills in the leafy village of Chalfont St. Giles, Buckinghamshire. His music and the effect on Oasis would also be significant. He wrote and demoed a few songs in his new home studio, the track titles taking on a more pensive edge, including 'Gas Panic', 'Cigarettes in Hell' and 'Revolution Song'. And the lyrical content was less righteous, more reflective.

It wasn't well reported at the time, but Noel couldn't and didn't stay out of the ring for long. Unannounced every night, he played as support act for his friend Paul Weller on a handful of UK dates. Comprising short acoustic sets of six or seven songs, he performed a variety of Oasis classics, and on the first night in Wolverhampton performed a cover of The Jam's 'To Be Someone (Didn't We Have A Nice Time)'. Noel also appeared alongside heroes and friends at a benefit gig for the Liverpool dockers, cunningly titled *Rock The Docks*, the highlight of the set a performance of 'Magic Bus' by The Who, alongside Pete Townshend and Steve Cradock.

In the latter part of the summer, the first official solo Noel Gallagher track was released, Noel having been asked to contribute a track to the soundtrack of *The X-Files* movie. A sombre, atmospheric, keyboard-led instrumental called 'Teotihuacan', inspired by his excursion in Mexico during the *Be Here Now* tour, and again demonstrating another side to his songwriting. Frustratingly for the fans, it was only available as part of the soundtrack album, meaning they had to fork out for the whole CD. He also spent time out as a drummer on a dreaded 'side-project', a collaboration with Mark Coyle called Tailgunner.

Even though their reputation was on the wane in the UK, Oasis' star was in the ascendancy in other international markets, including the Far East and South America. In those territories it was only possible to own the first three studio albums, and those wanting to dig deeper into the catalogue, finding the B-sides, would be forced to spend money on expensive European singles imports. So it was decided that a compilation album, consisting only of B-sides, would be released, fortuitously in time for the Christmas market. Entitled *The Masterplan*, it was originally sold as having a tracklist assembled via a fans' vote on their new-fangled website (an alien concept back in 1998), though this idea was later dismissed. Noel put together 14 original tracks (discounting live or alternative versions) from the B-sides released so far, with only two ('Stay Young' and 'Going Nowhere') selected from the *Be Here Now* singles. There was much debate about the omissions, which was testament to the strength and quality of the options.

As well as a radio-only single release of lauded B-side, 'Acquiesce', with accompanying video (using live clips from the *Be Here Now* tour), there were interviews conducted for the album's launch, all by Noel. Little nuggets for the hardcore following were revealed within, such as the previously-untold story behind the crowd noise on 'I Am the Walrus'. The song itself was faded and cut by three minutes, with 'Listen Up' also trimmed, reducing the guitar solo by four bars. 'Stay Young' was only included at Liam's insistence, Noel thinking it 'too poppy', while it was divulged that the drums on 'The Swamp Song' were lifted from their 1995 Glastonbury performance. Noel also revealed that the only time he'd ever intended to write a B-side resulted in 'Cast No Shadow'. As far as he was concerned, there were either good songs or bad songs, which would explain the inclusion of some of his greatest songs as B-sides.

During the interviews he also ruled out presumptions that 'Acquiesce' was about his relationship with Liam. Noel later put the cover - which featured a child looking not unlike the main Oasis songwriter teaching a room full of children - down to drugs. He'd only been off them a few months, so either the cover was signed off in early 1998 or the effects were still raging. In those interviews he also revealed that he was writing shorter songs, with no backing harmonies, and that brackets in the titles were the order of the day. And Noel gave an insight into what he anticipated to be the next single, revealing, 'It starts with a drum loop and you'll go, 'That's not Oasis.' It's really short and catchy, it hasn't got a guitar solo, and there are no backing vocals ... there's a sort of hole in the song where everything goes swirly and mental – backwards stuff from *Camberwick Green*, Windy Miller dialogue, and then there's like a false key-shift which kicks the song into a totally new gear.'

The Masterplan reached a very impressive No.2 in the UK album charts upon its release in early November, and No.51 in the US Billboard Chart. Another of the tracks ('Half the World Away'), was receiving regular public exposure as the theme tune to a new, Manchester-set BBC comedy, *The Royle Family*. Both were gentle reminders of the power and yet tenderness that made people love Oasis in the first place, before the headlines and the excess had become the default perception.

■ BREAKING NEWS: Yesterday's M.E.N. front page story revealing that Guigsy, second from right, had quit Oasis

Oasis in turmoil as a second star quits

We'll carry on – definitely, maybe

Shell-shocked Liam and Noel Gallagher yesterday told the world that the latest departure from their band would not be the end for Oasis. But with fatherhood around the corner and riches assured, how long will they want to continue?

By ADAM MOSS

ALL boys, even the bad ones, eventually grow up. It takes some longer than others, that's all. But even if they have distractions like sell-out world tours or, say, a fourth album to record, they all grow up into men. Family men. They become fathers. That's when boyhood dreams finally die. There's no room left to dream of being a footballer or a pop star when your hair is receding and waistline expanding.

That's what has happened to rock's ultimate bad boys – Oasis.

First Bonehead calls it a day and then Paul 'Guigsy' McGuigan follows suit and yesterday hangs up his bass guitar. They're tired of being men inside boys' bodies. And both have youngsters of their own to look after. They are dads and they want to give their children their full-time attention.

That's something neither can do when they are constantly on the road or recording albums abroad.

It's something former bandmates Liam and Noel Gallagher will discover soon enough. They're both fathers-in-waiting. This time next year we could well be asking "What's The Story?" once again when the fiercely competitive siblings decide there aren't enough hours in the day to juggle rock stardom and parenthood.

In the end, they will do justice to neither. Something has to give. And as children have an annoying habit of making themselves too beautiful to put down it's a safe bet that the Oasis rock 'n' roll empire will be the thing that crumbles. Back in 1994, when Liam was belting out "All I want is cigarettes and alcohol" teenagers sat up and listened. It was an angry anthem for an adrenaline-fuelled youth, a generation previously doomed to sugary ballads from sickly-sweet boy bands. They lapped it up, every word, every snarl. And when Noel and Liam took swipes at each other, both verbally and physically, it was confirmation that they were still young, brash, and bored. These days a Gallagher spat is about as newsworthy as a rainy day and probably less commonplace.

■ OASIS DESERTED: But Liam and Noel vow to continue yesterday

The reason? They're too old now. Liam's too far removed from his teenage years to be afforded teenage respect when he rages at the establishment. Today, if he spits angry comments at the authorities, he's just laughed at.

It's the same with Noel and the rest of the band. They can't condemn the establishment any more because they ARE the establishment, certainly in rock 'n' roll terms. Now there's a story – "Oasis in Mainstream Shock". It matters not. It's the circle of life. And they've earned their money. It's only the desperate men who hang onto their boyhood dreams. The ones who haven't made their mark, earned their crust. If Bonehead and Guigsy were still Burnage boys working down the factory, I dare say they would still be lugging amplifiers and guitars up the staircases of Manchester's grimiest venues and vigorously joining in the local band merry-go-round billing themselves as "the next big thing".

As it stands, they've done their bit. Both have recorded their parts for the group's forthcoming fourth album. But they have had enough. So they've left Liam and Noel – the identifiable face of Oasis in any event – to carry the Mancunian supergroup into the new millennium.

Back to 1994 again. Liam sang Live Forever and the song became one of the Oasis classics, a fans' favourite. Why? Because even though commonsense tells us different, everyone likes to think the good times will keep on rolling indefinitely. The truth is that everything comes to an end.

Bonehead and Guigsy have paid their dues, sacrificed their privacy for long enough and earned secure futures for themselves and their families. Now they want to enjoy what they have built.

As for Liam and Noel, give them a bit more time. They've the extra burden of being the most famous. It will be twice as hard to ditch their public personas and retire gracefully from the limelight. They have a bit more dreaming to do yet, a few more indulgences to satisfy. Then they'll discover Pampers.

1999

'LET'S ALL MAKE BELIEVE THAT WE'RE STILL FRIENDS AND WE LIKE EACH OTHER'

Four years on, Tony McCarroll still had unfinished business with Oasis. In the aftermath of his sacking, McCarroll commenced legal action against the band, claiming he was denied up to £18 million income, suing the band accordingly. Fortunately for all concerned, on the first day of the trial in March 1999, McCarroll settled, waiving all rights to Oasis material past, present and future. The settlement fee for Tony's share of future royalties on which he played was bought out for a figure in the region of £600,000.

Paul Ashbee: 'This legal battle he got into with them, he became obsessed with it. But it wasn't about the money. The poor lad was fucking lost. It was awful watching that. It was terrible. He was so badly advised, so for him to go back and do it again was crazy. He got lost, but it was understandable. When you come back to Burnage, Levenshulme, people hated Oasis because they were jealous. They'd hammer you for it. People were horrible.'

With enough new songs under his belt and feeling refreshed after his year off, despite the effects of cocaine withdrawal, Noel called the band to reconvene, rehearsing songs at Bermondsey's Music Band studios in London. Then, towards the end of March, Oasis decamped to the South of France to Chateau de la Colle Noire studios to begin recording sessions, Mark 'Spike' Stent brought in for production duties in an attempt to overhaul their trademark sound. Long had it been Noel's intention to revamp their signature style, and it seemed that his dalliances with Goldie and The Chemical Brothers had given him new ideas.

Spike had a few notable credits to his name, including U2's *Pop* two years earlier, and Noel opted to ditch all previously-used equipment, purchasing older guitars and pedals. The lack of a deadline, for the first time, allowed him to take his time.

Galvanised by getting back to the day job, Noel requested that Liam refrain from drinking alcohol throughout the entire period they were in France. Liam agreed, perhaps conscious of an opportunity for some creative control or that the opinions he offered when sober were more likely to be considered. Alternatively, it may have been that simply, in a first for the wild youngster, the band was deemed more important than the occupational hazards. Not only that, but he had a song of his own to offer, having penned an ode to his seven-year old stepson, 'Little James'. While a little simplistic, with some questionable lyrical choices, the song was an unheralded beauty, Noel believing it would be for the greater good to encourage Liam to contribute more in the songwriting department. And it was the first time a song written by a member of the band other than Noel was recorded and released.

It was decided that if Liam was abstaining it was only fair that the rest of the band should too. Marijuana was Guigsy's poison of choice, and it seemed it was unlikely to be a problem for him. It was for others though.

Records of their time in the South of France are scarce, particularly in comparison to the detailed analysis that now exists for the first three albums. It seemed that the sessions were rumbling along fine, but perhaps fuelled simply by boredom (Noel was even more hands on than before, no doubt aware that the personal content of the songs and structure required a much more attentive eye) Bonehead started drinking once more, his preferred tipple as always red wine. In the South of France, access wouldn't have been too difficult. In the aftermath Noel claimed Bonehead broke into a sound engineer's bedroom and poured red wine all over him while he slept.

Like several before him, Bonehead had become disillusioned with Oasis. It had become a business machine, a sad but inevitable result of their fame. The touring had taken its toll and having recently become a father, Bonehead was struggling with being away from his newly-enhanced family. The prospect of having to do so again in the near future, for a longer time, also held little appeal. In later years he would elaborate, explaining that he felt Oasis had stopped being fun and he would be betraying himself, the rest of the band and the fans by pretending otherwise. And so, in early August 1999 he quit and returned to England. It was described by all parties as amicable. A week later, the more introverted Paul McGuigan followed suit and returned to England, resigning by sending a fax to Ignition, announcing his desire to quit the rock'n'roll lifestyle. Noel never heard from him again.

Mary McGuigan: 'It's weird that Paul was quite shy and introverted yet was in what is seen as one of the biggest bands the world has ever seen. That seems a bit weird, but he was always at the back and kind of anonymous. He didn't like fame, didn't like the attention. He's just not that kind of person. I cannot believe, to this day, that he ever got up on stage. Any stage, even in a pub.'

Steve White: 'I can't speak for Guigs but I think people just expect to know everything about everything nowadays and why isn't he on Twitter? Because he doesn't want to do Twitter. And why isn't he on Facebook? Because he doesn't want to be on Facebook.'

Paolo Hewitt: 'It just became a machine, Oasis. Once Guigsy and Bonehead left, it was like when Ronnie Lane left the Faces, that was the end of them. They went on (for) another two years but that was the end of the Faces really. And once Guigsy and Bonehead left, that was the end of Oasis really.'

Mat Whitecross: 'It was originally his (Guigsy's) band. He was the one who had the idea about a band, before he even had an idea of how to pick up a guitar. He fell out with the management.'

Iain Robertson: 'The iteration of the band that made the most sense is the Alan White, Bonehead, Guigsy, Liam and Noel iteration. The point at which you lose people like Bonehead and Guigsy is when you've lost something intrinsic and really important. For me, and it's a subjective thing, that was kind of an end to it. I suspect, knowing Bonehead, it was as much as anything, 'This isn't fun anymore'. There's a machine to feed.

'Guigs and Bonehead were remarkably ordinary human beings. Always grounded, even with all the chaos around them, Guigs particularly. Guigs settled into a happy domesticity pretty early on, actually. I remember Guigs boasting to me that he'd just taken an apartment on the Finchley Road and he had two washing machines. What more does any man need?'

Mary McGuigan: 'It was always Bonehead's band. It will always be Bonehead's band. The day Bonehead left I cried like a baby. Because that was it. It was over. He was the spirit, the soul and the spine. He was everything. Without him it doesn't exist.'

Their departure resulted in Noel having to re-record Bonehead and Guigsy's parts on the record for legal reasons. With the benefit of hindsight, it's not difficult to see the way the wind was blowing. *Standing on the Shoulder of Giants* is arguably Noel's first solo album, as he plays every instrument on the album bar the drums, stoically provided by Alan White. But even they weren't untouched by Noel's influence, with loops on several tracks. For capable musicians this would have been frustrating, especially if there had been reservations about continuing at all. It stands alone in the Oasis canon, being unlike any of the albums before or after it. It's contemplative with luxuriant, perhaps excessive, production, and lyrically it's the perfect example of a 'comedown' album, 'Gas Panic!' gave an insight into the panic attacks Noel was experiencing post-cocaine, while 'Where Did It All Go Wrong?', 'Sunday Morning Call' and 'Roll It Over' discussed the travails and shallow nature of fame.

Nick Amies (writer and journalist): 'It kind of stands out because of its weirdness. It's not connected to the first part and it's not connected to the second. It was kind of, 'We need to regroup, recover and find a new way of being Oasis.' Maybe it was a false start. Most people considered it a stopgap.

'Noel said himself on numerous occasions he was creatively bereft at that time. When the main songwriter says the songs are not his best, what are you supposed to believe?

'They made that step and they took that chance to make something a bit different.

'That period has some very, very good songs which never made it onto that album. One of Noel's decisions to put the songs on the tracklist was when Liam came in with 'Little James.' He said, 'It goes on the album because if I say it's shit, he's never gonna write another one.' People may argue that Noel missed a trick there!'

Whatever the reasons, two founder members quitting in the space of two weeks smacks of a crisis, so a press conference was hastily called, at the Water Rats in London, where the band made their live London debut five years earlier, to calm the storm and put any speculation to bed. Liam and Noel for once put on a united front, never looking more like brothers, both clad in uniform sunglasses and long hair. Meanwhile, Alan White wasn't in attendance as he 'couldn't be arsed to get out of bed.'

Outlining the reasons for the double departure without revealing too much, Noel was as defiant and garrulous as ever, delivering the immortal line, 'It's hardly Paul McCartney leaving The Beatles.' The message was clear; Oasis were going to keep on rocking, as they always had. As far as Noel was concerned, from a musical perspective Bonehead and Guigsy weren't going to be missed too much, although unquestionably the dynamic of the band would change once more. The common perception of Oasis was that it was the Gallaghers plus others, and this was now affirmed internally as well.

But no band can exist with two people, and with another worldwide tour on the horizon, replacements were needed, and quickly. Subsequently, Colin 'Gem' Archer, formerly of Creation label-mates Heavy Stereo, was swiftly brought in, ostensibly on rhythm guitar, in time to film the video for lead single 'Go Let It Out.' Replacing Guigsy took a while longer, with auditions taking place over a week. As for who actually auditioned, we'll probably never fully know, although it was later confirmed by several people - including New Order's Peter Hook - that David Potts of the band Monaco (Hooky's side-project) was among the candidates. Potts later claimed he opted not to pursue the project, citing a not unjustified concern of being sacked within weeks.

MONEYBAGS Noel Gallagher may be one of the richest rockers in Britain, but Oasis are dobbing out a miserly £85-A-DAY to new guitarist Gem.

The former Heavy Stereo musician, who replaced Paul 'Bonehead' Arthurs last month, won't get **ANY** royalties from the fourth Oasis album Standing On The Shoulder Of Giants.

And worst of all, his services are only required full-time by the band until the end of this year!

Gem's paltry pay deal means he is on about £600 a week–give or take a few brass farthings for his bus fares . . .

An Oasis insider said last night: "Gem is on a flat wage of £600, paid into his bank account each week by Oasis management company Ignition.

"This will be increased to £1,200 when he's touring. But the only dates the band have secured are three radio station gigs in America."

The wage, which works out at £31,200 a year if the band don't tour is an insult compared to the millions the Gallaghers have raked in.

MILLIONS: Noel

Manchester City fan Noel, 32, is estimated to have earned a whopping £9 million last year while Liam, Bonehead, drummer Steve White and former bass player Paul 'Guigsy' McGuigan got a cool £2.7 million each.

Villa

Noel owns a £2 million mansion in Bucks, his £500,000 Supernova Heights pad in London and is trying to buy Mike Oldfield's £2 million villa in Ibiza.

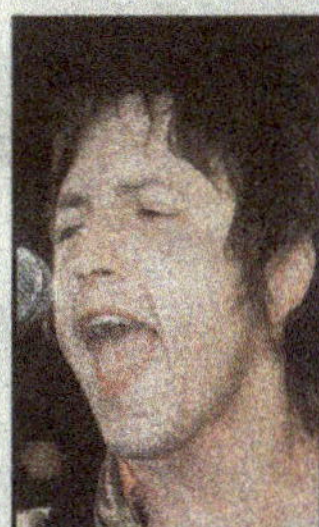

HARD-UP: Gem

The star also has a £10 million personal publishing deal with music giants Sony and earns £34 every time one of his songs is played on the radio.

Liam owns a £1.5 million home in London's Primrose Hill which he shares with wife Patsy and son Lennon.

Despite quitting the band in August, Bonehead and Guigsy will still receive royalties from the new album after its release on February 29 next year–as well as royalty cash for the first three LPs.

LOADED: Liam

Meanwhile poor newcomer Gem won't make any money because the album was written and recorded before he joined. And it still isn't clear if he will receive equal profits from touring and merchandise.

But it doesn't seem to bother the 27-year-old. He said: "Rehearsals with the band are going fine. It feels really good and natural. I like all the songs on the new album. Noel says there are two s*** ones, but I don't know what he's on about."

Gem's first live appearance with Oasis will be at a promotional gig for the US radio Station Y100 in Philadelphia on December 3, where the band will play just five songs. Gigs will follow in Chicago on December 4 and Detroit on December 5.

Gem is reluctant to confirm the job. He said: "Easy, easy. We'll see. I'm minding my ps and qs."

Don't bother, mate. Forget Wonderwall–if you ask me, you're getting Wunderpaid!

Additional reporting: MAXINE CREEDY

Upon hearing a radio announcement that Andy Bell, formerly of shoegaze pioneers Ride and latterly indie also-rans Hurricane #1 (arguably best known for two songs being used commercially; 'Only The Strongest Will Survive' featured on a TV ad for tabloid *The Sun*, and 'Step Into My World', as continuity music for *Match of the Day*) was joining London act Gay Dad, Liam proposed to Noel that they hijack the move and bring him in on bass. Noel wasn't sure if Bell played bass, but Liam put forward the argument that if he could play guitar, he could in all likelihood play bass. One phone call later their target understandably chose one of the biggest bands in the world over a band called Gay Dad.

Elsewhere in the summer of 1999, a further collaboration between The Chemical Brothers and Noel Gallagher saw the light of day, with 'Let Forever Be' taken from the dance act's third album and released as a single. While not as successful as 'Setting Sun' three years earlier, it still received considerable airplay and was a fillip for fans becoming starved of Oasis product.

Better still was to come later in the summer. For whatever reason, a tribute album to The Jam was compiled and released, *Fire & Skill: The Songs of The Jam* featuring cover versions of a number of their songs performed by contemporary artists, and bookmarking the album were two Oasis contributions. At the end was an acoustic, Noel-sung cover of *All Mod Cons*' 'To Be Someone (Didn't We Have A Nice Time)', the lyrics of the excesses and disappointment of the rock star lifestyle seemingly especially pertinent to Oasis' main wordsmith, who had covered the song live the previous year. And up front, the only single released from the LP (a double A-side with Buffalo Tom's take on 'Going Underground') was a version of *The Gift*'s 'Carnation', with Liam on vocals and Noel on guitar, Steve Cradock and Damon Minchella from Ocean Colour Scene, Steve White and Paul Weller himself on keys making up the band. The single reached No.6 in the UK Charts and the collective performed on *Top of the Pops*, the sight of Liam and Noel on television screens across the nation providing a nice teaser for the next album.

That December, Oasis played their first shows with their new line-up, a series of low-key dates in the US, the debut appearances of Gem Archer and Andy Bell taking place at Philadelphia's First Union Centre. The band did four short sets as part of some Christmas radio festivals, including *KROQ*. They didn't play any new songs, but included a cover of The Beatles' loud and dirty 'Helter Skelter'. During the same month the band also announced their live return to the UK, with a series of stadium shows to take place the following summer, including two nights at Wembley Stadium. As ever, the gigs sold out within a few hours, without a note of new music being heard. With the replacements in tow, rehearsals for the forthcoming world tour began, Noel confident in the new band, the latest additions arguably of considerably higher proficiency musically than the previous incumbents.

Despite high-profile shows at Dublin's Lansdowne Road and Bolton's Reebok Stadium, Wembley was where all roads were leading. Adding to the romance of playing the country's best-known venue ('It is *the* most prestigious gig in the world, along with Madison Square Garden,' claimed Noel in January 2000) was the realisation that the national stadium was due to be demolished shortly after, to make way for a more modern, purpose-built, entertainment arena.

Noel was typically bullish about the new line-up, confidently stating during the early rehearsals that 'by the time we get to Wembley, we'll be incredible.' It clearly meant a lot to him to be playing such an iconic and historic venue, his ambition dovetailing nicely with his sentimentality. Before that however, there was an album to be launched and promotion to undertake. But the problems were seemingly endless in that period, the latest being Creation's ceasing of operations in late 1999.

Since selling a large share of the company to Sony before signing Oasis, Alan McGee and Creation co-founder Dick Green were no longer enjoying the spontaneity of running a label where the artists came first, the label itself stumbling as guitar bands again became *de rigueur*. So the pair decided to wind up Creation Records, with the final release to be Primal Scream's forthcoming album *XTRMNTR*. It was said that Liam didn't take the news particularly well, feeling that McGee, in particular was abandoning the band just when they needed him. Noel, as ever, was more sanguine.

Ergo, one of the biggest-selling bands in the world found themselves in the unusual position of being essentially without a label. The fact that Oasis had always been part of Sony Records, a label very much solvent but licensed to Creation, always seems to be forgotten. Oasis were going to sign with Sony, 'over my dead body,' according to Noel, but one assumes the licensing and the fact that they were midway through a six-album deal must have caused complications. In the end it was decided that they had little choice but to set up their own label, Big Brother, to deal with the album release in the UK and Ireland, Sony looking after distribution as before.

That would have only added to the to-do list that already included publicity for the forthcoming album, promotion via singles and TV appearances, the album itself, and that worldwide tour. Indeed, Noel stated on several occasions that he had no time to commit to Big Brother and would have liked to set it up as a traditional label, i.e. signing bands. But he had pesky distractions to contend with, the first of which was the release of the lead single from the album, 'Go Let It Out.'

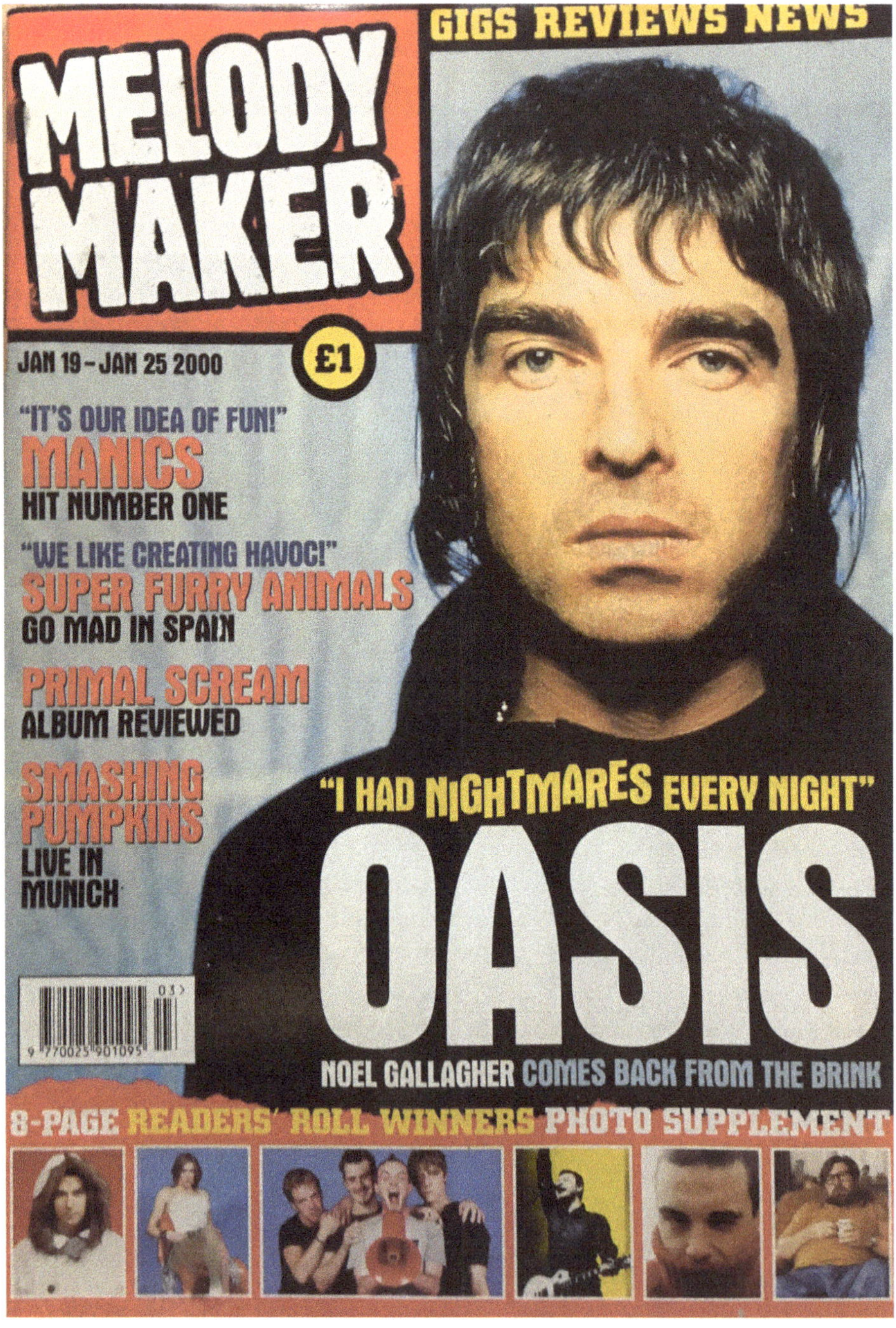
GIGS REVIEWS NEWS
MELODY MAKER
JAN 19 – JAN 25 2000
£1
"IT'S OUR IDEA OF FUN!"
MANICS
HIT NUMBER ONE
"WE LIKE CREATING HAVOC!"
SUPER FURRY ANIMALS
GO MAD IN SPAIN
PRIMAL SCREAM
ALBUM REVIEWED
SMASHING PUMPKINS
LIVE IN MUNICH
"I HAD NIGHTMARES EVERY NIGHT"
OASIS
NOEL GALLAGHER COMES BACK FROM THE BRINK
8-PAGE READERS' POLL WINNERS PHOTO SUPPLEMENT

2000

'IT'S WHERE WE BOTH BELONG, IT'S GONNA BE FULL ON'

If all that wasn't enough, the tide of public opinion had significantly turned against Oasis. In Britain, pop had once again regained its dominance, with the awfully-termed 'nu-metal' rap/rock output of bands like Limp Bizkit covering any guitar requirements labels had. In the indie sphere, Travis hoovered up all awards and accolades before them with second album *The Man Who*. Sensing the pendulum swinging away from them (or causing it to do so), the music and national press had the knives out for the Gallagher brothers.

The Guardian, hardly the biggest flagbearers for the band, wasted no time in panning 'Go Let It Out', declaring it as 'looking set to flop spectacularly... as retailers place small orders for the single.' They went on to quote Matthew Kreuzer of retail chain *Our Price* saying there was a 'general view the band had never moved on musically.' And later disgraced industry mogul Jonathan King was quoted as saying, 'Oasis have passed their sell-by date, I'm afraid.'

However, in February 2000 'Go Let It Out' debuted at No.1 in the UK and Irish singles charts, with all the usual bells and whistles of TV performances and video. Due to new chart rulings introduced during their sabbatical, it contained only three songs on the CD as opposed to the four that the band always included. Whilst the song was different enough but still recognisably Oasis, the B-sides ('Let's All Make Believe' and '(As Long as They've Got) Cigarettes In Hell') were indications of the album to come. The former stands out as one of Liam's best-ever vocal performances, doing justice to the lyrics, which seemed to be an insight into the breaking down of band relations. The video, filmed before Andy Bell joined, featured Noel on bass.

Three weeks later, *Standing on the Shoulder of Giants* was released. Despite mixed (at best) reviews, the album also went straight in at No.1, selling more than 310,000 copies in its first week. The title came, according to Noel, from his misreading of an inscription on the new £2 coin. The full and accurate Isaac Newton quote read, 'If I have seen further, it is by standing on the shoulders of giants.' Inspired (and drunk), Noel claims to have written the latter part on a cigarette packet as a reminder but omitted the 's' on shoulders. Undeterred, it became the title regardless.

Brian Cannon: 'It was all change at the office, basically. Half the band's gone, Owen didn't produce it, I didn't do the sleeve, Noel came up with a new logo. I think him and Gem did it. I think everyone's in agreement that was a bad idea.

It was a funny time. Looking back on it, I'm kind of glad that the last thing I did was what I did.'

As part of the promotion, Oasis had a special episode of *Later … with Jools Holland* dedicated entirely to them. They also played a live session on BBC Radio One, which included a competition in which listeners could nominate a song for the band to cover, with one of the options (finishing in second place) Blur's 'Country House'. The Who's 'My Generation' was the eventual winner.

More interesting to the media however was a brewing war of words between Liam and pop's golden boy, Robbie Williams. It all stemmed from a classic Noel barb about Williams being 'the fat dancer from Take That.' The highly-emotional, highly-competitive Williams responded with a funeral wreath, a note containing the message, 'To Noel Gallagher, RIP. Heard your latest album – with deepest sympathy, Robbie Williams.' For once Noel adopted a dignified silence, perhaps refusing to once again get into a war of words with another prominent pop star.

Colin Paterson: 'One of my first big jobs was working on (Channel 4's) *The Big Breakfast*. Around about the time of the fourth album there was a meeting between the record company and *The Big Breakfast*. The decision was that they would have access to that Oasis world tour. We would visit them constantly and the whole thing would be turned into a live DVD, made in conjunction with Oasis. I was the guy tasked with doing this. I was really young, and this was quite a big deal. So, they said, 'Just treat it as separate news reports and we'll see what we can get.'

'I went to the album launch party the night before I flew out to Japan with Oasis. I remember going to the party, doing interviews with people and asking Kelly Jones from Stereophonics, 'What have Oasis got?' And he went, 'Well, they're just AC/DC. Every song sounds the same … but it's a great song.' That was my memory of that party.

'The next day I had to fly to Japan with the band. I had to meet them at Heathrow and do those shots of Liam pushing the trolleys through (the airport). It was at the time that Robbie Williams - who had been their great mate, dancing with them at Glastonbury - and (the band) fell out. And then there was the whole Liam dating Nicole (Appleton) aspect. At this time, when *Standing on the Shoulder of Giants* came out. Robbie Williams sent a wreath to Noel Gallagher.

'At the airport I said to Liam, 'So, you're flying to Japan. What are the chances of you sending Robbie Williams a postcard?' He looked straight into the camera and went, 'You can tell that cunt that if I see him anywhere, I'm gonna break his nose. I'm angry about this, you're a dead man.' Something like that. I gave this tape to the runner, who took it back to *The Big Breakfast*. Absolute gold. Flying on the plane thinking, 'What are they gonna do with this?' *The Big Breakfast* led with it the next day.

'We arrived off the plane in Japan. It was the very early days of mobile phones. The PR was switching on this brick and the thing is going ballistic! While we've been on the plane to Japan, it's broken. It was the lead story; 'Liam challenges Robbie to a fight.' Then you'll remember Robbie Williams stands up at the Brits, wins an award and goes, '£100k of your money, £100k of mine, any time, any place, anywhere.' So, I caused that!

'I'd left the Oasis tour by the time of the Brits, but Noel told me at a later date Liam went absolutely crazy when that happened. I think there was a foot through a TV in Japan.'

What Williams was alluding to, during that Brit Award acceptance speech, was an offer to fight Liam in a boxing ring, with each putting £100,000 of their own money in, presumably with a winner takes all outcome.

Disappointingly at the time, but with hindsight thankfully, Liam refused, branding Williams a 'fucking idiot' and claiming it sent the wrong message to fans. It was probably the only time that year that Liam rose above a distasteful situation. However, Noel later commented that the first section of that tour was all about Liam and Robbie Williams, an early indicator of his dissatisfaction regarding Liam's antics.

The *Standing on the Shoulder of Giants* tour started at the end of February 2000, in Yokohama, Japan. A strange choice but perhaps somewhat indicative of the fragile state of the band's confidence (despite the usual soundbites, Noel was in a much more reflective mood, fatherhood no doubt playing on his mind). The gig proved to another indicator of the problems to come; after Liam fluffed a line on 'Stand By Me,' Noel rebuked him on stage, stating, 'If you turned up at rehearsals you'd know the words. Perhaps if we had the speakers plugged into the nearest pub, we'd be alright.' So far, so Gallagher.

Colin Paterson: 'I got to walk around Tokyo with them. We went to a shop which only sold Beatles and Oasis memorabilia, which was quite extraordinary. They sold Man City shirts in a shop in this market in Tokyo! We showed them around. They tried out guitars in a guitar shop. Then I got to interview them both at a Japanese garden in the hotel. I remember Liam was obsessed with *The Big Breakfast* newsreader at the time, he kept saying, 'Hello to Phyllis Gale.' I got to see them at the Yokohama Arena that night.'

'There was one other journalist with me - Dominic Mohan of *The Sun*. I don't think Oasis were so pleased that he was around. I remember Liam saying, 'I went into the toilet and he followed me in.'

The tour rolled through Asia, then on to North America via some small dates in Europe across April. On their third night in Japan, Liam had to stop singing because of vocal problems during the fifth song of the set, 'Acquiesce,' Noel picking up seamlessly then stepping up to provide lead vocals for the rest of the show.

In the States the band selected an unusual song for their performance on *The David Letterman Show,* the much-derided 'I Can See A Liar.' They had only performed the track on a handful of dates on the tour and it would never be played again. Meanwhile, the setlist was fine-tuned over the course of that leg of the tour, with 'Sunday Morning Call,' 'Some Might Say' and 'D'You Know What I Mean?' all receiving early airings but swiftly disappearing.

Zeb Jameson: 'I got a call from Mike Rowe (touring keyboard player) saying they needed someone to come out and cover for him and join the band. He was going off to write with Sheryl Crow. I was at a family party and the look on people's faces ... I said I'd have to call people back and work it out. No-one could believe I'd even said that; this is Oasis! You can't not go and play with Oasis. My name came from three different sources.

'It was a case of having a couple of sessions with him (Mike Rowe), flying out to the west coast of America, shadowing him for five shows and then jumping into the hot seat when we got to Vegas.

'I found it really inspiring hanging out with the guys. They were all so enthused by music. Backstage at the venues there would be a room with a studio, a room with a guitar and amp. There was a lot of writing on that journey. That's when Liam was writing a lot of songs. We were all supporting each other in our songwriting talents. It was a very constructive time in that way. Songwriting is about confidence, so if you're getting support from other musicians, you're going to get the best out of each other.

'When we were in Philadelphia I ducked into a studio and I was putting down some songs. There was one song, 'Jetsonian,' that Liam really loved. He was putting it on before each show. Noel was like, 'If you're going to play that song before every show, could you at least play the version without the click track?' I was recording them to send back home (to my band)!

'It was declared that it was dry bus. The reality of sharing a tour bus with the guys ... I was quite apprehensive. I was really put at ease, they were brilliant. The first thing I got on the bus was Noel saying, 'I'm going to call him Bez, because it's Zeb backwards.' I really didn't want to be the Bez of Oasis, to be honest!

'It felt like the *Sgt. Pepper* era of Oasis, with 'Go Let It Out,' 'Who Feels Love?,' 'Gas Panic' ... they were more theatrical songs. As a keyboard player there were some really great keyboard parts in that, and drum loops. It was a lot more experimental.

'If you watch the (*Familiar to Millions*) DVD, they worked live, those tunes. People loved them, it was a whole other dimension to the Oasis tunes. It felt very experiential, that psychedelic stuff that was going on.

'We were all hanging out together all the time. There was no going back to the hotel after soundcheck, it was as much about the sociality of being on tour together. We'd still be chatting about things as we walked on stage. It was literally, put your cup of tea down and walk on stage.

'(There was) no rehearsal stuff. I think I went outside to the studio in the country for rehearsal once in that time. We'd jam stuff in soundchecks. The songs had been decided. All the other music we were playing was just jamming. Noel would run through stuff, different tracks to experiment with. We were changing the set around a bit, so you were told which tracks were being played and then you learnt it.'

Colin Paterson: 'I was going to do interviews with them (Gem and Andy) later in the tour. I got to interview them once more in Hamburg but after that everything kicked off in Oasis. I think it was the beginning of them starting to fall apart, and we had all access to the tour revoked. *The Big Breakfast* documentary strangely didn't happen! You will never find that anywhere on YouTube. It got to Japan, and it got to Hamburg. Something was going terribly wrong on that tour. '

'I remember Alan White was very much on board by then. I was chatting to him and went, 'So when I do the feature on you later in the tour, what are your interests?' He went, 'How about filming me having a round of golf?' Perhaps I should have known that things were going to go wrong there!'

Meanwhile, back in the UK, *Standing on the Shoulder of Giants* prolonged its 'failure' with second single, 'Who Feels Love?' (backed with 'One Way Road' and their cover of 'Helter Skelter') charting at No.4 in April. Then, in May 2000 the tour moved on to mainland Europe, playing a date in each in Lisbon, Leganes and Marseille. On May 20, the band were due to play in Spain again, this time in Barcelona. At the soundcheck, in apparently good spirits, they swapped instruments and played some Beatles numbers. Liam was by all accounts, bizarrely, on drums. Unfortunately, drummer Alan White had problems with his arm, (it seized up) and the gig had to be pulled. The crew then had to go about dismantling the stage-set, and the band had a few hours to kill. There was also a full rider, containing San Miguel, vodka, and no doubt numerous other alcoholic possibilities. Boredom and alcohol are never a good combination, especially in a band that could be as toxic as Oasis.

Fuelled by booze, a fight broke out between Liam and Noel. The reasons weren't disclosed at the time, but there were rumours flying around within certain social circles that it related to disparaging remarks concerning Noel and his wife, Meg.

As the alcohol flowed, a jovial mood turned into something more sinister, Liam making a comment to Noel, or in Noel's presence. What was disclosed is that the altercation that followed was one of their more violent. What was described as a 'proper brawl' ensued.

Noel later recalled that, as he was on top of Liam, throwing punches and splitting his lip, the thought, 'He didn't really say that, did he?' was going through his head. That, no doubt combined with the other resentments and irritations that being in confined spaces for weeks at a time and copious amounts of alcohol coursing through the system will foster, resulted in Noel immediately quitting the tour.

It's worth noting at this point that both Liam and Noel were undergoing severe problems in their personal lives; Noel split up with Meg - the pair's daughter Anais having been born in January that year - shortly after, so one can presume their personal issues had become insurmountable and as such were ongoing at that point. As for Liam, his high-profile marriage to actress Patsy Kensit was in its death throes, so factoring in those issues as well as the hurdles Oasis were having to surmount, it's entirely understandable that tensions were high. They are only human, after all.

Zeb Jameson: 'We were at the hotel for three days while another guitarist was brought to cover Gem's parts, and then he covered Noel's parts. We carried on with Liam at the helm. It was disconcerting because they had their usual blow up. It came about because we couldn't play a show in Barcelona as Alan White had hurt his wrist. So we were just sat in the dressing room the whole time, hanging out and drinking. It just escalated. It was really hard to witness that, so I had to leave. Everything got rearranged. It was quite a traumatic thing. I left before the end of the debacle. I stepped outside of that very personal situation and just carried on doing my job. It was hard on everyone.'

Noel later went on to claim that the fallout wasn't about anything particularly important, but for the good of the tour he decided to quit (a unique take on events), although he probably felt justified in leaving Liam in the lurch with a tour to complete.

From a fan's perspective, the main concerns were (a) the summer shows, as several thousands of people had tickets and would have made plans for a big day, and (b) the band itself. Those fans had put all their stock and love into Oasis, and even though this situation of personnel changes within the band was familiar, it had been a few years since something so dramatic had happened mid-tour. Since the band had been through such upheaval recently it was felt that anything could happen - nothing was off the table. However, it will have given the faithful a

degree of satisfaction to hear that their beloved band were still making headlines and Noel would be re-joining for the UK dates, and the band would be carrying on after all.

Shortly after, press reported that Noel had quit the tour and possibly the band altogether. This had happened several times before, most notably in 1996, so the British press were having a field day. But in this instance, after pulling a couple of gigs, the remaining members of the band (i.e. Liam and Whitey, the others still being on salaries at this point) regrouped and then took the unprecedented step of carrying on, drafting in a replacement for Noel on lead guitar.

Utilising their networks, they found Matt Deighton, most recently of acid jazz quartet Mother Earth. Deighton had worked with Paul Weller, was immediately available and was a more than capable guitarist, so was drafted in at short notice. Once Gem (in the band for less than a year at this point) had given Deighton a crash course on the setlist, the tour re-commenced with Gem on lead axe. A statement was released shortly after that Noel had quit all overseas touring with immediate effect.

Naturally, another 'war of words' continued across the tabloids, desperate to milk this latest round of stories for all they were worth. Noel stated that he was not prepared to play outside the UK again, and that Liam had become 'too big for his boots.' Liam dismissed the row as nothing serious, perhaps attempting to defuse an already explosive situation. Noel returned to England and kept a low profile aside from an interview with Chris Moyles on BBC Radio 1, marking England's opening match of Euro 2000 against Portugal, where he described Liam as 'monkey boy.'

The first gig under the name Oasis without Noel since August 1991 took place at the FilaForum in Milan on May 30, 2000. The setlist was much the same, with no significant alterations (apart from the obvious removal of 'Acquiesce' and 'Don't Look Back in Anger'). But it was surely a surreal sight to see what was by then a completely different band (bar the singer and drummer) to a year previously, play such familiar songs. Reviews however were positive, the over-arching theme being that Noel wasn't especially missed. And so the tour rolled on, with a combination of festival dates and dates in Switzerland, Austria, France, Germany, Belgium, Denmark, Finland, Spain, and Norway. Truly, the show must go on, and go on it did.

A compromise had been agreed that Noel would return to play the shows scheduled in Dublin, Bolton, London and Edinburgh. This could be construed as Noel having his cake and eating it, but then being the lead songwriter must afford some privileges. And so he re-joined the fray for a stadium show at Lansdowne Road, Dublin. The show was heavily scrutinised, with any body movement or acknowledgement from either Gallagher towards the other taken as a sign of truce or continued resentment.

Ever the showman, and clearly aware that the world would be watching, after 'Acquiesce' Liam went over to his brother and put his hand out for a handshake, also probably aware of the symbolism of this act taking place in their ancestral homeland. Noel, fully knowing Liam's game but backed into a corner, responded in kind and the worlds of both press and fandom rejoiced. The *NME* declared that the show saw the band 're-emerge as one of the most vital groups in Britain.'

Big brother wasn't for turning, however, when it came to overseas commitments. Matt Deighton re-joined for a gig each in France and Greece, those shows going by without incident. Likewise, two dates at Bolton's Reebok Stadium, despite reports of sections of the crowd chanting 'no surrender to the IRA' and 'Heil Liam,' drawing unfavourable comparisons.

And so, to the home of football, Wembley Stadium. Anticipation for these dates was at fever pitch, representing a beautiful union of the people's game and the people's band. As Noel later commented, 'We were going to be the last band to play there; it was a symbolic thing.' Sadly, in a damning indictment of the corporate world, this dream was swiftly usurped by the powers that be looking to squeeze more money from the venue by booking poodle-rockers Bon Jovi as the final act to grace the original home of football. And the final British band to play the old stadium wasn't multi-million-selling giants Oasis, but flavour of the month Toploader.

The Wembley dates had clearly occupied thoughts throughout the entire tour, and Noel dropped the occasions into conversation at any opportunity. It was one of those glorious British summer weekends, the sun shining brightly and the lagers flowing endlessly. The support bill was strong as well, the recently-reformed Happy Mondays complementing the weather and atmosphere superbly, preceded by fellow Mancunians Doves, riding a wave following the positive response to their debut album.

The first night, as detailed on the *Familiar to Millions* DVD, went by without a hitch. The band were in ferocious form and Liam was typically confrontational, declaring Wembley a 'shithole' and insisting on female audience members' breasts being on screen (they were simpler times). Even Noel seemed to be thoroughly enjoying himself, swept up in the party atmosphere, leading the crowd in derogatory but playful singalongs towards his bandmates ('Who The Fuck Is Andy Bell?'), and shredding through 'Step Out' and a cover of Neil Young's 'Hey Hey, My My' (Into the Black), originally played stateside in tribute to Kurt Cobain , but by then a staple of the set.

The highpoint was 'Cigarettes & Alcohol,' sandwiched between the opening riff of The Beatles' 'Tomorrow Never Knows' and an outro of Led Zeppelin's 'Whole Lotta Love.' The former gloriously echoed through the stadium whilst building up the excitement perfectly, and the latter extended it. The good ship Oasis seemed to have been steadied. One down, one to go.

The second show on July 22, 2000 was broadcast live on Sky TV, with a potential audience reaching into eight digits. It was once again a beautiful day and spirits were high. In an early portent of things to come, during Happy Mondays' set Liam strolled out on stage to rapturous cheers, but simply sauntered around, stopping only to bearhug frontman Shaun Ryder and then disappear.

The cacophony of drums on 'Fuckin' in the Bushes' announced the imminent arrival of the band to a delirious crowd of around 80,000 people. The band walked onstage, with Noel looking smart in black leather, brown loafers, blue jeans and white t-shirt, Liam wearing all black, as if to reflect his (and later his brother's) mood.

Below is an edited transcript of the legible comments during the set:

Liam: 'If you think I'm over the moon to be here, you're fucking tripping. 'Cos this is for Bob Geldof. This is for fucking Simple Minds. This is for all those other fucking idiots who star ...

but I'm glad you made it. Fucking Live Aid. And I bet you wish it was fucking free and all.'

Noel: 'By the way, could I just say peace and love to every single person in the whole stadium, thank you very much. This one's called 'Go Let It Out.''

Liam: 'Says Lazy Arse, who's been sat on his back for a year.'

(during 'Go Let It Out')

Liam: 'Going there, took all the drugs, man, was like (gesture to indicate someone off his head) ... it's only a piece of furniture. Two. She takes this, she takes that, she takes this, she takes that. You fucking cow.'

(after song, as Liam goes and picks up a bag thrown on stage)

Liam: 'What am I, fucking Postman Pat? If you're gonna do Wembley last time, might as well do it pissed out of your arse, yeah?'

(during 'Who Feels Love?')

Liam: 'Gotta pay for it though, these days. 1, 2, 3, 4, 5 ... for love. Can't see your kid. Got a fucking lawyer involved. Rubbish. Arse.'

'I know you paid 30 for it, but you'd do the same if you were me. In and out of it, in and out of show business like that. In and out of it. I ain't no fucking celebrity. I ain't no fanny. I ain't no dickhead, man. I'm a rock star, I don't fucking arse about.'

'We've got Ivor the Engine down the front, trying to be cool. And it ain't right. This ain't us. This is not us. We're only here because of you.'

(during 'Supersonic')

Liam: 'If you expect to be professional, they'll be fucking on glue. 'Cos I'm arsed, (points to Noel) he's arsed (points to Andy and Gem), they're arsed. I'm Mancunian and I'm playing Wembley.'

'I'm Bruce Forsyth.'

'And if you think I could, you fucking must be on glue.'

(after song)

Liam: 'Been watching this football pitch, man, since I was about three and that. D'you wanna know what's good about it? I never thought I'd be here with a bunch of mates and that, having it fucking large. And I don't care about fucking ... 'You're a rock star, you're this, you're having it fucking large.' I'm playing Wembley Stadium, and I'm not ... I'm doing it with my mates. It's about time some fucking excitement happened in this fucking shithole now. About time someone done it proper.'

(during 'Shakermaker')

Liam: 'And this is going out to loads of knobheads all over the world. So why don't you give 'em all a big fuck-off.'

(Changes lyrics to, 'I'm arsed … shake along with me.')

'Are you listening to what I'm saying, then?'

'The way I'm fucking going wrong here, it'll be over in about 10 minutes.'

(after song)

'This is the last fucking rock'n'roll concert to go on in this shithole.'

(before 'Step Out')

Noel: 'This one's called 'Step Out,' if anyone's remotely bothered.'

(after song)

Liam: 'Shall we let Noel carry on? Yeah? Yeah? (Crowd cheers) Fucking cheeky bunch of bastards!'

Noel: 'No accounting for taste though.'

Liam: (to the crowd) 'I was gonna say, I'll come down there and join you. Eight fucking years and you're that arsed?'

Noel: 'It's actually nine years, but who's counting?'

Liam: 'Is it really professional, this gig? Yeah? Is it? Is it really fucking *Smash Hits*? Are we having a good time? Is it really fucking pro? Fucking hope not.'

Noel: 'Once again I would like to express my peace and love to everybody in the stadium, thank you very much for being here. This one's called 'Gas Panic!'.'

Liam: 'Whoa whoa whoa whoa whoa whoa whoa whoa. Hey hey, hey hey. Nah listen, listen. I dig all you, man. I dig all your offsprings. I dig all your pets. I dig everything. I just don't like shitholes.'

Noel: 'Pets is a bit over the limit, innit? Pets? Come on man.'

Liam: 'He's giving me a fuckin' bad name, man.'

(during 'Gas Panic!')

Liam: 'I'm not fuckin' scared. My name's not fucking Steven. And there she goes. With my furniture. Without leaving a fuckin' tea bag. How dare yer?'

(after song)

Noel: 'How does it sound over there? Does it sound loud enough over there?'

Liam: 'You don't want it to be professional, do you? Genesis.'

Noel: 'Hang on a minute. Don't fucking knock Genesis, man. Anyone who's got a bald-headed drummer who looks like a twat and can sing … I'm talking about Phil Collins.'

oasis
oasis
FAMILIAR TO MILLIONS
OUT NOVEMBER 13TH
OASIS LIVE AT WEMBLEY STADIUM.
DOUBLE CD, MC, MD AT SINGLE ALBUM PRICE.
TRIPLE LP. VHS & DVD.

Liam: (to Noel) 'I'll do it in your bedroom. This one's for all the alcoholics. And believe it or not, yeah, Noely G's more of a pisshead than I am. Ever been. So this one's for Noel.'

Noel: 'Now wouldn't that take some believing, eh? Eh? Y'know, if there was 40 cans of beer in our house, I was getting two, y'know what I mean? Which leads me nicely into the next song.'

(during 'Roll with It')

Liam: 'Don't believe in losing. That's for fucking knobheads.'

(after song)

Liam: 'Fuck all that losing nonsense.'

Liam: 'New boys are having a chat, discussion.' (Liam goes over to Andy and Gem. He puts his arm round Gem's shoulder and joins in the chat, pointing in Noel's direction)

Noel: 'See if I still took drugs, I'd be getting paranoid as fuck now. I'd be thinking Matt Deighton was gonna come on and kick me off and do my fucking bit, man. The mind boggles.'

(during 'Stand by Me')

Liam: 'I'm paying for the dodgy whore. Fucking does me every time.'

(after song)

Liam: 'Whoa whoa whoa whoa whoa whoa. It's a tradition. Breasts. On the screen. We're not doing a fucking tune till you get your stupid fucking bird to get her breasts out. On the screen. Come on. (Girl strips down to her bra) Hey hey hey, that's fucking catalogue shit. Get them out! Good job I'm not fucking married, 'cos I'd get a right thick ear. (points to Gem and Andy) He's gonna get a kick in the arse. (points to Noel) So is he. (points to Whitey) So's the other one.'

(during 'Wonderwall')

Liam: 'That'll be nice, do yourself a favour … If you think that's good, you're off your fucking head, man. It must be really fucking good when you're on it.'

(after song)

Liam: 'Noel's on it. You're on it Noel, aren't ya? You're on it, man? Alan's on it. Everyone's on it.'

Noel: 'I tell you what, I wish I was fucking on what you were on, anyway.'

Liam: 'What did ya say? What did you say? Tell all the nice rich people.' (Liam then makes out he's going to punch Noel, but instead walks over and gives him a kiss)

Noel: 'Don't fucking do it again. Little twat. (Noel then breaks into a smile) He just apologised profusely in my ear then. He did. I swear to you.'

Liam: 'Yeah, yeah. Apologising for making so much fucking money for him.'

Noel: 'You never have to apologise for that. Anyway, fuck that. This one's called 'Taxman.'

(during 'Cigarettes & Alcohol')

Liam: 'Turn it up ... so far the fucking show ... Straight in at No.1. Straight in at No.1! This week's climber. It's fucking charging.'

(before 'Live Forever')

Liam: 'This one's for my mate Dave ... Stick to your guns.'

Noel: 'You've been fucking singing all night. Free beer for Mr (Unknown) over there.'

Liam: 'This one's for my mate Dave. 'Live Forever.''

(before encore, the rest of the band leave the stage, but Liam stays on).

Liam: 'It's a real pain in the arse ... I'm in one of them fucking moods. Y'know them moods? That you get in? And you can't get out of. This really fucked up mood. It's true, I am a fucking twat.'

(before 'Champagne Supernova')

Liam: 'Is it Tracey? Tracey? Come on Tracey. Be sharper than that, Tracey.'

(during the song)

Liam: 'Without the fucking honey and lemon, I'd be here all fucking day getting off me fucking twat and that.'

(before 'Rock 'n' Roll Star')

Liam: 'Come on. Are you gonna be fucking sitting there all night?'

Noel: 'This is the last one tonight. It's called 'Rock 'n' Roll Star.''

Liam: 'Whoa whoa whoa. Noel's got somewhere to go. He's gotta be off there quick.'

Noel: 'I've got a bus to catch.'

Liam: 'You got a bus to catch?'

Noel: 'Yeah.'

Liam: 'Well I'm not going anywhere, till I've ...'

Noel: 'I've got a bus to catch. You've all got trains to catch, haven't you?'

Liam: 'This is the last one. 'Rock 'n' Roll Star.''

Noel: 'I just said that.'
Liam: 'But I fucking meant it.'

(during song)
Liam: 'Pulling the fucking place down. A shithole.'

After the gig Liam stayed on stage, throwing his beer into the crowd, then playing with Noel's guitar, finally standing and staring at the crowd, almost daring them to leave. It was all very surreal, it was great theatre, but perhaps not the best rock concert.

Zeb Jameson: 'He'd been up all night, having fun. When he arrived, 10 minutes before we went on it was like, me and Noel haven't even got time to get a couple of pints in. It was unfair! It was an incredibly entertaining show. If you bleeped out the swear words you wouldn't have had a show. It was disconcerting going on stage with him being very volatile. But he made the best of it, he was hugging cameramen, it was absolutely classic. But it was rock'n'roll. We were all holding on to our hats trying to keep up with him.'

Liam was incomprehensibly drunk and it's something of an achievement that he even managed to make it to the end of the gig, no matter how hilarious he was. He sounded bad, although not as bad as perhaps he should have done. He missed numerous cues and was out of tune more than once. His natural talent and sky-scraping larynx were invaluable that day.

Noel now claims that night to be the lowest point in Oasis' history, and that Liam should 'hang his head in shame'. But at the time Noel seemed quite chipper, at least at first. However, it was apparent that the joke became less and less funny as the night wore on and he refused to shake Liam's hand at the end of the show as he did in Dublin. In addition, the footage after followed both Gallagher brothers as they left the stage and Noel headed straight for a waiting car without stopping, with his body language telling all as he headed straight to his car and drove off. A few months later he gave his thoughts on the gigs, saying, 'Well, I thought the first night, the Friday night, was great. The second night was awful. It was one of the most awful experiences I've had in my fucking life. Liam hadn't been to bed the night before and I found that very disrespectful to the audience. Subsequently, that gig got reviewed and it was said to be one of the best performances by a British band in, like, God knows how many years, which makes me think that maybe I'm going a bit fucking mad and I don't know the state of my own band anymore.'

Noel Gallagher, summer 2000

The setlist for both Wembley Stadium shows was:

'Go Let It Out'
'Who Feels Love?'
'Supersonic'
'Shakermaker'
'Acquiesce'
'Step Out'
'Gas Panic!'
'Roll with It'
'Stand by Me'
'Wonderwall'
'Cigarettes & Alcohol'
'Don't Look Back in Anger'
'Live Forever'
'Hey Hey, My My (Into the Black)'
'Champagne Supernova'
'Rock 'n' Roll Star'

They again made headlines the following day, with some reports of Liam being 'out of control,' his antics suggesting he knew the band was coming to an end. It also came out in the press that Liam had been out drinking all day with new girlfriend Nicole Appleton, and his marriage to Patsy was officially over. Those in attendance and watching on TV had probably guessed as much.

And yet as the circus rolled on, so did the continuing troubles. Playing the Paleo festival in Nyon, Switzerland, the band (again minus Noel) were bottled off stage and left halfway through. The organisers of the festival claimed Liam's 'arrogant and provocative attitude' caused the siege of cans and coins, going on to claim that the singer 'insulted members of the audience' and the decision to cut the gig short was 'totally irrational and the result of a paranoid reaction.' Within a fortnight the same thing happened at Sudoeste Festival in Portugal, with Alan White being hit by a stone. No matter where, it seemed Oasis were cursed for the year.

Zeb Jameson: 'A lot of those festival shows we did after that ... there were these laid-back European festivals we were playing, but you had someone throwing a bottle at you. So you had to stop after three songs, went backstage and the promoters were going ballistic. Then you'd get in the van and the van was being rocked by the crowd. People would start throwing things and you would have to leave, it was dangerous. If you leave a show halfway through it gets a bit dark.

That happened quite a few times at those festivals. It must have been quite hard for Liam, because Noel wasn't there, so you're a man down and limping on a bit. Emotions were running high.'

In between the two incidents Noel, playing what must have been a particularly exhausting game of Hokey cokey for all concerned, was present for their last UK stadium gig at Murrayfield in Edinburgh. Meanwhile, the final single from *Standing on the Shoulder of Giants* was released in early July, and 'Sunday Morning Call' made the top-10, again reaching No.4. The band also appeared on *Top of the Pops*, Noel miming as a disinterested Liam played organ.

Matt Deighton played his last gigs with the band at Spain's Benicassim and Gijon festivals. Noel, meanwhile, was lined up to join Paul Weller on stage at the V2000 festival, but time limitations meant the chance was taken away no sooner than he walked on, in front of a very disappointed crowd. Somewhat ironically, Noel stated after that he was 'as pissed as a fucking arsehole.'

To wrap up the tour, Oasis headlined the Reading, Leeds and Glasgow's Gig on the Green festivals over the August bank holiday weekend. Reviews were mixed, although the BBC website led with 'Oasis take Reading by storm.' Noel declared onstage the gigs weren't a funeral, while Liam was in typically defiant form, saying, 'I'm gutted it's the last gig because it's been a bit of a fucking stupid tour.' Even the most ardent Oasis fan couldn't deny that.

By this point it seemed relations between the Gallagher brothers had thawed somewhat, the ever-contradictory Noel stating that he had been out on the booze with Liam very recently, and that, 'I wouldn't be going out on stage with him tonight (Reading Festival) if he wasn't my best mate.'

After such a dramatic sequence of events and with all tour commitments fulfilled, all went quiet in the autumn. Yet surprisingly the band, perhaps rejuvenated by new members and simple survival, went straight back into rehearsals, albeit without Noel. There was nothing sinister to this, as Noel was going through administration of his divorce with Meg Mathews. Once again, the solution to any problem Oasis had was to go back into the studio.

There was still some fun to be had and headlines to be made though. The *Q* Awards, the annual get-together of the great, good and not so good of the music industry came around in October, with Oasis nominated for Best Live Band. Also in attendance and lined up for an award was a certain Robbie Williams.

Whilst no details were made public, the fact that Liam had started seeing Williams' ex, Nicole Appleton, earlier in the year had logically only increased the friction between the two. It certainly would have damaged one of their egos. Williams' likely attendance at the awards no doubt spurred Liam on to attend, with the intention of writing a few wrongs.

As expected, Oasis won Best Live Act. After Noel insulted *The Sun* columnist Dominic Mohan, Liam took to the mic. and, after a dramatic pause, said, 'This one's for Robbie, as usual. He understands the letter Q.' Williams didn't react, and then when he accepted his own award later in the ceremony, he only took to the microphone to say he was going to keep quiet. Liam's indignant, disappointed face was a picture, but suffice to say he had won the latest round.

The final contributions Oasis made to the year 2000 included the release of their so-far only live album, *Familiar to Millions,* on all formats, including a DVD release in November. All versions featured the first show at Wembley which, whilst no doubt commercially the more sensible option, now seems like something of a missed opportunity. At the end of the month, Noel joined The Who onstage for a celebratory show, playing lead guitar on 'Won't Get Fooled Again.' Pete Townshend had in the past called him a very underrated guitarist, and despite his later claiming it was an inconvenience, Noel visually displayed awe and wonder that he was ticking off another achievement. Noel and Gem also joined Kelly Jones of Stereophonics onstage at an acoustic gig in Dublin to perform 'Live Forever' and the Welsh band's 'I Wouldn't Believe Your Radio.'

Lastly, to celebrate what would have been John Lennon's 60th birthday, the band contributed to a celebratory evening of his music on a Channel Four TV show. Noel performed an acoustic version of 'Tomorrow Never Knows' with Gem and old friend Johnny Marr, before performing a duet of 'I'm Only Sleeping' with Kelly Jones, as The Stereoasis All-Stars. All the performers on the night, including Ronnie Wood, ably supported as he sang 'All You Need Is Love' to close out the night. Liam meanwhile was also in attendance, opting not to perform but simply enjoy the occasion.

CITYBEAT WELCOMES
The Tour of Brotherly Love
THE BLACK CROWES
and
OASIS
with
SPACEHOG
May 21, 2001 * 7:00 pm
Riverbend Music Center
Cincinnati, Ohio

2001

'FOUND WHAT I LOST INSIDE. MY SPIRIT HAS BEEN PURIFIED'

It was expected that after such an eventful year a break for all concerned was in the offing for Oasis. Given the lukewarm reaction *Standing on the Shoulder of Giants* received, bunkering down and taking stock was the more logical strategy, and certainly what other artists in their position would do.

But their rehearsals led to Oasis playing the *Rock in Rio* festival and the Hot Festival in Buenos Aires in early January 2001, with Noel playing his first non-UK and Irish gigs since May, going back on his word. But as he put it, playing South America in January was a lot more appealing than spending the worst month of the year in Blighty. All the scars of the previous year had healed, at least for the short term. The setlists were watered-down versions of the stadium tours and were largely greatest hits shows.

Zeb Jameson: 'The last shows I did with Oasis were in South America. We did 'Rock In Rio', supporting Neil Young and Crazy Horse. There's 2,000 people at that festival and one stage. We all went to dinner afterwards. It was incredible, everybody was on great form.'

The band then re-emerged for the second half of awards season, with Noel presenting the Outstanding Contribution award to U2 at the Brits. Unusually wearing a traditional suit, perhaps marking the special occasion and adulation he felt for the band, he wasted no time in deriding the awards, saying, 'When A1 have won Best Newcomer, you know someone is taking the piss somewhere.'

The love-in with U2, themselves very much back in ascendance, continued the following week at the far more comfortable *NME* Awards. Liam also won Hero Of The Year (their only award of the night), and followed in the footsteps of compadre Richard Ashcroft by refusing to take to the podium to collect his award, leading to comedian Peter Kay having to walk to his table. As he returned to the podium, Peter Kay made a barbed remark about Liam's coat.

All the while rehearsals and recording for what would become the band's fifth album continued. Reviews coming from the studio were mixed, Noel claiming that future single 'Songbird', a Liam composition, was 'a waste of plastic, if you ask me.' Either his judgement, not for the first time, was off-kilter, or he and Liam were mid-argument. Noel also used the time in between tours to perform at a Steve Marriott tribute concert at London's Astoria, along with Gem, Paul Weller, and many others.

In an uncharacteristic move, in late-Spring 2001 Oasis embarked upon another American tour, a co-headline trip with Georgia's The Black Crowes. Fronted by the Robinson brothers, Chris and Rich, and therefore understanding the fragility and toxicity of working so closely with a sibling, The Black Crowes were kindred spirits to Oasis, despite sounding nothing like them. 'We are the Sex Pistols to their Lynyrd Skynyrd' as Noel said, which is more apt a description that I can come up with. The shows were dubbed, with no hint of irony, *The Tour of Brotherly Love.*

21 dates were pencilled in for one month, covering nearly 3,000 miles. The tour was the first of two that year, and the only times that the band went on tour without an album to promote, doing it just because they could. Both Gallaghers were newly divorced and seemingly determined to make the most of their respective freedoms. Alan White was carrying a thumb injury and was unable to make the tour, but his brother Steve, formerly of The Style Council and continuing to work with Paul Weller, stepped into the breach.

The tour was seemingly a blast, with Oasis playing before The Black Crowes and then Gem and Noel joining them onstage to play several covers, including:

Fleetwood Mac – 'Oh Well'
Pink Floyd – 'Lucifer Sam'
Bee Gees – 'To Love Somebody'
George Harrison – 'I Dig Love'
Neil Young – 'Everybody Knows This is Nowhere'
Rolling Stones – 'Can't You Hear Me Knocking'
Bo Diddley – 'Road Runner'
The Stooges – 'Down on the Street'

For their part, Oasis freshened up the setlist, reviving 'Slide Away', 'Columbia' and even dusting 'Fade Away' off for the first time in several years. 'I Am the Walrus' also returned as set closer, giving 'Rock 'n' Roll Star' a well-earned rest. Each night was a solid 70 minutes of Oasis in their purest form. The reviews were good and by all accounts the after-parties were good too. For a final flourish, the band also supported Neil Young in Paris in June. Having never hidden his adoration and respect for Young, one can assume that Noel wouldn't have so readily agreed to support many (or indeed any) other artists.

Steve White: 'We had a fairly kind of close history at that time and I went and did the Brotherly Love tour with Spacehog and The Black Crowes and loved it. I had an absolutely brilliant time.

'I had an afternoon's rehearsal, which wasn't very long, and I took some cassettes away, listened to some songs and asked a few questions when we got to

Las Vegas when we did the first soundcheck, and then we did it. We just went for it. I think there's some footage of us at the Greek Theatre on YouTube, with me playing with the band, and it sounded pretty good, I think.

'There was no problems. There was no tantrums. There was no falling out. I remember a lot of great nights of not only playing, but just seeing parts of America, and I remember going off in a taxi to watch *The Mummy 2* with Liam in Kentucky. And taking him out for Thai food in New York. It was quite a long tour, five or six weeks, I think. But it was really good fun. And yeah, I didn't know Oasis fans were particularly aware that I stood in for one tour, but it's nice to know they do know, because I've never been kind of mentioned in dispatches for my association with the band. Obviously, it's my brother that people associate with the band. It's nice to know it's out there, the gig's out there, that people can see it if they want to, because I really enjoyed it.'

Relations between the Gallagher brothers were strong outside of the band too, Noel stating that the brothers and wives would go for family dinners, and unexpectedly calling Liam 'a joy to be around.' Quite a contrast to 12 months previously.

Continuing their random touring arrangements, Oasis played Fuji Rocks in Japan and then in Thailand in late July. By this point, a new group of guitar saviours had emerged and were being devoured by press and fans alike - New York's The Strokes. The *NME* in particular were shouting about the quintet from the rooftops, in a way they hadn't done for anyone since Oasis. Always with his finger on the pulse, Noel was soon asked about them and, perhaps keen to nip another media frenzy over a 'Battle Of The Bands' in the bud, went out of his way to compliment the new guns in town, albeit with the caveat that there was a lot resting on their shoulders. In the same interview, Noel declared that normal service had been resumed, commenting that the forthcoming record was on hold as Liam was required to record some vocals 'if he can be bothered.'

On September 12, 2001, Liam and Noel were interviewed by the *NME* to honour their 10-year anniversary. Given what had happened the day before, the boys had much to discuss and, despite the World Trade Center tragedy aftermath, the brothers gave one of their best ever interviews. Topics covered include Damon Albarn (enjoying fresh success with the first Gorillaz album), modern footballers, and their own legacy. Not that they hadn't always been entertaining, but by this point Oasis interviews had become essential reading, once the new album promotion had been covered.

Moving into the autumn, the celebratory mood within the Oasis camp continued as they announced a UK tour, entitled *Ten Years of Noise and Confusion*. Hardcore World of Twist fans would have noticed the nod to the lyrics from their classic 'Sons of the Stage', while the rest of the music press nodded sagely at a very fitting name. So as to maximise anticipation and to add legendary status, only six dates were pencilled in - two dates each in London, Manchester and Glasgow.

The sets were designed purely for the fans and purists, with virtually all the classic Oasis singles and album tracks up to that point chosen. The sets varied slightly, with 'Whatever' and 'One Way Road' given rare outings. Noel took vocal duties for 'She's Electric' for reasons unknown, perhaps the high notes being out of Liam's live range. As if all this wasn't enough, the band took the then-unprecedented step of introducing two new songs to the set; 'The Hindu Times' and 'Hung In A Bad Place'.

The Glasgow Barrowland show is now the stuff of legend, fortunately recorded for posterity for later generations to enjoy. Elsewhere, old comrades Paul Weller and Johnny Marr came on stage at various points throughout this short UK jaunt, adding to the carnival atmosphere.

The setlist for the Glasgow Barrowland shows was:

'Go Let It Out'
'Columbia'
'Morning Glory'
'Acquiesce'
'Supersonic'
'Fade Away'
'The Hindu Times'
'Half the World Away'
'Whatever'
'The Masterplan'
'Gas Panic!'
'Cigarettes & Alcohol'
'Live Forever'
'Hung in a Bad Place'
'Slide Away'
'She's Electric'
'Champagne Supernova'
'Rock 'n' Roll Star'
'Don't Look Back in Anger'
'I Am the Walrus'
'Roll with It'

The gigs were unusual in that all tracks, including the traditionally acoustic Noel-sung numbers, were performed electrically. Not only that, but 'Roll with It' closed the gigs, the only time it would take such a hallowed position.

Despite not releasing any new music, 2001 was a very important year for Oasis, steadying the ship and then going back to their very essence, being a party band to soundtrack nights out. Freed from the constraints of carrying the entire band, Noel was able to enjoy himself at the same time as playing with much more capable musicians. Andy and Gem's confidence increased by being able to contribute music to the forthcoming album. Alan, sadly, was only able to contribute so much because of his injury but did so with his usual reliability. And Liam kept on doing what he did, which was provide the passion and the voice.

After the celebrations and consolidation of the preceding few months it was time for Oasis to get down to the serious business of finishing their new album. The original intention was to have a single out for late 2001, possibly to commemorate the band's 10-year anniversary celebrations. As ever in Oasis world, things didn't quite go to plan though, and the year went by without any new music.

In November, Noel put this down to the new band democracy, but as much as he had been eulogising about the positives of this new dynamic, it appeared that the negatives were now beginning to rear their heads; 'I can't tell anybody what to do in the band ... there's no referee and it looks like it's just going to drift. It'll end up in an almighty fight.'

oasis
LIVE AT YOYOGI TAIIKUKAN 29.09.2002

2002

'THERE'S A LIGHT THAT SHINES ON. SHINES ON ME AND IT KEEPS ME WARM'

Eventually the fifth album, produced solely by the band and called *Heathen Chemistry,* was completed and tour dates were announced, the first of which was a warm-up in Watford in February. The gig was dubbed as a tour warm-up but the setlist was much the same as the *Noise & Confusion* shows, with no new songs aside from forthcoming single 'The Hindu Times', while 'Hung In A Bad Place' was also given another airing. Paul Weller joined them on stage for 'Don't Look Back in Anger'. By this point, Oasis's stock had fallen somewhat in the eyes of the world, and as such they were on a par with the pleasant Travis, the solid Stereophonics, and newcomers Coldplay. The *NME* made a comparison to all three in their live review, with the backhanded compliment that they were still able to provide kicks in a live show.

Immediately after the Watford gig, Oasis played a benefit at the Royal Albert Hall, the first of what would become the annual *Teenage Cancer Trust* shows at the venue. This was the first step in Noel's long-running relationship with the charity. Meanwhile, mega-gigs were announced for the summer in Newcastle, Belfast, Hull and London's Finsbury Park. To the surprise of no-one, the gigs were the band's fastest-selling. Truly the band of the people, with the swings of the music pendulum making no difference to their live appeal.

In March, 'The Hindu Times' was unveiled to the world. Having no bearing on the content of the song whatsoever, Noel mentioned that he simply liked the title, having seen it on a T-shirt. The song itself was a simple, straightforward life-affirming party song that Noel could probably write in his sleep, the riff cribbing from, of all people, Stereophonics. The demo was much more industrial sounding and more of a departure, but Noel had taken Gem's advice in that the returning single should be 'exactly what everyone wants Oasis to sound like.' The video was probably the band's best up to that point, shot in black and white, with the quintet simply playing the song in a studio surrounded by meaningless props. It did, however, in the last chorus, feature Noel joining Liam on a double-mic to harmonise. Such a show of camaraderie hadn't been seen for a while ... and never would be again. So catching was the image that it was used on the CD of the album.

Once again Oasis reached the No.1 spot in the singles chart, and so the album promotion began in earnest. The usual run of TV appearances (*Top of the Pops, CD:UK*, et al) followed. In fact, Oasis were the subjects of a *Top of the Pops* special, showcasing the new album and also taking the opportunity to record their mandatory performance for the next single, 'Stop Crying Your Heart Out,' alongside band interviews. Never a fan of miming, despite having fun with it in the past, the band played live in the studio, a practise that was becoming more and more uncommon on the show. Following this, they jetted over to the US for a show in Las Vegas, and then to headline the Coachella festival in Indio, California.

Unfortunately, and unbeknown to the band, *Heathen Chemistry* had been leaked onto the internet three months earlier, an increasingly common problem. Nowadays it's part and parcel of releasing an album, and acts such as David Bowie and Beyonce used 'dropping' it with no notice as part of their promotion, but back in the early 21st century this was a disease in the music industry, of which there seemed to be little chance of a cure. As time elapsed people would realise this could be utilised to the artists' advantage. Indeed, for the fans in Vegas who were able to sing the words to several of the newer numbers, it was.

As was now becoming the norm, after hearing new music, the highlight of Oasis' album campaigns were their interviews, the latter actually more appealing to much of the media. In light of the confidence in the national football team's chances at the forthcoming World Cup, many English pundits were predicting ultimate glory. The scenario of *Heathen Chemistry* track 'Little by Little' soundtracking an England victory was put to Liam and, displaying almost psychic levels of foresight, the younger Gallagher declared, 'Piss off! It'll be 'Stop Crying Your Heart Out' coming out as a single and them lot crying their cocks off in Japan.'

Meanwhile, Noel was being interrogated on the new world order of music, specifically on bands' exploitation of the internet and consequently their relationship with their fans. Ever the romantic, Noel was scathing in his condemnation, saying, 'I think the more information you give people, the less magic there is in the music ... they better not be, in any way, expecting to speak to any members of the band ... well, it's none of your business, you know what I mean?' As with most things uttered by big brother, this stance would soften somewhat over time.

Noel was also (comparatively) gushing in his press for Liam's three contributions to the album - the wistful 'Songbird' (his 'Manc odyssey'), 'Born on a Different Cloud,' and the deep, dark 'Better Man.' To anyone who would listen, Noel was predicting that his younger brother would be the best songwriter in Britain within five years, although with the caveat that he was doing so to put pressure on him. He was even playing himself down; 'We (he and Liam) sat down and I said, 'Listen, I love you and you love me, what's the most important thing? One: the music. Two: the singer. Three: the cunt who writes the songs.'

Elsewhere in the interview, Noel claimed that he would never go solo because he didn't like being surrounded by session musicians, and that he would never make records without Liam. Slightly less dramatically but equally incorrect, Liam declared that he didn't believe in rock stars exercising and that he would never be caught doing such a thing. In 10 years, both Gallaghers would be doing exactly the opposite.

Amid the usual claims of greatness of the album (second only to *Definitely Maybe*, etc., etc.), Noel had seemingly made his peace with the fact that Oasis had gone out of fashion and were quite comfortable in their own niche; 'We always want our records to sound like Oasis.' Meat and drink for the cynics perhaps, but the records could speak for themselves.

And so they did. 'Stop Crying Your Heart Out' was released as the second single prior to *Heathen Chemistry*'s release, charting at No.2. The song was held off the top spot by one of the ubiquitous songs of that summer, a remix of lesser known Elvis Presley track 'A Little Less Conversation.' Having been held off the summit by Robson & Jerome in the past, some consolation would have been had by being denied by The King. And as Liam had sagely predicted, the single did indeed accompany footage of England's exit from the World Cup, its chorus sitting comfortably with images of David Seaman being lobbed and David Beckham in tears.

The release proper of *Heathen Chemistry* approached. Reviews were mixed as ever, but the record contained a lot more joy and verve than the previous two efforts. It was the perfect blend of all corners of the Oasis formula; life-affirming rock tracks ('The Hindu Times') sat alongside anthemic flag-wavers ('Stop Crying Your Heart Out', 'Little By Little') and swampier, grittier tracks ('Hung In A Bad Place', 'Better Man'). Johnny Marr was brought in to add some stardust to the cod-Stone Roses '(Probably) All in the Mind'. Reflecting their near-unique symbiosis at this point, Noel and Liam both contributed odes to their new partners which were very much cut from the same cloth; 'Songbird' and 'She is Love'. The former fitted in with Liam's Lennon fixation, the latter demonstrated Noel's easy journey into middle age. And *Heathen Chemistry* probably sits alongside *(What's the Story) Morning Glory?* as the most 'textbook' Oasis albums.

After a quick foray across Europe, taking in a gig each in France, Spain, Italy, Germany and Sweden, the UK dates began. Eschewing the normal cities for the first leg of the tour, Oasis played arenas in Belfast, Hull and Newcastle. And sandwiched between the northern dates were three enormous shows at Finsbury Park in North London.

Support for the dates was stellar, The Soundtrack of our Lives, The Coral, Proud Mary (one of the only other acts on the Big Brother label), Black Rebel Motorcycle Club and The Charlatans all contributing to a mini-festival.

Reflecting Noel's headspace at the time, they opened with 'Hello' before hitting the crowd with 'The Hindu Times' and 'Hung In A Bad Place'. Whatever one's opinions of the new songs, in a live environment they worked much better than anything from either *Standing on the Shoulder of Giants* or *Be Here Now*. Noel obviously thought so too, with only one song each appearing from those albums and seven from *Heathen Chemistry*. The icing on the cake was hearing their raucous version of The Who's 'My Generation', soon to be released as a B-side, as Noel dedicated it to one its original architects, John Entwistle, who had recently passed away.

With new communal anthems 'Stop Crying Your Heart Out' and 'Little by Little' sitting comfortably alongside 'Live Forever' and 'Don't Look Back in Anger', Finsbury Park felt like a rebirth. While everyone had their opinions on *Heathen Chemistry*, and the various criticisms would become the stock opinions for the remaining seven years of the band's lifetime ('doesn't hit the heights', 'Beatles'.... etc, etc), there was always grudging admiration for their live shows. And while the band would never want the moniker, the comparisons to the Rolling Stones, in that they would be a mainstay in the fabric of British music regardless of time, was becoming entrenched.

The setlists were:

'Hello'
'The Hindu Times'
'Hung in A Bad Place'
'Go Let It Out'
'Columbia'
'Morning Glory'
'Stop Crying Your Heart Out'
'Little by Little'
'D'You Know What I Mean?'
'Cigarettes & Alcohol'
'Live Forever'
'Better Man'
'She's Electric'
'Born on A Different Cloud'
'Acquiesce'
'Force of Nature'
'Don't Look Back in Anger'
'Some Might Say'
'My Generation'

The open-air gigs continued, with a T in The Park headline set in Kinross, north of the border, airing on BBC Radio One, then as July continued Oasis headed across Europe. So far, so good, with neither a cross word between the Gallaghers nor a crisis in the offing. The cross words were saved for indie outfit Starsailor, who at the Scottish festival became the latest to irk Liam. Predictably, Noel had insulted James Walsh, (labelling him 'a cock'), the Lancashire frontman taking umbrage and confronting Noel backstage. He couldn't even recall doing so, but Liam interjected and stood up for his brother, informing Walsh, 'If someone says you're a cock, then you are one.' Starsailor were very much in favour with the *NME* at the time, so they had a field day, going so far as to dub an article detailing band feuds *You Cock.*

The good luck and good spirits wouldn't last. As the tour moved on from Europe to the US, Lady Luck again abandoned our heroes. The first date was in Fort Lauderdale, but unfortunately after four songs Liam's voice started to give way. Again, Noel took over lead vocals, and those in attendance were given a real treat, Noel performing the majority of the set with an acoustic guitar, dusting off some classics, the mid-period set being:

'Whatever'
'The Masterplan'
'One Way Road'
'Talk Tonight'
'Live Forever'
'Cast No Shadow'
'Half the World Away'
'Wonderwall'

This would have become a legendary gig had it been in Britain, but the Americans again benefitted. Noel and the rest of the band then treated the audience to that rarest of occurrences; performing both parts on 'Acquiesce'. Crisis averted.

Even more serious problems followed. Travelling through Indianapolis, Noel, Andy and keyboard player Jay Darlington were in a taxi enjoying some leisure time before a show that night, when the taxi was involved in a head-on collision with another vehicle. Andy seemingly came away unscathed, but Noel and Darlington were taken to hospital with serious facial bruising and hand injuries respectively, as well as shock. The gig that night was immediately cancelled. Fortunately, the only lasting effect was Noel sporting a rather fetching beard for a few weeks. Peggy Gallagher, asked to comment on the incident, stated she was glad he was OK, then added, 'I don't know where Liam was. I assume he was in bed.' You can see where they get it from.

Completing a hat-trick of bad luck, prior to resuming the tour in New York, Noel lost his British passport, which threatened to prevent him from performing across North America. Fortunately, US embassy workers back home were able to rush through a visa application, so he was able to catch the flight with his bandmates.

The wheels were back on track for the remainder of the American tour, which ran for the rest of August. Moving into the autumn there were more UK dates, including a homecoming gig at the Old Trafford cricket ground in Manchester, the only incident of note being Liam's apparent insistence that all reference to Old Trafford (the home of their beloved City's rival Manchester United, albeit a different stadium) be removed. There was however one ghost from their past in the vicinity.

Paul Ashbee: 'We'd arranged a night out. I was close to all the City players. I got a box sorted out and put two limos on. City had beaten Villa that day. We pulled round the back to go backstage. Without realising, this box was hanging over the stage. I'd just taken them to court, which was a big mistake. I should never have gone down that road, but someone got in my head. It was a bad time, but whatever. Next thing, I've looked out the back of the car and Liam's clocked me. He comes bowling over to the car. I'm not knowing what to expect. He put his head in, grabbed hold of me and shook my hand passionately. And then he just went, 'What are youse up to?' I said, 'Playing cricket, you daft cunt, what do you think we're up to?' Then he started laughing and realised he had to tell Noel. He went in, fucking laughing and winding Noel up, telling him I was in the box with all the City players, hanging over the top of the stage, and he said I was going to bottle him or something. He told Noel that, taking the piss.

'Straight away, Noel got a load of minders and the next thing the door flies open with a bunch of meatheads. Noel, with his daft beard and glasses goes, 'Get that fucking cunt out of here.' Nicolas Anelka threw a gold chain under his top, thinking he was getting mugged. These cunts overpowered us, and four of them threw me down the stairs. Noel was like, 'Go on, you cunt.' And I said, 'You know what, mate? I'm having you for this. You're going to get fucked.' Next thing I was out of the door, and he was laughing. Liam's security guard came out and said, 'Listen mate, I'm so sorry, you don't deserve that.' I lost it and said, 'You've got a problem now,' and he really hurt me. I found out that they were staying in a hotel, but they moved hotel and everything. Like a dickhead I went to the police and they went and interviewed Noel. It was in the press the next day. What right has he got to come and do that to me in my box? Who does he think he is? Noel Gallagher?'

Continuing across the world as the nights drew in back home, Oasis played sold-out gigs across Asia and Australia before heading back to Europe for yet more shows. Seemingly everything went swimmingly, apart from one date in Manila, the Philippines, which had to be cancelled due to terrorist concerns, and a date at the Kokusai Center in Fukuoka, Japan, where Liam's voice gave in and his brother stepped in to finish the set.

Back in the UK, the third single from *Heathen Chemistry* was released, and for the first and only time the band released a double A-side, consisting of 'Little By Little' and 'She Is Love' (backed by their cover of 'My Generation', recorded two years earlier). The latter wasn't given any airplay and didn't even get an accompanying video, but the former was graced by having Scottish film star Robert Carlyle in the video. The single yet again just fell short and reached No.2, held off by another double A-side, covers of Elvis and The Beatles from ITV talent show *Pop Idol* winner and runner-up Will Young and Gareth Gates, arguably the Robson & Jerome of their day. Once again, Oasis were doomed to combat with a pop phenomenon.

One stop along the way was a charity gig for *Make Trade Fair* at the Astoria, where Noel played a short acoustic set of Oasis songs and then performed 'Live Forever', 'Yellow' and a cover of The Smiths' classic, 'Stop Me If You Think You've Heard This One Before' with Chris Martin (with whom Noel had become friendly) and Jonny Buckland of Coldplay. Conducting a round of interviews for the gig, Noel let slip that he was newly single (having been dating Scottish publicist Sara MacDonald for two years), the only time any insight into his personal life came to light.

All dates in Britain, France, Spain, Italy and Switzerland went by without a hitch in the autumn, and then two dates in Germany followed suit before one of the more infamous Oasis incidents, or more specifically Liam Gallagher incidents, took place. After a relatively quiet spell, he hit the headlines again and paid the price. In December, at the Bayerischer Hof nightclub in Munich, Liam was reportedly in an antagonistic mood on a night out with other members of the group (Noel not being one of them). Liam was said to be flicking peanuts at a group of estate agents drinking nearby, and the situation escalated quickly. The police were called, with Liam reportedly hitting one of them and receiving several punches for his trouble, one or more of which knocked out his front teeth. The leader of the five attackers was said to have knocked two Oasis bodyguards out with a brass ashtray, and '80' police officers from 10 police vans, were involved.

After the event Liam faced more legal proceedings, with the Chief Prosecutor quoted as saying 'He was the worst one in the entire episode. He assaulted a police officer who was trying to pull the other people apart.' Traces of cocaine were allegedly found in Liam's blood. The remaining dates of the ongoing tour of Germany were cancelled. The tour resumed in Cardiff 10 days later, with Liam dedicating 'Live Forever' to his new front teeth.

Noel was very matter of fact about the matter, saying, 'I don't need to say anything. He has very, very infamously had his teeth kicked out, right? I wasn't there, I don't know what happened. All I'll say is, if you're gonna pick a fight, make sure you're going to win. And, you know, it's very, very humiliating to be famously beat up. Maybe it'll teach him a lesson.' The incident was the inspiration for his song 'Ain't Got Nothin', which would surface a few years later. But, ironically, as the £35,000 fine would prove, they did have something on him.

A jaunt around the UK spanned mid-December, followed by two final Christmas presents for the fans, with a non-Oasis release from each Gallagher. 'Scorpio Rising', a Death In Vegas track from the album of the same name, was released as a single and featured Liam on lead vocals. A very rare foray outside of Oasis, the single featured one of his best vocal performances, the song containing a sample of 1968's 'Pictures Of Matchstick Men' by Status Quo, which in turn underwent a re-evaluation.

On Noel's part there was a much more pedestrian offering; his cover of Slade's Yuletide staple 'Merry Xmas Everybody', originally recorded for popular BBC show *The Royle Family*'s Christmas special two years previously, was given an official release as part of an *NME/War Child* charity album.

Heathen Chemistry is now regarded as a nadir in the band's output, yet 2002 saw Oasis reclaim lost ground in terms of commercial success, with a No.1 single and album as well as two No.2 single entries, sold out gigs all around the world (as ever), and the new version of the band fully up and running. As Noel himself said, 'If we lost it, we've definitely got it back.'

Noel Gallagher at the Zanzibar, 2003

2003

'A LITTLE SPACE, A LITTLE TIME. SEE WHAT IT CAN DO'

Nick Mercer (lead singer, Sergeant): 'Bands like The Strokes and The Libertines, they were ours. But there's something ingrained about Oasis that was different and was kind of inside you. I was a bit younger, but it was all around you when you were 10, 11, 12. It was just everywhere. Ultimately it was the way you dressed as school, the way you had your haircut at school. It was absolutely everything. They were always still the best. Nothing will beat that. We looked like them, and that was what it was. Everything.'

2003 was a very quiet one by Oasis standards, save for a bit of tour mopping up, i.e. the cancelled dates in Germany and Dublin in the early part of the year. Noel admitted at the time they were going through the motions with those gigs. He declared as those dates were wrapped up that he needed a break from the band and a break from music, and so the machine wound down again. He also said that he gave his career in Oasis another five years. He was only one year or so out.

Despite it being one of the quieter years since their inception, there was some activity, most notably in the early part of the year with the first (but by no stretch of the imagination the last) Britpop nostalgia piece.

Before that, a fourth single was lifted from *Heathen Chemistry*, the first time Oasis had released so many since *(What's the Story) Morning Glory*? It's well known within the music industry that if an album is doing well, the label will bleed it dry and release as many singles as possible, and so it was with the fifth album. With no real involvement, Noel took a back seat for the promotion and left it to the writer of the song. Liam came across as quite uncomfortable in all the interviews, perhaps unused to a different form of spotlight. This didn't make much difference to the single's success; 'Songbird' charted at No.3, (which as a fourth single was no insignificant achievement), with a beautiful accompanying B-side in '(You've Got) The Heart Of A Star', initially released on the Japanese version of the album.

Later that month the *NME* Awards took place in London, where Oasis picked up Best UK Band and Artist of the Year. More significantly, Liam picked up Best Haircut. Noel also performed at the Awards, with a solo version of 'Wonderwall', accompanied only by Gem and a string quartet. Noel was originally due to perform the song with American alt-rocker Ryan Adams, who had recently covered the track. Noel had been praising that version, going as far as to say

that Adams had made Noel understand the track for the first time and declaring Adams' version as superior. However, the US artist was unable to make the performance, and an unforgiving Noel called him a 'bottle job' when interviewed after.

Still in London, and once again for the *Teenage Cancer Trust* gig, Liam sang on 'C'mon People (We're Making It Now)' with old buddy Richard Ashcroft. Ashcroft's support was a supergroup consisting of Liam, Noel, Gem, Paul Weller, Kelly Jones of Stereophonics and Roger Daltrey, entitled Trust, playing a song or two each from each member's output. Always looking for a new opponent, Liam took the opportunity to have a go at Chris Martin, who was at the time heavily promoting the *Make Trade Fair* cause. Liam felt it was inappropriate to promote one cause when playing a gig for another.

Also in March, a documentary film called *Live Forever: The Rise And Fall Of Brit Pop*, written and directed by John Dower, was released to the world, a significant number of the population made to feel both nostalgic and old. While not entirely accurate, (*Trainspotting* wasn't set in Glasgow, as claimed, for example) it was a thoroughly enjoyable jaunt down memory lane, containing a wealth of interviews from '90s luminaries, including former Cabinet minister Peter Mandelson, *Vanity Fair*'s Toby Young, Massive Attack's 3D, artist Damien Hirst, and many others. Also involved were Britpop heavyweights Louise Wener of Sleeper, Jarvis Cocker and Damon Albarn, but of course the stars of the film were Noel and Liam.

Jarvis came across as pithy and as witty as you would want. Louise Wener was very matter of fact and insightful. Noel meanwhile fully played up to the working-class hero angle of the film, as the 'Battle Of Britpop' was once again hauled over the coals. Seven years on, he was clearly still revelling in Oasis' long-term victory over the 'middle-class fops', stating his soul was purer because he worked on a building site, etc. Damon Albarn still appeared fragile and bitter about the whole incident, but did provide a glimpse of stories untold, referring to 'other people' being involved in the war with Oasis.

Star of the show though was Liam, as the interviewer attempted to explain what 'androgynous' means, when describing the frontman. The interviewer tries to move on, but Liam doesn't let him off, continually pressing for an answer, eventually taking it to mean he's obsessed with his hair and going into a little diatribe about it. The film ends heartbreakingly, tracks by Robbie Williams and Steps offering a comprehensive full stop to the story, the first foray into what would later become a cottage industry complete.

In May, following his long and great support for the Merseyside music scene, Noel made a surprise appearance at the Zanzibar club in Liverpool, coming on with his mates The Stands then playing a short set himself, accompanied by Gem and Proud Mary's Terry Kirkbride on drums. In radio interviews earlier that day, Noel had waxed lyrical about his newest song, 'Stop the Clocks', his new *'best-ever'* song. The song (and indeed the gig) would very quickly become a myth, as it never made an Oasis record, although they did attempt it during the *Dig Out Your Soul* sessions, the track eventually surfacing on his debut solo album.

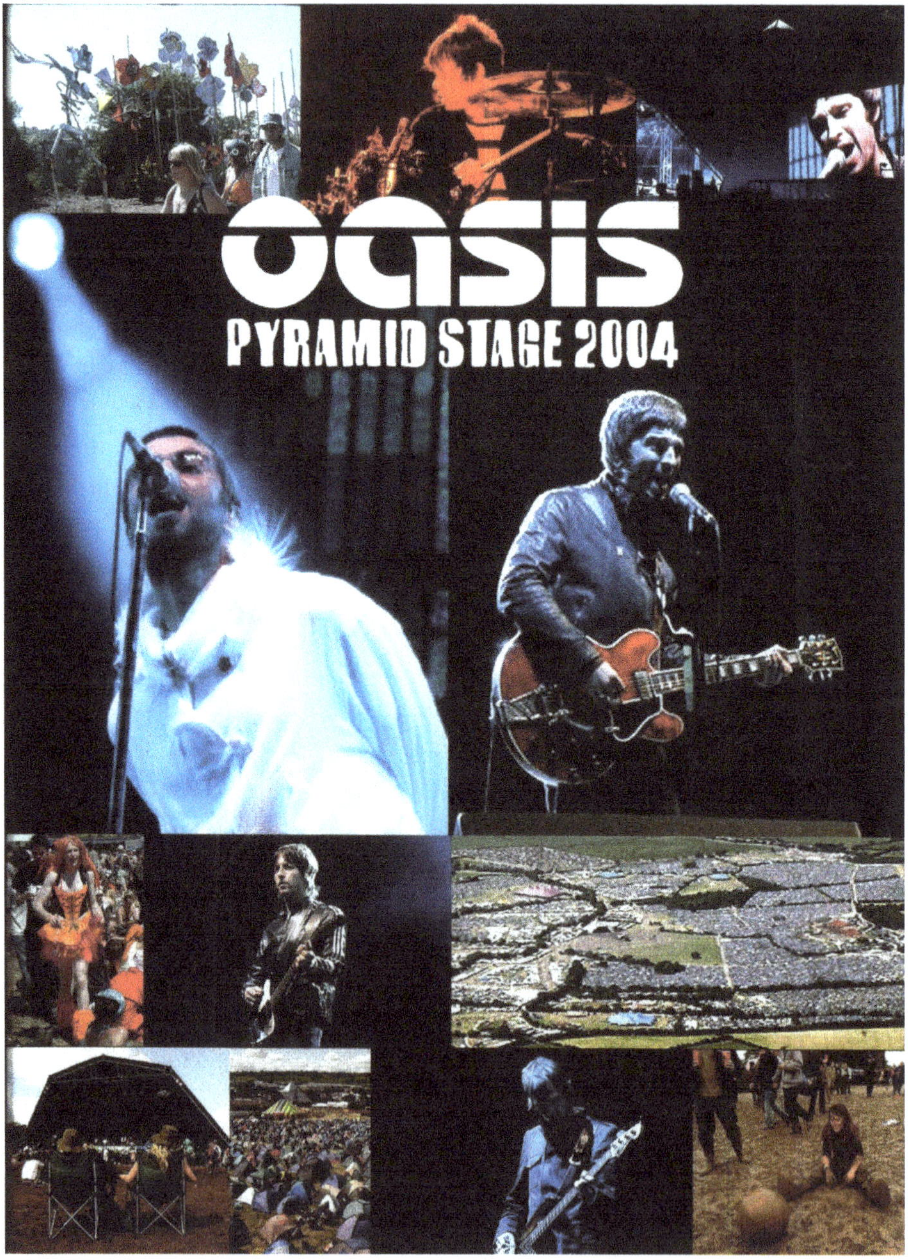
oasis
PYRAMID STAGE 2004

2004

'IT AIN'T NO PLACE TO BE KILLING TIME. I GUESS I'M JUST LAZY'

2004 began with the intriguing news that Oasis were to record their next studio album with Death in Vegas duo Richard Fearless and Steve Hellier, at Sawmill Studios in Cornwall. Presumably, Liam's collaboration with them back in 2002 led to this decision, and hopes were high. Death in Vegas had built an impressive array of work and pulled in some heavyweight names as well as Liam for their previous album, including Iggy Pop. Oasis had never really used a 'name' producer (although Mark Stent had worked with Madonna, U2 and Massive Attack), with the first three albums produced by Owen Morris and Noel, and *Heathen Chemistry* credited to 'the band.' The new creative spirit triggered by Gem and Andy's arrival seemed to show no sign of abating though. In interviews, Noel claimed that a single had already been chosen, song titles including 'Lord Don't Slow Me Down', 'Revolution Song' (again), and the aforementioned 'Stop The Clocks' being touted.

But yet again positivity and drama went hand in hand, as rumours started to fly that drummer Alan White, the sticksman since April 1995, had left the band. Initially the rumours stated that his arms weren't up to the job, but then an official statement was released by the band saying he had been asked to leave. Alan's brother Steve was the strong favourite to take over, but when asked, stated, 'Categorically no'. One other rumour doing the rounds was that Whitey was responsible for the *Heathen Chemistry* leak in 2002, but seeing as this didn't particularly affect album sales, that doesn't quite stack up.

This makes for one of the more mysterious stories in the Oasis saga. Shortly after, Noel claimed that the reason Whitey left was because of dispute between the drummer and Liam, and there was only ever going to be one winner there. Other reports claimed Whitey didn't attend band meetings (something Noel denied ever occurred) and as such his commitment was in question, so he was given the push.

More recently, Steve White made disparaging comments about Noel on social media, but Alan has stayed out of the public eye since. His departure was disappointing news, as White's drumming was the stable foundation on which the rest of the band could build from. That said, his drumming was never better than on *(What's the Story) Morning Glory?*, though this perhaps says more about what was asked of him than his talent.

Mat Whitecross: 'I don't know all the stories. I heard all kinds of stories, all contradictory, about him and Guigs, and why they left.'

Steve White: 'I'm actually documented as saying at the time what happened, and that's kind of the way that I see it. Once Alan was out of the band, he was out, and that door shut, and I don't think I'd be the sort of person that would get a call to do it. It's a shame really. All those doors were kind of slammed shut. I did run into Liam once at a gig and said hello to him, but our collective paths have never really crossed since then. That's just kind of how things worked out.

'I just don't think he feels the need to have to talk about it, or explain himself, and the media is such a strange animal that I just don't think he feels the need to ... he feels that his music and his drumming, his contribution to the band, said what it said and that was it. He's not going to do 'My Story' with *The Sun*. He doesn't want to do a book. He's not particularly interested. I think we both share a healthy distrust of the music business, business-wise. But the difference is that I've gone into other things and kept things going. Alan absolutely loved his time with the band, but once that chapter closed I think he thought that was it.'

Terry Kirkbride was believed to be the frame for the album sessions, as was Zak Starkey, sometime drummer with The Who and son of Ringo Starr. Noel and the rest of the band were said to have performed much of the drumming for the forthcoming album. Meanwhile, rumours started gathering pace of a headline slot at Glastonbury Festival, as well as some sort of celebrations for the 10th anniversary of *Definitely Maybe*.

Also bubbling along was a little spat between pantomime heroes The Darkness and Noel, although it was hardly headline deserving, Noel simply describing them as 'inoffensive'. For their part, in a bid to play with the big boys, the poodle-rockers took every opportunity to have a swipe at Noel in a bid to gain some headlines, but to no avail.

There were still positive noises surrounding the as-yet untitled sixth album, but the sessions with Death in Vegas proved to be unfruitful and were abandoned. The split seemed amicable, Noel later claiming, 'The songs weren't there, we were trying to polish a turd', and so the band reverted to type, with Noel and/or the band taking up the production reins. Going against their history, everything between Death in Vegas and Oasis was very civilised. Amid all this disarray, Zak Starkey was indeed working with Oasis, although he never intended for it to be a permanent arrangement, as he enjoyed being part of The Who.

One rumour was true; Oasis were confirmed to headline Glastonbury for the first time in nine years. In the build-up to the iconic West Country festival, Liam had seemingly taken a vow of silence, not doing any interviews and not appearing to get into any scrapes. Whereas Noel was his garrulous self, but as his heroes Paul McCartney and Morrissey were also on the bill, as well as hillbilly rockers Kings of Leon, sub-headlining beneath them, he had no-one to take swipes at.

Accordingly, the press made unsubstantiated claims about the brothers simply not talking and wanting to be kept apart from each other onstage.

One warm-up gig in Poole a few days before Glastonbury aside, the headline slot was their only show of the year. It was a strong setlist, with the usual classics mixed with more recent fare, and two new songs included (Gem's 'A Bell Will Ring' and Liam's 'The Meaning of Soul'). For whatever reason, the show failed to ignite though. Liam didn't seem particularly bothered, but nor was he shambolic. Noel appeared to be trying his hardest but couldn't seem to get going.

The band even looked disjointed; Liam looked glorious in a white parka, tidy beard and short hair, with Gem in an Adidas jacket and Andy a smart blazer, and Noel in regulation jeans and leather jacket. The latter said before that they would probably 'George Best' it, and it seemed he was proved right.

Liam told a journalist that he 'fucking hated' Glastonbury and was only there for the money. The festival's founder, Michael Eavis commented that he felt that the band didn't want to be there, and Kasabian frontman Tom Meighan revealed that the brothers had a row before their set. Sometimes these situations added fire to the band's performances, but by this point Oasis, much like the Rolling Stones and U2, were more suited to their own mega-gigs rather than festival headline slots. More inaccurately, it was reported that Noel was shocked by the reaction to the new songs and 'ordered' the band back to the studio. Strange then that both would appear on their next album.

Unusually, Noel took to commenting on various rumours about the sessions for the sixth album, releasing a statement to the *NME* that they were hoping to release new music by the end of the year and have the album out in February. Some new Gallagher-related music did shortly appear however, in the form of collaborations with some of their peers. Ian Brown put some lyrics and a melody over Noel's contribution to *The X-Files* movie from 1998, 'Teotihuacan', to release a glorious single called 'Keep What Ya Got', with an accompanying video depicting the two Mancunian titans trawling the streets of their hometown. A couple of months later in Manchester, Noel would join Brown onstage to play the song.

Noel also contributed to an album track on The Prodigy's long-awaited fourth long player, *Always Outnumbered, Never Outgunned,* playing bass on a raucous number called 'Shoot Down'. He was possibly coerced into doing so by Liam, who in turn was coerced to provide his punkiest-ever vocals to the track, by his then brother-in-law Liam Howlett, mastermind behind the Essex crossover electronic dance outfit. Both tracks would have been worthy additions to the Oasis canon. To promote 'Keep What Ya Got', Noel and Ian Brown performed on *Friday Night With Jonathan Ross*, but tellingly, despite the single being the first from Brown's forthcoming album, Noel was chosen to complete the formalities of the interview with the BBC 1 chat show host.

It wasn't just to promote the single though, as the 10th anniversary of *Definitely Maybe* was being marked with a re-release and a celebratory DVD. Most of the key figures from the time were interviewed, including Tony McCarroll (although Guigsy's absence is felt), as well as Gem, Andy Bell and Mani from the Stone Roses/Primal Scream. For super-fans there were a few nuggets of new information, one being that Noel had written 'Up in the Sky' as an anti-establishment tirade. Noel, Mark Coyle and Marcus Russell were unrepentant and still slightly bitter about Tony's limitations as a drummer, although this may have been something to do with being sued by him relatively recently.

Liam's contribution to the documentary was somewhat limited, but we finally got to see the legendary Digsy, who was far and away the highlight. Mad as a box of frogs but perfectly logical in his own way, he lived up to the myth.

Pete Deary: 'I can't even remember filming that, I was pissed. They were filming in Manchester and took me into town. The camera crew was arranged down by the dock, so they took me down and said, 'You'll have to wait here'. Free bar, so me and me mates got sozzled. By five o'clock I was rotten.'

The celebrations were acknowledged on BBC Radio 1, Channel 4 TV, and across the printed media, further proof if needed that the band had achieved Hall Of Fame status and were also part of the establishment. The celebrations also seemed to rewrite history, with most outlets deciding that the debut was the best thing they had ever produced, an accolade which was being geared towards *(What's the Story) Morning Glory?* up until that point.

All those celebrations and collaborations couldn't distract from the fact that a new album still had to be completed and, with the album becoming rudderless, manager Marcus Russell paired Oasis with producer Dave Sardy (who was to work with Noel for the next 10 years), a relative unknown who had produced Australian outfit Jet's first album *Get Born*. Part of this plan was to decamp to LA to finish the album off.

These sessions seemed to rejuvenate the album, and Noel started talking in grandiose terms once again, with the guitarist declaring new tune 'The Importance of Being Idle' one of the best things he had ever written. He also went back on his previous statement about not having the songs, claiming they were basically the same as those that had been recorded in the previous aborted sessions, although 'sonically' they hadn't been up to scratch. Zak Starkey was down to drum on the bulk of the album, although other reports claimed that Terry Kirkbride would be on skins. Kirkbride soon denied this, saying he helped them with demos, but what of his would be on the album was unclear.

With the album nearly complete Oasis started pencilling in dates for a tour the following year, the biggest UK and Irish dates being at Hampden Park in Glasgow, the City of Manchester Stadium, the National Bowl in Milton Keynes, and Dublin's Marlay Park. Once again, the gigs sold out in five minutes and additional dates were swiftly added, the faithful obviously not being as disappointed in their Glastonbury set as the majority. Around this time the band also put their back-catalogue on the internet for download.

Noel's influence continued to cascade among his fellow musicians, and he was also given a special thanks in the album notes of U2's latest album, *How To Dismantle An Atomic Bomb*, for inspiring Bono to write 'One Step Closer'. The story went that the Irish frontman told Noel his father had lost his faith and didn't know where he was going, to which Noel replied, 'Well, he's one step closer to knowing, isn't he?' Noel also provided backing vocals to a full recording of 'Freelove Freeway' by David Brent, comedian Ricky Gervais' greatest creation, the lead character of *The Office*. Strangely, to this day both Noel and Gervais ignore that this ever happened, despite the filmed evidence, perhaps as some private joke between the pair.

As Christmas approached, to commemorate the 20th anniversary of the Band Aid single 'Do They Know It's Christmas?', a new version was recorded with more contemporary stars, including Coldplay, Dido, Robbie Williams, and The Darkness. Noel Gallagher's name was one of those also heavily linked to the project, organiser and Ultravox frontman Midge Ure going so far as to claim he'd signed up. But this was swiftly disclaimed by his publicist, who said he was out of the country and disappointed not to be involved. Given his later comments on the following year's *Live8*, that was PR spin at its finest.

oasis
28/06 GLASGOW HAMPDEN PARK • 30/06 2/3/07 CITY OF MANCHESTER STADIUM
6/07 SOUTHAMPTON ROSE BOWL • 9/10/07 MILTON KEYNES BOWL
12/13/07 NEWCASTLE METRO RADIO ARENA • 16/07 MARLAY PARK DUBLIN

2005

'I CARRY A MADNESS EVERYWHERE I GO'

The album was announced for a May release, confirmed by Noel in an interview with BBC Radio 1 in January 2005. Rumours gathered pace in the tabloids that the first single would be called 'I Stand Alone'. Noel also let slip that the album was entitled *The Ear Has No Memory*. Not a strong title, but no worse than the eventual choice, *Don't Believe the Truth*. Liam came out of hibernation for a performance of 'Songbird' as part of Radio Aid, an on-air telethon for Asian tsunami victims in 2004, and was reported to have played the forthcoming LP to fellow hell-raiser Courtney Love, who was full of praise. Not a night out for the faint-hearted.

Continuing their American dalliances, the band announced a date at one of the most celebrated venues in the States, Madison Square Garden, which had long been on Noel's bucket-list and sold out rapidly. More US dates were pencilled in for later in the year. Meanwhile, Zak Starkey was finally confirmed as the drummer for the upcoming tour which, ironically, meant The Who had to delay any new music for a year.

Oasis again picked up a gong at the *NME* Awards, this time Best DVD for the *Definitely Maybe* re-release. In his acceptance speech, Noel made reference to the imminent expiration of their contract with Sony, which was due to be fulfilled with the release of the sixth album. Then in early March, there was finally some concrete news on music, with the new single confirmed as 'Lyla'. Ingeniously, the statement went on to say that Lyla was a sister of Sally, the protagonist of 'Don't Look Back in Anger', and the new track sounded like The Who, designed specifically for pogoing. They were also announced as headlining the V Festival in August. A full tracklist of the new album followed shortly after.

Eventually, after all the stories and all the hype, 'Lyla' received its first airplay, and the song lived up to all its writer's promises; an absolute monster of a party song, the band never sounding so mighty. During this period the indie and rock charts were dominated by more refined fare, including Franz Ferdinand and Bloc Party, and 'Lyla' was a stark, primal contrast to that. The video also ranks among their best, the band performing to a psychedelic rock circus, filmed at Hackney Chapel. No doubt about it, Oasis were most definitely back with a vengeance, the biggest cat in the rock jungle reasserting itself. Intriguingly, the choice of single wasn't made by Noel but by their label, yet given its success and impact that perhaps demonstrated that Big Brother wasn't always the best judge.

Noel started giving interviews about the album, and was characteristically effervescent in his praise; 'Part Of The Queue' sounded like nothing else they had ever written; 'Keep The Dream Alive' would be a live staple for years to come (it didn't even make the summer sets) and 'Let There Be Love' (which appeared in various forms over the years, notably during the *Standing on the Shoulder of Giants* sessions, as 'It's A Crime) could have gone on forever. The album was also 'the best since *Definitely Maybe*' (again).

During the round of interviews, Liam was also asked to give his opinions on the modern crop and produced some classic put-downs; Kaiser Chiefs were 'a bad Blur', Franz Ferdinand 'looked like Right Said Fred', and Bloc Party reminded him of 'a band off *University Challenge*.' His ire was mostly directed in the direction of former Libertines and current Babyshambles frontman Pete Doherty. Doherty was the most notorious rock star of the age, with his frequent appearances in the tabloids creating a media splash that hadn't been seen since Liam and Noel. Perhaps feeling usurped, Liam was particularly vicious, outlining his disdain for 'smackheads'.

Although they were often considered *de rigueur* by many contemporary rock outfits, such was the upturn in indie music (Britpop 2 was the very short-lived and imaginative title given), several other new bands cited Oasis as a key influence, including Las Vegas' finest, The Killers, Leicester psych-rockers Kasabian, and a new band starting to make noise across the media, Sheffield's Arctic Monkeys. Disconcertingly for Noel and Liam most of all, all these bands were children or teenagers when Oasis inspired them. It didn't stop the brothers, or specifically Noel, from happily taking the accolades and adulation though.

Upon its eventual release, 'Lyla' hit the No.1 slot in the UK singles chart, for one week only, as per usual. Oasis also announced a 'club' tour, with dates in small venues across London and other capital cities, the first destination of which was at the Astoria. The setlist was unsurprisingly heavy on the new album, with 'Turn Up The Sun' opening the set, immediate classic 'The Importance Of Being Idle' as well as 'Mucky Fingers' included and, thrillingly, 'Headshrinker', for the first time in 10 years. Sadly, that didn't appear in the setlist again. The set was chopped and changed across the club dates, with 'Champagne Supernova' and 'Bring It on Down' reappearing alongside 'Little By Little'. Also in May, the band picked up the acolyte of 'Most Successful Artist Of The Last Decade', as awarded by *The Book Of British Hit Singles And Albums.*

Don't Believe the Truth received mostly positive reviews in the music press prior to release (for what they were worth by this point), but no-one could deny that when the album did hit the heights, the songs stood alongside anything else in the canon. Reaching the top spot in the UK (obviously), selling 237,000 copies in the first week of sales, but also making a strong showing on the US Billboard chart, hitting the top-20, a first for the band. After all this time and, ironically with probably their most British sounding album, they were finally making headway across the pond. And it was released during a particularly strong period for albums, with The White Stripes, Coldplay, Foo Fighters and Gorillaz all unleashing new albums within weeks, but *Don't Believe The Truth* was able to hold its own.

Dates in Europe filled the diary for a few weeks as festival season being to kick into life, the only incident of note occurring when, in Italy at the Heineken Jammin' Festival, Liam walked off stage four songs from the end with vocal problems, Noel finishing the set as ever. The tour then moved on to the States, with all obligations successfully fulfilled, including that Madison Square Garden gig. The American media were lukewarm in their praise, calling the band's recorded output 'dronish' and the band themselves 'loutish'. That didn't stop the show at the Garden being rapturously received by those in attendance though, and even the press had to give some grudging admiration for the ferocity of their live show.

The band then returned to the UK for the first stadium show at Hampden Park, which seemed to go well, despite reports of the Glaswegian crowd fulfilling all expectations, being very raucous and unsavoury. The 'lad' crowd, or 'parka monkeys' as they would later become known, would never leave Oasis or either Gallagher behind.

Inevitably, given that it had been 20 years, an anniversary gig for *Live Aid* (this time called *Live8* in relation to the G8 summit) was to take place in London's Hyde Park in early July. A huge number of heavyweights were announced, including Coldplay, U2, Paul McCartney, The Who, and a temporarily reformed Pink Floyd. Notable by their absence were Oasis, who justified this through having dates at the City of Manchester stadium to fulfil. It should be noted that U2 and Coldplay also had dates pencilled in for the evening but were able to play the show early in the day. It was perhaps more down to Noel's cynicism of the whole shebang; 'I don't like the way that somebody suddenly decides that all the bands in England are going to fucking play, and everybody jumps to attention.'

As disappointing as it was not to see Oasis amid all the rest of the rock and pop glitterati, time has told us that the gig had little impact. And as shown in the DVD release of the gig, on the same night as *Live8*, it appeared that they had a far better and more productive time in Manchester. So imperious were they that before the third show had even started, the gig had to be delayed because of the barrier breaking at the front of the crowd, with Noel having to encourage the crowd to take a few steps back. Ever the raconteurs, Noel and Liam entered the 60,000 strong crowd for 25 minutes while the issues were resolved.

The setlist was:

'Turn Up the Sun'
'Lyla'
'Bring It on Down'
'Morning Glory'
'Cigarettes & Alcohol'
'The Importance of Being Idle'
'Little by Little'
'Acquiesce'
'A Bell Will Ring'
'Songbird'
'Live Forever'
'Mucky Fingers'
'Wonderwall'
'Champagne Supernova'
'Rock 'n' Roll Star'
'Guess God Thinks I'm Abel'
'The Meaning of Soul'
'Don't Look Back in Anger'
'My Generation'

The huge shows continued across midsummer in a congested season of outdoor shows. As well as Manchester, Milton Keynes, Southampton, Newcastle and Dublin were all ticked off successfully. So well were the tours going that the band scheduled large UK dates for December too, Cardiff and Belfast chosen among others, which broke their respective ticket records. The only blot on those dates involved Babyshambles having to pull out of a support slot at Milton Keynes Bowl, which gave Liam considerably more fuel to criticise their bohemian frontman, his taunts continuing across the remainder of the summer, including changing the lyrics to 'Bring It On Down' to 'But you don't care, because you're smoking crack.' The fact that Pete Doherty had been associated with one of Liam's old flames (Lisa Moorish) may have had something to do with his vitriol, but that aligned with the media attention Doherty received.

The band then moved on to festivals, initially headlining Benicassim in Spain, but then deciding to swap their slot with their spiritual proteges Kasabian. Such was the measure of success that they could wield such power. They also had a say in the line-up for the V Festival, with The La's, The Stands, Jet, and The Zutons all playing beneath them. Although The Streets and Maroon 5 also played, so it seems they didn't get it all their own way. The festival took place in August, at the same time as the second single lifted from *Don't Believe the Truth* was given an official release; 'The Importance Of Being Idle.'

That single was the second in a row to hit No.1, the first time Oasis had two singles from the same album hit the top slot since *Be Here Now* some eight years earlier. It would also turn out to be their final No.1 single. Despite operating in the same orbit as U2 and Coldplay at that very moment, neither of those acts saw such

success in the singles chart. For once Noel was also glowing in praise about the video, a memorable skit featuring Welsh actor Rhys Ifans, lifted from The Kinks' 'Dead End Street.' All was rosy in the Oasis camp.

Another reason for Noel's positive outlook was the completion of the band's contract with Sony, and the fact that they were reportedly the subject of a bidding war in the industry. However, as is standard practice when record contracts are fulfilled, the prospect of Sony cashing in and releasing a Greatest Hits package began to rear its head. Noel was dismissive of such a concept, saying, 'This is from the horse's mouth. We will only do a Greatest Hits when we split up.' The Chief, perhaps buoyed by their current successes, as well as having yet more ambitions fulfilled, also acknowledged the idea of a solo album again, saying he thought about it 'all the time.' He also made reference to a film soundtrack - presumably for the 2005 movie *Goal!* which would be out on the Big Brother label just a few

weeks after 'The Importance of Being Idle' was released as a single, featuring new mixes of 'Cast No Shadow' and 'Morning Glory', and a new song, 'Who Put the Weight of the World On My Shoulders?'

As if further proof were needed, Oasis completed an uneventful and consequently successful short tour of the US, including dates at the legendary Hollywood Bowl in LA, and the Red Rocks Amphitheatre in Colorado. They were teasing a collaboration with Kasabian, so blooming was their friendship, Noel referring to them as 'soul brothers.' Sadly, or perhaps fortunately, that is never came to light. The band were also nominated for a bumper five *Q* Awards, and won two, both prestigious; Best Album (beating Coldplay, Goldfrapp, Kaiser Chiefs and James Blunt), and the People's Choice award. Noel made a point of saying he was pleased with the album award, dismissing their previous Live Awards, saying, 'Yeah, brilliant, you can play guitar, nice one'. Liam was in a playful mood, goading Coldplay's Chris Martin as he took to the podium, with the brilliantly surreal barb, 'plant pot.' (2005 was a vintage year for Liam insults. Earlier on he claimed that Bono could 'talk a glass eye to sleep.') Martin played along and didn't take the bait as Robbie Williams had done five years previously, although this was no doubt down to his good friendship with Noel. Speaking to the press after, Noel claimed they were considering releasing a one-off single entitled, 'The Boy With the Blues.'

The tour re-commenced with dates in Europe, the Far East and Australia across November, and yet more shows were pencilled in for 2006. Eventually, the *Don't Believe the Truth* tour would be the longest album tour Oasis ever embarked on. 'Let There Be Love', the third single from the album, released in November, peaked at No.2, held off the top spot by Madonna's ABBA-sampling 'Hung Up', continuing their outstanding streak of success in the singles chart. And a final run of UK dates again saw out the year, including headlining a mini-festival at Cardiff's Millennium Stadium, where they were ably supported by Foo Fighters, Razorlight, and The Coral. The event was entitled *Noise and Confusion,* cribbed from their celebratory tour four years previously.

Popular opinion has it that Oasis peaked from 1994 to 1996, and never hit the same heights again. But the success the band enjoyed in 2005 fully puts that myth to bed, with two No.1 singles, one No.2, a No.1 album, and a sold-out tour. And for only the second time in the band's career, they also had critical acclaim and awards to go with the success. Don't believe the truth, indeed.

oasis
BIG BROTHER RECORDINGS LTD
presents
THE IMPORTANCE OF BEING IDLE
DVD SINGLE INCLUDES THE ACCLAIMED VIDEO
STARRING oasis WITH SPECIAL GUEST RHYS IFANS
DIRECTED BY DAWN SHADFORTH PLUS AN EXCLUSIVE
'MAKING OF' DOCUMENTARY. 7" & CD INCLUDE THE BRAND
NEW SONG "PASS ME DOWN THE WINE" PLUS BONUS TRACK ON CD
"THE QUIET ONES"
www.oasisinet.com
22:08:05

2006

'I KEEP PRAYING THAT THE LORD WON'T SLOW ME DOWN'

Plans for an EP continued into 2006, Noel confident that something could be released in the summer. He also took to commenting on the meteoric rise of Sheffield's Arctic Monkeys, praising their 'stunning' lyrics and mentioning their attire; 'I like the fact they don't wear shirts and ties.' The Yorkshire quartet were the first band since Oasis to have such an immediate impact, with both their first two singles and album hitting No.1, sales not seen in the indie genre since *Definitely Maybe*. Arctic Monkeys and Kasabian were cut from the same cloth as Oasis, and as such Noel was fully supportive and began offering his wisdom. Even Liam called the former 'a breath of fresh air' and dedicated songs to them later in the tour. The baton was beginning to be passed. Liam also made an on-stage appearance with Richard Ashcroft during the winter months.

In a slightly less positive indictment of the band's legacy, Oasis were announced to have agreed a $1million deal with US multinational telecoms giant AT&T. Noel apparently had reservations around corporate association, but Liam convinced him to take the money, especially as no-one would hear it in the UK. This came only a matter of months after Noel had taken Jack White to task about working with Coca-Cola, kicking him out of 'the club'. Strong rumours also gathered pace that Oasis were refusing to perform at the forthcoming Brit Awards, although given they were touring at that time (albeit in the UK), it was always unlikely. But the media were adopting the 'never let the truth get in the way of a good story' attitude. Or indeed, a story, full stop.

The tour included arena dates in Sheffield and Nottingham after European dates in January and then the next leg in the Far East again. They then moved on to their spiritual home, South America, and gave the audience a special treat, including 'Supersonic' in the setlist for the first time on this tour. The set had been much the same for nine months, in line with Noel's 'If it ain't broke ...' mentality and so it may have been as much for the band's sake as the fans. Yet more dates followed in North America, with Arctic Monkeys as support, and until the last show in Mexico at the end of March it seemed like Oasis were undertaking their own version of Bob Dylan's Never-Ending Tour.

Even though he was a key component of one of the band's most successful tours to date, Zak Starkey made no commitment to carry on as a full member, despite an official invitation. Given the way Alan White departed the band, had he heard the news that the door was open for his successor to come and go as he pleased, he may well have had a wry smile. But then Alan wasn't the son of a Beatle, merely a brother of a Style Councillor.

Free to enjoy their free time, the rest of the band re-commenced their personal lives for the rest of the year. Noel continued to praise the Arctic Monkeys and popped up as Italian footballer Alessandro Del Piero's lucky mascot for the 2006 World Cup Final. He also joined new compadres Kasabian on stage for a couple of their songs at a special gig to mark the 10th anniversary of *NME.com* at London venue Koko in early September. Liam was linked with an appearance on the next Gorillaz record, Damon Albarn even going so far as to say he would like it to happen. One of the Gallaghers working with one of Blur was still an incredibly unlikely proposition. Bizarrely, a completely fabricated interview with Andy Bell surfaced, where he supposedly talked of working on a solo album, with Gem assisting and Pete Salisbury, ex-The Verve, on drums. In June, *Definitely Maybe* was declared the Best Album of All Time in a joint poll of *NME* readers and the *Book of British Hit Singles*.

Inevitably, as Noel had predicted, Sony announced a Greatest Hits release for the autumn, the label not missing the opportunity of one last pay-out for one of their most lucrative acts. The compilation was to be entitled *Stop the Clocks* ('the title fits where we are now') and so the mainstream press reasoned that the title track, along with 'Boy With the Blues' would be included. They also incorrectly speculated that the band would be re-recording 'Acquiesce' for a single release. The track-listing was eventually unveiled, and the only arguments between fans were around the omissions rather than the inclusions. *Be Here Now* was completely ignored, and of the big hitters, 'Roll with It', 'Shakermaker' and 'Whatever' all failed to make the cut, but otherwise the selections would have pleased fans and the general public alike. It's top-loaded, with 14 of the 18 songs from before the year 1997, but Noel would have astutely known that the glory years would be the most appealing.

The artwork was designed by Peter Blake, designer of the Beatles' *Sgt. Pepper's Lonely Hearts Club Band* sleeve, and an EP (not a single and therefore not chart-eligible) was also released, consisting of the two biggest B-sides ('Acquiesce' and 'The Masterplan'), along with a demo version of 'Cigarettes & Alcohol' and a live version of 'Some Might Say'. Included in the album was a DVD interview with both Liam and Noel (the last time the two were interviewed together) and all the elements of their relationship were present. There was the mutual defiance - when taking the opportunity to discuss their peers the pair showed equal disdain for the competition. There was brotherly respect for the other's perspective on the chorus to 'Rock 'n' Roll Star'. There was the spikiness when discussing who has more money. And there was the earth-shattering news that it was actually Liam who came up with the line, 'So Sally can wait'.

oasis

A tour film, entitled *Lord Don't Slow Me Down*, directed by Baillie Walsh, following Oasis during their world tour of 2005/6, was given a special cinema screening, although it wouldn't be given a full release until the next year. Originally the idea was for Walsh to simply film crowd footage for the 'Let There Be Love' video, but Walsh stuck with the band throughout the remainder of the tour and was able to collate enough footage for a whole film.

As entertaining as the film is, it doesn't offer any surprises or new information; life on the road can be both extremely fun and extremely boring, interviewers often don't do their research, and Phil Smith and Scully (long-term friends of the band) have got the best gigs in the world. The most exciting thing about it was hearing the full title song, which had been recorded for the *Don't Believe the Truth* sessions but had yet to be heard, as well as a number in the soundcheck that would (much) later become 'God Help Us All.' There are telling moments, such as a few seconds of Noel and Liam arguing in a restaurant, and priceless footage of Liam having a dance with himself backstage, unaware of the camera. But generally, it almost suffers from being a document of a very successful, and therefore a very well-planned, tour.

Again, Oasis picked up gongs at the *Q* Awards; Best Act in the World Today (after an inactive few months), and Noel's Classic Songwriter award. To promote *Stop The Clocks,* Noel and Gem, along with Terry Kirkbride, played a short acoustic tour, including a benefit gig for drugs charity Focus, where Paul Weller joined him for renditions of 'Thick As Thieves' by The Jam and 'Strawberry Fields Forever' by The Beatles.

The tour also included a televised show at the Union Chapel in North London, dubbed *Sittin' Here in Silence (On My Own)* after the 'Let There Be Love' B-side, before going worldwide, with Noel and Gem stopping off in the US, Japan, Canada, Italy, France and Australia. The songs played on the tour weren't Greatest Hits, or those included on the compilation, rather tracks that worked well acoustically or could be reimagined. 'Cast No Shadow', 'Listen Up', and 'Fade Away' were all included, and tellingly Noel would open the sets with '(It's Good) To Be Free'. The pair also engaged in a competition on BBC Radio One, the winning entrant having the pleasure of seeing Noel and Gem play in their front room. He also took the unusual step of giving a revealing interview on *Parkinson,* opening up about his relationship with his family and even more uniquely, his father. Noel initially seemed taken aback by the host's knowledge of his past, but quickly reverts to the default setting of garrulous raconteur.

He hit the interview circuit hard. Never one to play the record company game, Noel was still mildly contemptuous of the compilation release, saying, 'If it was up to me, it wouldn't be coming out at all … but we were informed they were going to do a retrospective of some sort before Christmas. Did we want to get involved?

We were left with the dilemma of, 'Do you want to get involved and make sure it's done properly with the right songs, or not get involved? If there's Oasis records in the fucking shop, I want to be behind it.' Noel's quality control and personal pride would (generally) always take precedence over making a few quid, not that it was ever a choice for him.

In a curious twist of fate, *Stop the Clocks*' release date coincided with U2's latest best of, *U218 Singles*, and new Beatles compilation *Love*, their songs reimagined to a *Cirque de Soleil* soundtrack. The three rock giants went back and forth in the charts all week but unfortunately this was one chart battle Oasis couldn't win. Although they did top the triumvirate, all three lost out to Irish boy band Westlife. The irony of undoubtedly the strongest set of Oasis songs to be put to one album becoming one of only two that didn't go to No.1 is something that should not be overlooked.

On the brief tour, Noel managed to get into a bit of hot water with military personnel, stating, 'If you don't like being shot at, you shouldn't join the Army'. Ex-soldier Ben Wrench took exception to Noel's comment. It had been a while since there had been controversy with someone not in the public eye, so to be doing so during promotion of a retrospective was strangely fitting. He also offered advice to aspiring musicians, saying, 'Don't join your brother's band. If you're ever going to join a band, don't have any family members in it. It always ends in tears. Always.'

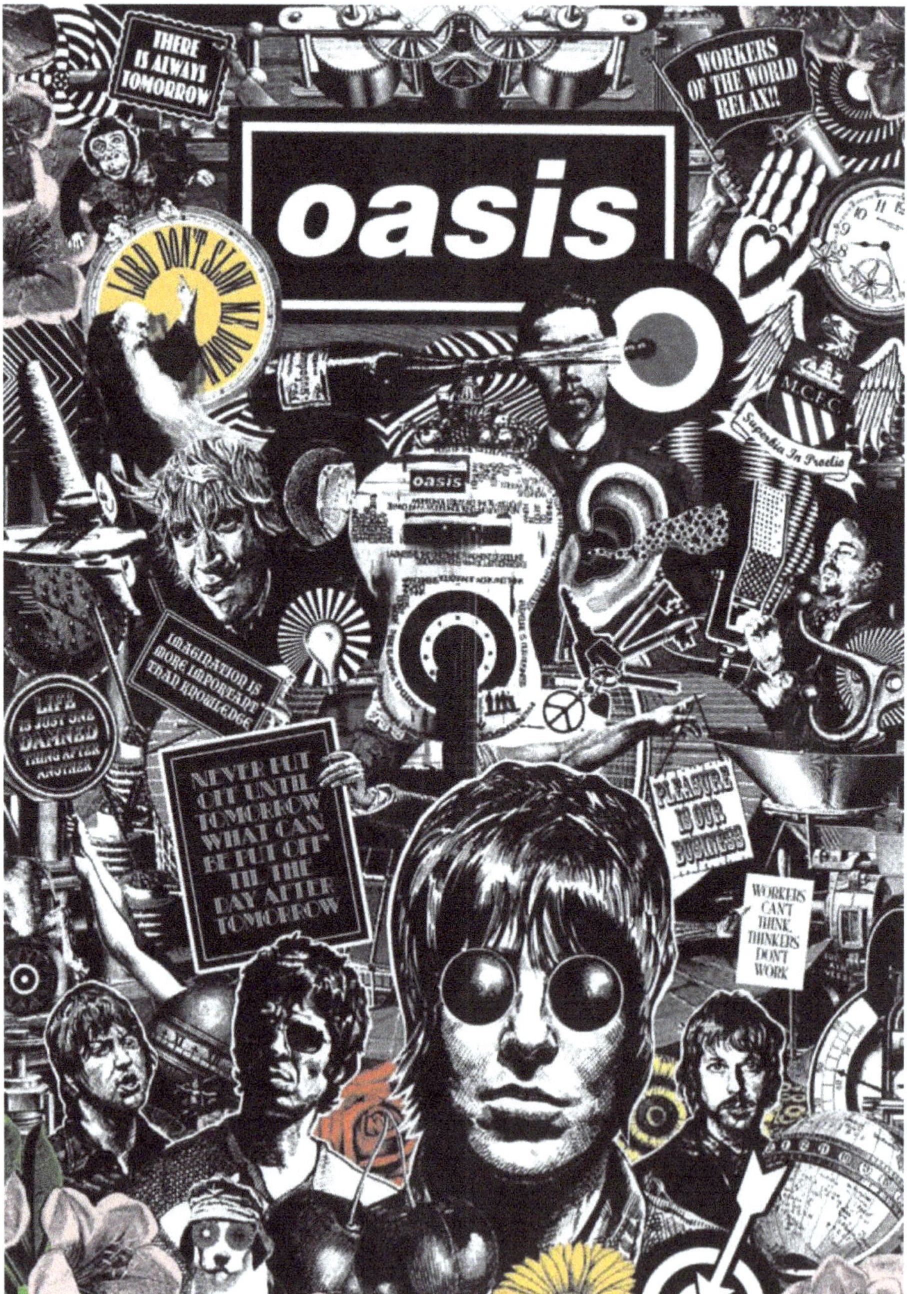
THERE IS ALWAYS TOMORROW
WORKERS OF THE WORLD RELAX!!
oasis
LORD DON'T SLOW ME DOWN
M.C.F.C.
Superbia In Proelio
oasis
IMAGINATION IS MORE IMPORTANT THAN KNOWLEDGE
LIFE IS JUST ONE DAMNED THING AFTER ANOTHER
NEVER PUT OFF UNTIL TOMORROW WHAT CAN BE PUT OFF TIL THE DAY AFTER TOMORROW
PLEASURE IS OUR BUSINESS
WORKERS CAN'T THINK, THINKERS DON'T WORK

2007

'MINING OUR DREAMS FOR THE SAME OLD SONG'

As had been speculated for several years, Oasis were to be the recipients of the Outstanding Contribution at the 2007 Brit Awards. It seemed that Noel was intent on tying up loose ends once the Best Of had been released, and he took great satisfaction in picking up the gong before the band hit their fifth decades. He said, 'With *Stop The Clocks* coming out we thought, 'This isn't gonna go away, so either we do it now or we *need* to do it in five years and look more like a bunch of old fellas. I'd like to do it before I'm 40. It means Oasis will be the youngest-ever band to get such an award. That's colossal.'

Doing the press rounds before the ceremony at London's Earl's Court, Noel was in typically witty, dismissive form, saying, 'We're finally up there with Eurythmics, Sting and Bob Geldof, so I'm not sure congratulations are in order.' On the night itself, Oasis had little fanfare upon receiving the award; unusually, there was no special guest to present the award, despite rumours of Ringo Starr doing the honours. Event host and friend of Noel's, Russell Brand, simply ran through a straightforward introduction, then the band accepted the award and ran through a short set; 'Cigarettes & Alcohol', 'The Meaning Of Soul', 'Morning Glory', 'Don't Look Back in Anger' and 'Rock 'n' Roll Star'.

'The Meaning of Soul' in particular seemed an odd choice, given that it wasn't even a single from their most recent album. But perhaps this was down to time constraints, or that the song had been used for Sky's Premier League coverage so had a place in the public conscience.

It was quite apparent that the band had been relatively inactive, as the performance was a bit rusty. Liam seemed to be in a foul mood, looking like he'd rather be anywhere else. Upon receiving the award, he kept it short, saying, 'Seeing as we don't get nominated for this shit anymore, this'll have to do.' As soon as he completed his vocals, he removed his in-ear mics and left the stage. What was heartening is how different the band were to anyone else on the bill, and indeed to most other recipients of the Outstanding Contribution gong. Uncompromising, the sound was moving into their later-period psychedelic, swampy rock music, a stark contrast to the casual viewer's memories of the band.

Meanwhile Noel continued his 'solo' jaunts with Gem in tow, including one night in Moscow, and booked in two nights at the Royal Albert Hall, again for the Teenage Cancer Trust. The shows mainly consisted of reworked versions of Oasis classics and some covers, including 'There Is A Light That Never Goes Out' by The Smiths, 'All You Need Is Love' and 'Strawberry Fields Forever' by The Beatles and

'The Butterfly Collector' by The Jam, with Paul Weller joining him. The two nights would go on to be released as a charity album for the Trust, entitled *The Dreams We Have as Children,* a few years later. The setlist included a wealth of lesser played songs.

'(It's Good) To Be Free'
'Talk Tonight'
'Fade Away'
'Cast No Shadow'
'Half the World Away'
'The Importance of Being Idle'
'The Butterfly Collector'
'All You Need is Love'
'Don't Go Away'
'Listen Up'
'Sad Song'
'Wonderwall'
'Slide Away'
'There Is A Light That Never Goes Out'
'Don't Look Back in Anger'
'Married with Children'
'Strawberry Fields Forever'

There was also an edited version of the set performed at the MEN Arena in Manchester, another charity gig, this time for Versus Cancer. The happy news that Noel was going to be a father for a second time led him to report in interviews that not much would be happening in Oasis-land that year, although he was never renowned for needing much reason not to go into the studio. He again started talking up the chances of a solo album, with a 'backlog' of songs ready to go, but this was swiftly dismissed by the band's website.

One bit of work did occur, although it took a stagnated release; to celebrate the 40th anniversary of The Beatles' seminal *Sgt. Pepper's Lonely Hearts Club Band,* a whole host of artists were invited by the BBC to record cover versions of some of the tracks, including The Magic Numbers, Razorlight, and Kaiser Chiefs. Obviously, Oasis were asked. Noel apparently had reservations but left it to Liam, who was up for it and decided to choose 'Within You Without You.' Pulling their weight, the band arrogantly insisted they would only record their version at Abbey Road Studios, using the original equipment.

Plans started formulating for the seventh album, Noel stating that some songs had been written and he was hopeful of having the album out for summer 2008,

although he acknowledged that was wishful thinking. Dave Sardy was again lined up to produce, and in August sessions started at Abbey Road, with Zak Starkey on drums. There was briefly some confusion as U2, also looking to record a new album, wished to use the studio time Oasis had already booked at the famous location. Noel bypassed the issue by paying for their recording time in cash, a method of payment preferred by the management team.

In their downtime, some of the then-current indie crop took the opportunity to take swipes at the band, including Bloc Party again, singer Kele Okereke claiming Oasis 'made being not aspirational cool.' The East London act would have a bigger part to play later in the story. Meanwhile, Noel joined Scouse psych-popsters The Coral during their performance at The Roundhouse, playing guitar on 'In the Rain' from the band's most recent album. Noel also participated in BBC Radio One's celebrations for their 40th anniversary, hosting a radio show, offering up gems from his record collection.

The year wasn't totally barren; a DVD release of *Lord Don't Slow Me Down* was finally announced in time for Christmas, which included footage of one of their triumphant gigs at the City of Manchester Stadium in summer 2005. Also released was an official single release of the title song, albeit as a download only, backed by live versions of 'The Meaning of Soul' and 'Don't Look Back in Anger', from the Manchester gig. Despite it being only a download, it still managed to continue their proud singles record, just about making it to No.10. Best of all was a commentary track by all four members of the band on the DVD, on which all were on good form and seemed to be getting on well. Mockery was rife, as you would expect from a group of men, but there was no animosity.

oasis
DIG OUT YOUR SOUL
06.10.08

2008

'I FEEL COLD BUT I'M BACK IN THE FIRE'

Noel saw in 2008 with Kasabian, again performing with them, this time for a special Hogmanay gig in Edinburgh, and the collaborations continued as it was rumoured, then announced that the elder Gallagher would be working with Paul Weller on a track for his upcoming ninth solo album. Noel had a bassline and drum beat he couldn't do anything with, so Weller wrote a song around it which became the first single from Weller's *22 Dreams* album; 'Echoes Round The Sun' (a double A-side with 'Have You Made Up Your Mind?'), even going so far as to appear in the video along with Gem Archer, despite Noel's notorious disdain for the process of filming promos. Noel also let slip on one of his semi-regular appearances on Russell Brand's BBC Radio 2 show that the new album would be out in October. Meanwhile, Liam took the opportunity of the break to marry long-term girlfriend Nicole Appleton.

Colin Paterson: 'I'm covering the Oscars. A guy I know from going to Scotland football matches, Gordon Smart, was an up and coming showbiz journalist at the time. He was already genuinely good mates with Noel, and I knew Gordon. We phoned each other and realised we were both in LA. He went, 'Oh right, where are you staying?' I went, 'The Roosevelt.' He was like, 'I'm there, with Noel Gallagher.' So I joined Gordon Smart, Ally Ross (*The Sun*'s TV critic) and Noel Gallagher. We sat there in the Roosevelt Hotel the day before the Oscars and I gave him my five funny stories. We got on well that day. I decided I wasn't going to interview him that day, he was off duty. I thought I'd get something better next time if I didn't. We had a fantastic afternoon.'

Recording for the new album was taken up a step, with further sessions at The Village Recorder studios in Los Angeles, followed by final mixing from January until March. Speculation was rife that because Oasis were without a record label, they may follow in the footsteps of Radiohead and release the album for free online. The Oxford band had shaken up the record industry by releasing their latest album *In Rainbows* on a 'pay whatever you want' model in late 2007, the idea being that fans could in theory have it for free, there being no obligation to pay, but were encouraged to pay whatever they think the music was worth. This was Radiohead's seventh album, having fulfilled their obligation to Parlophone, and as such many speculated that this model would become the norm and Oasis would adopt the same strategy. Liam Gallagher's response? 'Over my dead body.'

As the album neared completion, a few festival dates were announced for later in the year, the first being what would become the ill-fated slot at Toronto's Virgin Festival in September, followed by other dates in Canada. The band were also rumoured to be playing 10 nights at London's new O2 Arena, formerly known as the Millennium Dome. This was swiftly denied by Noel, who claimed it was 'the most soul-destroying venue I've ever been to,' although this didn't stop Noel performing there for his first arena tour as a solo artist.

Then, in April, Noel found himself at the centre of a storm as big as anything he'd been involved in since the turn of the 21st century.

Colin Paterson: 'It's the premiere of *Flashbacks of a Fool,* a film directed by Baillie Walsh, who did the 'Unfinished Sympathy' video for Massive Attack. He also did the *Lord Don't Slow Me Down* tour film and the 'Let There Be Love' video. This is a film very few people have seen.

'You get a tip sheet when premieres are happening, and it said Noel Gallagher will be there. I thought, 'He actually will be' because they'd done the work together, so he'd go and support him. So, I thought, 'What are the big news issues of the week? Oh yeah, Glastonbury tickets have gone on sale this week. Jay-Z's headlining and they haven't sold out. I'll ask him about that.

'He arrived and I asked a couple of questions about the film to be polite. Then you come in with the big one; 'Listen, I was just wondering, as a band who've headlined Glastonbury, why hasn't it sold out this year?' And then came the best answer I've ever had in my career. He just went, 'Well ...' there was a pause in that Noel way, and you think something gold's coming. 'It ain't broke, don't fix it. Jay-Z at Glastonbury? Hip-hop? I'm not having that. No way.' He talked about how sometimes there would be a curveball, with Kylie Minogue having been booked to play, and he went, 'I'm never sure about that, but hip-hop? No way, I'm absolutely not having that. No chance.' And it was one of those moments where you were like, 'Please let this have recorded.' And it had recorded. I remember I went 'round to my brother's to watch the Masters golf and said, 'I think I've just got the best story of my life.

'I was editing it and sending it to BBC Radio 5Live going, 'This is huge.' To be fair on them, they did run it as a story the next morning, but they didn't make it the phone-in or anything like that.

'It went quite big, but we didn't make the most of it. *The Asian Network*; hour long phone-in. (BBC Radio) 1Extra; hour long phone-in. The next day in the papers: 'Hip-Hop Glastonbury: Noel v Jay-Z.' It was absolutely huge. The *NME* put it on their cover maybe. It was genuinely a big, big news story. It was exciting being in the middle of it.'

Noel's comments made headlines across the music industry and to the wider world and caused outrage of comparison only to his AIDS comment over a decade earlier. The various unsavoury racist connotations were brought to the fore, with seemingly everyone having an opinion on the matter. Jay-Z himself was diplomatic, merely pointing out that headlining a festival was a natural evolution for rap music but he didn't throw any insults back.

Colin Paterson: 'Then two weeks before Glastonbury, I got the phone call. I picked up the phone and this guy went, 'Is this the acquisitions unit of the BBC?' I went 'yes.' 'A Mr Jay-Z's people have just phoned, wanting to license your interview for Glastonbury.' I was like; 'Yes, yes they can.' I don't care what my boss would say, they're having it. I didn't know what was going to happen. I cover Glastonbury every year, and it was one of my favourite moments ever. There was such a moment of anticipation around that. Would Jay-Z manage to pull it off? What would he do? I knew he would probably do something with the interview.

'This was never shown on TV because they couldn't clear the footage, but the lights went down on the main stage. The screens came up either side of the stage and there was a video Jay-Z had made. It started off with just, 'Jay-Z at Glastonbury? Hip-Hop? I'm not having that.' He really milked it too much; they had 'All You Need Is Love' playing and these vox pops of politicians from around the world giving their opinion on it. They also used other interviews I'd done, with Gwyneth Paltrow, who was big mates with Jay-Z, 'Noel doesn't know what he's talking about, Jay's going to smash it out of the park.

'So, there was this big video and I was standing there going, 'My interview is headlining Glastonbury! This is as good as it's going to get.'

It has to be said that the rapper played a blinder, making reference to the comments in his opening montage before taking to the stage. He proceeded to come onstage to 'Wonderwall', wearing a guitar, and singing along. Calling it singing is probably a stretch, but it set the tempo for an unforgettable show. Not that anyone came out of it badly. Sales of Oasis songs went up, Glastonbury sold out, and it was the highest-profile headline set for the festival for many years.

Noel was unrepentant after the event. While on the red carpet picking up an Outstanding Contribution at the Silver Clef awards, he stated, 'It appears my opinions offend people. Well, stop asking me fucking questions then.' Aggressively, he went on to state that he could just be like other 'two-bit' pop stars and claim everything was 'amazing.' To hammer home the point, he answered several questions with variations of the word 'amazing'. Noel, never being one to shy away from a subject, was asked for his thoughts on knife crime, at that point a hot topic, which also made the news. Later in the year, Noel had the last word on the Jay-Z debate, stating that he thought, 'It was pretty funny, but I'm not sure one should be seen in public with a white Stratocaster.'

Another Gallagher feud soon hit headlines; the meeting of mouths that the world didn't know it was waiting for took place in June: Liam appeared as support for his wife Nicole's appearance on *The F Word*, with celebrity chef Gordon Ramsay. Both Ramsay and Liam gave as good as they got in an expletive-laden exchange, although Liam had the upper hand by declaring Ramsay's sweet potatoes as 'bobbins.'

Amid this backdrop was the small matter of the Oasis machine grumbling into life. Three tracks had been leaked onto the internet over the summer; 'Ain't Got Nothing on Me' (as it was then supposedly titled), 'Record Machine' and 'Stop the Clocks.' A statement was issued that they were in fact demos from the *Don't Believe the Truth* sessions and wouldn't be part of the album (though 'Ain't Got Nothin' did actually make the cut).

Zak Starkey opted not to join the band for the forthcoming tour, despite recording the album, as it clashed with commitments he had already made with The Who. Chris Sharrock, formerly of The Icicle Works and The La's and most recently (and ironically) the drummer with Robbie Williams' live band, was drafted in. In other drummer-related news, Alan White's brother Steve threw a bit of light on the former's mysterious ejection from the band, informing *Zani* magazine that Alan received a call from the Oasis management team informing him he was out, that he had moved into property development, and was doing 'very well'.

On the business side, after all the derision Noel had thrown their way, came the somewhat surprising news that Oasis had re-signed to Sony for the release of the forthcoming album and two more. The deal was structured differently, with the music being released on Big Brother but under a profit-share agreement, which was no doubt lucrative for all concerned. Offering further clarification, Noel confirmed that Sony had signed Big Brother, but had given Oasis their back-catalogue.

Then finally (in the same week as Glastonbury) Oasis announced details of their new album and first single; the album was to be called *Dig Out Your Soul*, a Gem suggestion, with the first single to be 'The Shock of the Lightning.' There would be still be another few weeks until the public officially heard any new music, although the Chemical Brothers' remix of a track called 'Falling Down' was soon 'leaked,' if being played on mainstream radio can really be said to be leaked. BBC Radio One's Jo Whiley divulged that the remix would be included as a B-side on the forthcoming single, the first time Oasis had done so. As later stories would reveal, this may have been down to the paucity of songs, or that there was less input from the band. In another sign of the rapidly-changing music business, a video trailer for the album was released.

Brilliantly, even though it seemed that Oasis were very much part of the corporate world with such activity, the individuals within the band weren't quite so polished. In early August, as was custom, the first single received its first airplay on BBC Radio One, this time on *The Breakfast Show* with Chris Moyles. Sometimes in these circumstances a member of the band would come in for an interview to coincide with the first play. Noel had committed to doing so, but he had been playing a gig for competition winners the night before and had something of a wild night. As such, at 8am on national radio, Noel was interviewed blind drunk.

He was also hilarious, and ever the professional didn't swear once, a far cry from the halcyon days of insulting George Harrison and Keith Richards, which was broken up by expletives. Topics covered included Amy Winehouse, ('a destitute horse'), Gordon Brown ('texture like sun'), dogs ('is there anything funnier than dogs in hats?'), and producer Mark Ronson ('he wants to write his own songs instead of ruining everyone else's'). He also announced a UK tour for the autumn ('Is it a tour, or is it a promotional exercise?'), with arena dates in Liverpool, Sheffield, Birmingham, London, Bournemouth, Cardiff, Belfast, Aberdeen and Glasgow. All 180,000 tickets for the dates sold out in one hour.

The tour kicked off in Seattle in late August, the band playing only four songs from the forthcoming album ('The Shock of the Lightning', 'To Be Where There's Life', 'Ain't Got Nothin' and 'Falling Down'. This may have displayed a lack of faith in the new material but given that the album wasn't due for another two months it was more likely down to avoiding bootlegs. 'I Am the Walrus' was reintroduced as set closer after making way for 'My Generation' for a few years, and 'The Masterplan' found its way back into the set, as did 'Slide Away'. Other than that, the set contained few surprises for Chris Sharrock's first full gig, 'Lyla' and 'The Importance of Being Idle' cementing their places among the older material. The competition winners' gig a fortnight earlier held a few more treats, as well as a debut for 'Waiting For the Rapture', 'My Big Mouth' was given what was a rare performance at the time, although it did reappear in the main set before long.

The dates in Canada went by without a hitch, but it seemed that Lady Luck had used up her smiles on the band's last tour and re-emerged with a vengeance, specifically at the band's headline slot at the V Festival. Midway through the set, during 'Morning Glory', as Noel was focussing on the riff, stage left as ever, an attendee of the gig named Daniel Sullivan managed to make his way under the stage, through the back then on to it, and shoved Noel in the back, straight on to his speakers.

Noel immediately got up and exited the stage. Seemingly it took Liam a few seconds to realise what was happening as he witnessed the security guards wrestle Sullivan to the floor. Then, perhaps remembering he had a reputation to maintain, he threw a few punches Sullivan's way, though whether or not they connected, as there were two security guards between them, it's hard to tell.

This could have been a lot more serious, and Noel later said, 'Not to be too dramatic, but I thought I'd been stabbed', stating in a prepared statement at the sentencing that he felt as if he had been hit by a bus. The guitarist suffered three cracked ribs and the next few dates were postponed.

Surprisingly, given that in the past the band had no qualms about walking off stage if debris was thrown on stage, they re-emerged to finish the set. But the incident cast an early shadow over what was to be their final tour.

Writing on his *Tales From the Middle of Nowhere* blog on the official Oasis website, Noel was as flippant as ever, dubbing the security team, 'Trotters

Independent Security Service', with a nod to *Only Fools and Horses*, and describing it as 'a severe tickling.' Sullivan was charged and sentenced to house arrest 18 months later, his motives or mindset never revealed to the general public. The tour was put on hold, although dates in the US were pencilled in for the winter, as was a special show at the BBC *Electric Proms* in London.

The blog itself became a must-read over the course of the tour (and indeed later tours), Noel regaling his fans with amusing anecdotes, and also cryptic titles for his friends. His own title was 'General Dread', Andy was 'Tall Scratch', and Gem was 'Cool Prophet.' It also became a good insight into his headspace and a good outlet for press clarifications. He also divulged that he had a bad feeling about the gig in Toronto, demonstrating unerring psychic ability.

Disappointingly, when 'The Shock of the Lightning' was eventually released at the end of September, it stalled at No.3 in the top-40. This was quite significant, as it was the first lead single since their debut 'Supersonic' not to reach the top spot. This may have been due to being backed by remixes, the Oasis faithful no doubt preferring the option of new songs rather than alternative versions. It may also have been owing to the decline of physical sales; CD singles were dying by 2008 and, strangely (at the time) the track was released on download first, then a physical version followed the week after, which also cannot have helped its performance. To offset this, multiple versions of both single and album were announced, including various download packages and a deluxe vinyl box-set, which offered a number of exclusive tracks. Regardless, the times were changing, and Oasis were being left behind.

Not entirely though. Some of the marketing for the album was novel. Sheet music and lyrics were given to several busking bands in New York prior to release. Four songs ('The Turning', '(Get Off Your) High Horse Lady', 'Bag It Up' and 'The Shock of the Lightning') were performed across the Big Apple, the buskers selected after applying via the band's website. The *NME* also included a songbook and CD-ROM with band interviews and wallpapers. The album received a deluxe release, with an extra CD of songs, including more remixes and two new tracks; 'Boy With The Blues' finally saw the light of day, along with 'I Believe In All.' The pair were released digitally the following year.

Dig Out Your Soul was released in early October and, although mixed reviews were far from a new experience for Oasis, the write-ups this time were generally at polar ends of the spectrum. Some outlets declared it their best since *(What's the Story) Morning Glory?* while others took great satisfaction in deciding the band had finally run out of ideas. In truth, that reflects the album itself; six of the first seven tracks were as good as anything the band ever produced, but three of the last four rank among the worst among fandom. But, yet again and for the final time, an Oasis studio album went straight in at No.1, selling over 200,000 copies in the first week.

The tour re-commenced in early October, the day after the album's release, in Liverpool, heading onto Sheffield and Birmingham. On his blog, Noel was happy that the band had hit their stride. Two dates at London's Wembley Arena followed, one of which was broadcast live on MTV, and Oasis took the opportunity while in that part of town to announce two (later to become three) nights at the new Wembley Stadium the following summer, with Kasabian and The Enemy as support. In addition, there were mega-gigs for Heaton Park in Manchester, the Millennium Stadium in Cardiff, Sunderland's Stadium of Light, Murrayfield in Edinburgh, Coventry's Ricoh Arena and Slane Castle in Dublin. There wasn't a corner of the UK and Ireland that was untouched. All dates sold out within hours. Support on a handful of dates on the arena tour came from up and coming Scottish band Sergeant.

Nick Mercer: 'Noel heard one of our songs from someone, who gave him the record and was like, 'Check these out.' He heard it and basically phoned up and said, 'Get them on the tour.' That's how it works, which is pretty sweet. A lot of people don't realise you've got to pay for these things. So many support bands are paying to go on tours and nonsense like that. To actually be asked to do it was brilliant. It was everything.

"Turn up at this time and then on you go.' I think we played four nights with them. Two on, two off, two on. The first one was Aberdeen Exhibition Centre. We turned up, like little boys. Well, we were little boys! We were just in the moment, couldn't believe it was happening. We were literally living everything that we'd dreamt about.'

At the press conference announcing the stadium gigs, Noel was praising the quality of the line-up and, in a fashion that he later acknowledged was tongue-in-cheek, dismissed Glastonbury Festival and declared, 'This is where it's going to be at next year.' Which was partly true, although it was going to be another congested summer of live music. As well as the Oasis gigs and the usual run of festivals, Coldplay, U2 and a reformed Blur all had big open-air gigs pencilled in for summer 2009.

The UK arena tour went by without any more incidents before some dates in Europe. As was the theme for all acts performing at the *BBC Electric Proms*, it was an Oasis set with a twist, in this instance the band having backing on a select few tracks ('The Masterplan', 'I'm Outta Time', 'Wonderwall', 'Don't Look Back in Anger', 'Champagne Supernova', and 'I Am the Walrus') in the form of the Crouch End Festival Chorus, who would later go on to work with Noel on his first album. Sadly, such was the power of the band's performance that even a full choir couldn't really be heard on television, although people in the crowd after said otherwise.

Meanwhile, in an interview with *Billboard*, Noel revealed that he had already demoed songs for the next album, describing them as 'mid-era Kinks,' with a narrative around 'soldiers and religious people.' Along with the songs that hadn't made the cut on the last two albums, and other songs that were played in soundchecks, it seemed that virtually all his debut solo album was seemingly written by this point.

Nick Mercer: 'When we turned up, Noel was rehearsing on stage, and we stood at the side and watched. Then he came down and I think his words were, 'You must be the support band then.' That was the introduction. Everyone says, 'Don't meet your heroes,' but I kind of think the opposite. For every single one of them that was in that band, it was hugs from the beginning. Handshakes. Eat what you want, drink what you want. Go in any dressing room, whatever one you want. Just do what you want. That was pretty much how it worked. It was just hanging out for a week. That was pretty special. That was the realisation that your heroes, or people that are full-blown celebrities, and you realise, 'You're just the same as us.' That was awesome.

'The catering and the food bit was open, so anyone could be there at any given time. It wasn't like, 'This is the time you go for your dinner, this is the time they go for their dinner.' It was an open-planned thing. I remember sitting watching Lewis Hamilton win his first Formula One Championship with everybody in the room, because everyone was just ducking about.

'Chris Sharrock was in his element. He was recently on to that gig. It was an arena tour before they did their stadium tour. It was basically the smaller gigs of the tour, so he was just in his element. He was as excited as us!

'Every single night they stood at the side of the stage and watched us play. They thought it was great. I don't know if it was or not!

'With hindsight, you probably look back and think it was a bit bland. You watch videos and think, 'I didn't notice that,' but I guess you wouldn't, we were just living our dream, with our adrenaline and our rush. You were just in awe that you were on tour with them. Performance-wise, I didn't notice if anything was off. The production and the sound was really strong, the way that is sounded was great.'

The tour then crossed the Atlantic, first to Mexico and then up the West Coast of the USA. In early December, Noel and Liam were invited by boxer Ricky Hatton, himself a fierce Mancunian and Oasis fan, to carry his belts out for a World title fight with Paul Malignaggi in Las Vegas.

Ricky Hatton: '(Las Vegas) was one of my best moments. One of the highlights of my career. I think it's fair to say I beat better people than Malignaggi ... but the fact that the lads carried the belts in for me ... for a number of years, I'd always asked them if they'd do it for me, but they never got around to doing it because they always had a gig on or something, or they couldn't make it. But that time we actually did get the chance to do it, and it was something else. There's a picture

I have in my games room where Noel and Liam have both got the belts there, and I've got a belt around my waist. Liam, in typical fashion, is giving it the two fingers. It's the best picture I have in my games room. If ever there was a picture that personified Manchester ... You don't get much better than that. Working-class success stories. It was a brilliant occasion.

'Liam went up into Malignaggi's face. 'What do you bloody think about that, then?' It was funny.

'Then the following day we flew to Mexico City to watch them do their gig there. It wasn't just the fight that was the occasion, it was the whole weekend. They gave us a table on the stage where they were playing, and they gave us an ice bucket with cans of Guinness and cans of lager. We were only feet away from them. Liam got me up and introduced me to the crowd, and 40,000 Mexicans were there. It was a special weekend that will stay with me forever.'

Tellingly, at this point in his blog, Noel had started referring to Liam as 'wots'iz'name' rather than '*r-kid*' as he had previously. In an interview with *Mojo*, he also disclosed his dissatisfaction at his younger brother getting married during recording of the album, saying, 'I don't give a shit about the fact he didn't invite me to the wedding, but when it affects our work, it infuriates me.' The magazine also revealed that two tracks didn't make the album and had to be replaced with two which had been ear-marked as B-sides. Never before had the brothers' arguments knowingly had such an adverse effect on an album, Noel always insisting that the music be of the highest possible standard. Despite referring to Liam as the 'best rock and roll singer of his generation' some weeks earlier, with hindsight it is now easy to see this point as where the cracks began to show.

On their US dates, the general consensus with the American press seemed to be that the group were very grumpy and unimpressed. The media, stateside, always had an apathy at best towards Oasis (but the fans stayed loyal despite the gigs sometimes being unremarkable) despite another prestigious gig at Madison Square Garden. 'I'm Outta Time' was released as the second single from *Dig Out Your Soul* in early December, and sadly was the first Oasis single since 'Shakermaker' not to make the top-10, charting at No.12. As before, this surely wasn't helped by having no fresh material accompanying it, instead being backed by remixes of tracks from the album as B-sides across various formats.

oasis
FALLING DOWN
NEW SINGLE
9.3.09
7"/12"/CD/DIGITAL

2009

'WE LIVE A DYING DREAM, IF YOU KNOW WHAT I MEAN'

After the Christmas break the tour re-commenced in Europe, the band hitting France, Belgium, Germany, Austria, the Netherlands, Italy and Scandinavia, with one gig in Dusseldorf having to be postponed because of Liam's voice. Before Christmas, in his blog Noel had waxed lyrical about an act called Amorphous Androgynous and their *A Monstrous Psychedelic Bubble in the Head* series. The act had formerly been known as The Future Sound of London, and in early 2009 they took to social media to announce that Noel had been in contact and requested a remix of their next single 'Falling Down.' This would be the first step in an ultimately unfruitful relationship, despite enthusiasm from both parties.

Meanwhile, the band picked up an impressive seven nominations at the *NME* Awards, although one of those was Worst Band. They eventually picked up two gongs, Best Band and Best Blog, despite Noel proudly declaring he composed the blogs via text rather than on computer. Because of their touring commitments, they were unable to attend and were noticeably booed by the crowd for not doing so. Also, *The Dreams We Have As Children*, the live recording of Noel's performance for the Teenage Cancer Trust in 2007, was released via download and a CD version was given away free with *The Sunday Times*, which significantly increased their circulation for that week.

Rumours started circulating in the British press about Noel and Liam not communicating whilst on tour, taking separate transport and not seeing or speaking to each other outside of the performances. Ordinarily these sorts of stories were easy to dismiss, but with hindsight seem to be accurate. Noel barely mentioned Liam in his blog and in interviews he made no attempt to contradict the rumours. Liam meanwhile was preparing for a venture outside music; he was launching a fashion range, which was to be called *Pretty Green* after the song by The Jam. Liam's outlook was, 'I'm not gonna be putting anything out unless I'd wear it.' The younger Gallagher did a bit of publicity for the range, which was heavily influenced by Mod styles from the mid-60s onwards. It appeared that Liam was very hands-on with the range, although the idea of him offering insight into design seems a stretch. Liam also joined the new social media app, Twitter.

The tour continued to have various problems, with a gig in Paris having to be stopped twice because of sound issues and, more dramatically, Oasis were banned from performing in China, having had two dates booked for April. The reason given was Noel's performance at a *Free Tibet* benefit concert 12 years previously.

What would prove to be their final single, the Noel-sung 'Falling Down,' was released in March. Backed by a new track ('Those Swollen Hand Blues'), the single ensured Oasis' reign in the top-40 went out with some dignity, reaching No.10. By happy accident, the bi-annual BBC fundraiser *Red Nose Day* fell around the same time, and as part of their telethon a special version of sadly-retired cultural touchstone *Top of the Pops* (which stopped airing in 2006) was broadcast, with a performance of the single part of the programme. A firm advocate for the show, it was obvious from Noel's demeanour that he was pleased to be able to do the show one last time. Another box ticked. Meanwhile, Oasis were announced to headline the V Festival in August, for the second time.

Moving into the Far East, the band made a tweak to the set, adding 'Whatever,' in as a mainstay for the first time in years. It wasn't to be the full band version but performed acoustically by Noel. The tour touched all corners of the Far East, with nine dates in Japan, one each in South Korea, Taiwan, Singapore and Hong Kong. Noel called the South Korea date the best gig of the tour, although he did go on to say that a few times over the course of the year about other shows. Following this, they moved on to South Africa, for the first time, to play two festivals. In an interview in the May edition of *Q* magazine, Noel was in an intolerant mood with his little brother and seemingly snapped, 'He's never seen my little lad, just pictures (Noel and Sara had recently had a son). To a stranger it sounds ludicrous, but you wouldn't have him in the house if he spoke to you the way he speaks to me and my family. He's rude, arrogant, intimidating and lazy. He's the angriest man you'll ever meet. He's like a man with a fork in a world of soup.'

Significantly, Noel went on to say, 'We've arrived at the point I wanted to be at when Gem and Andy joined the band, and the last time we did that was at the end of *Be Here Now*.' He was also mentioning a five-year break for the band, and in the same interview again mentioned solo plans; 'Hopefully at the end of this tour I'm going to go and do something for myself.' On the blog, Noel referenced the *Q* magazine article but made no reference to his comments, seemingly confirming them.

Liam took to Twitter to snap back, 'Is it that time of the month again, r kid?,' dubbing Noel and Russell Brand 'a pair of old housewife's' (sic) when the pair were co-presenting a show for *Talk Sport*. And so the battle over social media began. Liam was engaging with fans in another way, by participating in short videos on YouTube entitled *Ask Liam* to promote the *Pretty Green* range. He couldn't deny the ructions with his brother, confirming things were, 'Not good. But this is the tension, it's like he wants to outdo me, and I want to outdo him.'

The band embarked on another leg of the tour, this time in South America, including a first gig in Peru. Details of the band's backstage demands were revealed, which were befitting of a band with Oasis' reputation, consisting of mainly booze and tea, and no outlandish requirements. The most diva-esque were simply that Guinness had to be in cans and chewing gum had to be flavoured peppermint or spearmint. Meanwhile, Noel alluded to, 'Bad times for the Oasis tour. Bad times. We are a rudderless ship at the minute. And there's a fuckin' shit-storm on the horizon. I guess all will be revealed in due course ... and there's a bit too much harrumphing going on for my liking.' To which Liam retaliated with, 'Don't know what tour you're on R KID.'

Knowing what was disclosed later, this may have been down to a dispute between Noel and Liam regarding *Pretty Green*. Noel later claimed that Liam wanted to advertise the line in the tour programmes, but Noel refused initially, although he then gave Liam the option of paying him to advertise, which Liam did not take well. Noel later put this disagreement down as the beginning of the end. Given that the line was due to launch in June, the timings may add up, although Liam vehemently denied this. The mood didn't affect Noel making the most of the tour though, declaring the gig at Estadio River Plate in Buenos Aires 'one of the best nights of all time.' He continued in a later post, 'The gigs are great. Could be better though. Anyway, 'nuff of that.'

Such was the way of the internet that more and more footage of Oasis performing started to make its way online, including from soundchecks, and every move could be scrutinised. Noel had always been known to play new material in soundchecks, and two new songs surfaced; 'If I Had A Gun', and 'Everybody is on the Run.' Liam was meanwhile taking swipes at The Enemy's Tom Clarke, who apparently made disparaging comments about Oasis' work rate, to which Liam responded, 'Do you want to go on 1st or what, you little fucker?' referring to their support slot for the forthcoming UK summer tour.'

Social media has its risks and in the age of instant reaction, in the hands of William Gallagher, it's positively disastrous to some. Clarke quickly and understandably rushed to deny the report and protest he was misquoted. Noel also took action to shut the rumours down, even going so far as to say it was the *NME* and if anyone from the paper was seen on site at the gigs, they would be escorted off.

And so, 'the summer of bigness' began, the first stop three homecoming gigs at Heaton Park, Manchester. In a strange irony, the park is now more famous for being the scene of The Stone Roses' comeback gigs, but Oasis were there three years earlier. The first night was a beautiful summer's evening, and the scene was set for a classic concert. The band took to the stage and opened with, as always, 'Rock 'n' Roll Star'... and got about two minutes in before the sound gave in. Mystified, both Liam and Noel attempted to speak to the crowd, but the speakers were completely dead. The band stayed on stage for a while, with the problem resolved 15 minutes later. They re-emerged to start again, this time going straight into 'Lyla.' On the second attempt they managed to get through to the last chorus before the sound cut out again. The band walked straight off stage, clearly furious. This time around there was a delay of half an hour. The screens projected apology messages, citing the cause as the generators.

Eventually the band re-emerged a second time, as both Liam and Noel individually informed the crowd that from there on it was to be a free gig, and the entire crowd could claim refunds. The rest of the show went by without a hitch, and the crowd were treated to the long mothballed 'Roll with It,' included in the set for the first time in eight years, as well as re-introducing 'My Big Mouth' and 'Live Forever,' which had been strangely absent for this tour. But it can't have made the band any cheerier. Noel, ever the businessman, admitted after that they may have overreacted in offering refunds, but he didn't go back on his word. He was also astonished that 20,000 people had asked for their money back. The next two nights went off without a hitch, as did the gig at Sunderland's Stadium of Light and at Cardiff's Millennium Stadium. Noel was effervescent in his praise of Kasabian each time, stating, 'If they're not selling out stadiums within two years, I will eat Joanna Lumley's shit.'

Edinburgh's Murrayfield was the next destination, via a stop-off in Lyon, then on to the annual Slane Castle Festival in the Irish Republic, where The Prodigy took over as main support from Kasabian. Both gigs were reported as being special, no doubt the Celtic connection with Oasis being a large factor, although Edinburgh suffered some trouble from crowds in the surrounding areas of the stadium, and reports of crowd congestion hit the headlines in Ireland. After a couple of headline festival slots at Rock Werchter in Belgium and Roskilde in Denmark, the travelling circus went back to England, firstly to Coventry and then, again, to Wembley Stadium. Oasis were one of the few bands to play both the old and new stadium, and although much had changed in the nine years since they last played there, it was much the same line-up, albeit two drummers having left in the intervening years.

Doing the round of press before the gig, Noel was adamant in his denial of the latest batch of rumours that Oasis were to split; 'I am Oasis. I'll never leave Oasis and Oasis will never leave me.' The first night of the three was beset by more technical problems, the sound giving in during 'Wonderwall.' Fortunately, the crowd were in fine voice and able to finish the song off, after which Noel stated categorically that there would be no refunds. The second and third nights went by without any such problems, and the stellar line-up of Reverend and the Makers, The Enemy, Kasabian and Oasis sent thousands of Londoners home happy. Noel himself declared Saturday as one of 'THOSE nights. What an atmosphere!' and Sunday to be, 'Another very special night ... Great, great gig. Not as good as the piss-up after though,' which was nice for paying guests to read. Wembley was followed by a rescheduled gig at the Eden Project in Cornwall, which was cancelled back in September because of Noel's injury.

Yet more sound problems hit the band's set at the Benicassim festival in Spain during their performance of 'Wonderwall', the PA once more blowing up. Again though, it didn't deter the crowd or the band, and they went on to conclude the set. It wasn't the only problem at the festival, and comparatively Oasis got away lightly; there was a huge fire on site and high winds caused the final two days to be cancelled. Then followed a gig at The Roundhouse in London as part of the iTunes Festival, where Liam seemed to be in a mightily bad mood, refusing to sing 'My Big Mouth' and generally abusing the crowd (although at certain points coins were thrown at the stage, so it wasn't entirely unjustified).

Despite appearing to be quite calm about the situation, Noel blogged, 'What'siz'name exploded with pretend rage the minute he walked on ... probably on his man period.' It appeared that Liam's behaviour was finally starting to take its toll.

Liam bit back on Twitter, with 'Regarding shortarse's comments on my behaviour at the Roundhouse - Pretend rage? It's called rock'n'roll, darling, you wanna try it sometime. Man period? You've been on since the first gig in Seattle! And as for the squares backstage, all your guests left with you.' It seemed that the rumours were true, and the brothers weren't even talking by this point, solely using social media to communicate, which of course the media absolutely lapped up. Relations between the brothers seemed to lurch from worse to even worse, Liam giving an interview to the *NME*, saying, 'It takes a lot more than blood to by my brother.'

Nick Mercer: 'The reality is, Noel and Liam were never in the same room at the same time. That's what everybody wants to hear or whatever, but that was the case. They weren't best mates, but they just weren't hanging out the way the other ones were. It wasn't that it was obvious that they weren't speaking to each other. That was all part of the story all along. Whether they seeped into the mood or the actual performance, I find it hard to pinpoint because the reality was that I wasn't paying attention. You'd never see them walk in, and then walk out because the other one wasn't there. It was almost like they took nights off on who was going to hang about.'

After some dates in the Far East and a short break, the last few dates of the tour were pencilled is as a warm-up for the V Festival in Bridlington Spa, then the two festival dates in Stafford and Chelmsford. The Bridlington gig, the last time Oasis ever played in front of their own fans, went ahead with no drama, as did the first date of the V Festival in Stafford. It was a subdued set - although the sound at the

oasis
plus special guests
KASABIAN
TheEnemy
Saturday 6 & Sunday 7 June 2009
MANCHESTER HEATON PARK
Friday 12 June 2009
CARDIFF MILLENNIUM STADIUM
Wednesday 10 June 2009
SUNDERLAND STADIUM OF LIGHT
Wednesday 17 June 2009
EDINBURGH MURRAYFIELD STADIUM
Saturday 11 & Sunday 12 July 2009
LONDON WEMBLEY STADIUM
Buy online for all shows from
www.oasisinet.com
www.gigsandtours.com www.ticketmaster.co.uk www.ticketline.co.uk
OASIS LO-CALL 24HR TICKETLINE 0844 412 4638
24hr Credit Card Hotlines 0871 2200 260 / 0871 230 6230 / 0871 424 4444
New album DIG OUT YOUR SOUL out now
TICKETS ON SALE AT 10am,
FRIDAY 24 OCTOBER

V Festival never helped - running through the staples of the entire tour.

The setlist was:

'Rock 'n' Roll Star'
'Lyla'
'The Shock of the Lightning'
'Cigarettes & Alcohol'
'Roll with It'
'Waiting for the Rapture'
'The Masterplan'
'Songbird'
'Slide Away'
'Morning Glory'
'My Big Mouth'
'Half the World Away'
'I'm Outta Time'
'Wonderwall'
'Supersonic'
'Live Forever'
'Don't Look Back in Anger'
'Champagne Supernova'
'I Am the Walrus'

The main set finished with 'Live Forever', and the last song of the night and the last song Oasis ever performed, fittingly given the constant comparisons to The Beatles throughout their career, was 'I Am the Walrus.' The tensions within the band were apparent from the crowd, the brothers not even acknowledging each other. Noel went on to say in the blog that he, 'Didn't enjoy it one bit. Dunno why. Couldn't get into it. Very strange.'

The same was expected on the next night in Chelmsford, but at the last minute it was announced that Oasis had to pull out due to Liam losing his voice to laryngitis. Already on the bill, Irish band Snow Patrol stepped into the breach. Several bands including Snow Patrol, Keane and MGMT performed cover versions of Oasis songs on the day. Liam took to Twitter a few days after with a message for the fans, 'First things first, V - I'm gutted, you're gutted. I'm sorry, what can I say? Fuck all at the moment.'

The previous week, columnist from *The Sun* Gordon Smart had published an article on Oasis, declaring the concluding dates would be their last ever. Liam took umbrage at this and posted (his grammar, not mine), 'Finally, reports in smartarses column about Oasis last British gig ever. The kid's talking out of his arse, I mean Rkids, beware of darkness.' Andy Bell conducted an interview with *Glasswerk* the same week and pointedly refused to discuss the brothers Gallagher.

Liam's voice had seemingly recovered by the end of the week, as a headline slot at the Rock en Seine festival in Paris was due to go ahead as planned. However, one minute before the band were due to go on, an announcement was made that the band were pulling the gig. It was left to Bloc Party, who were playing before the headliners, to gleefully tell the crowd that Oasis were pulling out and dedicated a song to 'those inbred twins.' Organisers then said it was because of a fight between Noel and Liam. Songstress Amy Macdonald, of all people, was the first to announce to the wider world on Twitter that the band were pulling out and that Liam had smashed Noel's guitar. Other rumours were flying, and then, in the early hours of the following morning, a short statement was released by Noel:

'It's with some sadness and great relief to tell you that I quit Oasis tonight. People will write and say what they like, but I simply could not go on working with Liam a day longer.

'Apologies to all the people who bought tickets for the shows in Paris, Konstanz and Milan.'

A statement was then released by a publicist for the group, stating, 'The rest of the band were considering whether or not to carry on without Noel.' Then, the following morning Noel posted a more detailed farewell message.

And that was that. The general public didn't hear from anyone within the band's circle for some time. Over the following years, as both Liam and Noel did press for their respective careers, more details of the incident were disclosed. Both brothers confirmed that the argument started over Noel's relationship with members of the press, Liam believing that too many journalists had entered the inner circle. The seeds of this had been blooming for several years. There's a scene in *Lord Don't Slow Me Down* which shows the brothers arguing over the same subject, Liam banging the table and admonishing Noel, saying, 'You should have a bit more respect for our band.'

As Liam stormed out of the dressing room, he apparently threw a plum across the dressing room in Noel's direction. In his version of events two years later, Noel singled out Andy Bell for his lack of support, claiming that during the altercation he was, 'looking at the floor, counting how many shoes he had on.' Liam then returned, apparently brandishing his own guitar - a present from his girlfriend and children - like an axe, swinging it around the room. Noel 'put the guitar out of its misery' and then left. The elder Gallagher sat in his car for a few minutes, contemplating what to do, then simply decided enough was enough and ordered the car to drive off. In that moment, and in his head, he had left the band.

Obviously, the news made headlines, with the world and his wife venturing opinions. The split took place while the Reading and Leeds Festival was in full swing and T-shirts were made up, and some of the bands playing the festival either paid tribute or gave some insight. American art-poppers Vampire Weekend informed the *NME* that they were in the dressing room next door, but it was Oasis' story to tell. Kele Okereke of Bloc Party continued to be ecstatic, saying from the stage, 'How are we all taking the news? One of the great British institutions is no more, the final series of *Big Brother*. Did you think I meant Oasis? Just kidding.'

The mainstream press was very glib about the whole affair, either commenting with an air that insinuated that the group were long past it or taking it with a pinch of salt as both brothers had been known to walk out on several previous occasions. The group's former mentor Alan McGee, ever the believer in the power of rock'n'roll, immediately called on Glasvegas to step into the breach, but also put forward the belief that the band would be back before long. Articles upon articles were written, either eulogising the band or already looking ahead to the 'inevitable' reunion. The fallout continued into the autumn. Apparently, Andy and Liam went on holiday to discuss the future, and Noel disappeared from public life for a short time.

The biggest rock'n'roll band of their generation were no more. Putting the pieces together, as referenced throughout despite his denials, it seems worth considering that Noel had always intended to call it a day following this tour. He often stated that his biggest regret was not disbanding Oasis after Knebworth, as he wanted them to go out on a high. A huge stadium tour, covering all corners of the United Kingdom, was as close to Knebworth as possible, it being a farewell tour in all but name. In the eyes of the critics, *Don't Believe the Truth* had generally been comparable to their highest points, as was, in certain corners, *Dig Out Your Soul*. Noel had mentioned that no-one had been capable of stepping into Oasis' shoes, but he was praising Kasabian at every opportunity throughout the summer, and he may have seen a band who could finally step into the breach to an extent. And commercially, despite being a No.1 album, the singles lifted from *Dig Out Your Soul* had not hit the heights of any of their previous work. Noel Gallagher is and was a proud man and may have wanted to go out on his terms.

Nowadays he also makes the point that there is very little point in reforming Oasis as, unlike The Stone Roses or The Libertines or numerous other reformed bands, they have no unfinished business, which is undeniable. No.1 singles and albums, sold-out tours, Wembley Stadium and Madison Square Garden both played twice, Outstanding Contribution awards. All achieved in their last few years. When you add all their achievements from their first three albums, very few British bands can claim to have anywhere near the same levels of success and dedication from a fanbase. As Noel reportedly divulged to Ian Brown, 'There's actually nowhere left to take it.'

'Dearly beloved, it is with a heavy heart and a sad face that I say this to you this morning.

'As of last Friday, August 28, I have been forced to leave the Manchester rock'n'roll pop group Oasis.

'The details are not important and of too great a number to list. But I feel you have the right to know that the level of verbal and violent intimidation to me, my family, friends and comrades has become intolerable. And the lack of support and understanding from my management and bandmates has left me with no other option that to get me cape and seek pastures new.

'I would like firstly to offer my apologies to them kids in Paris who'd paid money and waited all day to see us only to be let down AGAIN by the band. Apologies are probably not enough, I know, but I'm afraid it's all I've got.

'While I'm on the subject, I'd like to say (sorry) to the good people of V Festival that experienced the same thing. Again, I can only apologise – although I don't know why, it was nothing to do with me. I was match fit and ready to be brilliant. Alas, other people in the group weren't up to it.

'In closing I would like to thank all the Oasis fans, all over the world. The last 18 years have been truly, truly amazing (and I hate that word, but today is the one time I'll deem it appropriate). A dream come true. I take with me glorious memories.

'Now, if you'll excuse me, I have a family and a football team to indulge. I'll see you somewhere down the road. It's been a fuckin' pleasure.

Thanks very much.

Goodbye.

NG'

EPILOGUE

'THE FUTURE'S MINE AND IT'S NO DISGRACE, 'COS IN THE END THE PAST MEANS NOTHING'

Oasis changed the musical landscape without question, but even more than that, the public and media interest in the Gallagher brothers, be it as celebrity or rock star, was now firmly entrenched in the UK's consciousness. Indeed, six months after their split, Oasis were the recipients of the Best British Album of 30 Years award - decided by public vote via BBC Radio Two - at the Brit Awards in 2010. Liam broke cover to accept the award, thanking, 'Bonehead, Guigs, Alan White, and the best fucking fans in the world.' His brother may have mastered the art of grabbing a headline, but in not mentioning Noel, Liam proved he was no slouch when it came to garnering attention. He stated after that he wanted to acknowledge the other members, rather than the story always being about the Gallaghers. Although the story of Oasis was over, there were still plenty of tales to tell and plenty of merchandise to sell.

It was widely assumed and indeed a safe bet that Noel Gallagher would go solo, but first out of the traps with their intention to carry on were the rest of the band; Liam, Gem, Andy and Chris going straight into rehearsals to write some new music. The decision over whether or not to carry on as Oasis went on for a few months before it was agreed that the new project would need a new name, and in mid-2010 it was announced; Beady Eye. In late 2010 they released their first single, a bluesy piano-driven number called 'Bring the Light,' and the debut album *Different Gear, Still Speeding* was released in February 2011. It received very mixed reviews, the most positive sentiment being that it was noble for them to carry on without the main songwriter.

A great deal of intrigue and goodwill carried the band for a while. Their decision not to play Oasis songs live during their first tours was admirable, but unfortunately the songs included on the debut album weren't strong enough to sustain a lengthy tour, and by the end of 2011 they began to look very stale. However, with everything taken into account it was a relatively successful campaign. It was never likely to hit the heights of Oasis (even if Liam thought, in classic bullish fashion, that would be the case), but it was respectable. For the dedicated fan, the lyrics were scrutinised for references to the elder Gallagher, although few were apparent, the songs themselves largely made up of those that hadn't made the cut at various points during latter-period Oasis. For example, 'The Roller' had been kicking around for a decade. And 'Beatles and Stones' was perhaps a little too on-the-nose for some, in reference to their influences.

A new tack was attempted for their second album, with the band spreading their wings, bringing in Dave Sitek, a member of art-rockers TV On The Radio and a successful producer, to be responsible for the sound of their second album, entitled simply *BE*. The album was released in early summer 2013 but, despite a concerted effort to make No.1 (including a surprise appearance at Glastonbury Festival), it fell one place short again. It's a far more interesting album than the first though, both lyrically and sonically. For those seeking such things, 'Don't Brother Me' could only be about one person, and the textures of the album benefits from several listens. But it didn't increase their standing in any way, shape or form.

More seriously, Gem sustained a potentially damaging injury, falling down the stairs at home and fracturing his skull. His health was of paramount importance, but it also meant that the band were limited in how much touring they could do. Even though they played several European and other international shows, with a handful of Oasis songs included, Beady Eye only performed eight UK shows in 2013 in promotion of the album. After playing Australia in early 2014, Beady Eye then took a break.

During the downtime Andy started to demonstrate an interest in reforming Ride, which was seemingly the last straw for Liam, and he disbanded Beady Eye in November 2014. In his own words, the gigs were getting smaller and smaller. In summer 2013 Liam had been the subject of yet another tabloid sensation over his marriage to Nicole Appleton, the impending divorce taking up much of his time for the next few years.

For their part Ride enjoyed a successful comeback. To test the water, they embarked on a short UK tour in 2015, and their absence combined with the assent and importance of BBC Radio 6 Music gave them an excellent foundation on which to build. In 2017 they released new music in the form of an album entitled *Weather Diaries*, which made them arguably more successful than they were first time around. This was consolidated with the release of another album, *This is Not a Safe Place,* in 2019.

Noel kept a relatively low profile for some time. He was coaxed out of the wilderness to perform another two nights at the Royal Albert Hall in March 2010 for the Teenage Cancer Trust, yet the shows were very much greatest hits sets. He was also primarily responsible for the accompanying marketing for an Oasis singles compilation *(Time Flies ... 1994-2009)*, recording short interview videos for each song as well as providing DVD commentary for the video compilation. Noel's insights quickly became compulsory viewing, his opinions on the videos and often the songs themselves both hilarious and disparaging. For instance, he 'fucking hates' 'Sunday Morning Call' and the song is only included as a hidden track on the CD version of the compilation. Tellingly, he manages the impressive feat of generally ignoring Liam's presence throughout all 26 videos, only a couple of times referring to, 'the singer.'

To the surprise of no-one, Noel Gallagher did release a solo album in October 2011, two years after leaving Oasis. To launch his new project, Noel Gallagher's High Flying Birds, a press conference took place in July, arranged to avoid the rigmarole of having to repeat himself several tours on the interview circuit, and Noel went into detail about the incident in Paris and his regret at terminating the band. In terms of new music, as well as the self-titled debut album, Noel revealed that he had been working with Amorphous Androgynous in tandem and a collaboration album was in the offing. He was unfortunately being presumptuous as the album hadn't been finished when announced and was eventually scrapped. Once again, Noel talked of taking a psychedelic trip, but was grounded in the departure lounge.

But his self-titled debut album was an unmitigated success, going straight to No.1 and featuring a series of successful singles. For his High Flying Birds, he enlisted Jeremy Stacey on drums, former Zutons' bassist Russell Pritchard and guitarist Tim Smith, with semi-regular Oasis live member Mike Rowe supplying the keys. The album sold twice as much as Beady Eye's debut, a fact not lost on the press, and has at the time of writing sold nearly three million copies worldwide. It also had a very positive critical reception, the first time in a few years that Noel had been so popular in the eyes of the critics. The first tour started quite small, playing medium-sized venues in the UK, US, Europe, Asia and Oceania at the tail-end of 2011. However, when the tour re-commenced in 2012 the band were playing arenas. The success of the album would have been one factor, being one of the best-selling rock records of 2011.

Another factor was that the sets included a huge amount of Oasis songs. All the major Noel-sung compositions were included ('Don't Look Back in Anger,' 'The Importance Of Being Idle,' 'Talk Tonight,' 'Half the World Away,' etc), as well as other classics. Significantly, each show on the tour opened with his version of '(It's Good) To Be Free.' There was excitement among the devotees as to which songs Noel would select on his debut solo tour but, with the benefit of hindsight, it now looks like a very unsurprising setlist. That said, every now and again there were pleasant surprises; unheralded B-sides 'Angel Child' and 'Idler's Dream' both making fleeting appearances.

Again for the ardent fans, there were lyrics which could only have been ripostes to his younger brother, despite Noel claiming otherwise. 'Dream On,' the second track and fourth single lifted from the album, seems to be Noel's perspective on things. Likewise, 'Keep on Reaching' from his third album *Who Built the Moon?*

On launching Beady Eye, Liam had been very vocal to the press about his elder brother's underhand plans to quit Oasis. One line in particular ('the bitch keeps bitching and all, taking the shots as I fall') has to be directed at Liam, and the references to 'songbird' elsewhere in the track perhaps confirm this, as well as the title itself.

The biggest shock to anyone who fought in the Britpop wars took place in March 2013. Curating the *Teenage Cancer Trust* gigs for one year only (normal custodian Roger Daltrey undergoing surgery) as well as roping in his friends for sets (Kasabian, Primal Scream, Paul Weller), Noel also headlined one night himself. The support act for that show featured Blur's Damon Albarn and Graham Coxon with the author Michael E. Horowitz, performing an avant-garde poetry piece.

Noel and Damon Albarn had been on friendly terms since the former had left Oasis, the mutual consensus between the pair being that they were much older and wiser and had too much shared history to continue a feud. But what happened next had to be seen to be believed; after finishing their piece, Damon invited Noel onstage and the trio, along with Paul Weller on drums, performed the Blur hit 'Tender'. It was a remarkable sight, even Albarn appreciating the sense of occasion, smiling the whole way through. The past just gets further and further away.

Their friendship continues to this day; Noel featured on the fifth Gorillaz album *Humanz*, released in 2017, and there was talk of Damon appearing on Noel's albums if they could make the schedules work. Noel also started making unheralded appearances with a collective called Youth of the Apocalypse, an act which included Jeff Wootton, who had toured with Beady Eye, among its ranks. Noel never speaks of the project though and being in the background seems to suit him.

In early 2015 Noel released his second solo album, *Chasing Yesterday*, which consolidated the success of his debut, with some boundaries slightly pushed; 'The Right Stuff' could only be described as psychedelic jazz (although it was a leftover from the Amorphous Androgynous sessions), and 'Riverman' featured the scourge of rock music, the saxophone. The accompanying tour was also successful, stretching out over 18 months (albeit including a six-month break), continuing to sell out arenas worldwide. The album also hit No.1.

For his third album, recorded concurrently with *Chasing Yesterday*, having produced his first two albums himself, along with Dave Sardy, Noel opted for a different approach, working with Northern Irish producer David Holmes, famous for his soundtrack and electronic work. Rather than utilising his more traditional approach of writing the songs then heading to the studio, Holmes insisted that Noel fly over to his studio in Belfast armed with nothing more than effects pedals and some guitars. Whilst lengthy, the sessions resulted in his most diverse and poppy album yet; *Who Built the Moon?* Once again, the album made No.1, his 10th album in succession to do so, a new record. And he followed it up with a hugely successful tour.

Across 2019 and early 2020, Noel broke from tradition to release a series of EPs (*Black Star Dancing, This Is The Place,* and then *Blue Moon Rising*) rather than an album, continuing his new experimental approach, albeit pilfering from David Bowie and acid house. The songs continued to receive a mixed response from his fanbase, which Noel seemed to revel in. And his collective continued to tour the world, including a homecoming show at Manchester's Heaton Park that summer.

However, it wasn't all plain sailing for the *Who Built the Moon?* album campaign. As well as the constant (and usual) barrage of questions about when Oasis would reform, this time there was fresh meat for the press - the return to the limelight of his brother.

Liam had opted to keep a low profile for a few years while he negotiated his divorce, as well as pondering his next move after Beady Eye. He had long been an advocate of being the singer in the band rather than a solo star but had infrequently written songs over the years. Eventually, encouraged by his partner Debbie Gwyther, he approached Warner Music with his songs, who in turn enquired as to whether or not he would be interested in releasing a solo album. Liam made the good point that he only had a few written, certainly not enough for an album. But the label flew Liam over to LA to work with songwriters, notably Greg Kurstin, who had collaborated with Adele and Beck among others. After a few weeks they had enough songs for an album, and Liam made the announcement that he had signed a deal in late 2016 and was due to record in early 2017. Having previously scoffed at the idea of being a solo artist on Twitter ('I'm not a cunt'), even the man himself had to backtrack somewhat ('It's official, I'm a cunt').

Liam began easing himself back into the public eye with press appearances in early 2017, before announcing a short tour and new single, 'Wall of Glass.' In the same week came a devastating terrorist attack in his home city, at Manchester Arena, with 23 people killed, many of them children, as they made their way out of the arena shortly after a concert by pop star Ariana Grande. A benefit concert was hastily arranged, taking place two weeks later at the Old Trafford home of Lancashire County Cricket Club, and Liam made a surprise appearance, performing three songs, including a highly emotional version of 'Live Forever' with Coldplay.

Being their home city, Oasis were closely aligned with the healing process, with 'Don't Look Back in Anger' sung by attendees of a vigil the day after the tragedy. The song became ubiquitous for a short period, and Coldplay covered the song at the benefit concert, and with no publicity, Noel donated the royalties of the song to associated charities. Later in 2017, Noel also headlined a special concert to mark the re-opening of Manchester Arena.

The *One Love* concert in May was broadcast live on BBC1, and as such it thrust Liam Gallagher back into the public eye. While no-one would be so crass as to say this was a publicity stunt, the scenario couldn't have worked out better for Liam's comeback. The joint factors of his appearance being a surprise, the nostalgia elements of the songs and the simple virtue of absence making the heart grow fonder, set Liam up for the forthcoming campaign.

Not taking any chances, he was everywhere for the remainder of 2017 and for most of 2018. He performed at Glastonbury Festival a few weeks after *One Love* and sang 'Don't Look Back in Anger' a cappella. As entertaining as his comeback interviews were, and as good as it was to have him back, it has to be said that nostalgia played a huge part; Oasis songs comprised the main body of his sets. Despite Noel performing many of them himself, those songs being performed as nature had intended (i.e. sung by Liam) proved a huge draw.

Liam's solo album was announced for October 2017, to be called *As You Were*. By sheer coincidence, his big brother had pencilled in a November release for *Who Built the Moon?* And so, rivalry as to whether one was a Liam or a Noel fan was finally given a focal point. Even though the albums were very different in sound, with Noel's third effort much more diverse and more focussed on production compared to Liam's more straightforward rock'n'roll, comparisons were inevitable. *Who Built the Moon?* sold well, shifting 78,000 units in its first week, and was well received critically, but *As You Were* broke 102,600 combined sales in the same period, with an additional accolade of boasting the highest vinyl sales for 20 years. For the first time since Oasis disbanded, Liam Gallagher had the upper hand.

And the younger Gallagher brother made the most of his rebirth, playing a seemingly endless tour, with highlights including sell-out shows at London's Finsbury Park and back at Old Trafford cricket ground. The setlists were quite varied, with fan favourites such as 'Listen Up', 'Rockin' Chair' and 'Bring It on Down' making appearances. On numerous occasions, Liam was joined by Bonehead to perform Oasis numbers. Capitalising on his success, a documentary film was released in the early summer of 2019, *As It Was*, timed to capitalise on the launch of his second album and released in cinemas the day before the first single, 'Shockwave' (which like much of his post-Oasis output was a scathing diatribe aimed in the direction of his brother). The film itself was a rewarding watch, spanning the moment Oasis disbanded to the present day, and pulled few punches in outlining the self-destructive nature of Liam's character.

There was a drip-feed of singles prior to the release of his second solo album, *Why Me? Why Not.* (dubbed after a pair of John Lennon doodles betrothed to him by Yoko Ono) in September 2019. And that followed another successful summer, which included a big slot at Glastonbury Festival, sub-headlining the iconic Pyramid Stage. And in 2020 he was all set to play further large outdoor shows, including a homecoming gig at Manchester's Heaton Park in June and topping the bill back at Reading and Leeds festivals in late August.

For his part, Noel kept on doing what he does, but for the live shows his High Flying Birds significantly expanded, employing Chris Sharrock on drums and drafting in Gem Archer to replace Tim Smith on lead guitar following Beady Eye's disbandment. Including keyboard player Mike Rowe, the High Flying Birds now included four touring members of Oasis, all bar Rowe with the final live incarnation.

For Oasis fans, this was the best of both worlds, the beauty being that they didn't even have to choose, despite it being imposed on them by social media. While it can never be ruled out, an Oasis reunion looks increasingly unlikely. Liam was honest in his comeback, stating that he would much rather be conducting interviews as the lead singer of Oasis than solo. But Noel has been consistent throughout the decade, even going so far as to say, 'Not if all the starving children in the world depended on it.'

It's not hard to see why Noel feels this way. Not only does he now have total control and not have to fulfil the democratic obligations that being in a band requires, but he has a significant legacy to protect. It surely can't be coincidence that, in the 21st century, there have only been a handful of seminal British bands not to have reformed, two of those being The Jam and The Smiths. And Noel is good friends with Paul Weller, Johnny Marr and, to a lesser extent, Morrissey. Unlike The Stone Roses or The Libertines, he certainly doesn't need the money. Between Noel and his younger brother, most fans have easy access to hearing the songs live.

The ongoing clamour for an Oasis reunion has to be at least partially fuelled by the lack of a replacement. Since the mid-1990s, only Arctic Monkeys can claim to have had anywhere near the cultural impact and excitement. The Libertines had tabloid notoriety and fan dedication but lacked the songs, and since their reformation they have become part of the establishment. Coldplay have sold more than Oasis, but their mass appeal is an entirely different prospect. Yet when the annals of Great British bands are written, all three will pale in comparison to Oasis. Some of the hysteria which greeted The Stone Roses' reunion in 2011 demonstrated two things; the dearth of contemporary bands of any equal, and the huge hole that Oasis have left. The mega-gigs that the Roses put on were simply following a template that Oasis had mastered; large communal gatherings to sing songs of defiance and joy.

There would also need to be a significant improvement in brotherly relations.

If their interviews are to be believed (and there is little reason to doubt them), relations between Noel and Liam have never been worse. They have apparently run into one another a handful of times over the last few years, mainly while watching their beloved Manchester City. It was said that those brief exchanges were cordial. But Liam has been consistently scathing of his brother since 2009, blaming the Oasis break-up solely on him, insinuating he had a solo career in the works for much longer than Noel claims.

Being the wildly-unpredictable character he is, Liam has also held out the olive branch to his brother on quite a few occasions, but swiftly follows these up with further insults. Since the launch of his solo career, Liam's vitriol has also been directed at Noel's wife Sara MacDonald and his children. For a period, Noel largely maintained a dignified silence, the odd barb aside, but when asked by interviewers, he's always quick to give a withering comment. Sadly, this hasn't prevented Liam from continuing his vendetta, the prospect of an Oasis reunion getting further and further away.

But does it matter? In this era of instant gratification, all Oasis songs are readily available at the press of a button. The first three albums have all been reissued, with *Be Here Now* the pick of the bunch. Not only are the Mustique demos included in the box-set, but two new songs ('If We Shadows' and an untitled number) also. It's surely only a matter of time until the remaining four albums receive the same treatment.

Furthermore, in the decade since the final Oasis album, there have been seven Gallagher-related albums, three EPs and a clutch of B-sides, plus two Ride albums. That's twice as much as was released in the preceding 10 years. It's unlikely any year will go past without the opportunity to see either Gallagher brother live. There have been remix albums, live DVDs, the wonderful *Supersonic* film, too many TV appearances to mention, and last but most definitely not least, *The Oasis Podcast.* While the demand for Oasis is as high as it has been since the 1990s, there is enough readily-available material to placate the masses.

And yet, all we know is that we don't know how it's gonna be.

Mark Feltham: 'I do acoustic shows, and after the shows young guys who are mid- to late-30s or early-40s say, 'I love what you did with Oasis. What were they like?' I get it all the time, and I'm thinking, 'I didn't really do a lot with them!' It's followed me around since then.'

Johnny Sharp: 'The very fact that, even in the dying days of the *NME*, the person they would have on the cover like a shot was either of the Gallaghers. This is 25 years after their supposed peak. Still, no-one could hold a candle to them in terms of star power. In terms of charisma, quotability, just entertainment value. Even someone like Morrissey, who was a fantastic interview, quickly became a parody of himself. Being a rock star in terms of being a gobshite ... the Gallaghers are without compare in their generation.'

Brian Cannon: 'I know lads that weren't even born when *Definitely Maybe* was recorded, but they are massive Oasis fans.'

Simon Mason: 'Back when I was a young man, everyone said I should quit the Rolling Stones and that. But they're still making music and their last album was fantastic. They don't care. No-one's going to be telling Keith Richards he shouldn't be making music. In the same way, no-one's going to tell Liam Gallagher, 'You're too old to be a musician.' That is the legacy.'

Nick Amies: 'One of the saddest things about the whole split is the regret of not knowing where they went after that. For me (*Dig Out Your Soul*) was a really great album and a good idea. They were growing up, they were trying to push things and try something different.'

Ricky Hatton: 'It's a shame, them not being together now, I have to go and see them individually. I see Noel at Noel's gigs or Liam at Liam's gigs.

'People probably say to Liam and Noel, 'You only get one brother,' but it's easy for people to say that when your life's rosy. You don't know the ins and outs of what happened, so I just think it's for the best to leave it. If I were to sit them both down, I'd give them a slap and say, 'Get your arses in gear, we had so many great times and so many memories,' which they will have from those days. I just hope they're both happy and succeeding where the path takes them. All Oasis fans hope they patch up, but if they don't, they don't. If they do, it would be lovely, but family's family. It's difficult, isn't it?

'Because I've become friends with Noel and Liam, and people don't know them from a personal perspective like I do, I couldn't give two shits about the music now. The music will live forever. That's not a pun. We'll be playing those tunes until the day we die.'

Tony McCarroll: 'You can't deny the force of that band and the influence they had on people's lives.'

Jeff Slate: 'You can argue with the method. You can certainly sit with printed lyrics and nit-pick them. But how does that record make you feel? It's making a lot of people feel a lot of things.'

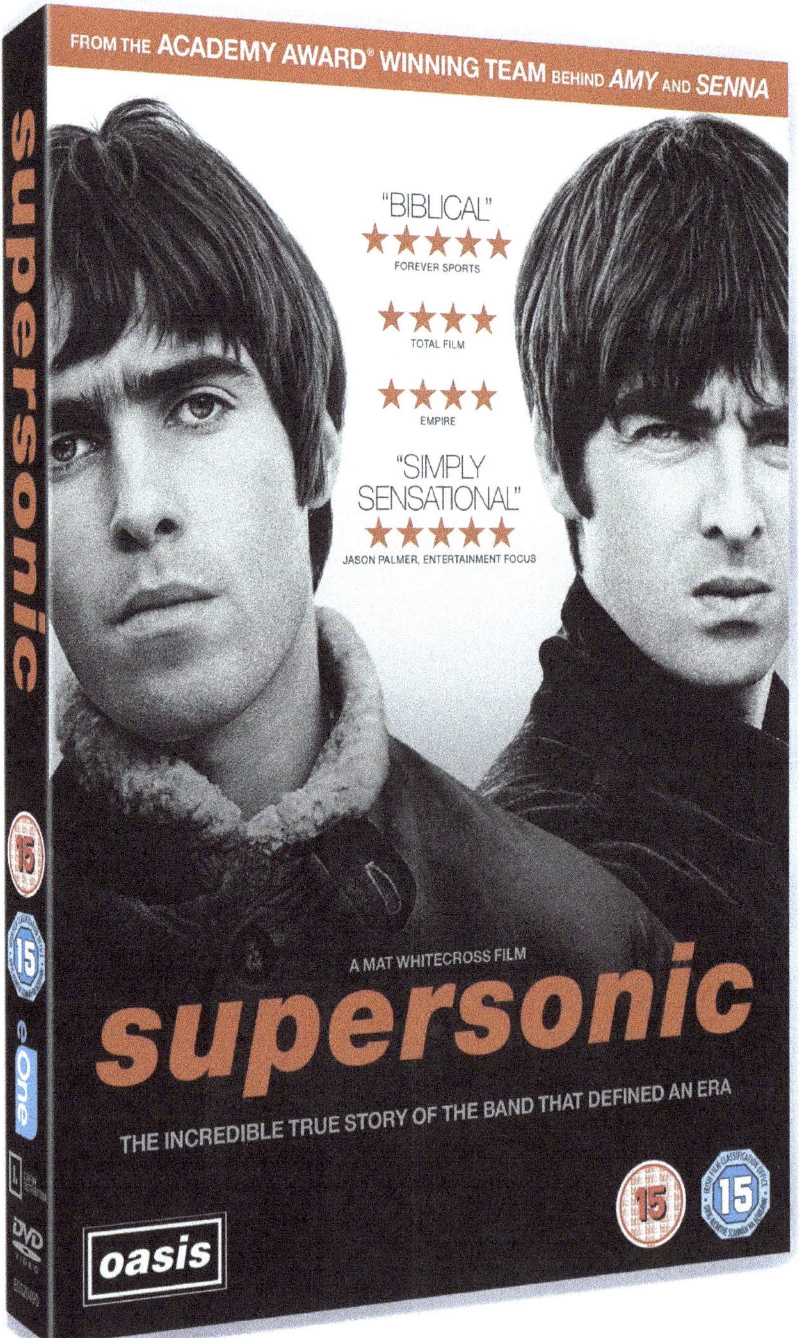
FROM THE ACADEMY AWARD® WINNING TEAM BEHIND AMY AND SENNA
"BIBLICAL"
★★★★★
FOREVER SPORTS
★★★★
TOTAL FILM
★★★★
EMPIRE
"SIMPLY SENSATIONAL"
★★★★★
JASON PALMER, ENTERTAINMENT FOCUS
A MAT WHITECROSS FILM
supersonic
THE INCREDIBLE TRUE STORY OF THE BAND THAT DEFINED AN ERA
15
15
oasis
supersonic
eOne
DVD

EYEBALL TICKLERS

Acclaimed rock and art photographer and music video director Michael Spencer Jones shares his thoughts on his time working with the phenomenon that was Oasis.

On that first exposure to the band, and falling in love with their music

"Going back to Spike Island, there's a big car park and I was sort of walking through it to the main entrance and saw this van, and it was really interesting because it had been painted in this sort of Jackson Pollock style - you know, how The Stone Roses had been doing their artwork. So I took a photograph and thought, 'Yeah, that looks interesting,' it went in the souvenir issue of *Uptown*, and I thought nothing more of it. Then I bumped into Bonehead at this Verve gig, maybe eight or 10 years later, and someone had dug out this magazine and shown it to him. And he said, 'That's my van!' I went back and got the negative out, printed it and blew it up, and on the side of the van it says, 'Paul Arthurs, plasterer,' with his phone number! That was my first introduction. Spike Island, you know I think a lot came out of that.

"Before Oasis, I was doing The Verve and I did a shot for a single called 'All in the Mind' (1992) and did a kind of Hieronymus Bosch-style surrealist shot on infra-red. That got me a lot of work, and then the follow-up to that, 'She's A Superstar,' using a neon sign in a waterfall, caught the attention of Mr. Noel Gallagher, who was working with Inspiral Carpets. I was working with a designer, Brian Cannon, and his office was in the same building as Inspiral Carpets, so Noel had seen my photos on the cover of The Verve's stuff and thought, 'Yeah, I'll get this guy in.'"

"I was given a demo of *Definitely Maybe* and at the time I was working with The Verve, so my head space was more with them and doing all their covers. So when Oasis came along, it was kind of a distraction almost, because The Verve are this great band and obviously there can't be two great bands! I got this cassette and it was then like, 'Wow!'. Especially the demo version, it was just absolutely incredible! Tracks like 'Live Forever,' that was my first real introduction, and you knew then it was gonna be massive. I remember, back then, I lived in a flat and during the summer I just used to blast the album on my stereo with the windows wide open. I blasted 'Live Forever' to the world way before it was even released. In fact, there's a funny story, I got some complaints from the neighbours and I've got *Definitely Maybe* turned to 11, and apparently the police had arrived and I had it up so loud they'd been banging on the front door. I only heard them when the album finished. They'd been there for 20 minutes. There was this policewoman outside, who said, 'You are so lucky. If you hadn't answered the door in the next two minutes, we were gonna smash the door in and arrest you.'"

On creating the debut album's iconic cover image

"My photography was location-led, so I used to spend days, sometimes weeks, looking for the right locations, especially with The Verve, you know, driving around everywhere just taking pictures. When it came to *Definitely Maybe* I actually thought it was going to be a location-led photograph. The band had this meeting, they decided they were going to have this photograph taken in Bonehead's house in West Didsbury. They'd seen the back cover to a collection of Beatles oldies and it's a photograph of The Beatles which I think was taken in 1966 in Japan, around this table. They'd seen this photograph and thought, 'Yeah, that's it, we want us 'round a table.' Anyway, I went 'round to Bonehead's house to do a recce, and they said, 'Yeah, we're gonna do it here,' and it's in the kitchen and there's a table and there's a window and it's like, 'What are you thinking of?.' I could not see it at all. I'm looking around Bonehead's house, thinking, 'Oh God, of all the places to do an album cover, why choose this place?'

"But if you looked in the opposite direction - because Bonehead's house was open-planned, there's a big bay window. I said, 'The only way this is gonna work is if we take it in there and use the light coming through the bay window as a source of illumination. Let's use that as the feature.' So we shoot into the light, that room is incredibly tiny, I mean you look at the album cover and it looks ginormous. And it's funny because I went back with Noel and Liam for the 10th anniversary and everyone walked in the room and we were all so used to looking at the album cover that that's the sort of size it was; it was a bit like going back to your old school and seeing how small all the chairs were. When we walked in the room, no one could believe how small it was. To overcome that problem, I had to whack on a wide-angle lens to get everyone in, and when I did that there was all this strip-flooring and it sort of became this huge expanse. Basically, you had a photograph that was just 80% floorboards, so the real problem was how do you get the band into that room. A couple of days before, I'd been down to the Science Museum to the Egypt section, so had this notion of lying in state. I thought I'd get Liam lying on the floor as if he's in some transcendental state sort of meditating or something, because the only other alternative would be to have him sat cross-legged looking into the camera, and that wasn't gonna work. I think that was one of the key elements. On the day of the shoot I told him what I wanted him to do, to lay on the floor with his eyes closed, but I knew if he said no it would be a serious problem - the whole shoot was reliant on that. But when I asked, he said, 'Great, yeah, I'll do that,' So he seemed to get it.

"If you're looking at the construction of that album cover, having Liam laid on the floor, it had never been done before that. It looks right, but it's not a normal request to get the lead singer of a band to lay on the floor with their eyes closed. I used to do a thing called cross-processing, where I got colour film and you put it through the wrong chemicals to process it, and that would create a sort of surrealist effect. You'd get different colours and hues. But I think one of the main things which created the whole dynamic of the shoot change was that one of the roadies brought in a globe, which was reminiscent of Spike Island when Ian Brown came onstage with a globe. The minute I saw that, I thought yeah. It was kind of lacking, it just needed something else. They put it in the corner of the room, and I was looking down the camera, thinking that's not looking right, then I came up with the idea – that's the moment the shot changed. And I had this invisible thread I'd had in my camera bag from college that I'd never used and thought this is the day when I can use it! So we hung the globe from the ceiling and because the film I was using was quite slow film, I think the exposure was two seconds, so it was a long time to keep still. But I thought, because it's a two-second exposure, if I spin the globe when the camera shutter is open, it's gonna appear blurred, and if it appears blurred it's gonna capture movement. I think at that point, if you look at the cover, you get a sort of triangle, so there's the globe, there's Liam lying on the floor, and there's Noel on the settee. The globe spinning is the catalyst, then suddenly you're into a sort of surrealist aspect of imagery. I think the colours of the globe mirrored the colours of the room - the blues and the yellows - so it just seemed to work.

"I knew it was an important album and I knew if you take a photograph for a magazine and it's not very good, no one's gonna care about it a month later, because it's in the bin. But I knew if this was a bad photograph, it's gonna be there forever. So it's a bit of a weight on your shoulders. Whenever you do a shoot - I think this is the difference between a good, average, or bad photographer – you're trying to hit some kind of target and create an image that looks great, but to get to that point is a struggle. And when I got the globe spinning, I just looked down and I was the first person to see that cover on the viewfinder, and it was like, 'Whoah,' I knew I'd got it. I was buzzing. You know you've reached the point, then you can relax a bit.

"The great thing about working with Oasis was that someone would come up with an idea, so with *Definitely Maybe* it was to copy the back cover of that collection of Beatles oldies. If you look at those two images, they're nothing alike, but we took inspiration from it. I like to work in an organic way, so you start off with a germ of an idea, someone develops it, and it slowly grows. It's not predetermined."

On creating those memorable sleeve photographs for 'Some Might Say' and 'Wonderwall'

"With 'Some Might Say', Noel wanted to represent the lyrics of the song on the single cover. There's all these references to stations, and I think he said, 'Let's do a photograph at Piccadilly Station'. I thought it was boring, and said, 'Let's get a disused station with a collection of people waiting, and the train is never gonna arrive, and the platform could act as a stage, and go from there.

"That was an interesting one, 'Wonderwall', because if someone comes to me with an idea and I don't like it, then there's no way I'm gonna do it. Noel had come up with this idea, and said he wanted a picture of a girl in a picture frame, and I'm thinking I can't see it working. At the time I was at the Marriott Hotel with Liam, saying, 'I'm not into this idea at all, I think you should be on the cover'. I thought he'd make a great subject on his own for a single or album cover, and he said he was up for it. So we walked down to Primrose Hill and had a couple of gold frames, set up shop, and I can remember there was some heckling going off – I think someone had recognised Liam – and I'm trying to ignore it, and then the next minute there's this taxi screeching down the road and this guy shouting out the window really loudly. The shouting got louder, and then the taxi stopped and this guy got out and came up to the railings, which were about 15m from the shoot, still shouting, and I turned around and it was Noel, who just happened to be passing! He said we were wasting our time, it was a love song and we needed a woman, so we packed up shop and left. But it really freaked me out, so bizarre! So I shot it the following day, got this girl called Anita (Heryet) who worked at Creation Records, but to overcome this issue of an objectified woman on an album cover, I shot it in black and white, infra-red. Then she becomes part of her environment, almost a dreamscape, part of the narrative."

On the inspiration behind the Be Here Now cover images, and how things were changing

"When it came to *Be Here Now*, it's a lavish statement, but I do like the cover and I think it's appropriate to that album. There's nothing subtle about it; it plays on the whole album cover's semiotic symbolism. When someone said, 'We've got three helicopters, it's like, 'Are you sure? What are you making?' The whole band had got a bit darker, a bit fractious, with so much money swirling around, and that started to have an effect. The working environment changed, it wasn't protected. They were always great to work with though, they're the greatest people you could possibly wish to work with - they're creative, fun and comedic.

"It's quite difficult to define, I remember at the time I was speaking to someone and they were saying the music was nothing new, but I kinda disagreed with that. The testament to that is if you put *Definitely Maybe* on now, it's like freshly-baked bread that was made that day; time hasn't dated it. It's about an energy that is indefinable. A track like 'Columbia' sounds like a dirty, dangerous rock'n'roll track. That energy was new, never heard it before.

"I remember I went 'round to meet Noel and Liam's mum, Peggy. They'd just come from a gig in Blackpool. So funny because the Rolls Royce came to pick us up, like winning the lottery! The juxtaposition of the Rolls Royce with the council estate."

On the future of rock music, the album cover, and having an eye for that iconic image

"There's an argument, if you want to get deep into the whole art form of rock'n'roll, that not only do bands like that not come around very often, but they might not come around ever again, because it was a product of the culture. I liken it to Renaissance Italy, the whole rock'n'roll movement that started with Elvis in '56, the '60s, '70s, '80s, '90s. In Renaissance Italy, why was everyone painting so many great paintings at that time? That was the culture. And in the '60s and '70s everyone was in a band, and they're not anymore. Oasis may be the last late, great rock'n'roll band. Only time will tell.

"People say vinyl died when the cd came along and that marked the end of the album cover, but I'm like, 'Hang on, when did the album cover come in? Between 1958 up until, really, '67, all dreadful. No one had considered using the album cover as an art form until The Beatles with *Sgt. Pepper.* So it's not necessarily the vinyl or the gatefold, it's to do with the temperament. You can still create an image to go with the music on Spotify, if a band want to put the effort in; there's still opportunity to create an image to go with a song. Because the thing about music, you can't see it, touch it, smell it, it's ethereal, it only exists at the time it's being played. It needs this kind of link to the real world with a photograph or image. I say to people who don't think sleeve art is important - think about The Beatles' *Abbey Road,* I know you're thinking of a zebra crossing. They're inextricable. And how important is that image to culture?

"I'm not searching for the perfect shot, but being a photographer you tend to walk around as if you're a tourist, looking at things slightly from an abstract view; looking for things that are unusual or beautiful. Great photography is the capacity to see what other people cannot see."

North Yorkshire-born, Los Angeles-based music video and film director Nigel Dick – who started out in the business as a press officer for Stiff Records and whose past promo successes also include Band Aid's 'Do They Know It's Christmas?' and Britney Spears' '... Baby One More Time)' – on working with Oasis.

"I made a total of five videos with Oasis, of which 'Wonderwall' was the second. Of course, you never really know if something is going to be a hit or not. I usually don't have any perspective on that. I make the video, and you leave that stuff to the other people. If you have a strong opinion – 'this is going to be a hit' – that's the end.

"Sony thought I could connect with the band, because no one in New York could understand their accents and they were kind of scared of them and their fighting. I was under strict instructions - don't make them 'act,' or they will leave the set.

"Noel apparently wanted black and white with splashes of colour. That was the band's one specific note. We were all concerned about them getting bored – which is why we had the football table and the showgirls in high heels and stockings. Keep them entertained. Much like rap videos, really.

"The band really related to The Beatles. I 'borrowed' the idea of the showgirls from *A Hard Day's Night*. The people playing saws also comes from that English music hall and vaudeville world. There is also a lot of that in *A Hard Day's Night* – definitely part of growing up in England in the 1960s.

"We shot in a disused factory in London. The only place we could find on short notice, it actually had the white walls. My producer's wife was pregnant and gave birth halfway through the video - leaving me to finish the video myself.

"The Gallagher brothers had one of their distinctive battles on the set. They argued over something, I'm not even sure what about. It lasted five minutes and then we were shooting again. Unlike 'Champagne Supernova,' where Liam stormed off and was gone for hours, this was just a few minutes. In retrospect, it was a good day.

"On a side-note, the clowns fought. The clowns didn't like each other!

"The band hated doing videos. They were not engaged in the process. It was something they *had* to do. They were loath to appear and left as soon as they could. I gave one of them a newspaper, someone else a guitar, and lined them up for the first shot. Once the camera started rolling, they started acting their hearts out.

"There is actually an early version of the video that is just a single take of them sitting side by side on those chairs, switching places around and staring at the camera for the whole song. That's not the kind of thing that you can put down on paper, but when you saw it you wondered why you'd want to have anything else.

"I've not watched that video in years. I only watch my old work if I have to. By the time the video gets released, it has achieved its primary goal. It's for other people to watch and get some insight into the band and hopefully be entertained. It's found its place in the world. If someone wants to buy the record, I've done my job."

Acclaimed photographer, director and cinematographer Peter Walsh was the man behind the lens for many iconic Manchester images, including shots of the Hacienda and Spike Island. Here, tells us about the first Oasis photo session, in 1992.

When was the shoot?

The photo was taken on 10th July 1992, in Castlefield, Manchester. It's the first ever session of the band together. They are stood on one of the columns of the viaduct, which is now the Metrolink tramline. I directed them for each of the images that I wanted to capture.

What were your first impressions of the band?

I knew Noel from him working with The Inspiral Carpets. They looked really confident, and Noel seemed like he knew what he was doing with the band. He had all the experience of touring and being with the Inspirals, so he knew the business, and knew what he wanted.

What was the thinking behind the picture?

I took the band to Castlefield, and I took some shots around the viaduct. I walked under one of the legs of the viaduct, and looked up, and I thought this image of the band up there would look great.

I asked the band to climb up and once up there, look down into the camera and the final image looks amazing.

In cinematography, low angle shots, when the camera points upwards from below makes people, and things, bigger, stronger and more important.

The band looking straight down into camera, which made them really strong, powerful and important, just as they became in the following years.

Did you have an idea of how big they would become?

I didn't know they would become as big as they did, but there was something about them, the confidence, the swagger, which made you think 'this band could be big.'

ALBUM BY ALBUM

DEFINITELY MAYBE (aka The Purist's Favourite)

What can be said about this album that hasn't been said before?

Well, quite a bit actually. British music was doing very well in 1994, thanks very much. The notion of Britpop was starting to build up a head of steam, with Blur and Suede leading the charge. British guitar music had found its voice after being suffocated by grunge and the all-conquering Nirvana who had, especially after Kurt Cobain's death, cemented their place in the pantheon of rock. The bands lumped under the umbrella term of Britpop all had voices, opinions and sounds that could only herald from these isles and were tapping into a feeling that resonated among the younger generation.

Then *Definitely Maybe* arrived.

The quality of the album wasn't a huge surprise. Oasis were generating so much hype amid the music press for their incendiary live performances, must-read interviews and, not least of all, a strong brace of singles prior to its release. But the impact was seismic, the like of which only the Sex Pistols and forebears The Stone Roses could relate to. It's an awful cliché but every track could have been a single, indeed two tracks have weaved themselves into the culture as normally only singles can do.

'Rock 'n' Roll Star' was everything you ever wanted a song with such a title to be; abrasive, obnoxious and unifying. There's a reason Liam still opens every gig with it today. It's his *modus operandi,* it only sounds right coming from his lips and he delivers a performance that knows it. Not to be outdone, Noel's judgement on when to provide backing vocals is spot-on from the off. It's a sparkling statement of intent, four undiluted minutes of rock music, and then, from nowhere, it transforms into a whirling dervish, psychedelically sliding from view as Liam reminds us that it is just rock'n'roll.

At the other end of the record, 'Slide Away' is a yearnful, questioning romantic number and sets the benchmark for every other Noel Gallagher track of this kind, although he's yet to deliver anything comparable. It never fails to hit you in the gut. To put a track with lyrics that expose the heart, with a soaring melody, against a backdrop of clattering drums and deafening guitars shouldn't work. But it does, building and building until the coda breaks your heart. If you don't stand to attention on hearing the introduction, then perhaps you should check your pulse.

Not that the rest of the band let up anywhere else on the album. An evolved 'Columbia' loses none of its magic by adding guitar layers and beefing it up, as it slowly lumbers into action, Bonehead gleefully going over the same chord sequence ad nauseum. It may still be going, somewhere in the ether. The 'come on/yeah yeah yeah' codas were so inspiring that the band pilfered from themselves a few years later for the title track on *Be Here Now*. Legend has it that Noel played the bass guitar for much of the recording of the album, which is simple yet functional but importantly allowed Guigsy to perfect it live. This album isn't about flourish or wizardry, it's about power.

Tony McCarroll's drumming on 'Bring it on Down,' almost incandescent with controlled rage, was undoubtedly his high point and provided a punk energy that the band lost once he left. As snotty as they ever were, for once Liam sounds reserved while the rest of the band vent their frustrations. Not to mention the political statements ('you're the outcast, you're the underclass'), of which there are several on the album. 'Up in the Sky' refers to the elite or the establishment and invites them to take a walk on the wild side. If you think it's tough up there, try spending a day in these shoes. The first Brexit anthem? Let's not think about that too much. And of course, there's that line on 'Cigarettes & Alcohol' ('is it worth the aggravation to find yourself a job when there's nothing worth working for?') that is as true today as it was then, and even before.

The working classes had been driven into the ground by Thatcherism and were now fighting back. Not with anger or malice, but with defiance and hope. Enter 'Live Forever.' Perhaps about Peggy Gallagher, perhaps about best friends, it doesn't really matter. An intimate conversation between two people ('we'll see things they never see') or a clarion call for the masses, it works on all levels, with a wonderful melody, fist-pumping chorus and an outstanding guitar solo. After the last chorus you think the song has nowhere else to go, but it turns on its axis for the last minute. Defiance set to music, time and overexposure have not dulled its power. Masterful songwriting in every way.

Fourth and final single 'Cigarettes & Alcohol' has suffered from featuring on virtually every rock compilation since 1994. Slower than you think it is, the guitar feedback gives the song a rough edge that it warrants and it's hard not to hear the songs it steals from. But it's the style of song that Liam was born to sing, and Rod Stewart should hang his head in shame for even trying it on his cover in 1998. No Oasis gig was complete without it.

'Live Forever' was designed to be the band's trump card after the first two singles had set the scene, yet it's doubtful Noel would have predicted that 'Supersonic' now runs it very close in the fan's affection. It's lyrically inane but that doesn't matter; when the opening line strikes such a chord, anything that followed would pale in comparison, so you may as well write about Alka-Seltzer and farting dogs. The guitars are slowed-down punk, and you sense the solo could go on forever, backed by excellent tambourine - one of Liam's unheralded skills (presuming it's him). Features backing vocals by The Real People, the few external contributors to the album.

'Shakermaker' on the other hand is rarely granted in such status. Perhaps an ode to Noel's youth (a Shakermaker was a kids' toy from the 1970s), like 'Supersonic' it's lyrically nonsensical, apart from the Mr Sifter line. One senses the nods to The Jam's 'Mr Clean' and Steve Harley's 'Mr. Soft (revived for a Trebor ad in the mid-'80s) are only included because they rhyme. And yet that middle-eight ('I'm sorry but I just don't know'...) is better than most bands' choruses. The structure is simple, 12-bar blues with added gusto and it was what it was; a throwaway pop single (as The New Seekers would bear witness to). Noel would better the formula, but there's nothing else in their canon that sounds quite like it. Equally dispensable is 'Digsy's Dinner', Oasis doing Blur without even knowing it, far too chirpy for this writer's liking. But once again, that chorus taps into something primal.

Although the album is one long slap in the face, there are moments to breathe. 'Sad Song', only on the vinyl edition, finds Noel with acoustic guitar and mellotron, alone in a room and pressed up against your ear. His continual theme lyrically in the early years was a wish to escape his circumstances, but 'Sad Song' puts a different spin on the idea, trying to talk someone else out of the idea while sharing their frustration. At least that's one take on it. The genius of Noel Gallagher is that the lyrics are individual to everyone. Closer 'Married with Children' surely holds the title of driest Oasis song, both in the crispness of the acoustic guitar and the humour in the lyrics. After delivering an album that he knows to be great, the lyric, 'Your music's shite, it keeps me up all night' acts as a wink to the listener.

The album is built on guitar rhythms that are incessant but vital, 'Up in the Sky' and 'Shakermaker' being the best examples. Kudos to Bonehead, a talented musician, for knowing that was what the songs needed, rather than adding more distractions. A further word also for Tony McCarroll; several songs in his short era, including stone-cold classics like 'Live Forever', open with his incessant drumbeat, without which the songs would hold less gravitas, likewise his cymbal work on 'Cigarettes & Alcohol' and 'Slide Away'. Time has fortunately been a healer for Tony's reputation, and justly so.

The reissue in 2014 provided an official release to early track 'Strange Thing', part of the *Live Demonstration* EP, another cod-Stone Roses track that is full of charm but lacking in guile, but it would have held its own as a B-side.

In the 25-plus years since Definitely Maybe crashed into our lives, only Arctic Monkeys on their debut (*Whatever People Say I Am, That's What I'm Not*) can lay claim to creating such an immediate impact in British guitar music. Play loud.

Accompanying Tracks

'Supersonic'

Not quite at the stage where Noel was writing classics for fun, the B-sides from this single are representative of a songwriter finding his feet. 'Take Me Away' is a slight, fragile acoustic ballad, with Noel singing almost insecurely, literally finding his voice. Slightly too long perhaps, but the acoustic builds before slowing down, drawing breath. Liam is in similar territory on 'I Will Believe (Live)', something of a hidden gem, the angelic voice of the early demos still present. A chorus ('but when I find my own piece of mind I, I will believe') is a splendid combination of words and melody, complementing each other perfectly. Also includes the white-label version of 'Columbia'.

'Shakermaker'

'D'Yer Wanna be A Spaceman?' is the first of only a handful of times that Liam provided backing vocals for Noel and has a naïve charm that detracts from its faults in production and lyrics. It's also one of the songwriter's personal favourites, so of course Liam has performed it live since Oasis split up, Noel also doing so on his early solo shows. 'Alive' (demo) sounds exactly that, vibrant but tinny, and deserved more attention from the band. An opportunity lost but given the strength of the other songs available to the band at the time, not a great tragedy. 'Bring it on Down' (live) showcases the band's ferocity on the stage but sounds comparatively tame considering the monster it would become.

'Live Forever'

Releasing arguably the weakest set of B-sides of their entire output as support for what is now regarded as one of their best songs is classic Oasis. On strength of songs it's fine, but there's very little value for money here. 'Up in the Sky' gets the acoustic treatment, now woozier and more psychedelic than the electric version, and it was always exciting to hear how Noel would deliver a song in comparison to his brother. 'Cloudburst' is a beefier offering with a great riff, and ironically sounds like something from The Stone Roses' second album (*Second Coming*), which came down the tracks four months later. Good taken in isolation, but not including it on the parent album was a wise move. A blistering live version of 'Supersonic', complete with surly introduction from Liam ('this is gonna be the single, so go and buy it.') rounds off the set.

'Cigarettes & Alcohol'

Released on cassette in a mock cigarette packet, the collection of songs present is where the mythology of the Oasis B-sides commenced. They manage to make The Beatles' 'I Am the Walrus' their own, a lesson in how to cover a classic; make it different. A relatively repetitive song, the thundering breakdown of the 'English garden' section aside, like 'Columbia' it goes on for longer than it should be but is no weaker because of that, the rhythm section and Bonehead bludgeoning the listener to death then back to life while Noel unleashes on the guitar and speaker. 'Listen Up' somehow manages to be a re-tread of what's gone before but is the finest case of all. The drums are reminiscent of 'Live Forever' and the guitar cribs from 'Supersonic'. It once again touches on the recurrent lyrical theme ('one fine day, gonna leave you all behind') as verse, bridge and chorus are all repressed and solemn, but Liam's skyscraping vocal whitewashes any repetition and make the song transcendent. Early-Oasis operating at maximum capacity, 'Listen Up' is sublime. 'Fade Away', a contender for inclusion on *Definitely Maybe*, may steal its melody from Wham!'s 'Freedom', but once Liam rattles through the lyrics in an almost staccato fashion he completely owns it. One of their fastest pace songs, with not an ounce of fat on it, it's a paean to lost youth delivered with a sneer. This collection is essential.

'Whatever'

The acoustic opening may have been the musical equivalent of the face that launched a thousand ships (not least by Noel himself), but that doesn't detract from 'Whatever's appeal. Carefree and now with added strings, it represents an immediate leap in the band's ambitions, only four months after *Definitely Maybe*. It's also a hark back to Noel's clubbing days, the structure and message being more in line with dance music than the surrounding indie fields. For anyone who has left a job, or a relationship, or just broken up for a holiday, this should be the first song played. It captures the mood perfectly, just veering on the right side of cheesy. Whatever you do, whatever you say, I know it's alright.

'(It's Good) To Be Free', while operating from the same manifesto, is a darker beast. Moody, crunchy, feedback high guitars merge with organs and piano as Liam sings in a low key until midway through the second verse, when he decides to bring things up a notch (or key). A nagging tambourine is persistent throughout and for once the bass takes centre stage. Yet it ends with Morris dancing squeezebox and clapping. Wonderfully bizarre.

'Half the World Away' now occupies treasured status, yet for this writer it's a poor cousin to what went before. I am aware I'm in the minority here (it's now a regular staple of Noel Gallagher's sets and regularly features in 'best of' song lists), and it's not without merit; it oozes melancholia, the brushed-stick drumming and organ add more texture, but in this case overexposure has worked against it.

(What's the Story) Morning Glory? (aka The Game Changer)

When someone asks the question, 'What's the best Oasis album?', my instinct is always to say this one. It's certainly the one that means the most to me, and to a lot of people. Oasis were well on their way to becoming one of the biggest bands in Britain after an incredible year in 1994. Each single rose higher up the charts than its predecessor, and 'Whatever' was the icing on the cake. Demonstrating a work ethic and hunger that put their peers to shame, there was a quick turnaround for their sophomore album but the step up in terms of arrangement, production and songwriting belies the 14 months that separated it from *Definitely Maybe*'s release.

It blew the doors off. The backlash had started already (an inevitable British trait), down in part to both their popularity and their 'loss' to Blur. The reviews for the album weren't great either. But people didn't care; it sold in droves in its first week. Oasis were already a pop phenomenon, with loyal fans who didn't care much for the opinions of music journalists. The people's band. Then 'Wonderwall' was released, followed by the majestic 'Don't Look Back in Anger', and it all got gloriously out of hand. It will outlive you and me and even now, trying as best we can to separate it from the historical baggage, it's an unbelievable piece of work.

Lead single 'Some Might Say' is the curio of the piece, the last single recorded with Tony McCarroll on drums, and for that reason alone it stands apart from the rest of the album. His drumming once again suits the track, which felt like a new dawn on its arrival in the spring of 1995. The lyrics on the verses are great, the chorus not so much, but it's notable by the bridge, Noel seeming to realise that can effectively be a chorus in itself. Building up and up, the second chorus seems somehow more important than the first, even though they are the same. He also steps his backing vocals up a notch, the call and return of the outro marking new territory. Like 'Whatever', it served as a bridge to new lands rather than working within the context of the album, it's placing on the tracklist (midway through the album) only accentuating its difference.

And for all the improvements in other areas, the stand-out departure from what went before is in the drumming. Alan White's train of thought across the album seems to be; if's there's a space, fill it. On 'Hello' his work overpowers the rest of the band, who almost seem incredulous that someone exists that can play louder than them. They quickly get their act together for 'Roll with It', matching him toe-to-toe in volume terms, but he's never anything other than mighty.

The former track now brings to mind certain negative connotations (the chorus sample lifted from Gary Glitter's 'Hello, Hello I'm Back Again'), but that shouldn't detract from its glorious, glam-tinged racket. The neat track of lulling the listener into a false sense of security by opening the album with a quiet acoustic strum (which would appear in full form two tracks later), thereby prompting you to turn up the volume so the full blast hits you square in the ear canal, is cheekiness in extremis. The latter track too has associations it cannot control (The Battle of Britpop) and it's fair to say that Damon Albarn's famous comparison to Status Quo isn't entirely without substance. Yet it's not supposed to be anything other than what it is; pure rock-pop with a simple yet effective structure, guitars clashing all around it. Like 'Some Might Say' it features the hallmark of the new era; extended repetition of a chorus or a line to finish the song. 'I think I've got a feeling I've lost inside,' Liam cries, eight times.

Indeed, the trope is sprinkled all across the album. Most, if not all, tracks repeat themselves or go further than is necessary, which was a method that would bite them in the backside on the next album, yet here the noise is so glorious and crisp that Oasis get away with it. The guiltiest candidate is 'Hey Now!,' the weakest track on the album (even including the short interludes), a marauding beast of a song but with a nursery-rhyme melody. The melodramatic guitar over the chorus adds an intriguing dimension to it, but otherwise it's lumpen and sits very much in the lower tier of their output. Everyone knows it but nobody talks about it.

'Hey Now!' holds less affection than even 'Bonehead's Bank Holiday,' included only on the vinyl release. If one didn't know better one could suspect this is Noel consciously trying to write a Blur song. It's a ridiculous lark that comes across like it was rattled off in the time it took to record, although Bonehead's West Country accent is hilarious. 'She's Electric' is equally as jaunty, a tale of the protagonist working his way through a family, saved by a Liam's vocals and an earworm of a melody. More glorious but disposable pop (and not a single).

Speaking of Liam, the younger Gallagher really evolves into a singer across the album. His sneer (one of *Definitely Maybe*'s most effective weapons) is still present and correct, but he adds knowing subtlety to his range. 'She's Electric,' the companion piece to 'Digsy's Dinner,' doesn't require the microphone to receive a battering so it doesn't get one. He's even better on the acoustic-led numbers, pitching his volume and tone just right.

And what numbers they are. 'Cast No Shadow' pushes the listener into new directions. Heart-breaking lyrics ('as they took his soul, they stole his pride' – we've all been there), sumptuous bass and yearning backing vocals all make the song greater than the sum of its parts. Its only weakness is, yet again, the repetition of the lyrics. Verse, chorus, repeat, but that one extra chorus line at the end somehow pushes the emotion to near-breaking point. And then of course there's 'Wonderwall.'

What is it about this song? Is it its simplicity? Anyone can sing the chorus and it works in a communal atmosphere (as any football match-goer can testify to) but it's not particularly spine-tingling in comparison to say, 'Live Forever.' Is it the arrangement, the intricate acoustic guitar dominating and then giving way to cello and the rest of the band? As good as it is, better arranged songs have nowhere near the mass appeal. No. It's the sentiment. It's ambiguity, hinting at love but not outright declaring it, managing to tap into the (largely male) psyche and vocalise it in a way that was previously lacking. We, as humans, are loath to reveal our emotions unless we have to, and the 'there are many things that I would like to say to you, but I don't know how' line happens to be positioned over the most heart-tugging musical section of the song, at least for this listener. Other people will feel differently and there of course is the beauty of it. It's no-one's and everyone's.

Oh, and it's followed by 'Don't' Look Back in Anger'. Basically now the British national anthem, at least by the measurement of passionate delivery of the everyman, it doesn't really matter what we think of it anymore. Technically speaking, it's luxurious, the guitars and strings performing different functions but lightly overlapping wonderfully. The reason it bears repeated listens is that there's so much going on; the guitars go mad on the second bridge when they didn't on the first. Alan White is almost showing off, demonstrating his proficiency, his solo threatening to steal the show before the last chorus. Noel opts to bellow rather than sing and delivers the chorus differently each time ('as were/as she's walking on by'), another tic of the album. The irony of the line, 'Please don't put your life in the hands of a rock'n'roll band' has often been discussed yet, like 'Wonderwall', the song transcends any analysis, so it's best to give in to its dominance.

So, the lows are lower than what went before, but the highs undoubtedly higher. One of the many reasons *(What's the Story) Morning Glory?* is special is that, like all classic albums, it operates in its own world while also hinting at other realms within. As on *Definitely Maybe*, there are little snippets that add nothing to the song but add to the intrigue. A cough here, a scratch of the guitar there, it's best exemplified in the two interlude sections, which come and go and were for a few short weeks frustrating, until the main track was given a full release.

The second interlude separates two tracks that are so fully ingrained in the British psyche that it's hard to imagine life before them. The quasi-title track is a monster, a straining riff accompanying driving guitar and bass with whip-crack drums while Liam gleefully plays his part. You can hear him revelling in his delivery of 'wake-up', like the No.1 Oasis fan he's always been. It's the sound of the band reassuring anyone worried they'd gone soft by providing their loudest song yet. If you don't do the riff when you hear a helicopter flying overhead, you should probably put this book down.

Lastly there's 'Champagne Supernova', its sheer scale befitting such a title. It's got everything; the warm, gentle acoustic followed by military drumming and then an explosion of music. The lyrics are, ahem, open to interpretation, but feature one killer, perhaps because it's only used once: 'wake up the dawn and ask her why a dreamer dreams, she never dies.' Paul Weller, then in his Modfather pomp, enters the fray to give his take on events, and just when it's reached its crescendo it goes for one more lap. Liam, determined not be left out amidst the drama, delivers his best vocal yet. Not the first time Noel Gallagher had laid his lusty eyes on the kitchen sink, but the first time he grabbed it with both hands. Gargantuan.

And then it's over. An album that a quarter of a century on still sounds so alive and hangs together as a complete piece of work better than any other in the Oasis canon. You own it. Your grandparents own it. Your grandkids will own it. The dog probably has a copy stashed away. If you haven't already, you may as well just succumb to it.

Accompanying Tracks

'Some Might Say'

One of the single releases that could rival the quality of what was on offer on 'Cigarettes & Alcohol,' all three of the extra tracks are held in high affection by the fans, and rightly so. 'Talk Tonight,' written while Noel was on 'sabbatical' in 1994, is arguably his greatest acoustic track, the writer sounding almost devastated when faced with the possibility that his band was no more against the rounded guitar. Armed with a simple, unromantic sentiment, a melody and a six-string, there's few who tap into the soul better. 'Acquiesce' was a source of mystery for a while, with an unknown acoustic track which plays at the beginning and end ('Morning Glory'). That could wait though; a gritty guitar blows it away on the verse then becomes a great sequencing into the chorus. As it's a duet, and therefore a competition, both Gallaghers give it their all. Liam obviously digs the track and responds to the music accordingly, and Noel - managing to hit 'that' note in the chorus - never fails to impress. For years it was the 'real' fan's best-kept secret. And then Tony McCarroll's last hurrah, 'Headshrinker.' Like the Faces on speed, even Liam at his peak could only sing this once at a time, so shredding would the effect on his larynx be. Absolutely brutal.

'Roll with It'

The weakest single from its parent album gets the weakest collection of B-sides. When that includes 'Rockin' Chair' you know we are in a golden age. A sister piece to 'Listen Up' with an abnormal structure (the solo comes straight after the first chorus, and is an acoustic solo at that), it's back to that theme of aspiring for greatness, but it's done in such style, and with an outstanding vocal (excuse the repetition but it can't be stated enough, especially at this point in their career). Liam's delivery of the title on the second chorus is perfection, and 'Waiting for my memories to come and play' stands alongside Noel's best-ever lyrics. Unusually it fades in and out. 'It's Better People' on the other hand is joyful but disposable, its fast pace setting it apart from other tracks of its ilk, but with little else to live long in the memory. Lastly the performance of 'Live Forever' from their Glastonbury headline set a few weeks' previously is marked by Alan White's thundering drums, giving the song a menacing air, although Noel's backing vocals do sound a bit off.

'Wonderwall'

Something of a lad's anthem, the Mancunian romp that is 'Round Are Way' is all bounce and bluster, albeit with titanic drums. The kitchen sink was well and truly deployed now, post 'Champagne Supernova.' When played live the coda was filled with 'Up in the Sky', a little treat for fans that it would have been nice to have seen more of (there was probably lots of other times it could be done in the Oasis oeuvre). Sadly forgotten ever since 'Fuckin' In The Bushes' stole it's crown for 'Best Oasis Instrumental', the interludes on the parent album get their full reveal as 'The Swamp Song' here. Little more than a romp, it stops and starts then does it again, essentially a vehicle for Paul Weller to play guitar, with more than able support from Messrs Arthurs, McGuigan and White. Like all Noel Gallagher's truly great songs, and despite the criticism he gets, 'The Masterplan' couldn't be by anyone else. With admirable restraint, the song gradually builds, starting slowly with dub bass before the strings sweep to a higher plane on the chorus. It takes up then back down again. The chorus is one of reflective hope ('dance if you wanna dance'). As Noel himself believes, everything just clicked.

'Don't Look Back in Anger'

The glorious, shining guitars on 'Step Out' reflect this period of Oasis well. Noel was now confident enough in himself to handle some heavier tracks, with the rest of the band delivering in such an uninhibited fashion, and it's a free-wheeling rocker that encourages the listener to drink away any problems. That said, it's a blessing that it was left off *(What's the Story) Morning Glory?* (even though this wasn't by choice) as it ranks as a good B-side and would perhaps tip the balance of the well-judged album. 'Underneath the Sky' on the other hand, wouldn't be out of place; it carries an air of dread via a haunting piano solo from Bonehead and broadens their trademark sound without running the risk of alienating the hardcore. The backing vocals at the end of the chorus wash over the rest of the track, and some stupendous scanning ('I'll be making a start with my brand new heart') mark it out as a gem. Lastly, it's the hairdryer blast of their cover of Slade classic 'Cum on Feel the Noize', all furious guitars and clashing cymbals. A riot to listen to and, as the rest of the lads joining in at the end reveal, most probably a riot to record. An uncomplicated rock stomp, and a fitting closer to this period.

Credited to 'Oasis & Friends' and recorded during the *War Child* sessions in late summer 1995, 'Fade Away' gets the semi-acoustic treatment, with Noel on lead vocals imposing a different slant on the song. Liam's delivery for the backing vocals are only slightly softer than his delivery on the electric version, with Kate Moss *et al* only adding to the campfire vibe. Noel's other effort on the album, a dream-team collaboration with Pauls McCartney and Weller (as Smokin' Mojo Filters) is an ever-so-slightly beefed-up version of 'Come Together'. Weller and Macca do what they do best but it's hard to discern what contribution Noel makes, although he makes a better fist of a Beatles cover with 'You've Got to Hide Your Love Away'. But it's still a straight-forward copy, although Gallagher enunciates better than John Lennon. Noel also plays acoustic guitar on Weller's cover of Dr John's 'I Walk on Gilded Splinters' from *Stanley Road*. And of course, there was 'Setting Sun', a smash-hit single with The Chemical Brothers in late-1996, Tom Simons and Ed Rowlands taking the original demo and alchemy happening.

Be Here Now (aka The Black Sheep)

There's much maligned, and then there's *Be Here Now*. That title has become a byword for overblown, cocaine-addled arrogance and indulgence. It's a critique that's hard to defend, and time has not been kind to the 72 minutes of extravagance that Oasis indulged in for their third album.

But kindness wasn't in great supply back then either. *Be Here Now* stood apart from everything that surrounded it as Father Time started wielding his scythe over Britpop. The success of *(What's the Story) Morning Glory?* and Knebworth had gone to everyone's heads, and no-one dared question the wisdom of adding a 32nd layer of guitar to an already dense album.

And yet. Strip away the bombast (or don't) and there is much to appreciate here. As indulgent as it is, comeback single 'D'You Know What I Mean?' needed to be big just to match the sheer anticipation, and big it was. Brooding menace and intriguing messaging that begged to be explored but came to naught (the Morse code was quite literally meaningless and the backwards lyrics were lifted from other parts of the song, as revealed by the ambitious video), it's full of individually exciting moments; the mysterious little break before the solo, the NWA sample (which in turn sampled the Amen break), *that* bridge. For a couple of weeks in 1997, it was the most exciting thing that had ever happened. Oasis had actually done what they threatened to do and advanced their sound.

Yes, it's too long, and yes, the chorus is unimaginative (and repeated three times). In an ideal world the chorus line would feature once, then twice on the second chorus, and then three times for the big finale. But it's colossal, and no-one can tell me otherwise.

Unfortunately, the chorus line problem is a recurring theme throughout the album. The same thing happens on second single 'Stand by Me', designed to be the big emotional flag-waver but too over-egged to really connect (although the middle eight, with its rising strings and lift guitar never fails to send a shiver down the spine). 'Made a meal and threw up on Sunday' is no way to start a power ballad. By the time the third chorus arrives, boredom at hearing the title has kicked in. Shrewdly, when performing it live, Liam has opted to trim it down. If even he's bored of an Oasis song, then we are in trouble.

And that's the real problem. There are some good (and some great) songs crying out to be freed from their layered (and layered) shackles. Despite its reputation, 'Magic Pie' is a decent song for three minutes and would have been a good acoustic track, but it descends into an imitation of 'Cast No Shadow'. All the fat that was missing from *Definitely Maybe* and *(What's the Story) Morning Glory*? could be found in these seven minutes. You could make a cup of tea, come back in the room and the song still wouldn't have developed, the Mott the Hoople drum-fill (also used on 'Stand by Me') draining all enthusiasm. Noel's ability to tap into the human psyche comes in handy here too, shouting 'shut up' at the end. We hear you.

'The Girl in the Dirty Shirt' bounces along well, carries a lovely sentiment ('to me it doesn't matter if your hopes and dreams are shattered'), and is probably the nearest equivalent to 'Digsy's Dinner' and 'She's Electric', and therefore does not need to be six minutes long, with Liam pushed to the limits of his vocal range.

In fact, Liam comes out of the whole album well, significantly better than his brother, with enough experience under his belt to remove the naivety but resist the temptation to go hell for leather while knowing that he could. It was ever so slightly downhill from here. Being 'just' the singer, all he needs to do is match the noise as best he can, and he delivers the goods once again. He does well to rise above the noise on 'My Big Mouth', all forewarning vocals and Bonehead's rhythm turned up the maximum. A two fingers up to the perils of fame, with Whitey barely making an effort, the track feels long but is succinct compared to what surrounds it.

After making such a seismic impact on the previous album, Alan White was always going to struggle, but here he approaches certain tracks with almost ambivalence, or perhaps his wings had been clipped. Bonehead's contribution is so loud as to be white noise, and if Guigsy was present in the studio, based on what we hear he may as well have not been, so devoid is the album of bass.

Yet on 'I Hope I Think I Know' both Whitey and Liam are truly towering, matching the guitarists, here and on the title track, which perfectly encapsulates where the band were at that point: overblown, bombastic, obnoxious and stealing from themselves with some lyrical gems, but Liam is the star performer. Both tracks should have been the benchmark for the album. The former, with its cacophonous drums recalls the defiant insecurity of years gone by. You betcha!

'It's Getting Better (Man!!)' is slightly new territory for Oasis. Yes, that territory is a bit poodle-rock (the guitar sounds too close to Guns N' Roses for comfort) but it's got swagger and a solo you can lose yourself in. And then they repeat the title as an outro 33 times (I counted so you don't have to). More interesting still is 'Fade In-Out' which, perhaps due to Johnny Depp's riff, sounds like nothing on the album or their wider canon. It feels almost like a western score, as Liam bellows, 'Coming out of nowhere, singing rhapsody' (one of Noel's personal favourite lines) against a dusty backdrop. Then it breaks free and all bets are off. One of the few tracks on the album that could justify its length by virtue of being different.

But if we're talking about length, and we must, then step forward 'All Around the World.' One of Noel's oldest songs, left for the third album as he wanted the budget to warrant the ambition, its age shows - the song style having a wistful charm that got lost over time. It's very, very simple, the key changes failing to cover the lack of ideas in the melody. The kitchen sink is long gone by the time the first minute passes, and by the eighth minute the extension is being ripped from its foundations. Even the guitar playing is simplistic. But if you're going to go big, you may as well redefine the word. Kudos to Oasis for playing it live on the tour too. The reprise on the other hand has an elegance and paucity that could have come in useful elsewhere, but the slamming of the door (signifying the end of this era of the band) comes at the right time.

In stark contrast is 'Don't Go Away', also one of the older tracks, and a thing of beauty. Soaring guitars (albeit deployed similarly on 'Slide Away'), carrying a wonderful melody, it's a rare moment of restraint, the subtle introduction of horns on the second chorus going unashamedly for the heartstrings. If, as Noel stated, it was written about the boys' Mum, Peggy, then Liam surely knew, bringing his A-game. His delivery of the last 'time' on the last chorus is unbearably emotional, and by the time the fragile coda ends we're in floods. And Noel was, ironically, never more eloquent than with the line, 'Damn my education, I can't find the words to say.' Whatever its other faults, the album contains a real step-up in lyrics. 'Don't Go Away' sits alongside 'I Hope I Think I Know' as the best songs on the album.

Paradoxically, the could-have-been great tracks present are now hard to imagine as anything other than excessive. The verses are strong, but the bridges and choruses are twice as long as they need to be and dulled with overexposure. When Noel purported to remix the whole album, *Let It Be Naked* style, back in

2016, even he knew it was a fool's errand. It was never going to cure cancer. It was never going to save us. It is what it is; a moment in time and an insight into the biggest band in the world going absolutely hell for leather.

Accompanying Tracks

'D'You Know What I Mean?'

Many radio stations preferred to play the poppy, catchy 'Stay Young' over the single, and it's not hard to see why; the care-free chorus taps into the mindset of the young; 'Stay in bed and sleep all day as long as it's Sunday', and obviously, 'Stay young and invincible'. Does exactly what it says on the tin. 'Angel Child' was listed as a demo (recorded during the Mustique sessions), which teased the fans, expecting a full release that it never got, and it's a jolly yet melancholic thing which doesn't really go anywhere. The fragile keys at the end segue straight into the blast of a cover of David Bowie's 'Heroes'. It has its detractors, but the direct romance of the lyrics correlates well with Noel's general mindset. 'We could be heroes' is the basic message that informs everything the man writes. The rhythm section comes out well. All in all, this collection isn't particularly reflective of the parent album and is more in line with what went before (pop number, acoustic, cover).

'Stand by Me'

Such a clarity of thought doesn't last over the remaining two singles. '(I Got) The Fever' is gigantic, a menacing verse with a chorus full of hope, Liam's voice soaring as suggested on the lyrics but the line, 'It's got me on my knees' pre-solo takes it elsewhere. It's somewhat limited (the solo is the melody and no more) but the outrageous fills from Whitey and the overall joy lift it. To be clear, this sort of behaviour is acceptable for a B-side. It closes out to a nod from *The Fast Show*, which Noel was asked to appear on but declined (a decision he subsequently regretted). 'My Sister Lover' is cut from a similar cloth, Noel clearing out his closet with an unused verse from early Oasis track 'Lock All the Doors'. The Hammer horror piano adds an air of dread, but with an inconsequential chorus, it doesn't really go anywhere for six minutes. Presumably held back for similar reasons as 'All Around the World', i.e. lack of budget, 'Going Nowhere' sees Noel fully embracing his Burt Bacharach fantasies, with wholesome horns and pleasant strings. It stands out for its lyrical themes, Noel returning to his favourite topic of aspiration pre-1996.

'All Around the World'

Offering no alternative to the bombast that preceded them, the three tracks here can only be played loud. 'The Fame,' similar in spirit to 'Step Out,' strips away just enough of *Be Here Now*'s scale yet retains its other problems (too long, bridge better than chorus, etc.) but is pitched well overall. At last orders the bass finally buys a drink, entering the fray just as the mid-section lets loose. 'Flashbax' meanwhile, plods along unspectacularly until some trippy production spins it on its head at the chorus, with stinging guitar. Lyrically it tells a story, repeating the phrase 'lost and lonely' from 'Headshrinker' (Coincidence? Probably) and being quite literal in its title. Features a whistling solo drowning in cymbals. Then for one last hurrah, we get their cover of 'Street Fighting Man,' Liam sounding like he's come straight from hell. All fizz and brio, as the last official release of the *Be Here Now* era it's fitting that it fades out, Oasis in search of yet another party. This writer always thought Bonehead was decrying 'lawyers' rather than 'wires' at the beginning, which I still prefer given the context.

The *Be Here Now* reissue in 2016 delivered some new tracks; 'If We Shadows' is telling and insightful ('nobody knows what's wrong 'cept me and my brother') but that's probably why it didn't see the light of day for nearly two decades. 'Untitled' is easy to imagine with the full band treatment, but as it is, it's a bit insubstantial, the middle-eight aside. Noel's solo reinterpretation of 'Help!' really works, recorded live and as such with nowhere to hide, he's almost soulful here, sounding stark and raw in an arena environment. Recorded during the album tour, Noel knew which way the wind was blowing. 'Setting Sun' began life as an early demo before being reinterpreted by The Chemical Brothers, presented here as a mid-western drawl, which is acceptable. The Mustique demos gave us an instrumental which carries an air of the melody of 'The Girl in the Dirty Shirt,' showing just what a beautiful track that could have been, almost tear-jerking.

The 'Don't Go Away' single included 'Cigarettes & Alcohol' live at Manchester G-Mex and reiterates that, whatever else they were in the late 1990s, Oasis were a hurricane on the stage. Noel's remix of 'Devil's Haircut' by Beck from 1996 also comes recommended, although in truth he doesn't add much to the mix, merely some heavier beats and barely discernible garage guitar. Nice work if you can get it. He pops up again playing guitar on Britpop also-rans Smaller's track 'Is,' and his performance of 'Cast No Shadow' at the *Tibetan Freedom Concert* was released for posterity.

Liam also had a couple of external forays, co-writing 'Love Me and Leave Me' with John Squire for The Seahorses' debut album, as well as providing backing vocals on 'Nothing Lasts Forever' by Echo & the Bunnymen and The Verve's 'Come On.' Both Liam and his brother pop up on Ocean Colour Scene's *B-sides, Seasides & Freerides* compilation album on a live version of 'Day Tripper', while Noel plays guitar on a live take on Travis' 'All I Want to do is Rock' from their *More Than Us* EP in 1998.

Standing on the Shoulder of Giants (aka The Transitional One)

Unlike before, the party was over and everyone knew it, no-one more so than Noel Gallagher. Even their comrades knew it, Bonehead and Guigs departing midway through the recording sessions. Alan White aside, Noel and Liam were left alone to fly the flag at the worst possible time; Noel was now free of drugs but experiencing writer's block, with little choice but to lay bare his soul via his work. The presence of Liam, a steadfast believer in rock'n'roll, by his side was likely reassuring for once. The two of them put on a united front, at least at first, to the rest of the world. Music had moved on, but Oasis were determined to prove there was still room for them at the top table.

In an attempt to overhaul the sound, Noel made a point of not using any of his previous recording equipment and instead purchased older musical paraphernalia, including vintage pedals and smaller amps. It's sonically the most interesting Oasis album, awash with sitars, mellotrons, samples, drum loops and garnished with backwards guitars. The songs may be lacking, but it sounds like an appreciator of the wonders of music fully enjoying the lack of a deadline.

Any lack of confidence isn't immediately apparent, as a bang of drums announces 'Fuckin' in the Bushes'. It belies both what was to follow and what had gone before, more vital than anything from *Be Here Now* and more confident than most of the album. Frantic drumming, aping 'Little Miss Lover' by Jimi Hendrix, it has the same air of ecstasy as The Prodigy's 'Breathe' and is no less exciting. Pointing to the immediate future, there is a speech taken from the Isle of Wight festival in 1970 and the deployment of a gospel choir, Noel's new favourite trick, which both contribute to a brazen opening. There's a reason it currently adorns soundtracks and sporting events, not to mention being the entrance for Liam Gallagher's solo shows.

The statement of intent continues with lead single 'Go Let It Out', as wired acoustic guitars, a McCartney-esque bassline and shuffling drums continue to herald the new era. The sabbatical has added a gravelly tone to Liam's voice, which complements the bristling sound that grooves along nicely. It's got a clarity that had been missing from the previous album, and the psychedelic mellotron leading into the band kicking in for the last chorus, signposted by a whistle and stinging guitar, rank amongst the most exciting Oasis moments.

Sadly all the good work is undone immediately. 'Who Feels Love?' has interesting sonics, ragga style, and another strong bassline, but by jingo it's dull. Liam tries his best with a bumblebee in his throat but it's a hangover from the *Be Here Now* era, by virtue of its length and repetitive style. It would have struggled as a B-side in years gone by, let alone as a single, but Noel is at least pushing himself lyrically.

Along with the production, the lyrics are far and away the album's strength. Where he's forlorn on 'Where Did It All Go Wrong?,' he's soul-searching on 'Sunday Morning Call.' The perils of fame have finally dragged him down. He's also scorning on 'Roll it Over' ('look at all the plastic people who live without a care/try to sit with me around my table but never bring a chair'), but it's on 'Gas Panic!' where he flies. The words could almost be poetry and are a fascinating and disturbing insight into cocaine withdrawal.

'Gas Panic!' is a haunting and intense listen, almost suffocating. It's not often you hear this, but the mouth organ is utilised perfectly, it's discomforting tones perfectly suiting the mood before the final soothing minute, which feels almost as if the drugs are leaving the system. It's the type of song that only Liam should sing and as great as it is, it almost comes as a relief when it concludes. Meanwhile on 'Roll It Over,' Oasis go fully widescreen, evoking a heavy Pink Floyd complete with intricate guitar, combined with a blitzkrieg of a chorus on which even Liam nearly struggles. The heavenly voices and the slow meditative mid-section are so light it feels like walking through mist, until it builds towards a huge crescendo. A 'lost' classic.

The two Noel-fronted efforts (bizarrely sequenced consecutively) are two sides of the same coin, equally demonstrating his flaws and strengths. The self-analysis of 'Where Did It All Go Wrong?' is cynical and exposing over a great piece of music, with a speaker-slicing solo that goes so high it nearly breaks. It's perhaps a little too on the nose, and something of a relief that the album didn't end up with the same name (as was proposed). The press would have had a field day. Released as a radio single in the US, it was another strange decision not to give it a full release back home.

Especially considering what the UK was given instead. 'Sunday Morning Call' rights some of the wrongs of 'Who Feels Love?' but is still too lumpen for a single. More subdued and weary than the previous track, it's something of a slog until, from nowhere, the mid-section and solo add some much needed energy, but it sounds like it's from a different song.

Energy is not something that's lacking on the rockier numbers. The swirling, loaded production on 'Put Yer Money Where Yer Mouth Is' sadly can't bury the paucity of the song itself, which doesn't really go anywhere but doesn't need to. The choir adds to the drama supplied by the nagging riff and organs. Meanwhile 'I Can See a Liar' (coming straight after 'Sunday Morning Call,' the relief on hearing Liam again is palpable) turns everything up to 11. The boisterousness is a thing to behold; Alan White finally gives himself a workout (by this point he had settled on his style and rarely pushed the boat out) and even Noel sounds like he's enjoying letting his hair down on guitar. It's a bit AC/DC but we all need that in our life sometimes, and the only let-down is the awful chorus line ('I can see a liar sitting by the fire').

However, we can't mention lyrics without discussing 'Little James.' Sigh. Alan McGee argued around the time that it should have been a single, his logic being that overexposure would have dulled the frankly naff lyrics, but 20 years later they still generate a wince. And it's a real shame because the epic soundscapes and arrogant guitar outro are excellent, and at points it's so fragile that it feels like it could fall apart. But it holds it together just long enough to sail away splendidly. It's ironic that on the first self-penned song Liam Gallagher ever recorded, his presence is the weakest element (lyrically, not vocally. Never vocally.)

Sadly, some great lyrics and excellent production (arguably their best) aren't enough to rank *Standing on the Shoulder of Giants* alongside their strongest work. Noel Gallagher was trying to push himself and should be applauded for that, although having the greatest singer feature on only seven tracks betrayed his still-questionable judgement at the time. Overall, it's a real shame they didn't pursue this musical style, as there are some flickers of genius and lots of promise.

Accompanying tracks

'Go Let It Out'

The Masterplan should have been a lesson for Noel Gallagher, that all good songs should go on albums, but in 2000 he was still to learn that. 'Let's All Make Believe' is better than 80% of its parent album, earnestly chilling in tone, with Arabian-style production. The shimmering guitar and Whitey's tinny drums accompany an ode to lost friendships, presumably about the departure of the original members of the band. Liam's impassioned but distant delivery (the only B-side on which he appears in this era) is the foundation that allows the brittle music to evoke memories that you've never had. Truly magnificent. '(As Long as They've Got) Cigarettes in Hell' is a different beast entirely, with poetic lyrics about socialites and the surrounding chaos, but Noel just wants to sit back and observe. Again the production is layered and grandiose, the over-zealous coughing at the end perhaps a nod to earlier B-sides. We've come a long way since 'Take Me Away.'

'Who Feels Love?'

Paul Weller was a huge fan of 'One Way Road,' even going so far as to cover it for his album *Studio 150* in 2004. A strange choice, given what else was available, as it's something of a plodding number bereft of drama or significance. Their least energetic cover, The Beatles' 'Helter Skelter' follows. It still manages to storm a few barns but Alan White keeps himself restrained when it's begging for some elaborate fills, the kind of which he supplied without prompt just five years earlier. Although Noel sounds more like Paul McCartney, it's begging for Liam to be unleashed upon it.

'Sunday Morning Call'

One of Noel's first ponderings on religion ('faith in any god will only bury us all'), 'Carry Us All' features a strong vocal performance from the man himself, singing at the top of his lungs, with some excellent wordplay. It swells rather than explodes but is all the better for it, while the crunching 'Full On' is an out-and-out epic yet simple stomper of the kind that's wired and watertight, but once again begging for a wrecking-ball Liam performance. Yet another missed opportunity.

Recorded and released in 1998, 'Teotihuacan' is a haunting instrumental featuring a nagging keyboard riff and breakbeats that doffed their cap to Noel's involvement with the electronic artists of the age. It later took on a new form as the basis for his collaboration with Ian Brown, 'Keep What Ya Got', but the original still has merit.

Twin covers released on the *Fire & Skill: The Songs of The Jam* compilation in 1999, 'Carnation' and 'To Be Someone (Didn't We Have a Nice Time?)', get both Gallagher barrels. The former is daunting and bouncing (no doubt due to the contributions by some uber-mods) with added wooziness as Liam reinterprets and then completely owns the song, while the latter is transformed into a half-paced acoustic strum. It's not difficult to surmise that Noel took to this song because of the subject matter, which he slightly tweaks ('Did I have a nice time? I can't remember if I had a nice time') to better fit his own experiences. Earlier that summer Noel collaborated with The Chemical Brothers again on the hit single 'Let Forever Be', a slice of modern psychedelia, while the year previously he added scrunching guitar to Goldie's 'Temper Temper'.

Available only as a live version on *Familiar To Millions,* Noel originally performed 'Hey Hey, My My (Into the Black)' as a tribute to Kurt Cobain in the Nirvana frontman's home city (at the Paramount Theater, Seattle) but he was so taken with it that he opted to keep it in the set for the remainder of the *Standing on the Shoulder of Giants* tour, as well as sporadically playing it during the *Heathen Chemistry* tour. As a Neil Young superfan, Noel pays due deference. You can hear the foundations for 'Fuckin' in the Bushes' being laid on his collaboration with UNKLE, 'The Knock-On Effect' (1999) with pounding drums, wired guitar flute and some scatting thrown in for good measure. He also offered up his drumming skills on the dreaded side-project Tailgunner, an album of the same name being released in 2000, which offers some glimpses of talent but is over-indulgent, as most side-projects are.

Heathen Chemistry (aka The Back-to-Basics One)

With Gem Archer and Andy Bell now firmly established and having passed the initiation that was the gruelling 2000 world tour, Oasis re-entered the studio with a renewed sense of purpose and, significantly, a new band democracy that would sustain until the split some nine years later. And *Heathen Chemistry* was the first true band effort, four of the five members contributing to songwriting duties.

Noel was relieved of the pressure and seemed freed but primarily reverted to type, his ambitions of evolving the sound put back on the shelf. By this point he had perhaps realised that the anthems were a vital component of the band's unique appeal in uniting the masses. Now critic-proof, fans would keep attending Oasis shows for the communal experience but would expect to be moved by the songs in the process.

As such the Chief played a straight bat and gave them what they wanted without trying too hard. 'Stop Crying Your Heart Out' is now rightly revered as one of the all-time Oasis classics, a direct statement that goes straight for the heart. It's unashamedly earnest but as ever Liam's masculine vocals prevent it from becoming too slushy. With a strikingly simple piano, sparse chords and subtle strings that don't drown the song as once they may have, Noel reaps the rewards of not over-complicating things. As always, it's the melody alongside a motivational message ('take what you need and be on your way') that makes it a success, with a beautifully-desperate coda sealing the deal.

'Little by Little' is cut from the same anthemic cloth, but with a much more philosophical subject matter. Asking questions of himself and the fanbase ('now you'll have to accept the life inside your head I gave to you'), in trying to be grandiose it's a bit stodgy, but that matters not a jot. Two bellowing choruses and then we're off into an excellent mid-section, which ratchets up the tension before exploding into one last burst of euphoric righteousness which befits the question, 'Why am I really here?'

It was an offcut from the *Standing on the Shoulder of Giants* sessions, as was 'Force of Nature', which was originally unveiled on the soundtrack to Britflick *Love, Honour and Obey* with no fanfare. A solid if underwhelming track, with a drumbeat eerily similar to Iggy Pop's 'Nightclubbing', it's a bar-room brawl of a song with strangled guitar and wailing vocals. Rumoured to be about Noel's then-wife Meg, a claim he immediately refuted citing timeline discrepancies (it was recorded before the pair split), it's another swipe at the superficial side of fame and its hangers-on.

Comeback single 'The Hindu Times' on the other hand is about nothing at all, which was what made it appealing. Like the last two albums didn't happen (aside from the choir), it's a loose and ragged burst of rock-pop which effectively announced the commencement of Oasis Mk. 2. Feedback heavy, with a riff that sounds uncannily like Stereophonics' 'Same Size Feet,' it's distilled joy in a bottle and its simplicity is its strength. Perhaps not a classic but a very good Oasis single in the vein of 'Roll with It.'

'(Probably) All in the Mind' however is simple to the point of being forgettable, which is surprising given the effort that went into it. Another good McCartney-esque bassline (specifically 'Rain'), with genuine dual vocals (delivered waspishly by Liam), some great fills and cymbal clashing by Whitey and a nice little jam at the end, it should be better than it is. Even a guest appearance by Johnny Marr doesn't elevate the song, perhaps because it's a little too close to The Stone Roses for comfort. Oasis could never quite master the psychedelic thing.

The last of Noel's efforts is the cheesiest thing he's ever put his name to, but given he was in the heady first flush of romance one can allow him such an indulgence. 'She Is Love' is a straight-forward love song (as the name suggests), with even the added bells and handclaps sounding smitten. At three minutes it's succinct, but even then it's probably a little bit much.

Equally infatuated was Liam on the first of his three contributions, 'Songbird,' yet unlike his brother he exercises some restraint, with nothing other than an acoustic guitar, an organ piano and his vocals. With a topsy-turvy melody it's a slight thing, over before it's begun, but quite the step-up from 'Little James.' Even Noel must have been impressed, signing off on its release as a single.

'Born on a Different Cloud' is the younger Gallagher's attempt at 'Happiness is a Warm Gun' (and steals lyrics from 'Working Class Hero' just for good measure) and while it falls short, there is still much for the listener to get their teeth into. An eerie opening and an effect-heavy Liam vocal give way to chugging piano and stomping drums, making up the first two parts of an opus, before Johnny Marr re-enters the fray to contribute slide guitar and join the band as they sail away to sea, in a fog of 'nahs.' Epic in a downtrodden sort of way.

His final effort ('Better Man') is much more of a straight-forward dirty rocker, which must have filled the rest of the band with glee when it was presented. It shuffles and rattles along nicely, with not much in the way of lyrics or melody, but Gem, Andy and Noel (who also played drums, oddly) all get to wig out without pressure. Featuring Johnny Marr once more, this time on backing vocals.

Gem adds a sense of purpose and purity with the snappy 'Hung In A Bad Place,' a Stooges-style rocker with focussed guitar that is surely a reference the troubled recent years of Oasis ('hung in a bad place for too long'). The absolute filth of the track clearly impresses Liam, who sneers and snarls accordingly. 'A Quick Peep' is a small slice of lightweight fluff that serves well as an interlude, Andy's sole contribution bouncing by briefly. Along with hidden instrumental track, 'The Cage,' a jam that simply meanders along to nothing, it does little aside from demonstrating the new musical proficiency in the band.

Oasis needed to make *Heathen Chemistry* to rediscover their sense of purpose, and for that it should be judged for what it is. They no longer had the expectations of the music world on their shoulders (The Strokes *et al* had seen to that) but had to strike a fine balance to keep the fans interested. And a sense of freedom inhibits the album, with some outstanding tracks but with better things to come.

Accompanying tracks

'The Hindu Times'

'Just Getting Older' was another hangover from the *Standing on the Shoulder of Giants* sessions, and it feels like it. Everything about it, from the half-baked drums to the vocal delivery, sounds lethargic, but then that is the point of the song, essentially just a list of concerns about the passing of time. Some of the lyrics feel like they were just holding patterns but fittingly, Noel couldn't be bothered to change them. In contrast 'Idler's Dream' is a beautiful piece of work, one of only a handful of piano-led tracks released under the name Oasis. A strong vocal performance by Noel ('I hope you don't break my heart of stone'), it starts off cold then becomes warm to *Abbey Road*-era harmonies, hymnal-like in delivery. A gorgeous little thing that belongs to the fans and the fans alone.

'Stop Crying Your Heart Out'

The screeching guitars of pleasant rocker, 'Thank You for The Good Times' are at odds with the good vibe (see title), a competent track which Liam brings up a notch. Gem and Andy still sound wired and pleased to be there, while Alan White is little more than stoic, his enthusiasm for the band perhaps now spent. 'Shout It Out Loud' suggests gusto within, but there is little to be found here. It's got some intriguing lyrics ('Hope at last we get some peace'), but while sufficient it's not wholly satisfying.

'Little by Little'/'She is Love'

Everyone steps up to the plate on their cover of The Who's 'My Generation'; Alan White is back to his old filling best (although it was recorded in 2000), Gem crunches away, and Andy emulates John Entwistle's bass perfectly. Disciples of classic rock, the band are aware that it would be unwise to add much to a classic and don't, revelling in the carnival outro. Even Liam's voice slightly fracturing towards the end doesn't put a dampener on things, adding to the spontaneous feel of the recording.

'Songbird'

'(You've Got) The Heart of a Star' is the sound of someone walking away from a period of their life, whether good or bad ('if you could see what I could, then maybe we could all get along, and maybe I could justify the bad things in life that I've done.'). The organ and horn section give it an air of finality. and it's quite mournful and evokes regret, but with that Noel touch of reassurance outlined in the title.

On 'Merry Xmas Everybody,' released in 2002 as part of another *War Child* compilation, Noel manages the feat of making a cheery song (Slade's festive staple) sound depressing, in contrast to his usual technique. Also featured on a Christmas episode of 'The Royle Family,' which may explain its maudlin tone, it's certainly their weakest cover.

Noel was a gun for hire in the early part of the 21st century, popping up to add his by now distinctive guitar tones to The Who's 'Won't Get Fooled Again' on their *Live at the Royal Albert Hall* album, as well as on Cornershop's 15-minute epic 'Spectral Morning.' He and Gem also produced the debut album by Proud Mary, *The Same Old Blues,* as well as providing back-up on various instruments in the studio. He recommenced his fruitful relationship with Paul Weller offering on 'One X One' from his album *Illumination,* as well as being part of a supergroup with Weller, Ian McLagan and Kenney Jones on a selection of tracks on *Mustn't Grumble: The Steve Marriott Memorial Concert 2001,* including lead vocals on 'Here Come the Nice.'

Both Noel and Liam are front and centre on 'Shoot Down' from The Prodigy's fourth album *Always Outnumbered, Never Outgunned,* Noel delivering incessant bass high in the mix as Liam delivers a vocal from the gods over a dance-punk maelstrom. It's bettered only by 'Scorpio Rising,' Liam's collaboration with Death in Vegas in late 2002. Sampling Status Quo's 'Pictures of Matchstick Men,' it's a contender for one of the youngest Gallagher's best-ever vocal performances, certainly of the decade. Almost rapping at points, it demonstrates that when Liam was sufficiently inspired by a song, he could leave all other singers for dust.

Don't Believe the Truth (aka The Return to Form)

It's hard to reconcile Noel's claim after Oasis split that people 'had stopped listening' when thinking about their penultimate album. *Don't Believe the Truth* shifted nearly a quarter of a million units in its first week, and while a lot of that could be put down to the fiercely loyal fans following old habits, purchasing it on day one, it was primarily down to the fact that it's also one of their best albums. The only album to have two consecutive No.1 singles (in the same calendar year to boot), the brothers and others were firing on all cylinders here.

Not only that, but the main songwriter had rediscovered his mojo and started exploring musical avenues he perhaps wouldn't have in the recent past. 'The Importance of Being Idle' was an immediate classic, timeless British pop with a wry wistfulness, Noel finding a key that perfectly suited his singing style, as well as undergoing some vocal effects which add to the kitchen sink vibe. It has a dusky timbre, reminiscent of 'Clean Prophet' by long-standing Gallagher favourites The La's, with circus-ring guitars and precise lyrics that make sense. Noel claims he knew soon after finishing that it was a No.1 single in waiting, a brave call but justified. 'The Importance of Being Idle' is perfectly balanced, perfectly paced and knows when to leave, with their best-ever video (Rhys Ifans dancing like a loon) as an added bonus.

Noel channels the 1960s throughout his five contributions to the album. 'Mucky Fingers,' originally suggested as lead single, is his take on The Velvet Underground's 'I'm Waiting for the Man,' a driving number built around incessant drums and simple chords. It's the only track where Terry Kirkbride provided drums, and it's noticeable; different from Zak Starkey's clear sound, his contribution simple but essential to the persistency of the song. Gem's ear-splitting harmonica solo sounds like a train, and the wobbly bass towards the end keeps things going until the last. It features interesting lyrics too; 'You get your history from the Union Jack' seemed almost irrelevant at the time, but in this post-Brexit world it's eerily prescient.

This seems a good point to reference the album's title. It seemed incredibly naff back in 2005, both contradictory and obvious, as Noel claimed it was a reference to the machinations of media (specifically addressing the conflicts in the Middle-East of the time). Now we live in a post-truth age, it's one of the few times he can be accused of being ahead of his time.

He continued his rich vein of form on 'Part of the Queue.' Although this one borrows from The Stranglers' classic 'Golden Brown' (in Noel's hands it's a lot noisier), it's ostensibly about the mundanity of the supermarket experience. As on 'Mucky Fingers,' he goes for the minimalist approach when it comes to the verse melody, but with a steep jump up as he belts out a rallying chorus. He's primarily going for the observational approach here and can't help but be cynical, the effects of middle-age now in full throe. Zak Starkey, brought in to cover the drumming vacancy, adds a vitality that had been missing for a good few years. This is speculation, as perhaps Noel was dictatorial when it came to all areas of instrumentation, but Alan White had settled into a drumming pattern that was night and day compared to what went before, and as this album proves, sometimes enforced change has benefits.

Noel could also take comfort in the knowledge that, now the band was a democracy, 'traditional' Oasis songs wouldn't be hard to come by. He was right. Andy puts his experience to good use, writing songs in a style that fitted The

Voice. 'Turn Up the Sun' is a beast, opening with twinkly guitars before exploding into life, blowing away any cobwebs that may have formed from three years out of action. It has the epic feel of the sun (fittingly) rising on day of mischief, alive and booming from the speakers. Similarly, his other effort, 'Keep the Dream Alive' features a soul-scraping and righteous delivery from Liam and is a paean to keeping one's soul intact. Fitting the tone, Gem delivers *Revolver* razor sharp guitars with metallic drumming not unlike his dad (Ringo) from Zak on 'A Bell Will Ring'. Meanwhile, Liam, unsurprisingly, digs that Beatles vibe.

But of course, no-one can do anthemic rock-pop better than Noel Gallagher. 'Let There be Love' was originally written in the late '90s, going through various iterations (better known as 'It's a Crime' amongst fandom for a few years) but is a lesson in not over-egging the pudding. It's far too slow and, although designed to be low-key, plods along without the spark of electricity it so desperately needs. Arguably their most Beatlesy number both in production (that piano comes straight from *Abbey Road*) and message, it's interesting only in that it was performed just twice (once for an Italian radio session and again with Noel closing a gig in Santiago, acoustic-only), and is a proper duet between what were by now co-frontmen.

Lead single 'Lyla' is a different proposition entirely. Re-recorded at the very last minute, Noel wasn't even convinced it should go on the album but had his mind changed by the label. Just as well; it's a monstrous call to arms, encouraging everyone listening to go mental. Incessant drums and cymbal work, a berserk mid-section and closing wig-out contribute to what at first listen could be a lost single by The Who. Oasis operating at maximum capacity.

Liam's offerings are a bit more pedestrian than his previous work, suggesting he'd hit a glass ceiling in terms of ambition, i.e. going beyond 1972 (his year of birth). 'The Meaning of Soul' is a diatribe of spat-out vocals, with dry drumming via a cereal box and wooden spoons. As he's a self-taught guitar player, the chord sequences are unusual, and the track manages to fit a lot in, given its length. 'Love Like a Bomb' is interesting in that he opts to push himself vocally, straining his nasal passage and larynx towards a direction that strains his voice (given the simplicity of the rest of the song he would be forgiven for staying in his comfort zone) with fiercely struck acoustic guitars. Sadly, he attempts a falsetto that he can't really deliver anymore, and the track is a bit aimless.

The suggestively-spelled 'Guess God Thinks I'm Abel' (perhaps it's all a show and he's not as illiterate as he makes out) twists and swirls with a simple verse and strong chorus, but saves its best for last with an explosion of noise that is both cathartic and frustrating. If only he tried writing on the electric guitar sometimes.

So comfortable were Oasis in this period that all responsibilities were shared, and the musicianship was mixed, so much so that the band struggle to remember who played what instrument. That's perhaps surprising given *Don't Believe the Truth*'s gestation was the most troubled since *Definitely Maybe.* Death in Vegas came and went, then the band tried to produce it themselves and drew a blank, eventually bringing in Dave Sardy for production duties, who convinced the band to decamp and start again in L.A. Strange then that it's the most British sounding album of the Oasis oeuvre, thoroughly indebted to the 1960s (more so than usual), and extremely popular with the critics of the time. Justly so.

Accompanying tracks

'Lyla'

Sadly, the quality was lacking in the other songs of the period, 'Eyeball Tickler' aside. It's a rip-roaring slice of garage rock written by Gem, a mini-tidal wave with wired vocal that doesn't outstay it's welcome. In contrast, on the self-penned 'Won't Let You Down' Liam delivers one of his worst-ever vocals, his nasal delivery trying far too hard to evoke his hero John Lennon. It makes the skin crawl and it's hard to defend.

'The Importance of Being Idle'

'Pass Me Down the Wine' has at least a bit more gumption about it, but contains dreadful rhyming couplets (thunder/hunger, etc.) with nothing to make it stand apart from any other Liam Gallagher composition. 'The Quiet Ones' by Gem is even worse, dull as dishwater and instantly forgettable.

'Let There be Love'

Even Noel had caught the B-side virus; 'Sittin' Here in Silence (On my Own)' is obviously stronger than the others, but at less than two minutes feels little more than a demo, the singer ruminating whilst backed with simple piano and drums. His equivalent to 'Her Majesty.' Backed with a pulsating version of 'Rock 'n' Roll Star' from the City of Manchester stadium gigs.

Of the three 'new' tracks featured on the *Goal!* Soundtrack, only 'Who Put the Weight of The World on my Shoulders?' is worthy of attention. A by-the-numbers widescreen ballad, the strings are much more melodramatic than on other Oasis tracks, suggesting they were provided by an external source. It's another of Noel's attempts to ape Burt Bacharach and unfortunately falls somewhat short, even sounding slightly flat, and it features the more lumpen drumming technique that came before 2005. The remixes of 'Cast No Shadow' and 'Morning Glory,' by UNKLE and Dave Sardy respectively, don't bring much new to the table, although Noel delivers, performing lead vocals on the former. Recorded during the album sessions. 'Can Y'See it Now? (I Can See it Now!)' is another of those Noel meanderings, only his repeat of the title preventing it from becoming an instrumental. He was obviously listening to a lot of krautrock at the time, judging by its vibe.

The aforementioned 'Keep What Ya Got,' a co-write with Ian Brown, was given a single release in 2004, Brown adding his usual metaphysical lyrics to a beefed-up version of 'Teotihuacan' with added guitar. One of Brown's best singles, it's so strong that only one of Noel's heroes was worthy of being gifted it. Noel also popped up to provide backing vocals on 'Freelove Freeway' by David Brent (Ricky Gervais) in summer 2004, reaching a note so high that no mortal man should even attempt it.

Dig Out Your Soul (AKA The Last Hurrah)

Emboldened by the positive response to *Don't Believe the Truth* and having taken stock of their past in 2006-7 via Best Of album *Stop the Clocks* and their Outstanding Contribution award at the Brits, Oasis were at a crossroads before what would prove to be their final album. The previous LP captured the imagination of the public in a way not seen since *(What's the Story) Morning Glory?* and what followed needed to be averted at all costs. On the other hand, as artists of every ilk will testify, there is little reward in ploughing the same furrow.

Dig Out Your Soul is a swampier, heavier beast than its predecessor. Their live showing at the Brit Awards gave some notice to where they were headed; their performance may have included mainstream classics, but the delivery was something else entirely, more grizzled than ever. It's also an album of two halves, Noel providing the songs for six of the first seven tracks before leaving the rest of the band to get on with it, almost unconsciously setting the scene for Liam's Beady Eye.

You can see the lineage clearly; 'I'm Outta Time' is Liam's favourite of his efforts, unsurprising given how much it sounds like John Lennon, even going so far as to feature an interview extract from the man himself playing over the fade-out. However, there are worse people to copy, and the dreamy opening and piano break up the album very effectively. The whispering mellotron and music box ending are mournful touches on his most direct tribute to his hero.

'Ain't Got Nothin,' written while Liam was working on the rigs in late 2002, is ferocious yet simple - all venom, attitude and vigour, with booming drums and ripped guitar. Closer 'Soldier On' is notably downbeat for the last track on an Oasis album, and for that reason alone is worthy of our attention. It's quite haunting, petering out gradually, Noel oddly on drums (perhaps Zak, who after being made permanent promptly upped sticks before the tour, gave his notice too early) offering an almost funereal affair, fittingly. It was apparently rediscovered when The Coral were recording in Wheeler End Studios and given a polish. Ironically it brings to mind the early work of Gorillaz, complete with spooky harmonica. A message from Noel (by putting it at the end) perhaps?

Gem's 'To Be Where There's Life' is stronger, but that's mainly down to Liam, who's clearly impressed with the sitars and bongos (because, y'know, The Beatles did it, so it must be good), giving his best vocal on the album (his cry of the album title in the mid-section is particularly special). When a paint-stripping vocal is required, look no further. Unfortunately, the song itself is too close to pastiche to be considered special. Meanwhile, Andy Bell's 'The Nature of Reality' contains a good groove and blistering guitars but is a bit of a dirge overall.

And there's the rub. Noel was evolving at a faster pace than his bandmates could keep up with, and the growing gap was becoming cavernous. The first half is much stronger, and the fact that's entirely Noel-driven is surely no coincidence. Opener 'Bag It Up' is a shifty and shuffling opener, with allusions to 'freaks', 'the Monkey Man' and having his 'heebie-jeebies hidden in a bag'. Who knows what he's on about, but I'll have some of what he was having. It appears Noel had given up trying to soundtrack our lives, setting his sights on our dreams and nightmares instead.

'The Turning' is the first of two Oasis songs in the 'classic' mode. It starts with a vaguely dubby bass line before the trademark wall of sound unleashes itself. A glorious, biting guitar solo that evokes the early years is truly sky-kissing, before a calming piano brings things back down to earth, leading into a pastiche of 'Dear Prudence'. To reiterate a simile from earlier, it feels like dusk. Lyrically the whole album has an apocalyptic theme; 'the rapture' is first mentioned here, although quite what he means by, 'Shake your rag doll baby' is anybody's guess. It sounds great though.

The pumping lead single, 'The Shock of the Lightning' sounds like 'Headshrinker's unruly younger brother and has the same spirit and urgency. It's got a drum solo then a guitar solo. Finally, a decade and a half after the comparisons were first made, Oasis truly sound like the Sex Pistols covering The Beatles, circa 1967. A majestic, frantic way to begin a final hurrah, and the fastest thing Noel had written in years.

Sandwiched between those behemoths is 'Waiting for the Rapture', which may very well be the dirtiest Oasis song ever. The riff screams carnal desire, so it's ironic that the lyrics are a wistful stroll down memory lane, its composer reminiscing about meeting the love of his life for the first time. It's bluesy in a way they'd never dared, complete with a furious solo. As such, Jack White would have been within reason to ask for his sound back.

'(Get Off Your) High Horse Lady' was originally earmarked as a B-side, but apparent issues with his brother led to Noel promoting it to the album. It's a strutting stomp with a western vibe, his effect-heavy voice twisting and turning around the speaker, and it serves as a good palette cleanser before we enter the second half.

And while the album does fall away, its high-water mark midway through is spectacular. It mystifies this writer that 'Falling Down' isn't heralded as one of the greats. A glimpse into Noel's mind, it features (one suspects) one of his most personal set of lyrics. It seems he's recalling his upbringing (born to Catholic parents and attending a Catholic school) from a distance and still wants to believe there is a God, but the world-weary lyrics suggest he's just about given up on the concept; 'If you won't save me, please don't waste my time.' The spine of the song is Zak Starkey's plucky drumbeat (riffing on 'Tomorrow Never Knows'), but it's a cacophony of glorious noise with a beautiful melody to complement it. The final Oasis single, it's quite the journey from 'Supersonic' all those years ago.

Dig Out Your Soul has the same spirit of early Oasis work in places ('The Turning', 'The Shock of the Lightning') and so in a way it brings things full circle, while also confirmation that Oasis had evolved into a psychedelic rock beast. Arguably and ironically, they had no peers in that field, either in the modern era or in rock'n'roll history. But hindsight teaches us that it was probably a good place to stop. Noel always had a strong sense of vision that can only be indulged with complete control, and when comparing his efforts of controlled experimentation to the rest of the band's - specifically Liam's - more direct approach, one can hear that democracy isn't conducive to creativity. A parting of ways now seems like it was always the logical outcome.

Accompanying tracks

Perhaps as a sign of the times (CD singles becoming obsolete) or as a sign of a band not doing more than was necessary, there's a real paucity of additional tracks by now, most of which are included on the special-edition boxset version of the album. Only 'Those Swollen Hand Blues' on the 'Falling Down' single was a traditional B-side and a throwback to the internal musings of the *Standing on the Shoulder of Giants* era. 'I wished I'd learned to play piano, if only I could keep myself sober for more than a day', Noel sings against an odd mix of music hall-esque piano and mellotron-fused atmospherics. Just weird.

'Boy with the Blues' and 'I Believe in All' were Liam compositions, the former a gospel-tinged plea to 'come on together' with a huge array of instrumentation (orchestra, organs, the lot). The latter was rockier and more energetic but sadly fell short again because of Liam's infuriating deference to rhyming couplets ('there's a fire in the sky, I don't need no alibi'). Noel even left Gem to provide backing vocals, with both tracks a precursor to Beady Eye.

'Lord Don't Slow Me Down' was recorded during the *Don't Believe the Truth* sessions but took on a life of its own when it accompanied the film of the same name. Including it as part of the *Dig Out Your Soul* package was a wise move, as it sounds too similar to 'Lyla.' That's no bad thing of course; the track could be The Yardbirds rattling as if full of pills, posture and vigour. As a single release it only charted at No.10 but as it was only available as a download, that was an impressive achievement. As much as Noel tried his best, it was the type of track far more suited to his brother, a version of which is available online. Meanwhile, the single was backed with two further songs from the City of Manchester gigs in 2005 ('Don't Look Back in Anger' and 'The Meaning of Soul').

As compensation there were a glut of remixes and alternate versions available; 'The Turning (Alt. Version #4)' much bouncier but because of the strength of the final version, little more than a curio. Likewise, 'Waiting for the Rapture (Alt. Version #2),' is little more than a demo, devoid of the power it finished with.

Some heavyweight names were brought to the table for remixes, to mixed results; Neon Neon (better known as Gruff Rhys and Boom Bip) and Richard Fearless of Death in Vegas tackled 'To Be Where There's Life,' the latter's additions adding some power and depth while the former's were inconsequential. Primal Scream gave 'The Shock of the Lightning' the once-over, opting not to rock further but to twinkle brighter, and on '(Get Off Your) High Horse Lady (the May 29th version)' Devendra Banhart added some campfire vibes. Furthermore, Jagz Kooner and Twiggy Ramirez also tackled a handful of tracks.

'Falling Down' got the full works, with a demo, mixed by Gibb (bland) and The Prodigy (cavernous), and there was even a 22-minute version by Amorphous Androgynous. Best of all though was The Chemical Brothers' take; completely different from the main track and unmistakably them, it felt like a companion piece to 'Setting Sun,' all siren wails and blasts but with exquisite house piano. 'Leaked' in the summer of 2008 with excellent timing, it carried a Balearic quality.

In 2007 Oasis (*sans* Noel) took to covering The Beatles' 'Within You Without You,' opting not to change much apart from replacing the drums with those from 'Tomorrow Never Knows,' although it has to be said that Liam's voice worked really well against sitar. And the following year we heard the results of Noel finally commit to writing a song with Paul Weller, 'Echoes Round the Sun,' with able support from Gem. And as well as providing bass loop for Weller to add to, Noel also contributed mellotron, wurlitzer and guitar to the most vibrant offering on the Modfather's *22 Dreams*.

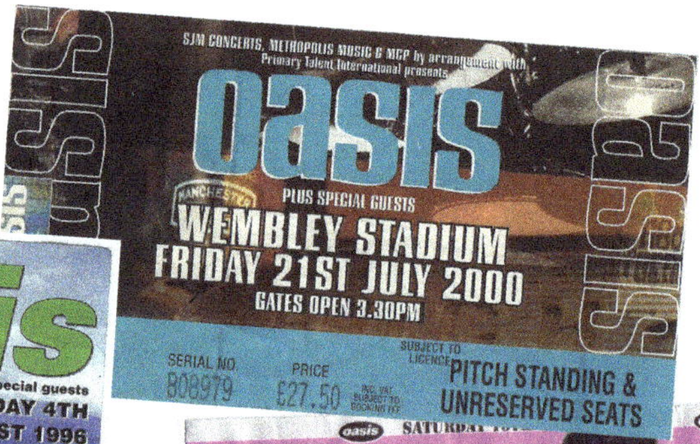

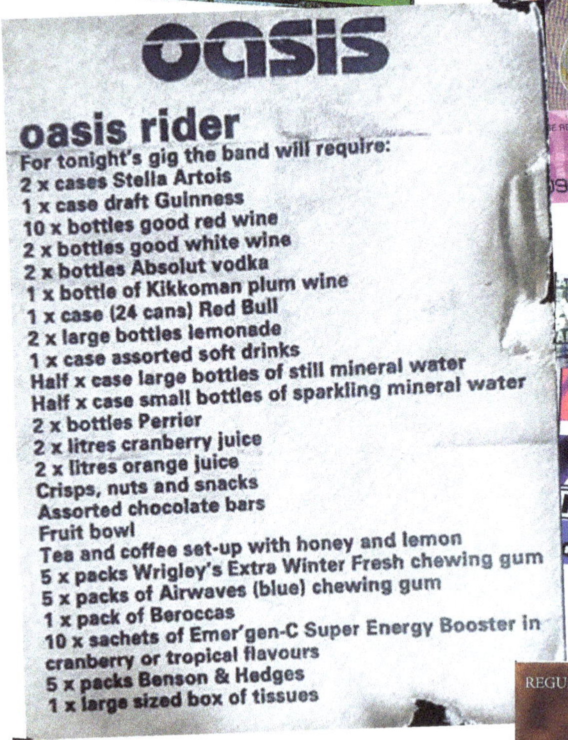
oasis

oasis rider

For tonight's gig the band will require:
2 x cases Stella Artois
1 x case draft Guinness
10 x bottles good red wine
2 x bottles good white wine
2 x bottles Absolut vodka
1 x bottle of Kikkoman plum wine
1 x case (24 cans) Red Bull
2 x large bottles lemonade
1 x case assorted soft drinks
Half x case large bottles of still mineral water
Half x case small bottles of sparkling mineral water
2 x bottles Perrier
2 x litres cranberry juice
2 x litres orange juice
Crisps, nuts and snacks
Assorted chocolate bars
Fruit bowl
Tea and coffee set-up with honey and lemon
5 x packs Wrigley's Extra Winter Fresh chewing gum
5 x packs of Airwaves (blue) chewing gum
1 x pack of Beroccas
10 x sachets of Emer'gen-C Super Energy Booster in cranberry or tropical flavours
5 x packs Benson & Hedges
1 x large sized box of tissues

DISCOGRAPHY

Studio Albums:

DEFINITELY MAYBE **(CREATION)**
Released: 29 August 1994
Highest UK chart position: 1
Worldwide sales: 15,000,000

Tracklist:
'Rock 'n' Roll Star'
'Shakermaker'
'Live Forever'
'Up in The Sky'
'Columbia'
'Supersonic'
'Bring It on Down'
'Cigarettes & Alcohol'
'Digsy's Dinner'
'Slide Away'

'Married with Children'
(vinyl release also included 'Sad Song')

2014 reissue B-sides/rare tracks
'Columbia' (white label demo)
'Cigarettes & Alcohol' (demo)
'Sad Song'
'I Will Believe' (live)
'Take Me Away'
'Alive' (demo)
'D'Yer Wanna Be A Spaceman?'
'Supersonic' (live)
'Up in the Sky' (acoustic)
'Cloudburst'
'Fade Away'
'Listen Up'
'I Am the Walrus' (live at the Glasgow Cathouse, Glasgow, Scotland, June 1994)
'Whatever'
'(It's Good) To Be Free'
'Half the World Away'
'Supersonic' (live at Glasgow Tramshed, Glasgow, Scotland, 7 April 1994)
'Rock 'n' Roll Star' (demo)
'Shakermaker' (live Paris In-Store Performance)
'Columbia' (Eden Studios Mix)
'Cloudburst' (demo)
'Strange Thing' (demo)
'Live Forever' (live Paris In-Store Performance)
'Cigarettes & Alcohol' (live at Manchester Academy, Manchester, England, 18 December 1994)
'D'Yer Wanna Be A Spaceman?' (live at Manchester Academy, Manchester, England, 18 December 1994)
'Fade Away' (demo)
'Take Me Away' (live at Manchester Academy, Manchester, England, 18 December 1994)
'Sad Song' (live at Manchester Academy, Manchester, England, 18 December 1994)
'Half the World Away' (live at Tokyo Hotel Room)
'Digsy's Dinner' (live Paris In-Store Performance)
'Married with Children' (demo)
'Up in the Sky' (live Paris In-Store Performance)

'Whatever' (Strings Only)
'Live Forever' (live Gleneagles June '94)*
'Digsy's Dinner' (live Gleneagles June '94)*

download only

(WHAT'S THE STORY) MORNING GLORY? (CREATION)
Released: 2 October 1995
Highest UK Chart position: 1
Worldwide sales: 22,400,000

Tracklist:
'Hello'
'Roll with It'
'Wonderwall'
'Don't Look Back in Anger'
'Hey Now!'
'Untitled 1' (The Swamp Song – Excerpt 1)
'Some Might Say'

'Cast No Shadow'
'She's Electric'
'Morning Glory'
'Untitled 2' (The Swamp Song - Excerpt 2)
'Champagne Supernova'
(vinyl release also included 'Bonehead's Bank Holiday')

2014 reissue B-sides/rare tracks
'Talk Tonight'
'Acquiesce'
'Headshrinker'
'It's Better People'
'Rockin' Chair'
'Step Out'
'Underneath the Sky'
'Cum on Feel the Noize'
'Round Are Way'
'The Swamp Song'
'The Masterplan'
'Bonehead's Bank Holiday'
'Champagne Supernova' (Brendan Lynch mix)
'You've Got to Hide Your Love Away'
'Acquiesce' (live at Earls Court, London, 4 November 1995)
'Some Might Say' (demo, recorded at soundcheck Cub Quattro Tokyo Japan, 14 September 1994)
'Some Might Say' (live at Roskilde Festival, Denmark, 30 June 1995)
'She's Electric' (demo, recorded at Mauldeth Road West Studio, Manchester)
'Talk Tonight' (live at Bath Pavillion, 22 June 1995)
'Rockin' Chair' (demo, recorded at Mauldeth Road West Studio, Manchester)
'Hello' (live at Roskilde Festival, Denmark, 30 June 1995)
'Roll with It' (live at Roskilde Festival, Denmark, 30 June 1995)
'Morning Glory' (live at Roskilde Festival, Denmark, 30 June 1995)
'Hey Now!' (demo, recorded at soundcheck Club Quattro Tokyo, Japan, 14 September 1994)
'Bonehead's Bank Holiday' (demo, recorded at soundcheck Club Quattro Tokyo, Japan, 14 September 1994)
'Round Are Way' (MTV Unplugged, Royal Festival Hall, London, 23 August 1996)
'Cast No Shadow' (live at Maine Road, Manchester, 27 April 1996)
'The Masterplan' (live at Knebworth Park, Hertfordshire, 10 August 1996)

BE HERE NOW **(CREATION)**
Released: 21 August 1997
Highest UK chart position: 1
Worldwide sales: 8,000,000

Tracklist:
'D'You Know What I Mean?'
'My Big Mouth'
'Magic Pie'
'Stand by Me'
'I Hope, I Think, I Know'
'The Girl in The Dirty Shirt'
'Fade In-Out'
'Don't Go Away'
'Be Here Now'
'All Around the World'
'It's Getting Better (Man!!)'
'All Around the World (Reprise)'

2016 reissue B-sides and demos/The Mustique Sessions

'Stay Young'
'The Fame'
'Flashbax'
'(I Got) The Fever'
'My Sister Lover'
'Going Nowhere'
'Stand by Me' (live at Bonehead's Outtake)
'Untitled' (demo)
'Help!' (live in L.A.)
'Setting Sun' (live radio broadcast)
'If We Shadows' (demo)
'Don't Go Away' (demo)
'My Big Mouth' (live at Knebworth Park, August 1996)
'D'You Know What I Mean?' (NG's 2016 rethink)
'D'You Know What I Mean?' (Mustique demo)
'My Big Mouth' (Mustique demo)
'My Sister Lover' (Mustique demo)
'Stand by Me' (Mustique demo)
'I Hope, I Think, I Know' (Mustique demo)
'The Girl in the Dirty Shirt' (Mustique demo)
'Don't Go Away' (Mustique demo)
'Trip Inside' (Mustique demo)
'Fade In-Out' (Mustique demo)
'Stay Young' (Mustique demo)
'Angel Child' (Mustique demo)
'The Fame' (Mustique demo)
'All Around the World' (Mustique demo)
'It's Getting Better (Man!!)' (Mustique demo)

STANDING ON THE SHOULDER OF GIANTS **(BIG BROTHER)**
Released: 28 February 2000
Highest UK chart position: 1
Worldwide sales: 3,000,000

Tracklist:
'Fuckin' In the Bushes'
'Go Let It Out'
'Who Feels Love?'
'Put Yer Money Where Yer Mouth Is'
'Little James'
'Gas Panic!'
'Where Did It All Go Wrong?'
'Sunday Morning Call'
'I Can See A Liar'
'Roll It Over'

HEATHEN CHEMISTRY (BIG BROTHER)
Released: 1 July 2002
Highest UK chart position: 1
Worldwide sales: 3,500,000

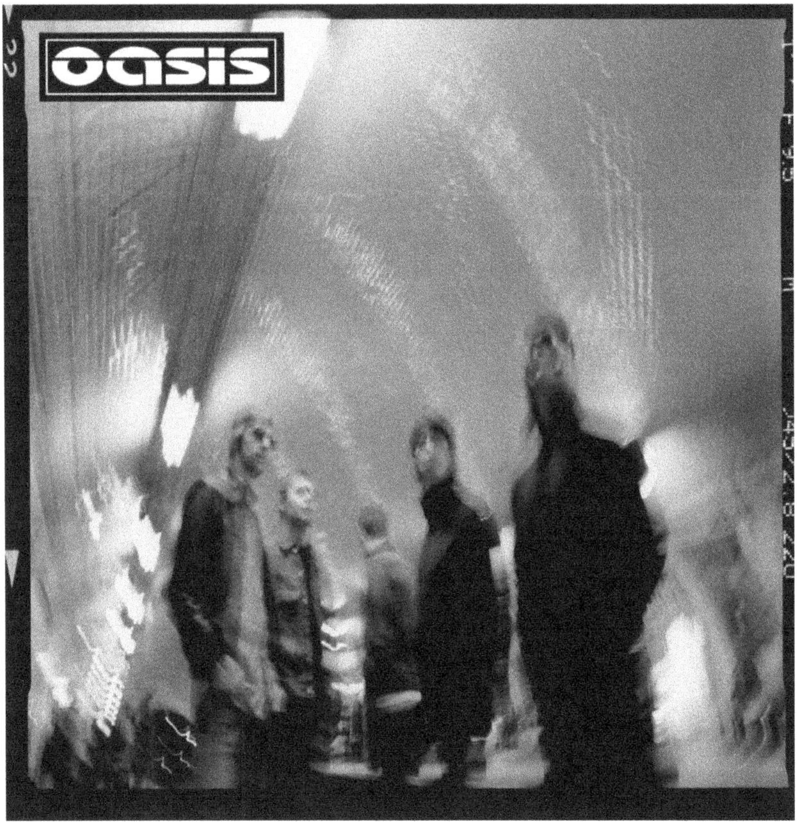

Tracklist:
'The Hindu Times'
'Force of Nature'
'Hung in A Bad Place'
'Stop Crying Your Heart Out'
'Songbird'
'Little by Little'
'A Quick Peep'
'(Probably) All in The Mind'
'She Is Love'
'Born on A Different Cloud'
'Better Man'
(hidden track 'The Cage')

DON'T BELIEVE THE TRUTH (BIG BROTHER)
Released: 30 May 2005
Highest UK chart position: 1
Worldwide sales: 7,000,000

Tracklist:
'Turn Up the Sun'
'Mucky Fingers'
'Lyla'
'Love Like A Bomb'
'The Importance of Being Idle'
'The Meaning of Soul'
'Guess God Thinks I'm Abel'
'Part of The Queue'
'Keep the Dream Alive'
'A Bell Will Ring'
'Let There Be Love'

DIG OUT YOUR SOUL **(BIG BROTHER)**
Released: 6 October 2008
Highest UK chart position: 1
Worldwide sales: 1,600,000

Tracklist:
'Bag It Up'
'The Turning'
'Waiting for The Rapture'
'The Shock of The Lightning'
'I'm Outta Time'
'(Get Off Your) High Horse Lady'
'Falling Down'
'To Be Where There's Life'
'Ain't Got Nothin''
'The Nature Of Reality'
'Soldier On'

Bonus CD:
'Lord Don't Slow Me Down'
'The Turning' (The Jagz Kooner Remix)
'Boy with The Blues'
'Falling Down' (The Chemical Brothers Remix)
'The Shock of The Lightning' (The Jagz Kooner Remix)
'I Believe in All'
'To Be Where There's Life' (A Richard Fearless Production)
'The Turning' (Alt. Version #4)
'Waiting for The Rapture' (Alt. Version #2)
'The Shock of The Lightning' (Primal Scream Remix (Italian Version Only))

Live Albums:

FAMILIAR TO MILLIONS **(BIG BROTHER)**
Released: 13 November 2000
Highest UK chart position: 5
Worldwide sales: 1,000,000

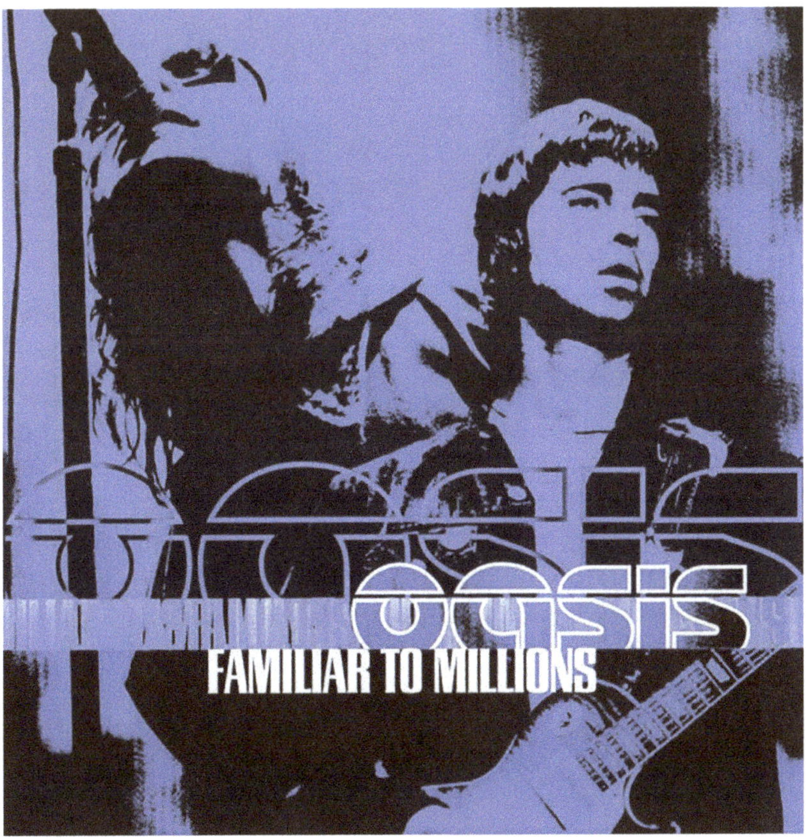

Tracklist:
'Fuckin' In the Bushes'
'Go Let It Out'
'Who Feels Love?'
'Supersonic'
'Shakermaker'
'Acquiesce'
'Step Out'
'Gas Panic!'
'Roll with It'
'Stand by Me'
'Wonderwall'
'Cigarettes & Alcohol'
'Don't Look Back in Anger'
'Live Forever'
'Hey Hey, My My (Into the Black)'
'Champagne Supernova'
'Rock 'n' Roll Star'
'Helter Skelter'

Compilation Albums:

DEFINITELY MAYBE: SINGLES **(CREATION)**
Released: 5 November 1996
Highest UK chart position: 23
Features 'Supersonic,' 'Shakermaker,' 'Live Forever' and 'Cigarettes & Alcohol' CD singles

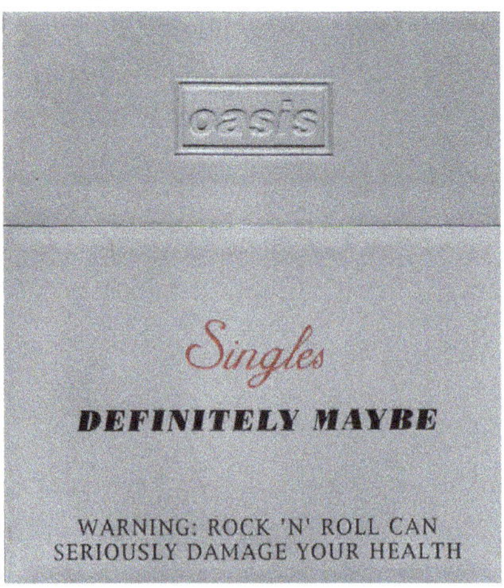

(WHAT'S THE STORY) MORNING GLORY?: SINGLES **(CREATION)**
Released: 10 November 1996
Highest UK chart position: 24
Features 'Some Might Say', 'Roll with It', 'Wonderwall' and 'Don't Look Back In Anger' CD singles

THE MASTERPLAN **(CREATION)**
Released: 3 November 1998
Highest UK chart position: 2
Worldwide sales: 2,000,000

Tracklist:
'Acquiesce'
'Underneath the Sky'
'Talk Tonight'
'Going Nowhere'
'Fade Away'
'The Swamp Song'
'I Am the Walrus (live)'
'Listen Up'
'Rockin' Chair'
'Half the World Away'
'(It's Good) To Be Free'
'Stay Young'
'Headshrinker'
'The Masterplan'

STOP THE CLOCKS **(BIG BROTHER)**
Released: 20 November 2006
Highest UK chart position: 2
Worldwide sales: 3,000,000

Tracklist:
'Rock 'n' Roll Star'
'Some Might Say'
'Talk Tonight'
'Lyla'
'The Importance of Being Idle'
'Wonderwall'

'Slide Away'
'Cigarettes & Alcohol'
'The Masterplan'
'Live Forever'
'Acquiesce'
'Supersonic'
'Half the World Away'
'Go Let It Out'
'Songbird'
'Morning Glory'
'Champagne Supernova'
'Don't Look Back in Anger'

TIME FLIES … 1994-2009 **(BIG BROTHER)**
Released: 14 June 2010
Highest UK chart position: 1

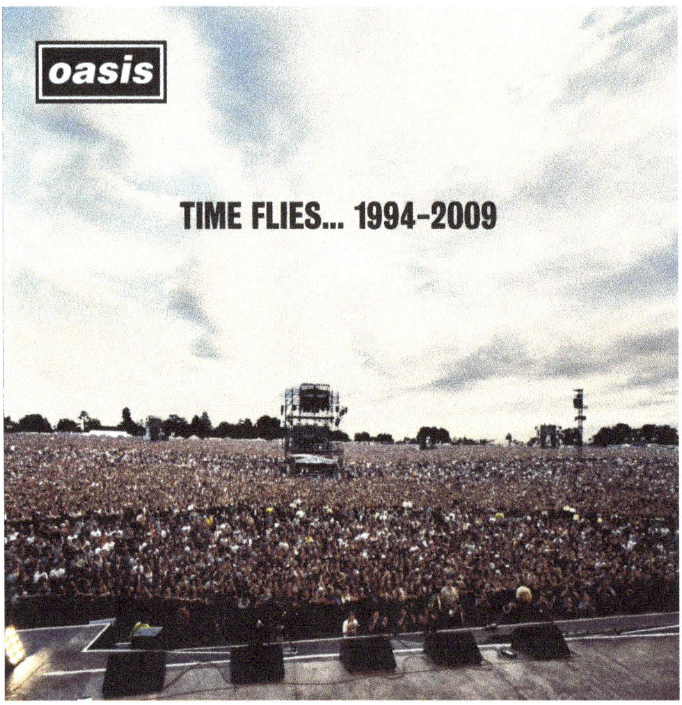

Tracklist:
'Supersonic'
'Roll with It'
'Live Forever'

'Wonderwall'
'Stop Crying Your Heart Out'
'Cigarettes & Alcohol'
'Songbird'
'Don't Look Back in Anger'
'The Hindu Times'
'Stand by Me'
'Lord Don't Slow Me Down'
'Shakermaker'
'All Around the World'
'Some Might Say'
'The Importance of Being Idle'
'D'You Know What I Mean?'
'Lyla'
'Let There Be Love'
'Go Let It Out'
'Who Feels Love?'
'Little by Little'
'The Shock of The Lightning'
'She Is Love'
'Whatever'
'I'm Outta Time'
'Falling Down'
'Sunday Morning Call' (hidden track)

Extended Plays:

Stop the Clocks EP **(Big Brother)**
Released: 13 November 2006

Tracklist:
'Acquiesce'
'Cigarettes & Alcohol' (Demo)
'Some Might Say' (live 1995)
'The Masterplan'

Singles

'SUPERSONIC' (CREATION)
Released: 11 April 1994
Highest UK chart position: 31

Tracklist: 'Supersonic', 'Take Me Away', 'I Will Believe' (live), 'Columbia' (white label demo)

'SHAKERMAKER' (CREATION)
Released: 13 June 1994
Highest UK chart position:
Tracklist: 'Shakermaker', 'D'Yer Wanna Be A Spaceman?', 'Alive' (8-track demo), 'Bring It on Down' (live)

'LIVE FOREVER' (CREATION)
Released: 8 August 1994
Highest UK chart position: 10
Tracklist: 'Live Forever', 'Up in The Sky' (acoustic), 'Cloudburst', 'Supersonic' (live)

'CIGARETTES & ALCOHOL' (CREATION)
Released: 10 October 1994
Highest UK chart position: 7
Tracklist: 'Cigarettes & Alcohol', 'I Am the Walrus' (live at Glasgow Cathouse, June'94), 'Listen Up', 'Fade Away'

'WHATEVER' (CREATION)
Released: 18 December 1994
Highest UK chart position: 3
Tracklist: 'Whatever', '(It's Good) To Be Free', 'Half the World Away', 'Slide Away'

'SOME MIGHT SAY' (CREATION)
Released: 24 April 1995
Highest UK chart position: 1
Tracklist: 'Some Might Say', 'Talk Tonight', 'Acquiesce', 'Headshrinker'

'ROLL WITH IT' (CREATION)
Released: 14 August 1995
Highest UK chart position: 2
Tracklist: 'Roll with It', 'It's Better People', 'Rockin' Chair', 'Live Forever' (live at Glastonbury '95)

'MORNING GLORY' (CREATION, EPIC)
Released: 18 September 1995
Highest UK Chart Position: N/A
Tracklist: 'Morning Glory', 'It's Better People', 'Rockin' Chair', 'Live Forever' (live at Glastonbury '95)

'WONDERWALL' (CREATION)
Released: 30 October 1995
Highest UK chart position: 2
Tracklist: 'Wonderwall', 'Round Are Way', 'The Swamp Song', 'The Masterplan'

'DON'T LOOK BACK IN ANGER' (CREATION)
Released: 19 February 1996
Highest UK chart position: 1
Tracklist: 'Don't Look Back in Anger', 'Step Out', 'Underneath the Sky', 'Cum on Feel the Noize'

'CHAMPAGNE SUPERNOVA' (CREATION)
Released: 13 May 1996
Highest UK chart position: (N/A)
Tracklist: 'Champagne Supernova', 'Slide Away'

'D'YOU KNOW WHAT I MEAN?' (CREATION)
Released: 7 July 1997
Highest UK chart position: 1
Tracklist: 'D'You Know What I Mean?', 'Stay Young', 'Angel Child' (demo), 'Heroes'

'STAND BY ME' (CREATION)
Released: 22 September 1997
Highest UK chart position: 2
Tracklist: 'Stand by Me', '(I Got) The Fever', 'My Sister Lover', 'Going Nowhere'

'ALL AROUND THE WORLD' (CREATION)
Released: 12 January 1998
Highest UK chart position: 1
Tracklist: 'All Around the World', 'The Fame', 'Flashbax', 'Street Fighting Man'

'DON'T GO AWAY' (CREATION/SONY MUSIC JAPAN)
Released: 19 February 1998
Highest UK chart position: (N/A)
Tracklist: 'Don't Go Away,' 'Cigarettes & Alcohol' (live), 'Sad Song,' 'Fade Away' (WarChild Version)

'GO LET IT OUT' (BIG BROTHER)
Released: 7 February 2000
Highest UK chart position: 1
Tracklist: 'Go Let It Out,' 'Let's All Make Believe,' '(As Long as They've Got) Cigarettes In Hell'

'WHERE DID IT ALL GO WRONG?' (EPIC)
Released: 29 February 2000
Highest UK chart position: (N/A)

'WHO FEELS LOVE?' (BIG BROTHER)
Released: 17 April 2000
Highest UK chart position: 4
Tracklist: 'Who Feels Love?,' 'One Way Road,' 'Helter Skelter'

'SUNDAY MORNING CALL' (BIG BROTHER)
Released: 3 July 2000
Highest UK chart position: 4
Tracklist: 'Sunday Morning Call,' 'Carry Us All,' 'Full On'

'THE HINDU TIMES' (BIG BROTHER)
Released: 15 April 2002
Highest UK chart position: 1
Tracklist: 'The Hindu Times,' 'Just Getting Older,' 'Idler's Dream'

'STOP CRYING YOUR HEART OUT' (BIG BROTHER)
Released: 17 June 2002
Highest UK chart position: 2
Tracklist: 'Stop Crying Your Heart Out,' 'Thank You for The Good Times,' 'Shout It Out Loud'

'LITTLE BY LITTLE'/'SHE IS LOVE' (BIG BROTHER)
Released: 23 September 2002
Highest UK chart position: 2
Tracklist: 'Little by Little', 'She Is Love', 'My Generation'

'SONGBIRD' (BIG BROTHER)
Released: 3 February 2003
Highest UK chart position: 3
Tracklist: 'Songbird', '(You've Got) The Heart of A Star', 'Columbia' (live)

'LYLA' (BIG BROTHER)
Released: 16 May 2005
Highest UK chart position: 1
Tracklist: 'Lyla', 'Eyeball Tickler', 'Won't Let You Down'

'THE IMPORTANCE OF BEING IDLE' (BIG BROTHER)
Released: 22 August 2005
Highest UK chart position: 1
Tracklist: 'The Importance of Being Idle', 'Pass Me Down the Wine', 'The Quiet Ones'

'LET THERE BE LOVE' (BIG BROTHER)
Released: 28 November 2005
Highest UK chart position: 2
Tracklist: 'Let There Be Love', 'Sittin' Here in Silence (On My Own)', 'Rock 'n' Roll Star' (live)

'LORD DON'T SLOW ME DOWN' (BIG BROTHER)
Released: 21 October 2007
Highest UK chart position: 10
Tracklist: 'Lord Don't Slow Me Down', 'The Meaning of Soul' (live), 'Don't Look Back in Anger' (live)

'THE SHOCK OF THE LIGHTNING' (BIG BROTHER)
Released: 22 September 2008 (download), 29 September 2008 (physical)
Highest UK chart position: 4
Tracklist: 'The Shock of The Lightning', 'Falling Down' (Chemical Brothers Remix)

'I'M OUTTA TIME' (BIG BROTHER)
Released: 1 December 2008
Highest UK chart position: 12
Tracklist: 'I'm Outta Time', 'I'm Outta Time' (Twiggy Ramirez remix), 'The Shock of The Lightning' (Jagz Kooner remix), 'I'm Outta Time' (demo) (download only), 'To Be Where There's Life' (Neon Neon remix) (7" only)

'FALLING DOWN' (BIG BROTHER)
Released: 9 March 2009
Highest UK chart position: 10
Tracklist: 'Falling Down' 'Those Swollen Hand Blues', 'Falling Down' (The Gibb Mix), 'Falling Down' (The Prodigy Version), 'Falling Down' (Amorphous Androgynous A Monstrous Psychedelic Bubble remix), 'Falling Down' (demo, download only)

Miscellaneous:

THE HELP ALBUM
Released: 9 September 1995
'Fade Away' (Oasis and Friends)

NME IN ASSOCIATION WITH WAR CHILD PRESENTS 1 LOVE
Released: 14 October 2002
'Merry Xmas Everybody '

GOAL! SOUNDTRACK
Released: 30 September 2005
'Who Put the Weight of the World on My Shoulders?', 'Morning Glory (Dave Sardy Mix), 'Cast No Shadow' (UNKLE Beachhead Mix)

CAN Y'SEE IT NOW? (I CAN SEE IT NOW!) (WHITE LABEL PROMO)
Released 2005. Later appears on compilation *Various – Brand Neu* (2009)

'(GET OFF) YOUR HIGH HORSE LADY' (THE MAY 29TH REMIX)
Released: 9 June 2009 (download only)

FILMOGRAPHY:

***LIVE BY THE SEA* (EPIC)**
Released: 28 August 1995
Highest UK video chart position: 1

***...THERE AND THEN* (EPIC)**
Released: 14 October 1996
Highest UK video chart position: 1

***FAMILIAR TO MILLIONS* (BIG BROTHER)**
Released: 13 November 2000
Highest UK video chart position: 2

***DEFINITELY MAYBE* (BIG BROTHER)**
Released: 6 September 2004
Highest UK video chart position: 1

***LORD DON'T SLOW ME DOWN* (BIG BROTHER)**
Released: 29 October 2007
Highest UK video chart position: 1

***TIME FLIES... 1994-2009* (BIG BROTHER)**
Released: 14 June 2010
Highest UK video chart position: N/A

***OASIS: SUPERSONIC* (ENTERTAINMENTONE)**
Released: 31 October 2016
Highest UK video chart position: 1

DVD Documentaries
Noise & Confusion (2002) (Three part documentary series on *Heathen Chemistry* DVD singles)
Can You See It Now? (2005) ('Lyla' DVD single)
Don't Believe the Truth Documentary (2005) (featured on special editions of album)
Lock the Box EPK (2006) (featured on special editions of *Stop the Clocks)*
Gold & Silver & Sunshine EPK (2008) (featured on special editions of *Dig Out Your Soul*)

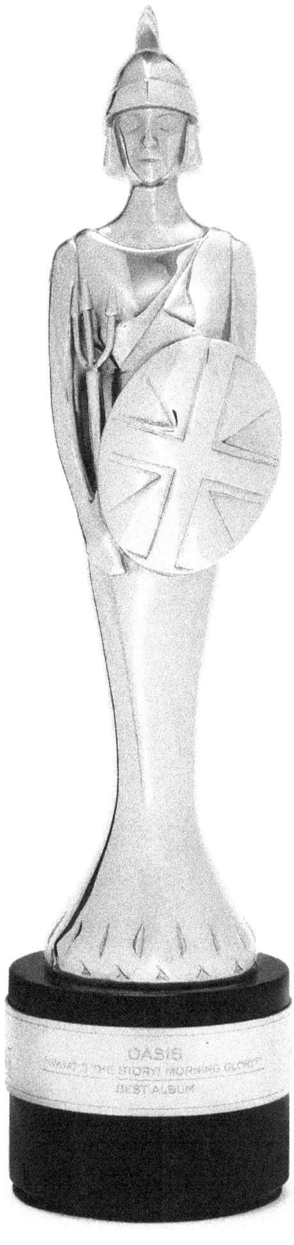
OASIS
BEST ALBUM

AWARDS:

1994

Q Awards: Best New Act

1995

Brit Awards: British Breakthrough Act
Ivor Novello Awards: Songwriters of the Year
MTV Europe Music Awards: Best Song for 'Wonderwall'
NME Awards: Single of the year for 'Live Forever'
NME Awards: Album of the year for *Definitely Maybe*
NME Awards: Best New Band
Q Awards: Best Live Act

1996

Brit Awards: British Group
Brit Awards: British Album of The Year for *(What's the Story) Morning Glory?*
Brit Awards: British Video of the Year for 'Wonderwall'
Ivor Novello Awards: Songwriters of the Year
MTV Europe Music Awards: Best Group
NME Awards: Best Single for 'Wonderwall'
NME Awards: Best Album for *(What's the Story) Morning Glory?*
NME Awards: Best Live Band
NME Awards: Best Band
Q Awards: Best Act in the World Today

1997

MTV Europe Music Awards: Best Rock Group
NME Awards: Best Music Event for Knebworth
NME Awards: Band of the year
Q Awards: Best Act in the World Today

2000

Q Awards: Best Live Act

2002

MTV Video Music Awards Japan: Best Live Act

Top of the Pops Awards: Best Rock Act

2003

NME Awards: Best UK Band
NME Awards: Artist of the year

2005

NME Awards: Best Music DVD for *Definitely Maybe*
Q Awards: Best Album for *Don't Believe the Truth*
Q Awards: People's Choice Award

2006

NME Awards: Best Video for 'The Importance of Being Idle'
Q Awards: Best Act in the World Today
Q Awards: Noel Gallagher Classic Songwriter Award

2007

Brit Awards: Outstanding Contribution to Music
Vodafone Live Music Awards: Best Live Music DVD

2009

NME Awards: Best British Band
UK Music Video Awards: Best Editing in a Video for 'Falling Down'
UK Music Video Awards: The Innovation Award for *Dig Out Your Soul*

2010

Brit Awards: British Album of 30 Years for *(What's the Story) Morning Glory?*

2017

NME Awards: Best Music Film for *Oasis: Supersonic*
NME Awards: Best Reissue for *Be Here Now*

GIGOGRAPHY

UK dates unless shown

Pre-*Definitely Maybe* Tours

1991

Boardwalk - Manchester - 18th August - supporting Sweet Jesus

1992

Polytechnic - Dartford - 19th April
Hippodrome - Oldham - 20th April - supporting Revenge
Club 57 - Oldham - 5th May - supporting The Ya Ya's
Boardwalk - Manchester - 14th July
Boardwalk - Manchester - 19th August
The Venue - Manchester - 13th September
Boardwalk - Manchester - 22nd November - supporting the Cherries

1993

Boardwalk - Manchester - 5th January - supporting The Essence
La Bateau - Liverpool - 1st March
Krazyhouse - Liverpool - 1st April
Boardwalk - Manchester - 1st May
King Tut's - Glasgow - 31st May - supporting 18 Wheeler
Manchester University - Manchester - 1st June
La Bateau - Liverpool - 1st July
Boardwalk - Manchester - 3rd July
Duchess - Leeds - 11th September
Canal Bar - Manchester - 14th September

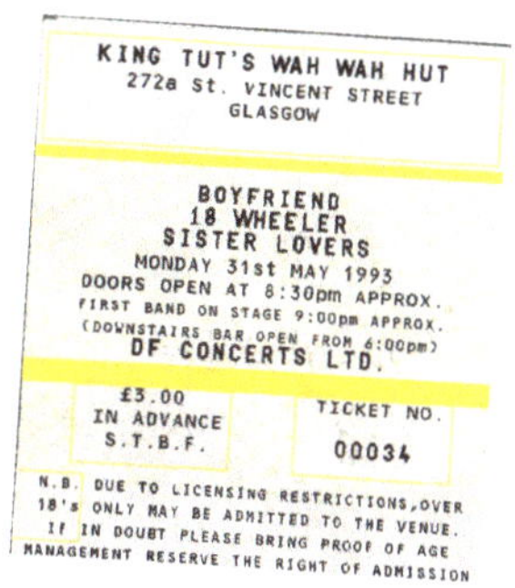

Manchester University - Manchester - 7th October - supporting Liz Phair
Manchester University – Manchester - 14th October
- supporting Milltown Brothers
Keele University - Keele - 27th October - supporting BMX Bandits
Sheffield University - Sheffield - 28th October - supporting BMX Bandits
Wherehouse - Derby - 1st November - supporting BMX Bandits
Wulfrun Hall - Wolverhampton - 3rd November - supporting BMX Bandits
Powerhaus - London - 4th November
Sheffield University - Sheffield - 28th November - supporting CNN

Institute - Birmingham - 1st December - supporting Saint Etienne
Plaza - Glasgow - 2nd December - supporting Saint Etienne
Warwick University - Warwick - 4th December
Wulfrun Hall - Wolverhampton - 8th December - supporting The Verve
Manchester University - Manchester - 9th December - supporting The Verve
Cathouse - Glasgow - 10th December - supporting The Verve
The Mill - Preston - 11th December - supporting The Verve
Riverside - Newcastle - 13th December - supporting The Verve
King's Hall - Bradford - 14th December - supporting The Verve
Krazyhouse - Liverpool - 16th December - supporting The Real People

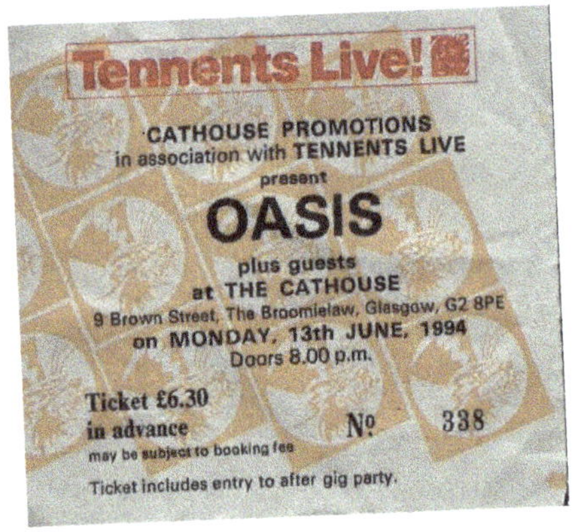

Definitely Maybe Tour (1994–95) (UK unless marked)
The Water Rats - London - 27th January
Gleneagles - Scotland - 6th February
Angel - Bedford - 23rd March
100 Club - London - 24th March
Forum - Tunbridge Wells - 26th March
Polytechnic - Oxford - 27th March
Jug of Ale - Birmingham - 28th March
The Joiners - Southampton - 29th March
Fleece & Firkin - Bristol - 30th March
Moles - Bath - 31st March
Lucifer's Mill - Dundee - 5th April
La Belle Angel - Edinburgh - 6th April
Tramway -Glasgow - 7th April
Arena - Middlesbrough - 8th April
Wheatsheaf - Stoke - 11th April
Duchess - Leeds - 12th April
Lomax - Liverpool - 13th April
Adelphi - Hull - 29th April
University - Coventry - 30th April
Wedgewood Rooms - Portsmouth - 2nd May
TJ's - Newport - 3rd May

Wherehouse - Derby - 4th May
Charlotte - Leicester - 6th May
Old Trout - Windsor - 7th May
Roadmenders - Northampton - 8th May
Army And Navy - Chelmsford - 10th May
Boat Race - Cambridge - 11th May
New Cross - London - 13th May
Leadmill - Sheffield - 14th May
Edwards 8 - Birmingham - 1st June
University - Cardiff - 2nd June
Island - Ilford - 3rd June
Royal Albert Hall - London - 4th June

Arts Centre - Norwich - 6th June
Marquee - London - 8th June
Hop and Grape - Manchester - 9th June
Avenham Park Festival - Preston - 11th June
Cathouse - Glasgow - 12th June
Cathouse - Glasgow - 13th June
Erotika - Paris (France) - 16th June
(East Wing) Centre - Brighton - 18th June
Glastonbury Festival - Somerset - 26th June
Wetlands - New York, NY (USA) - 21st July
T in the Park Festival - Hamilton - 31st July
Riverside - Newcastle - 9th August
Irish Centre - Leeds - 10th August
Wulfrun Hall - Wolverhampton - 11th August
Hultsfreds Festival - Hultsfred (Sweden) - 13th August
Rock City - Nottingham - 15th August
Forum - London - 16th August
Astoria - London - 18th August
Lowlands Festival – Biddinghuizen (Netherlands) - 28th August
Tivoli - Buckley - 31st August
Gino - Stockholm (Sweden) - 2nd September
Limelight - Belfast - 4th September
Hacienda - Manchester - 5th September
Logo - Hamburg (Germany) - 8th September
Arena - Amsterdam (Netherlands) - 9th September
Quattro - Tokyo (Japan) - 13th September
Quattro - Tokyo (Japan) - 14th September
Quattro - Tokyo (Japan) - 15th September

Quattro - Tokyo (Japan) - 16th September
Quattro - Osaka (Japan) - 18th September
Quattro - Nagoya (Japan) - 19th September
Moe's - Seattle WA (USA) - 23rd September
Satyricon – Portland, OR (USA) - 24th September
The Whiskey - Los Angeles (USA) - 29th September
Bottom Of The Hill - San Francisco CA (USA) - 26th September
Melarky's - Sacramento CA (USA) - 27th September
The Whiskey - Los Angeles CA (USA) - 29th September
Uptown Bar - Minneapolis MN (USA) - 14th October
Metro - Chicago IL (USA) - 15th October
St Andrews Hall - Detroit MI (USA) 16th October
Grog Shop - Cleveland OH (USA) - 18th October
Lee's Place - Toronto (Canada) - 19th October
Local 186 - Allston MA (USA) - 21st October
Met Cafe - Providence RI (USA) - 22nd October
JC Dobbs - Philadelphia (USA) - 23rd October
9:30 Club - Washington DC (USA) - 26th October
Maxwell's - Hoboken NJ (USA) - 28th October
Wetlands - New York (USA) - 29th October
La Cigale - Paris (France) - 4th November
Transbordeur - Lyon (France) - 5th November
Theatre Du Moulin - Marseille (France) - 6th November
Palladium - Stockholm (Sweden) - 16th November
Cue Club - Gothenburg (Sweden) - 17th November
Dairy - Lund (Sweden) - 18th November
Loft - Berlin (Germany) - 20th November
Markthalle - Hamburg (Germany) - 21st November
Batchkapp - Frankfurt (Germany) - 23rd November
Luxor - Cologne (Germany) - 24th November
Paradiso - Amsterdam (Netherlands) - 25th November
Zeche Carl - Essen (Germany) - 27th November
Botanieve - Brussels (Belgium) - 28th November
Guildhall - Southampton - 30th November
Octagon - Sheffield - 1st December
Corn Exchange - Cambridge 4th December
Barrowlands - Glasgow - 7th December
Civic Hall - Wolverhampton - 11th December
Astoria - Cardiff - 12th December
Hammersmith Palais - London - 13th December

Royal Court - Liverpool - 17th December
Academy - Manchester - 18th December
Barrowlands - Glasgow - 27th December
(East Wing) Centre - Brighton - 29th December
Town Hall - Middlesbrough - 30th December
DV8 - Seattle WA (USA) - 28th January
Commodore Ballroom - Vancouver (Canada) - 29th January
Roseland Theatre - Portland OR (USA) - 30th January
Fillmore - San Francisco (USA) - 1st February
The Palace - Hollywood CA (USA) - 3rd February
SOMA Live - San Diego CA (USA) - 4th February
Nile Theatre - Mesa AZ - 5th February
Bar & Grill - Salt Lake City UT (USA) - 7th February
Bluebeard Theatre - Denver CP (USA) - 9th February
Deep Ellum Live - Dallas TX (USA) - 11th February
Liberty Lunch - Austin TX (USA) - 12th February
Urban Art Bar - Houston TX (USA) - 13th February
New Daisy Theatre - Memphis TN (USA) - 15th February
Cat's Cradle - Carrboro NC (USA) - 17th February
Masquerade - Atlanta GA (USA) - 18th February
Stone Pony - Ashbury Park NJ (USA) - 3rd March
Wust Music Hall - Washington DC (USA) - 4th March
The Abyss - Virginia Beach VA (USA) - 5th March
Theatre Of Living Arts - Philadelphia PA (USA) - 7th March
The Academy - New York NY (USA) - 8th March
Lopo's - Providence RI (USA) - 10th March
Avalon - Boston MA (USA) - 11th March
Club Soda - Montreal (Canada) - 12th March
Phoenix Theatre - Toronto (Canada) - 14th March
The Odeon - Cleveland OH (USA) - 15th March
St Andrews - Detroit MI (USA) - 16th March
Tyndale Armory - Indianapolis (USA) - 18th March
Vic Theatre - Chicago IL (USA) - 19th March
Orbit Room - Grand Rapids MI (USA) - 20th March
First Ave - Minneapolis MN (USA) - 24th March
Rave At Eagles Milwaukee WI (USA) - 25th March
Cliffs Pavilion - Southend - 17th April
Bataclan - Paris (France) - 20th April
Arena - Sheffield - 22nd April

(What's the Story) Morning Glory? Tour (1995–96)
Pavilion - Bath - 22nd June
Glastonbury Festival - Somerset - 23rd June
Roskilde Festival (Denmark) - 30th June
Piazza Stuparich - Milan (Italy) 3rd July
Fauvier festival - Lyon (France) - 5th July
Out In The Green Festival - Frauenfeld (Switzerland) - 7th July
Eurokeenes Festival - Belfort (France) - 8th July
Badesee - Duren (Germany) - 9th July
Beach Park - Irvine - 14th July
Beach Park - Irvine - 15th July
Plaza De Toros De Las Ventus - Madrid (Spain) - 18th July
Zeebruggers Beach Festival (Belgium) - 21st July
Slane Castle - Dublin (Ireland) - 22nd July
Kawasaki Club - Citta (Japan) - 21st August
Kawasaki Club - Citta (Japan) - 22nd August
Liquid Room - Tokyo (Japan) - 23rd August
Garden Hall - Tokyo (Japan) - 25th August
Garden Hall - Tokyo (Japan) - 26th August
Imperial Hall - Osaka (Japan) - 28th August
Imperial Hall - Osaka (Japan) - 29th August
Empress Ballroom - Blackpool - 2nd October
Trentham Gardens - Stoke - 3rd October
International Centre - Bournemouth - 5th October
Leisure Centre - Gloucester - 6th October
Hammerjack's - Baltimore MD (USA) - 10th October
Roseland Ballroom - New York NY (USA) - 11th October
Tuxedo Junctions - Danbury CT (USA) - 13th October
The Orpheum - Boston MA (USA) - 14th October
Metropol - Pittsburgh PA (USA) - 16th October
La Luna - Brussels (Belgium) - 31st October
Earls Court - London - 4th November
Earls Court - London - 5th November
Zenith - Paris (France) - 7th November
Grosse Freiheit - Mamburg (Germany) - 10th November
Live Music Hall - Koln (Germany) - 12th November
Trocardiere - Nantes (France) - 14th November
Aeronef - Lille (France) - 15th November
Granby Hall - Leicester - 17th November

Annexet - Stockholm (Sweden) - 20th November
KB Hallen - Copenhagen (Denmark) - 24th November
NYMEX Arena - Manchester - 26th November
KNDD Holiday Festival - Seattle WA (USA) - 2nd December
WHFS Holiday Festival - Washington DC (USA) - 7th December
Q101 Holiday Festival - Chicago IL (USA) - 8th December
KEGE Holiday Festival - Minneapolis (USA) - 9th December
Liberty Warehouse - Toronto (Canada) - 13th December
Live 105 Holiday Festival - San Francisco CA (USA) - 15th December
KOME Holiday Festival - San Jose CA (USA) - 16th December
KROQ Holiday Festival - Los Angeles CA - 18th December
Viper Room - Hollywood CA (USA) - 19th December
Music Centre - Utrecht (Netherlands) - 10th January
Terminal 1, Munich (Germany) - 12th January
Huxley's - Berlin (Germany) - 14th January
Bielefeld (Germany) - 15th January
Whitley Bay Ice Rink - Tyne & Wear - 19th January
Royal Highland Centre, Ingliston - Edinburgh - 21st January
Royal Highland Centre, Ingliston - Edinburgh - 22nd January
Memorial Hall - Kansas City MO (USA) - 23rd February
American Theater - St Louis (MO) - 24th February
Orpheum Theater - Minneapolis MN (USA) - 26th February
Aragon Ballroom - Chicago IL (USA) - 27th February
Eagle's Auditorium - Milwaukee WI (USA) - 1st March
Theater - Detroit MI (USA) - 3rd March
Egyptian Room - Indianapolis IN (USA) - 5th March
GMU Patriot Center - Fairfax VA (USA) - 7th March
Tower Theater - Philadelphia PA (USA) - 9th March
Strand Theater - Providence RI (USA) - 10th March
Paramount Theater - New York NY (USA) - 13th March
International Arena - Cardiff - 18th March
International Arena - Cardiff - 19th March
The Point Depot - Dublin (Ireland) - 22nd March
The Point Depot - Dublin (Ireland) - 23rd March
Stradhalle - Offenbach (Germany) - 26th March
Terminal 1 - Offenbach (Germany) - 27th March
Piazza Stuparich - Milan (Italy) - 29th March
Summum - Grenoble (France) - 31st March
Zeleste - Barcelona (Spain) - 2nd April

Pacific Coliseum - Vancouver BC (USA) - 10th April
Mercer Arena - Seattle WA (USA) - 11th April
Bill Graham Civic Auditorium - San Francisco CA (USA) - 13th April
Mammoth - Denver CO (USA) - 18th April
Bronco Bowl Auditorium - Dallas TX (USA) -20th April
Austin Music Hall - Austin TX (USA) - 21st April
Maine Road - Manchester - 27th April
Maine Road - Manchester - 28th April
Balloch Castle Country Park - Loch Lomond - 3rd August
Balloch Castle Country Park - Loch Lomond - 4th August
Sjohistoriska Museet - Stockholm (Sweden) - 7th August
Knebworth Park - Stevenage - 10th August
Knebworth Park - Stevenage - 11th August
Paric Ui Chaoimh - Cork (Ireland) - 14th August
Paric Ui Chaoimh - Cork (Ireland) - 15th August
Royal Festival Hall - London - 23rd August
Rosemont Horizon - Rosemont IL (USA) - 27th August
Palace - Auburn Hills MI (USA) - 30th August
Molson Park - Toronto (Canada) - 31st August
Corestates Center - Philadelphia PA (USA) - 2nd September
The Centrum - Worcester MA (USA) - 6th September
Jones Beach Theatre - Long Island NY (USA) - 7th September
Jones Beach Theatre - Long Island NY (USA) - 8th September
Nissan Pavilion - Bristow VA (USA) - 10th September

Be Here Now Tour (1997–98)
Weenie Roast - Irvine CA (USA) - 14th June
Coliseum - Oakland CA (USA) - 18th June - Supporting U2
Coliseum - Oakland CA (USA) - 19th June - Supporting U2
Spektrum - Oslo (Norway) - 8th September
Globe - Stockholm (Sweden) - 9th September
Forum - Copenhagen (Denmark) - 10th September
Westpoint Arena - Exeter - 13th Septemeber
Westpoint Arena - Exeter - 14th September
Arena - Newcastle - 16th September

Arena - Newcastle - 17th September
Exhibition & Conference Centre - Aberdeen - 19th September
Exhibition & Conference Centre - Aberdeen - 20th September
Arena - Sheffield - 22nd September
Arena - Sheffield - 23rd September
Earls Court - London - 25th September
Earls Court - London 26th September
Earls Court - London - 27th September
National Indoor Arena - Birmingham - 29th September
National Indoor Arena - Birmingham - 30th September
Hammerstein Ballroom - New York NY (USA) - 7th October
Hammerstein Ballroom - New York NY (USA) - 8th October
Zenith - Lille (France) - 3rd November
Pabellon Principe Felipe - Zaragoza (Spain) - 8th Novemeber
Palacio De La Comunidad - Madrid (Spain) - 10th November
Palau Dels Esports - Barcelona (Spain) - 11th November
Arena - Geneva (Switzerland) - 13th November
Palasport - Bologna (Italy) - 15th November
Forum - Milan (Italy) - 16th November
Forum - Milan (Italy) - 17th November
Olympichalle - Munich (Germany) - 19th November
Sportovni Hala - Prague (Czech Republic) - 21st November
Festhalle - Frankfurt (Germany) - 22nd November
Messehalle - Hannover (Germany) - 24th November
Festhalle - Frankfurt (Germany) - 25th November
Earls Court - London - 26th November
Brabanthallen - Den Bosch (Netherlands) - 27th November
Arena - Oberhausen (Germany) - 28th November
The Point - Dublin (Ireland) - 3rd December
The Point - Dublin (Ireland) - 4th December
The Point - Dublin (Ireland) - 5th December
SE & CC - Glasgow - 7th December
SE & CC - Glasgow - 8th December
Indoor Arena - Cardiff - 10th December
Indoor Arena - Cardiff - 11th December
GMEX - Manchester - 13th December
GMEX - Manchester - 14th December
The Water Rats - London - 16th December

Wembley Arena - London - 17th December
Wembley Arena - London - 18th December
Sony E Center - Philadelphia PA (USA) - 8th January
Patriot Center - Washington DC (USA) - 9th January
Palumbo Center - Pittsburgh PA (USA) - 10th January
Continental Airlines Arena - Rutherford NJ (USA) - 12th January
Maple Leaf Gardens - Toronto (Canada) - 15th January
Rosemont Horizon - Rosemont IL (USA) - 17th January
Northrop Auditorium - Minneapolis (USA)
- 18th January
GM Place - Vancouver (Canada) - 23rd January
Seattle Center Arena - Seattle WA (USA) - 24th January
Bill Graham Civic - San Francisco CA (USA)
- 26th January
Universal Amphitheater - Los Angeles CA (USA)
- 27th January
Universal Amphitheater - Los Angeles CA (USA)
- 28th January
Bronco Bowl Auditorium - Dallas TX (USA)
- 31st January

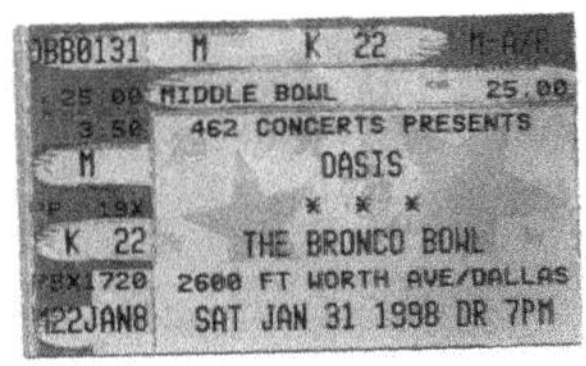

Theatre At Bayou Place - Houston TX (USA) - 1st February
WPB Auditorium - Palm Beach FL (USA) - 5th February
UCF Arena - Orlando FL (USA) - 6th February
Fox Theatre - Atlanta GA (USA) 8th February
Budokan - Nippon (Japan) - 18th February
Budokan - Nippon (Japan) - 19th February
Budokan - Nippon (Japan) - 20th February
HKCEC Hall 3 - Hong Kong (China) - 22nd February
Entertainment Center - Perth (Australia) - 26th February
Entertainment Center - Adelaide (Australia) - 28th February
Entertainment Center - Melbourne (Australia) - 1st March
Entertainment Center - Sydney (Australia) - 3rd March
Entertainment Center - Brisbane (Australia) - 6th March
Carter Holt Pavilion - Auckland (New Zealand) - 9th March
Queens Warf Event Center - Wellington (New Zealand) - 10th March
San Carlos Apoquindo Stadium - Santiago (Chile) - 14th March
Luna Park - Buenos Aires (Argentina) - 17th March
Luna Park - Buenos Aires (Argentina) - 18th March
Meropolitan - Rio De Janiero (Brazil) - 20th March
Polo De Arte E Cultura De Anhembi - Sao Paulo (Brazil) 21st March

Sports Palace - Mexico City (Mexico) - 24th March
Sports Palace - Mexico City (Mexico) - 25th March

Standing on the Shoulder of Giants Tour (1999-2001)
First Union Centre - Philadelphia (USA) - 3rd December
Allstate Arena - Rosemont IL (USA) 4th December
Cobo Arena Detroit MI - (USA) - 5th December
The Pond - Anaheim CA (USA) 11th December
Yokohama Arena - Tokyo (Japan) - 29th February
Rainbow Hall - Nagoya (Japan) - 1st March
Marine Mese - Fukuoka (Japan) - 3rd March
Yokohama Arena - Tokyo (Japan) - 5th March
Yokohama Arena - Tokyo (Japan) - 6th March
Yokohama Arena - Tokyo (Japan) -7th March
Castle Hall - Osaka (Japan) - 9th March
World Hall - Osaka (Japan) - 11th March
World Hall - Osaka (Japan) - 12th March
Green Hall - Hiroshima (Japan) - 14th March
Army Hall - Sendai (Japan) - 16th March
Bataclan - Paris (France) - 21st March
Ancienne Belgique - Brussels (Belgium) - 23rd March
E-Werk - Koln (Germany) - 25th March
Paramount Theater – Seattle WA (USA) - 5th April
Schnitzer Auditorium - Portland OR (USA) - 6th April
Berkeley Community Theater - San Francisco CA (USA) - 8th April
Universal Amphitheater - Los Angeles CA (USA) - 9th April
Hard Rock Hotel - Las Vegas NV (USA) - 11th April
Auditorium Theater - Denver CO (USA) - 13th April
State Theater - Minneapolis MN (USA) - 15th April
Riverside Theater - Milwaukee WI (USA) - 16th April
Chicago Theater - Chicago IL (USA) -18th April
State Theater - Detroit MI (USA) - 19th April
EJ Thomas Hall - Akron OH (USA) - 21st April
Murat Center - Indianapolis IN (USA) - 22nd April
Palace Theater - Columbus OH (USA) - 24th April
Tower Theater - Philadelphia PA (USA) - 26th April
Orpheum Theatre - MA (USA) - 27th April
Maple Leaf Gardens - Toronto (Canada) - 29th April
Radio City Music Hall - New York NY (USA) - 1st May
Patriot Center – Fairfax VA (USA) - 3rd May

Music Midtown - Atlanta GA (USA) - 5th May
Sports Palace - Mexico City (Mexico) - 8th May
Praca Sony - Lisbon (Portugal) - 17th May
Plasa De Toros La Cubierta De Leganes - Leganes (Spain) 19th May
Filaforum - Milan (Italy) - 30th May
Zurcher Saalsporthalle - Zurich (Switzerland) - 31st May
Wiener Stadthalle - Vienna (Austria) - 2nd June
Haus Auensee - Leipzig (Germany) - 3rd June
C.O.S "Torwar" - Warsaw (Poland) - 5th June
Arena - Berlin (Germany) - 7th June
Rock AM Ring - Nurburg (Germany) - 9th June
Pinkpop Festival - Landgraaf (Netherlands) - 10th June
Rock Im Park - Nurnburg (Germany) - 11th June
Hultsfred 2000 - Hultsfred (Sweden) - 15th June
Heineken Jammin Festival - Imola (Italy) - 18th June
Le Dome - Marseilles (France) - 19th June
Fete De La Musique - Paris (France) - 21st June
Sporthalle - Hamburg (Germany) 22nd June
Werchter Festival - Werchter (Belgium) - 30th June
Roskilde Festival (Denmark) - 1st July
Ruisrock - Turku (Finland) - 2nd July
Palacio De La Comunidad - Barcelona (Spain) - 4th July
Quart 2000 Kristiansand (Norway) - 6th July
Lansdowne Road – Dublin (Ireland) - 8th July
Eurokeenes Festival - Belfort (France) - 9th July
Rockwave Festival - Athens (Greece) - 12th July
Reebok Stadium - Bolton - 15th July
Reebok Stadium - Bolton - 16th July
Wembley Stadium - London - 21st July
Wembley Stadium - London - 22nd July
Paleo Festival - Nyon (Switzerland) - 26th July
Murrayfield Stadium - Edinburgh - 29th July
Benicassim Festival - Benicassim (Spain) - 4th August
Sudoeste Festival - Odemira (Portugal) - 6th August
Sziget Festival - Budapest (Hungary) - 8th August
Skanderborg - Skanerborg (Denmark) - 12th August
Gijon Festival - Gijon (Spain) - 23rd August
Reading Festival - Reading - 25th August
Glasgow Green Festival - Glasgow - 26th August

Leeds Festival - Leeds - 28th August
Rock in Rio - Rio (Brazil) - 14th January
Hot Festival - Buenos Aires (Argentina) - 18th January
Caracas Pop Festival - Caracas (Venezuela) - 21st January

Tour of Brotherly Love (2001)
Hard Rock Hotel - Las Vegas NV (USA) - 11th May
Barbara Bowl - Santa Barbara CA (USA) - 12th May
The Greek Theater - Los Angeles CA (USA) - 14th May
The Greek Theater - Los Angeles CA (USA) - 15th May
Fiddler's Green - Denver CO (USA) - 17th May
Xcal Energy Center -St Paul MN (USA) - 19th May
New World Music Theater - Chicago IL (USA) - 20th May
Molson Amphitheater - Toronto (Canada) - 22nd May
Riverbend Music Theater - Cincinnati OH (USA) - 24th May
Blossom Music Center - Cleveland OH (USA) - 25th May
SNET Oakdale Theater - Wallingford CT (USA) - 27th May
A.J. Palumbo Center - Pittsburgh PA (USA) - 29th May
Tweeter Center - Philadelphia PA (USA) - 30th May
Verizon Wireless Music - Indianapolis IN (USA) - 1st June

Pine Knob Music Theater - Detroit MI (USA) - 2nd June
Darien Center P.A.C. - Darien Center NY (USA) - 3rd June
Merriweather Post Pavilion - Baltimore MD (USA) - 5th June
Radio City Music Hall - New York NY (USA) -7th June
Radio City Music Hall - New York NY (USA) - 8th June
Radio City Music Hall - New York NY (USA) - 9th June
Tweeter Center - Boston MA (USA) - 11th June
Bercy - Paris (France) - 24th June
Rock Festival - Fuji (Japan) - 27th July
Bangkok - Bangkok (Thailand) - 31st July

Ten Years of Noise & Confusion Tour (2001)
Shepherd's Bush Empire - London - 7th October
Shepherd's Bush Empire - London - 8th October
Apollo Theatre - Manchester - 10th October
Apollo Theatre - Manchester - 11th October
Barrowlands - Glasgow - 13th October
Barrowlands - Glasgow - 14th October

Heathen Chemistry Tour (2002–03)
Watford Coliseum - Watford - 5th February
Royal Albert Hall - London - 6th February
Watford Coliseum - Watford - 8th February
Hard Rock Hotel - Las Vegas NV (USA) - 26th April
Coachella Valley Music & Arts Festival - Indio CA (USA) - 28th April
Piazza San Giovanni - Rome (Italy) - 1st May
Transbordeur - Lyon (France) - 17th June
Razzmatazz - Barcelona (Spain) - 19th June
Vox Club - Modena (Italy) - 21st June
Columbiahalle - Berlin (Germany) - 24th June
Circus - Stockholm (Sweden) - 26th June
Odyssey Arena - Belfast - 29th June
Odyssey Arena - Belfast - 30th June
Arena - Hull - 2nd July
Arena - Hull - 3rd July
Finsbury Park - London - 5th July
Finsbury Park - London - 6th July
Finsbury Park - London - 7th July
Telewest Arena - Newcastle - 10th July
Telewest Arena - Newcastle - 11th July

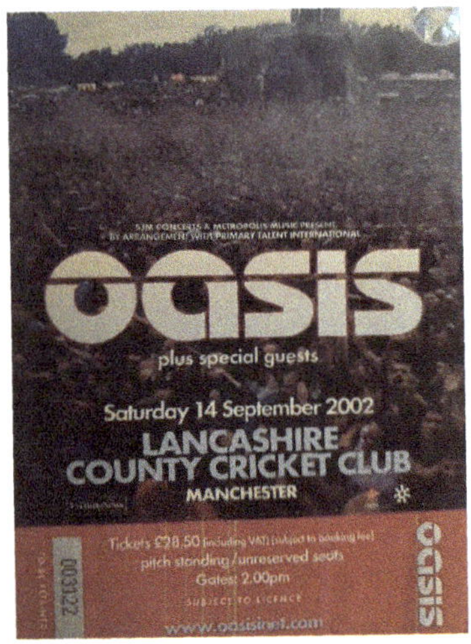

T In The Park Festival - Kinross - 13th July
Witnness Festival – Fairyhouse Racecourse, Ratoath (Ireland) - 14th July
Stadio Comunal - Vicenza (Italy) - 16th July
Piazza Napoleone - Lucca (Italy) - 17th July
Gurten Festival - Bern (Switzerland) - 19th July
Calvia Festival Isladencanta - Mallorca (Spain) - 21st July
Plaza De Toros La Glorieta - Salamanca (Spain) - 23rd July
Parque De Castrelos - Vigo (Spain) - 24th July
Foro Italico Centrale Del Tennis Stadium - Rome (Italy) - 26th July
Foro Italico Centrale Del Tennis Stadium - Rome (Italy) - 27th July
Pompano Beach Amphitheater - Ft. Lauderdale FL (USA) - 2nd August

Hard Rock Live - Orlando FL (USA) - 4th August
Tabernacle - Atlanta GA (USA) - 5th August
Murat Center - Indianapolis IN (USA) - 7th August
Tower Theater - Philadelphia PA (USA) - 9th August
Fleet Pavilion - Boston (USA) - 10th August
Roseland Ballroom - New York NY (USA) - 11th August
Beacon Theater - New York NY (USA) - 13th August
Beacon Theater - New York NY (USA) - 14th August
Molson Center - Montreal (Canada) - 16th August
Molson Amphitheater - Toronto (Canada) - 17th August
Chicago Theater - Chicago IL (USA) - 20th August
Fox Theater - Detroit MI (USA) - 21st August
Prehen Playing Fields - Derry (Ireland) - 7th September
Exhibition & Conference Centre - Aberdeen - 9th September
Exhibition & Conference Centre - Aberdeen - 10th September
Corn Exchange - Edinburgh - 12th September
Lancashire County Cricket Club – Old Trafford, Manchester - 14th September
Lancashire County Cricket Club - Old Trafford, Manchester - 15th September
Zenith - Paris (France) - 17th September
Yoyogi Taiikukan - Tokyo (Japan) - 25th September
Yoyogi Taiikukan - Tokyo (Japan) - 26th September
Yoyogi Taiikukan - Tokyo (Japan) - 28th September
Yoyogi Taiikukan - Tokyo (Japan) - 29th September
Kokusai Center - Fukuoka (Japan) - 1st October
Castle Hall - Osaka (Japan) - 2nd October
Castle Hall - Osaka (Japan) - 3rd October
Miyagi-Ken Taiikukan - Sendai (Japan) - 5th October
Sun Plaza - Hiroshima (Japan) - 7th October
Rainbow Hall - Nagoya (Japan) - 8th October
Enmore Theatre - Sydney (Australia) - 11th October
RNA Showgrounds - Brisbane (Australia) - 12th October
Royal Theatre - Canberra (Australia) - 14th October
Civic Theatre - Newcastle (Australia) - 15th October
The Forum - Melbourne (Australia) - 17th October
Melbourne Park - Melbourne (Australia) - 19th October
Moore Park - Sydney (Australia) - 20th October
The Forum - Melbourne (Australia) - 23rd October
Araneta Coliseum - Manila (Philippines) - 24th October
Indoor Stadium - Singapore (Singapore) - 26th October
Arena - Nottingham - 10th November

Arena - Nottingham - 11th November
Braehead Arena - Glasgow - 13th November
Braehead Arena - Glasgow - 14th November
Zenith - Lille (France) - 16th November
Le Liberte - Rennes (France) -17th November
Pabellon Wutzburg - Salamanca (Spain) - 19th November
Pabellon De La Casilla - Bilboa (Spain) - 20th November
Forum - Milan (Italy) - 22nd November
PBA Palas - Pesaro (Italy) - 23rd November
Hallenstadion Arena - Zurich (Switzerland) - 25th November
Messe B - Stuttgart (Germany) - 28th November
Jurhunderthalle - Frankfurt (Germany) - 29th November
Zenith - Munich (Germany) - 1st December
Color-Line Arena – Hamburg (Germany) - 2nd December
Philipshalle - Dusseldorf (Germany) - 4th December
Pier 2 - Bremen (Germany) - 5th December
CIA - Cardiff - 8th December
CIA - Cardiff - 9th December
Centre - Brighton - 11th December
Pavilions - Plymouth - 12th December
Arena - Sheffield - 14th December
Royal Court - Liverpool - 16th December
NIA - Birmingham - 18th December
NIA - Birmingham - 19th December
The Point - Dublin (Ireland) - 5th March
The Point - Dublin (Ireland) - 6th March
Color-Line Arena - Hamburg (Germany) - 8th March
Philipshalle - Dusseldorf (Germany) - 9th March
Zenith - Munich (Germany) - 11th March
Arena - Berlin (Germany) 12th March

Summer 2004
Poole Lighthouse - Dorset - 23rd June
Glastonbury Festival - Glastonbury - 25th June

Don't Believe the Truth Tour (2005–06)
Astoria - London - 10th May
Alcatraz - Milan (Italy) - 12th May
Usher Hall - Edinburgh - 15th May
Clapham Grand - London - 22nd May

Olympia - Paris (France) - 23rd May
Coronet - London - 25th May
Carling Apollo Hammersmith - London - 26th May
Aqualung - Madrid (Spain) - 1st June
Ancienne Belgique - Brussels (Belgium) -4th June
Columiahalle - Berlin (Germany) - 6th June
Hurricane Festival (Germany) - 10th June
Southside Festival (Germany) - 11th June
Heineken Jamming Festival Imola (Italy) - 12th June
The Molson Amphitheatre – Toronto - (Canada) - 17th June
Meadow Brook Amphitheatre - Detroit (USA) - 18th June
UIC Pavilion - Chicago IL (USA) - 20th June
Madison Square Garden New York - NY (USA) - 22nd June
Tweeter Center Boston MA (USA) - 24th June
Festival Pier Penns Landing, Philadelphia PA (USA) - 25th June
Hampden Park - Glasgow - 29th June
City Of Manchester Stadium - Manchester - 30th June
City Of Manchester Stadium - Manchester - 2nd July
City Of Manchester Stadium - Manchester - 3rd July
Rose Bowl Stadium - Southampton - 6th July
National Bowl - Milton Keynes - 9th July
National Bowl - Milton Keynes - 10th July
Newcastle Metro Arena - Newcastle - 12th July
Newcastle Metro Arena - Newcastle 13th July
Marlay Park - Dublin (Ireland) - 16th July
Sudoete Festival - Odemira (Portugal) - 5th August
FIB Heineken Festival - Benicassim (Spain) - 7th August
Summer Sonic Eve Show - Nagoya (Japan) - 11th August
Summer Sonic Festival - Osaka (Japan) - 13th August
Summer Sonic Festival - Tokyo (Japan) - 14th August
Frequency Festival - Saltzburg (Austria) - 18th August
V Festival - Hylands Park, Chelmsford - 20th August
V Festival - Weston Park, Staffordshire - 21st August
General Motors Place - Vancouver (Canada) -8th September
Everett Event Center - Seattle WA (USA) - 9th September
Shoreline Amphitheatre - San Francisco CA (USA) - 11th September
Hollywood Bowl - Los Angeles CA (USA) - 12th September
Coors Amphitheatre - San Diego CA (USA) - 14th September
House Of Blues - Las Vegas NV (USA) - 15th September
Glen Helen Pavilion - Los Angeles CA (USA) 17th September

Dodge Theater - Phoenix AZ (USA) - 18th September
Red Rock Park Amphitheatre - Denver CO (USA) - 20th September
Smirnoff Music Center - Dallas TX (USA) - 22nd September
Austin City Limits - Texas TX (USA) - 24th September
HIFI Buys Amphitheatre - Atlanta GA (USA) - 27th September
Merriweather Post Pavilion - Baltimore MD (USA) - 29th September
Blossom Music Center - Cleveland OH (USA) - 30th September
Staten Island - New York NY (USA) - 2nd October
House Of Blues Club - Atlantic City NJ (USA) - 3rd October
Alsterdorfer Sporthalle - Hamburg (Germany) - 20th October
Valbyhallen - Copenhagen (Denmark) - 21st October
Rouen Zenith - Rouen (France) - 23rd October
Forest National - Brussels (Belgium) - 24th October
The Zenith - Paris (France) - 26th October
Jahrhunderhalle - Frankfurt (Germany) - 27th October
Tresivo Palaverde - Treviso (Italy) - 29th October
Milano Forum - Milan (Italy) - 30th October
Phillipshalle - Dusseldorf (Germany) - 1st November
Heineken Music Hall - Amsterdam (Netherlands) - 2nd November
Pavello De La Vall D'Hebron - Barcelona (Spain) - 4th November
Palacio De Deportes De La Comunidad - Madrid (Spain) - 5th November
Osaka Catle Hall - Osaka (Japan) - 17th November
Yoyogi Taiikukan - Tokyo (Japan) - 18th November
Yoyogi Taiikukan -Tokyo (Japan) - 20th November
Yoyogi Taiikukan - Tokyo (Japan) - 21st November
Entertainment Centre - Brisbane (Australia) - 26th November
Hordern Pavilion - Sydney (Australia) - 28th November
Hordern Pavilion - Sydney (Australia) - 29th November
Festival Hall - Melbourne (Australia) - 1st December
Festival Hall - Melbourne (Australia) - 2nd December
Rock It Festival - Perth (Australia) - 4th December
Millennium Stadium - Cardiff - 10th December
AECC - Aberdeen - 12th December
SECC - Glasgow - 14th December
SECC - Glasgow - 15th December
Odyssey Arena - Belfast - 18th December
Odyssey Arena - Belfast - 19th December
The Point - Dublin (Ireland) - 21st December
The Point - Dublin (Ireland) - 22nd December
Spektrum - Oslo (Norway) - 25th January

Hovet - Stockholm (Sweden) - 26th January
Zenith - Lille (France) - 29th January
Summum - Grenoble (France) 30th January
Gasometer - Vienna (Austria) - 1st February
Eulachhallen AG Winterthur - Winterhur (Switzerland) - 2nd February
Zenith – Toulouse (France) - 4th February
Mandela Forum - Florence (Italy) - 6th February
Palalottomatica - Rome (Italy) - 7th February
Sheffield Hallam FM Arena - Sheffield - 9th February
Sheffield Hallam FM Arena - Sheffield - 10th February
Nottingham Arena - Nottingham - 13th February
Nottingham Arena - Nottingham - 14th February
100 Rock Festival - Bangkok (Thailand) - 18th February
Lakeside - Bangkok (Thailand) - 19th February
Olympic Hall - Seoul (South Korea) - 21st February
Indoor Stadium - Singapore (Singapore) - 23rd February
Asiaworld Arena - Hong Kong (China) - 25th February
Hot Festival - Buenos Aires (Argentina) - 10th March
Velodrome - Santiago (Chile) - 12th March
Credicard Hall - Sao Paulo (Brazil) - 15th March
Air Canada Centre - Toronto (Canada) - 20th March
Riverside Theatre - Milwaukee WI (USA) - 22nd March
Murat Theater – Indianapolis IN (USA) - 23rd March
Taft Theatre - Cincinnati OH (USA) - 25th March
Ryman Auditorium - Nashville TN (USA) - 26th March
Verizon Wireless Theatre - Houston TX (USA) - 28th March
Sports Palace - Mexico City (Mexico) - 31st March

Stop the Clocks Acoustic Tour (2006-07)
KOKO – Camden, London - 2nd November
Danforth Music Hall - Toronto (Canada) - 7th November
Wadsworth Theater - Los Angeles CA (USA) - 9th November
Union Chapel – Islington, London - 26th November
Le Cabaret Sauvage - Paris (France) 28th November
The Forum - Melbourne (Australia) - 10th December
The Chapel - Melbourne (Australia) - 11th December
Tivoli - Brisbane (Australia) - 12th December
Enmore Theatre - Newton (Australia) - 14th November
Perth Concert Hall Perth (Australia) - 16th November
BRITS - London - 14th February

Club B1 - Moscow (Russia) - 23rd March
Royal Albert Hall - London - 26th March
Royal Albert Hall - London - 27th March
MEN Arena - Manchester - 30th March

Dig Out Your Soul Tour (2008–09)
WaMu Theater - Seattle WA (USA) - 26th August
GM Place - Vancouver (Canada) - 27th August
Rexall Place - Edmonton (Canada) - 29th August
Pengrowth Saddledome - Calgary (Canada) - 30th August
MTS Centre - Winnipeg (Canada) - 1st September
Scotiabank Place - Ottawa (Canada) - 4th September
Bell Center - Quebec (Canada) - 5th September
Toronto Island Park - Toronto (Canada) - 7th September
Liverpool Echo Arena - Liverpool - 7th October
Liverpool Echo Arena - Liverpool - 8th October
Sheffield Arena - Sheffield - 10th October
Sheffield Arena - Sheffield - 11th October
Birmingham NIA - Birmingham - 13th October
Birmingham NIA - Birmingham - 14th October
Wembley Arena - London - 16th October
Wembley Arena - London - 17th October
Bournemouth BIC - Bournemouth - 20th October
Bournemouth BIC - Bournemouth - 21st October
Cardiff International Arena - Cardiff - 23rd October
Cardiff International Arena - Cardiff - 24th October
The Roundhouse – Chalk Farm, London
- 26th October
Belfast Odyssey Arena - Belfast - 29th October
Belfast Odyssey Arena - Belfast - 30th October
Aberdeen Exhibition Centre - Aberdeen - 1st November
Aberdeen Exhibition Centre - Aberdeen - 2nd November
Glasgow SECC - Glasgow - 4th November
Glasgow SECC - Glasgow - 5th November
Gloria Theatre - Cologne (Germany) - 7th November
Falkoner Teatret - Copenhagen (Denmark) - 8th November
Bataclan - Paris (France) - 10th November
Sports Palace - Mexico City (Mexico) - 26th November
VFG Arena - Guadalajara (Mexico) - 28th November

Arena - Monterrey (Mexico) - 29th November
Oracle Arena - Oakland CA (USA) - 3rd December
Staples Center - Los Angeles CA (USA) - 4th December
The Pearl - Las Vegas NV (USA) - 6th December
Broomfield Events Center – Denver CO (USA) - 8th December
Target Center – Minneapolis MN (USA) - 10th December
Allstate Arena – Chicago IL - 12th December
Palace Of Auburn Hills – Detroit MI (USA) 13th December
The John Labatt Centre - London (Canada) - 15th December
Madison Square Gardens - New York NY (USA) - 17th December
Susquehanna Center - Camden NJ (USA) - 19th December
GMU Patriot Center – Washington WA (USA) - 20th December
Zenith - Nantes (France) - 12th January
Forest National - Brussels (Belgium) - 13th January
Messehalle - Dresden (Germany) - 15th January
Sporthalle - Hamburg (Germany) - 16th January
Arena - Berlin (Germany) - 18th January
Heineken Music Hall - Amsterdam (Netherlands) - 21st January
Heineken Music Hall - Amsterdam (Netherlands) - 22nd January
Forum - Copenhagen (Denmark) - 24th January
Scandinavium - Gothenburg (Sweden) - 25th January
Spektrum - Oslo (Norway) - 27th January
Globe - Stockholm (Sweden) - 28th January
Zenith - Lille (France) - 30th January
Medoquine - Bordeaux (France) - 31st January
Datchforum - Milan (Italy) - 2nd February
Philipshalle - Dusseldorf (Germany) - 4th February
Palacio de Deportes de La Comunidad - Madrid (Spain) - 12th February
Pavello Olympic de Badalona - Barcelona (Spain) - 13th February
Atlantico Pavilion - Lisbon (Portugal) - 15th February
Zenith - Toulouse (France) - 17th February
Le Dome - Marseille (France) - 18th February
Palalottomatica - Rome (Italy) - 20th February
Palaverde - Treviso (Italy) - 21st February
Palaonda - Bolzana (Italy) - 23rd February
Mandela Forum - Florence (Italy) - 24th February
Stadthalle - Vienna (Austria) - 26th February
Zenith - Munich (Germany) - 27th February
Hallenstadion Arena - Zurich (Switzerland) - 1st March
Bercy - Paris (France) - 3rd March

Gaishi Hall - Nagoya (Japan) - 18th March
Makuhari Messe - Tokyo (Japan) - 20th March
Makomanai Ice Arena - Sapporo (Japan) - 22nd March
Intex - Osaka (Japan) - 24th March
Intex - Osaka (Japan) - 25th March
Makuhari Messe - Tokyo (Japan) - 28th March
Makuhari Messe - Tokyo (Japan) - 29th March
Olympic Gym # 1 - Seoul (South Korea) - 1st April
Exhibition Hall 4F, Taiwan World Trade Centre Nangang - Taipei City (Taiwan) - 3rd April
Singapore Indoor Stadium (Singapore) - 5th April
AsiaWorld Arena - Hong Kong (China) - 7th April
Riversands Farm - Johannesburg (South Africa) - 10th April
Lourensford Wine Estate - Cape Town (South Africa) - 13th April
Estadio Nacional - Lima (Peru) - 30th April
River Plate Stadium - Buenos Aires (Argentina) - 3rd May
Movistar Arena - Santiago (Chile) - 5th May
Citibank Hall - Rio de Janeiro (Brazil) - 7th May
São Paulo Arena Anhembi - São Paulo (Brazil) - 9th May
Expotrade - Curitiba (Brazil) - 10th May
Porto Alegre Gigantinho - Porto Alegre (Brazil) - 12th May
Heaton Park - Manchester - 4th June
Heaton Park - Manchester - 6th June
Heaton Park - Manchester - 7th June
Stadium Of Light - Sunderland - 10th June
Millennium Stadium - Cardiff - 12th June
Théâtre Antique de Vienne - Vienne (France) - 14th June
Murrayfield - Edinburgh - 17th June
Slane Castle - County Meath (Ireland) - 20th June
Rock Werchter - (Belgium) - 2nd July
Roskilde Festival - Roskilde (Denmark) - 3rd July
Ricoh Arena - Coventry - 7th July
Wembley Stadium - London - 9th July
Wembley Stadium - London - 11th July
Wembley Stadium - London - 12th July
Eden Project - Cornwall - 14th July
Benicàssim Festival - Castellón (Spain) - 16th July
Gurten Festival - Berne (Switzerland) - 18th July
Melt Festival - Gräfenhainichen (Germany) - 19th July
iTunes Festival - London - 21st July

Fuji Rock Festival Naeba Ski Resort - Naeba (Japan) - 24th July
Jisan Valley Rock Festival - Jisan Valley (South Korea) - 26th July
Bridlington Spa - Bridlington - 20th August
V Festival – Weston Park, Staffordshire - 22nd August

RECOMMENDED VIEWING:

Live Forever: The Rise and Fall of Brit Pop documentary (John Dower, 2003)
Liam Gallagher: As It Was documentary (Charlie Lightening & Gavin Fitzgerald, 2019)
Upside Down: The Creation Records Story documentary (Danny O'Connor, 2010)
Oasis: Right Here Right Now documentary (Mike Connolly, 1997)
Standing on the Edge of the Noise concert film (Dick Carruthers, 2008)

RECOMMENDED READING – BOOKS AND ONLINE SOURCES

Getting High – The Adventures of Oasis by Paolo Hewitt (Dean Street Press, 1997)
Forever the People: Six Months on the Road with Oasis by Paolo Hewitt (Boxtree, 1999)
Take Me There: The Story by Paul Mathur (Bloomsbury, 1996)
Brothers from Childhood to Oasis: The Real Story by Paul Gallagher and Terry Christian (Virgin Books, 1996)
Oasis: What's the Story? by Iain Robertson (Music Press Books, 1996)
Oasis the Truth: My Life as Oasis's Drummer by Tony McCarroll (John Blake Publishing, 2010)
Don't Look Back in Anger: Growing Up with Oasis by Christopher Hutton and Richard Kurt (Simon & Schuster Ltd, 1997)
Where Did It All Go Wrong?: Oasis and the Millennium Meltdown 1995-2000 by Nick Amies (Lipps-Amies Publishing, 2015)
Giving it the Big 'Un: Oasis, Manchester, Football and Me by Paul Asbee (New Haven Publishing, 2019)
Lunch with The Wild Frontiers: A History of Britpop and Excess In 13 ½ Chapters by Phill Savidge (Jawbone, 2019)
Don't Look Back in Anger: The rise and fall of Cool Britannia, told by those who were there by Daniel Rachel (Trapeze, 2019)
Isle of Noises: Conversations with great British songwriters by Daniel Rachel (Picador, 2014)
The Last Party: Britpop, Blair and the Demise of English Rock by John Harris (Harper Perennial, 2003)
Going Deaf for A Living by Steve Lamacq (Omnibus Press, 2019)
Supersonic: Personal Situations with Oasis (1992-96) by Stuart Deabill (Marshall Cavendish International Asia Pte Ltd, 2013)

ONLINE SOURCES

Stopcryingyourheart.com – the best and most comprehensive Oasis website around, with details of all the band's output, gigs, bootlegs and other miscellany. Put together by the No.1 Oasis fan and helpfully divided between Oasis, Beady Eye, Noel Gallagher's High Flying Birds and Liam Gallagher with up-to-date news on all. Look no further: http://www.stopcryingyourheartout.co.uk/

Oasisfanclub.com – alternative viewpoint, an unofficial fan club with articles and album info: https://www.oasisfanclub.com/

Live4Ever.com – a dedicated Oasis forum with hundreds of different topics covering all areas of the band past and present. Useful for both tidbits of information or wild speculation, a chance to converse with other diehard fans: http://live4ever.proboards.com

Oasisrecordinginfo.co.uk – unofficial fan site with detailed breakdowns of the Oasis recorded archive: http://www.oasis-recordinginfo.co.uk/

Oasisinet.com – The official band website, offers detailed if not comprehensive images and videos, mainly from the band's early years, including official music videos and famous interviews. Also includes the online store, the first port of call for Oasis merchandise: https://www.oasisinet.com

Thanks to all the following publications and media, which we would like to thank for quotes used throughout this book:

Supersonic (directed by Mat Whitecross), *Britpop!: Cool Britannia and the Spectacular Demise of English Rock, Uncut, NME,* All Owen Morris quotes taken from Richard Buskin interview (2012), *The Face, San Francisco Chronicle, Lock the Box* (DVD), *Supanet, Oasis What's the Story* (by Iain Robertson), *The Guardian, Q Magazine,* BBC Radio 2, *The Jonathan Ross Show, Western Mail, The O Zone, Newsnight, The Independent, Spin, Live Forever* (directed by John Dower), *Oasis Magazine, Forever the People* (by Paolo Hewitt), *GQ Magazine, Heat Magazine, The Evening Session, The Sun, Rolling Stone, City Life,* MTV Europe, *Daily Mirror, Daily Telegraph, Billboard, Female First, Toronto Sun,* The Brit Awards, *Lord Don't Slow Me Down* (directed by Baillie Walsh), interviews with Michael Spencer Jones and Nigel Dick interviews taken from *This Day In Music* Podcast.

I think that's everything. You may be perplexed that I haven't covered certain things to the extent they deserve, and you'd be right. 'The Masterplan' deserves a chapter all of its own, for example. Perhaps I missed out certain details in the Oasis story. I certainly hope not, but it's inevitable that I have somewhere along the way.

We haven't even discussed the bootlegs that are available, or the best ever Oasis gigs. But I didn't go to every Oasis gig, and every person's experience is different. My best ever gig could be someone else's worst experience. The unique thing about fandom is that it's subjective. Similarly, I haven't gone into huge analysis about the key songs or lyrics. Even more so than with gigs, Noel Gallagher leaves that experience to the listeners. For example, I always thought 'Supersonic' was about a conversation at a party, yet no-one has ever proposed that as an interpretation, nor has anyone suggested anything better. The songs and the lyrics speak for themselves, however you want them to. That's why they have mass appeal, and that's while they will, if you'll forgive the obvious, live forever. Better writers than I have analysed those songs to within an inch of their lives, so it would be foolish to even try.

If you feel short-changed, or you notice that I have missed something out, feel free to let me work it out for myself. Or write your own fucking book.

Writing this book has been a real labour of love but also a team effort, and thanks aren't enough for everyone who has helped out. However, it's all I've got.

Firstly, I'd like to thank the following for sending in pictures. Not all of them were used as you can see, but the efforts were appreciated nonetheless. Thanks to Hendrik Elfenthal, Kevin Fahey, Neil Hogg, Sarah Larizza, Robert Mason, Matheus Mendes, Andrew Middleton, Kelly Panter, Andrew Quinlan, Jamie Rosney, Kevin Smith, James Tanner, Travis Tee, Chris Tuffen and David Walker. God bless social media.

Big thanks to Paul Bachmann for his excellent photographs (cheers Boss!).

Thanks for Amy Feltman for her transcription efforts, hope you can see they were worthwhile! Thanks also to those people who helped out and I've now got to know through the Podcast world; Brandon Arend, Dan Best, Kyle Dale, Brian Garcia, and Katy Georgiou. May your smiles shine on. Speaking of which, stopcryingyourheartout.com can never be thanked enough for not only the pictures but as an Oasis resource, it's unbeatable. Keep the dream alive. Special thanks to Richard Buskin for being kind and allowing us to use the Owen Morris interview he conducted back in 2012.

A medal goes to Malcolm Wyatt for his patience and mentoring during 'deadline' phase. You taught me some valuable lessons! Thanks to Neil and the team at This Day in Music for taking a punt on an unpublished upstart. And of course, thanks to James Corcoran for allowing me to pilfer the interviews and generally for all the work that goes into the Oasis Podcast.

In the real world, big thanks to my brother Andrew for getting me into Oasis (less so for being an arse when I listened to your CDs), and my wonderful mother Joanie (and Ian) for not banning them from the house. And to my darling Debbie, who's been a patient and supportive Gallagher widow for over two years (considerably longer than that when you add pre-book. Sorry to say that's not changing anytime soon). The only god that I will ever need.

In a bit.

RB

Photo credits: Front cover image - Kevin Cummins, Page 3 and page 366 - Paul Bachmann, Page 91 - Brian Garcia, Page 148 - Graham Spooner, Page 171 - Katy Georgiou, Page 198 - Simon Howitt Sears-Piccavey, Page 218 - Dave Martin, Page 245 - Marc Rossiter, Page 317, 319, 321 album cover photos by Michael Spencer Jones

Milton Keynes UK
Ingram Content Group UK Ltd.
UKHW020336181123
432766UK00002B/35

9 781838 379834